AUTOCOURSE
INDY CAR™
1994-95

HAZLETON PUBLISHING

WE EVEN HELPED PAINT THAT SMILE ON HIS FACE

PPG CONGRATULATES AL UNSER JR., WINNER OF THE 1994 PPG CUP

Al certainly has good reason to smile. After compiling enough wins and near-wins on the Indy Car circuit this year, he was awarded the coveted PPG Cup. And PPG was with

him all the way. As the official automotive finish of the Indy Car circuit, PPG makes every car look like a winner. Which means we give every driver good reason to smile.

PPG

The world leader in automotive finishes.

CONTENTS

PUBLISHER
Richard Poulter

EDITOR
Jeremy Shaw

ART EDITOR
Steve Small

PRODUCTION MANAGER
George Greenfield

HOUSE EDITOR
Peter Lovering

BUSINESS DEVELOPMENT MANAGER
Simon Maurice

SALES PROMOTION
Elizabeth Le Breton

CHIEF PHOTOGRAPHER
Michael C. Brown

Additional photographs
have been contributed by:
Jori Potiker
Formula One Pictures
Popperfoto

US Advertising Representative
Barry Pigot
12843-A Foothill Boulevard
Sylmar, California 91342
Telephone and fax: (704) 322 1645

INDY CAR 1994-95
is published by
Hazleton Publishing,
3 Richmond Hill,
Richmond, Surrey
TW10 6RE, England.

Color reproduction by
Barrett Berkeley Ltd., London, England.

Printed in England by
Butler and Tanner Ltd.,
Frome.

ISBN: 1-874557-85-3

Michael C. Brown

ACKNOWLEDGMENTS
The Editor and publishers wish to thank the following for their assistance: Andrew Craig, Andy Deas, Randy Dzierzawski, Kirk Russell, Nancy Lewis, Cathy Lyon, Jeff Kowalczyk, Dave Elshoff, Tamy Valkosky, Chris Mears, Gordon Kirby and David Phillips.

DISTRIBUTORS

UNITED KINGDOM
Bookpoint Ltd.
39 Milton Park
Abingdon
Oxfordshire OX14 4TD

NORTH AMERICA
Motorbooks
International
PO Box 1
729 Prospect Ave.
Osceola
Wisconsin 54020, USA

AUSTRALIA
Technical Book and
Magazine Co. Pty.
289-299 Swanston Street
Melbourne
Victoria 3000

NEW ZEALAND
David Bateman Ltd.
'Golden Heights'
32-34 View Road
Glenfield
Auckland 10

SOUTH AFRICA
Motorbooks
341 Jan Smuts Avenue
Craighall Park
Johannesburg

"One thing you learn in racing is that they don't wait for you." *Roger Penske*

When he was fourteen years old, Roger Penske's father took him to see his first Indianapolis 500. "The crowd, the excitement—it just got to me," Penske recalls. "I said to myself, 'Someday I'm going to compete here.'"

Eighteen years later he made it to Indy as the leader of Team Penske. To date, they have won ten Indy 500 victories, and are the most successful team ever.

In addition to managing his racing team, Penske runs an international multi-billion-dollar transportation business. "I try to teach my people that it's up to them to innovate, to make things happen."

Roger Penske combines a focus on results with attention to detail. "What I like about Rolex," he explains, "is that they don't compromise either. That's why I've worn a Rolex for over two decades."

ROLEX

Rolex Oyster Perpetual Day-Date Chronometer in 18kt gold with matching concealed-clasp President bracelet.
Write for brochure. Rolex Watch U.S.A., Inc., Dept. RLX, Rolex Building, 665 Fifth Avenue, New York, N.Y. 10022-5383.
Rolex, ♔, Oyster Perpetual, Day-Date and President are trademarks.

FOREWORD
by Al Unser Jr. 1994 PPG Cup champion

Michael C. Brown

When I began my racing career I had three main goals. Two of them were to win the PPG Indy Car World Series championship and the Indianapolis 500. The other was to drive for Roger Penske.

Winning the PPG Indy Car World Series championship and the Indianapolis 500, both for the second time, took place during my first season with Marlboro Team Penske.

A driver can never take full credit for any of his successes. The accomplishments we achieved could never have taken place without much dedication and teamwork. We all worked together toward a winning season with one common goal in mind – to put a #1 on one of our Marlboro cars. Many thanks to everyone associated with Marlboro Team Penske for making this happen.

Most of all, thanks to my wife, Shelley, and my three children, Al, Shannon and Cody, for their support and the sacrifices they've made which go along with this lifestyle.

The Indy Car series is the best in the business. I'm proud to be a part of it and look forward in the seasons to come to competing against some of the greatest drivers in the world.

As you page through this book, know what an honor it is for me to be a small part of what I consider to be the greatest sport in the world – racing.

Formula1DriverMikaHakkinenduringpre-qualifying.

BOSS
HUGO BOSS

MEN AT WORK.

EXCITING TIMES

All's well for Al Unser Jr. *(right)* as he gives thanks to his crew after scoring yet another victory *en route* to his second PPG Cup title.

Left: Marlboro Team Penske was a dominant force, yet Emerson Fittipaldi, Paul Tracy and Al Unser Jr. enjoyed some thrilling battles during the season.

Photos: Michael C. Brown

Nigel Mansell came, saw and conquered in 1993. This season has not been so auspicious. Now his 'incredible adventure' is over and Mansell is turning his back on the Indy Car scene and returning to Formula 1.

The PPG Indy Car World Series has exhibited a startling pattern of growth in recent years. In particular, the sport has benefited enormously from the brief but spectacular participation by Nigel Mansell. Almost single-handedly, in the course of just two seasons, he became responsible for raising worldwide interest in the series to hitherto almost unimaginable levels. He has been the focus of attention wherever he has gone. The crowd surrounding his Texaco Havoline motorhome at every race track bore testimony to that.

When Mansell won, as he frequently did in 1993, the news was splashed across banner headlines not only in his native England but around the globe. When he crashed, which he seemed to do with some regularity during 1994, in his surprisingly ineffective bid to retain the PPG Cup title, Mansell was also big news. He was fortunate to emerge uninjured from his altercation with the hapless Dennis Vitolo at Indianapolis, yet spectacular photographs accompanied by stories proclaiming 'Mansell cheats death' appeared in newspapers as far afield as Adelaide and Oslo, Tokyo and Milan. Make no mistake: if any driver other than Mansell had been involved in the accident, the story would not have been nearly so newsworthy.

But perhaps times are a-changing. The new popularity enjoyed by Indy Car racing has come in large part due to extensive television coverage. The viewership has expanded rapidly – again, aided considerably by Mansell's exploits – but the point is that many new fans have been won over. And the chances are that even without Mansell, who has apparently committed himself to a return to Formula 1 in 1995, the sport of Indy Car racing will continue to reap the rewards.

The PPG Cup races have proved to be exciting to watch. The action is often spectacular. There is plenty of overtaking. And the sheer variety of the circuits ensures an ever-changing perspective.

For Mansell and, indeed, the majority of the drivers involved in Indy Car racing, it is the diversity of the series that provides one of its primary attractions. To achieve success, both team and driver are required to perform with equal prowess on road courses, street circuits, short ovals and superspeedways.

In 1994, no one did so better than Al Unser Jr. Armed with a Marlboro Penske-Ilmor/D, which proved to be by far the fastest and most consistent car-chassis combination, Unser swept all before him. Unser, 32, won eight races *en route* to clinching his second – and Roger Penske's record-extending ninth – PPG Cup crown with two races remaining.

Team-mates Paul Tracy, with three victories, and Emerson Fittipaldi, who won once, underlined the dominance of Nigel Bennett's Penske PC23 chassis and Mario Illien's Ilmor Indy 94 engine. When Tracy took the checkered flag in the season finale at Laguna Seca Raceway, securing the team's 12th win of the year and a sweep of the top three positions in the PPG Cup standings, he broke the tie with Vel's Parnelli Jones Racing and STP Granatelli Racing, both of which earned 11 wins in 1969 and 1970 respectively.

Unser's performance was all the more impressive given the fact he was the newcomer on the team at the beginning of the season. Nevertheless, he settled in quickly, worked harmoniously with his own group of engineers and mechanics, and took full advantage of the vast pool of technical resources and experience at his disposal.

'If you've got all the horsepower in the world and you can't put it to the ground, it doesn't do you any good,' noted Unser after claiming the pole at Cleveland in July. 'And on the other hand, if you've got the horsepower but your chassis isn't working, you can't do too well either. So it's a real combination. You need the best equipment and the best people. It's a real team effort.'

Unser went on to win the race that weekend, his fifth out of six starts, and in doing so stretched his PPG Cup points lead to 41 over Fittipaldi. Already he had marked himself as the hot favorite for seasonal honors. But Unser, in his customary style, refused to take anything for granted.

'There's actually more pressure on me now than there's ever been,' he said. 'Roger and the boys demand perfection, and so it's a great challenge to me because I've always demanded perfection from my race team. The main thing on my mind is just to do the best job I can do, and if I can do that, we'll be OK.'

No problems there. Unser performed magnificently and with hardly the hint of a mistake. His only retirements came as a result of engine failures at Surfers Paradise (on the very last lap), Toronto and Michigan, and a transmission

9

Above: Mario Andretti takes center stage as his 31-year career in Indy Car racing draws to a close.

Rookie of the Year Jacques Villeneuve *(left)* spearheaded the fresh Reynard challenge at Indianapolis.

Right: From drawing board to test bed in just 26 weeks, the success of the Mercedes-Benz 500I V8 engine added another chapter to the fabled history of the Indianapolis 500.

Photos: Michael C. Brown

problem at Laguna Seca. He finished either first or second in every other race, with the exception of Detroit, where he was inadvertently punted out of the lead (by Tracy) and fell back to tenth. By any account, it was a remarkable year.

Unser emerged during the season as a true all-round performer, arguably for the first time in his career. In the past, there had always been a question mark regarding his ability during qualifying. Indeed, prior to the 1994 season, he had but three poles to his credit after 11 full seasons of Indy Car racing (and two of those poles had come at Long Beach). This year, Unser put that to rest by claiming his first pole on an oval track – at Indianapolis, no less – then followed up by annexing the inside front row grid positions at Portland, Cleveland and Mid-Ohio.

'In my eyes, most of [the reason] is the car – and the team,' he declared. 'I've had more time with this race team, and with the testing, to concentrate on my driving and what I can do to help that aspect of it – get smoother and all that sort of thing. It's given me a chance to be a better driver.'

There's no question that Penske Racing has raised the standard in Indy Car competition. The team's level of professionalism, as Mansell put it, 'is at least as good as anything in Formula 1.' No stone has been left unturned in the quest for speed.

A case in point was the remarkable story of the Ilmor-designed Mercedes-Benz 500I V8 engine, which was developed specifically for Indianapolis – and in total secrecy. Many of the crew members in Reading knew nothing of the engine's existence until only a very short time before its launch in April, mere weeks before its debut at Indianapolis. And yet a clandestine operation had been under way for a couple of months, based in another building just a few hundred feet away from the main race shop. A separate crew handled the testing duties. An extensive dyno program on the engine was carried out during the overnight hours.

The stunning success of the Mercedes/Ilmor, which was designed to take advantage of what was, effectively, a loophole in the regulations for the Indianapolis 500, has led USAC, which, uniquely, sanctions the largest jewel in the PPG Cup series crown, to reduce the maximum allowable turbo boost pressure for all similar engines. This year the limit was 55 inches, some ten inches

more than was permitted for all 'conventional' four-cam race engines, such as the Ilmor/D and Ford/Cosworth XB. Soon after this year's '500,' USAC announced the boost for 1995 would be reduced to 52 inches; then, upon further reflection and in light of an all-new formula which is slated to be introduced in 1996, USAC back-pedalled some more, leaving the new figure at 48 inches.

On face value, the boost reduction certainly spelled good news for the majority of Indy Car teams, as the competitiveness of their regular engines now should be assured, at least for 1995. Conversely, if the old rules had remained, all of the top contenders would have been obliged to invest in the new breed of pushrod 209 engines simply in order to be competitive. But the decision still irked several different parties, including Ilmor Engineering, which, by the time the final rule-change had been made public, had already placed an order for 30 new cylinder blocks and other expensive ancillaries in anticipation of going ahead with further development of the 1993 Indy motor. In addition, Cosworth Engineering had spent several months undertaking both a full-scale study and an initial design for a similar engine; and John Menard, whose team traditionally competes only at Indy, had given the green light to yet another pushrod concept.

Nevertheless, in the overall scheme of things, the USAC decision seems to be a sound one.

Rather more worrying, however, is the potentially disastrous effect of the Indy Racing League, an independent series of races to be centered upon the Indianapolis 500. It is due to commence in 1996. The notion was conceived by Indianapolis Motor Speedway President Tony George, who for years has held a running battle with the board and management of CART/IndyCar, the sanctioning body for the PPG Indy Car World Series.

As of the end of the 1994 season, no firm outline for the IRL had been made public, other than to confirm it will be administered by USAC, which governed the sport of Indy Car racing prior to the formation of CART (now IndyCar) in 1978. A complete set of regulations has yet to be finalized, although USAC has settled upon an engine formula which will demand 2.2-liter, overhead-camshaft turbocharged engines running at 45 inches of boost – i.e. almost identical to the current

11

Miami will return to the PPG Cup schedule in 1995, thanks to the efforts of race promoter Ralph Sanchez *(left)*.

Below: Firestone has conducted an exhaustive test and development program with Patrick Racing in preparation for its return to the Indy Car wars.

Photo courtesy of Firestone

Photos: Michael C. Brown

Tasman Motorsports team-mates Steve Robertson and Andre Ribeiro were the class of the field in the PPG-Firestone Indy Lights Championship, the 'Official Development Series' for Indy Car racing.

Close racing, strong sponsorship and broadening international appeal are paving the way toward a bright future for the PPG Indy Car World Series.

In memoriam

Sam Hanks, who died June 27 aged 79 at his home in Pacific Palisades, California, after a long illness, was one of the nation's most successful race car drivers in the 1930s, '40s and '50s. Both before and after serving his country during World War II in the Army Air Corps, Hanks won numerous races and titles at the wheel of a variety of midgets and stock cars. He also won the AAA National Championship in 1952, and in his 12th appearance in the Indianapolis 500, in 1957, he finally achieved his lifetime goal by racing to victory at the wheel of George Salih's trend-setting lay-down roadster, the Belond Exhaust Special. In his emotional moment of triumph, Hanks promptly announced his retirement from driving Indianapolis-type cars, although he did fulfill his stock car commitments to Ford by finishing the season and claiming his second straight Pacific Coast crown. Hanks retained close links with the sport in a number of capacities, including serving as director of racing at Indianapolis from 1958 to 1979.

---

breed, except for a downsizing from 2.65 liters to 2.2.

The engine regulations have led those teams participating in the thriving PPG Cup series to perceive a glimmer of hope that some kind of reconciliation will be reached between IndyCar and the coalition between the Indianapolis Motor Speedway and USAC.

That scenario apart, the PPG Cup series has continued its upward spiral in 1994. The total number of entrants rose to a new all-time high, with an average of 32 cars attending each of the 16 races (or 30.87 even without Indianapolis, which this year attracted 49 participants during official practice). That figure has increased by more than 25 per cent, from 24 cars per race, since 1991. This season, for the second straight year, the overall percentage of cars reaching the checkered flag has remained above 60 per cent, which also reflects improved reliability and a better overall standard of preparation. There has been a more sustained involvement, too, with no less than 24 drivers contesting each of the 16 races in 1994, up 50 per cent over the corresponding total in 1991.

The signs are equally good for the future, with more and more teams looking to enter the series. Next season, Patrick Racing, which can boast three Indianapolis 500 victories and two National Championship titles, will return in association with Firestone tires, which will challenge Goodyear's monopoly for the first time in 20 years. The Patrick/Firestone combination has undertaken an exhaustive test and development program over the past 12 months, with Scott Pruett clocking up thousands of miles at a variety of race tracks.

Firestone's comeback has been carefully orchestrated, with a victory at Indianapolis viewed as the ultimate goal. For 1995, however, Bridgestone/Firestone Motorsports Manager Al Speyer will be content with more modest achievements.

'We want to race without significant difficulties,' he says. 'We obviously want to win some races. From the data we have accumulated so far, we think we will be in the thick of it and win our fair share.'

Another name familiar to Indy Car fans over the past decade or so, Steve Horne, former co-owner of TrueSports Racing, also will be back on the PPG Cup circuit in 1995. Horne has guided his newest venture, Tasman Motorsports, to consecutive PPG-Firestone Indy Lights

Championships in 1993 and 1994. Along the way to winning 19 out of 24 races, Horne has set a new standard of preparation among the 'Official Development Series' for Indy Car racing. Tasman will be a worthy addition to the series, as will its highly rated young Brazilian driver, Andre Ribeiro.

Dan Gurney, too, is planning to be back at the pinnacle of North American auto racing with his famed All American Racers team. For the past year or so, Gurney has been conducting an extensive development program in concert with Toyota. An all-new, all-American Eagle chassis also is under construction. If all goes to plan, look for it to debut before the end of the 1995 season.

A new venue also is to be included on the PPG Cup schedule for 1995, with a visit to Miami, Florida, for the season-opener on March 5 marking the series' return to the prestigious south-eastern marketplace for the first time since 1988. The event will be held on a temporary circuit based around Bicentennial Park, on the edge of the downtown area, although the long-term plan calls for the race to be relocated once the exciting new Homestead Motorsports Complex, which will include a 1.5-mile oval, is completed.

The commitment to Miami represents one of the many positive steps taken by Andrew Craig since his appointment as President and Chief Executive Officer of Championship Auto Racing Teams/IndyCar on April 1. Craig also has succeeded in finalizing long-range contracts with 13 other venues currently hosting PPG Cup events, as well as pledging to include a race on the proposed California Speedway facility, which is scheduled for completion by 1996. The stability afforded by these obligations will undoubtedly provide other benefits as the sport continues to grow in the coming years.

These are indeed exciting times for the Indy Car World Series, which in 1994 celebrated its 15th year in association with title sponsor PPG Industries.

Over the years, PPG has played a vital role in helping to attain the series' current status. So, too, has a huge cast of others, among them numerous officials and drivers. In addition to Nigel Mansell having been instrumental recently in spreading the word about Indy Car racing, particularly onto the continent of Europe, fellow Formula 1 champion Emerson Fittipaldi also has become

The end of an era

When, at Laguna Seca, Mario Andretti turned the final page on an Indy Car career that began 31 years earlier, he also closed the book on an entire era of the sport. For much of his career, but especially in the 1960s and 1970s, when a rich mixture of dirt and paved ovals provided the battleground, Andretti was embroiled in a fierce rivalry with four other drivers who shared the same passion and commitment. Their names: A.J. Foyt, Al Unser, Bobby Unser and Johnny Rutherford.

Even now, Foyt, Andretti, Al U. and Bobby U. remain as the top four winningest drivers in the history of Indy Car racing. Rutherford ranks eighth on the all-time list. Between them they can account for an incredible 220 race victories, 17 National Championships and 15 Indianapolis 500 crowns.

The older of the Unser brothers, Bobby, has been watching from the sidelines for more than ten years, although he remains actively involved, working as an analyst for ABC Sports television. In 1993, Foyt decided the time was ripe for retirement. This year, of course, Andretti has participated in a phenomenally successful 'Arrivederci, Mario'

Tour. Amid rather less fanfare, 'Big Al' Unser and 'Lone Star JR' also decided it was time to hang up their helmets after long and illustrious careers.

Both veterans made their decisions during a typically dramatic month of May at Indianapolis. Unser, now 55, reached his conclusion first, having come to the realization he was more concerned about watching and helping his son, Al Jr., than he was about attempting to make his own 28th start in The Greatest Spectacle in Racing.

'I finally realized that I'm not doing what I should be doing [in the car],' said an emotional Unser. 'I always said when that day came I'd back down.'

Four days later, Rutherford, 56, took one last lap around the hallowed Brickyard aboard the same #14 Lola in which Foyt bade his farewell in 1993.

'It's tough. Boy, it really is tough,' said the gritty Texan, who had so desperately wanted to qualify for his 25th Indianapolis 500. '[But] there comes a time when the old guys have to move over and let the young guys come through.'

Michael C. Brown

an influential figure, introducing the sport to a huge and appreciative audience in South America. But perhaps nothing over the past 30 years has enlivened the competition as much as the intense rivalry between A.J. Foyt and Mario Andretti. Between them, the notorious duo won everything there was to win, many times over. They established their reputations in Indy Car racing, yet they were also equally successful in a variety of other categories.

In 1993, Foyt bid a fond and emotional farewell at Indianapolis as he officially announced his retirement from driving. This year Mario Andretti capped his own sensational career by undertaking a popular season-long salute: the 'Arrivederci, Mario' Tour. Following a solid performance in his 407th and final Indy Car race, Andretti took one last lap of honor at Laguna Seca Raceway in the Oldsmobile Calais PPG Pace Car painted in, you guessed it, Andretti

Red, a new color formulated specially by PPG Automotive Refinishes. It was a fitting tribute to one of the sport's most enduring and endearing characters.

Before departing for the Newman-Haas team's traditional end-of-season party, which this year, of course, took on an extra-special significance, Andretti took some time to reflect upon how Indy Car racing has changed over the years. And how it has prospered. And about how he feels its present management structure, headed by IndyCar President and CEO Andrew Craig, is headed in the right direction: 'I'm happy to report that I leave the sport in very good hands and probably enjoying the best times in its history,' said Andretti. 'No question. There's a lot of depth in the field and I think the future's bright and very strong. I just wish [Indianapolis Motor Speedway President] Tony George would understand that . . .'

Here's to Al Jr., Paul, Emmo, and their crews
for a season full of victory.

16 mg "tar," 1.1 mg nicotine av. per cigarette by FTC method.

SURGEON GENERAL'S WARNING: Cigarette
Smoke Contains Carbon Monoxide.

1995 PPG INDY CAR WORLD SERIES SCHEDULE

March 5	Bicentennial Park Street Circuit, Miami, Florida
March 19	Surfers Paradise Street Circuit, Queensland, Australia
April 2	Phoenix International Raceway, Phoenix, Arizona
April 9	Long Beach Street Circuit, California
April 23	Nazareth Speedway, Nazareth, Pennsylvania
May 28	Indianapolis Motor Speedway, Speedway, Indiana
June 4	Milwaukee Mile, West Allis, Wisconsin
June 11	Belle Isle Park Street Circuit, Detroit, Michigan
June 25	Portland International Raceway, Portland, Oregon
July 9	Road America, Elkhart Lake, Wisconsin
July 16	Exhibition Place Circuit, Toronto, Ontario, Canada
July 23	Burke Lakefront Airport Circuit, Cleveland, Ohio
July 30	Michigan International Speedway, Brooklyn, Michigan
August 13	Mid-Ohio Sports Car Course, Lexington, Ohio
August 20	New Hampshire International Speedway, Loudon, New Hampshire
September 3	BC Place Circuit, Vancouver, British Columbia, Canada
September 10	Laguna Seca Raceway, Monterey, California

Subject to alteration

TEAM PENSKE

CHAMPIONSHIP YEAR
1994

We can all be proud of the remarkable success achieved by Marlboro Team Penske in the 1994 PPG Indy Car World Series. While success can be attributed to the combination of a good car, a reliable engine and fast drivers, more than anything, it is the result of commitment, a great team and dedication to hard work.

The key was the total effort made by the entire organization working together – the people at Penske Cars in Poole, England; Ilmor Engineering in Brixworth, England; and Penske Racing in Reading, Pennsylvania.

Auto racing is the common thread throughout our companies. In racing, as in business, you must manage by anticipation. You have to be prepared – no one waits for you to be ready and you get your report card on Sunday afternoon.

This year Marlboro Team Penske won its tenth Indianapolis 500. We also earned a record 12 wins and a clean sweep of first, second and third places in the 1994 PPG Cup championship. It was a fitting reward for a lot of hard work by the whole team.

In today's world, we get paid for performance. This has been a record year for all of us, but we cannot rest on our laurels. We must now look forward to the challenges of the future.

Mark Donohue *(right)* paved the way for Penske Racing at Indianapolis by winning in 1972. Twenty-two years later, Al Unser Jr. *(below)* swept to the team's 10th triumph in the world's most prestigious single-day sporting event.

Karl Kainhofer can clearly recall the first time he met Roger Penske. It was at a long-defunct race track in Vineland, New Jersey. The date was April 12, 1959. At the time, Austrian-born Kainhofer was employed as a technician with the Porsche factory on assignment in the United States. He was working for Harry Blanchard, a well-known amateur Porsche driver. One R. Penske also was competing with a Porsche RS Spyder, and when he sought some advice, Kainhofer was quick to oblige.

The pair struck an immediate rapport. Penske, just 22 years old and still studying business administration at Lehigh University, was impressed by Kainhofer's technical prowess as well as his attention to detail and willingness to help. Kainhofer, meanwhile, a few years older, immediately recognized Penske as an ambitious, honest and forthright young man who also possessed clear talent in a race car.

In many ways they were kindred spirits.

'It's remarkable,' says Kainhofer. 'For 35 years we have never lost sight of each other.'

A year later, toward the end of May, 1960, on a particularly hectic weekend, Kainhofer and Penske traveled to Canada for a sports car race on Saturday, then hurried south to Bridgehampton, Long Island, in time for another race the next afternoon. As if that wasn't enough, the pair drove into New York City, 'cleaned ourselves up,' as Kainhofer puts it, then caught a flight to Indianapolis for the Memorial Day classic: the Indianapolis 500.

'He said to me then, "Some day, Karl, I'm going to have a car in this race, and if I don't drive it myself, somebody else will."'

Penske was true to his word. Al Unser Jr.'s sensational drive in the 1994 Indianapolis 500 in a Marlboro Penske powered by Mercedes-Benz was Penske's record-breaking 10th victory as a car owner in the world's most prestigious auto race. Kainhofer, now general manager of Penske Racing, has been involved in every single one of them.

Success, of course, is nothing new to Penske. His race team has been winning since its earliest days, initially with Penske himself behind the wheel.

Now, just as it did more than three decades ago, Penske Racing stands out from the rest. From the very beginning, Penske was a stickler for detail, a perfectionist who wanted to be associated with nothing but the best. It was a quality to which Kainhofer was particularly attracted.

'I have a trophy at home,' he says proudly, 'the only one that means anything to me, and I won it at a sports car race in Pensacola, Florida. Roger won the driver's award and I got the trophy for the best prepared car.

'Appearance meant so much to us then, and in those days no one else cared about appearance. A good-looking car, to me, was always a good-running car. Reliability comes with looks and attention to detail.

'Oh, sure,' says Kainhofer with more than a hint of pride but absolutely no trace of arrogance, 'you can come up with occasional success, but to be a consistent winner you must have something in your system that nobody else has – or you must do it better than anybody else does.'

It's no wonder their partnership has been so successful. Penske himself retired from driving in 1964. At the same time he left his job as a sales engineer for Alcoa and took the position of general manager of McKean Chevrolet in Philadelphia, focusing all his energy on becoming successful in business. Auto racing, he decided, would have to wait. One year later he purchased the auto dealership when its owner retired, then formed Penske Corporation, whose subsidiaries now employ more than 13,000 people worldwide and generate annual revenue exceeding $3.6 billion.

But Penske's yearning for auto racing remained. In the spring of 1966, at the Sebring 12 Hours race in Florida, Penske and Kainhofer renewed their association on more formal terms: Kainhofer would run the newly formed Penske Racing team. It was the start of what is arguably the most successful relationship in the history of auto racing. The duo's quest for excellence has continued, unbroken, to this day.

Mark Donohue, one of the nation's most promising young stars, was the first full-time driver employed by Penske Racing. A gifted engineer as well as a racer, Donohue won in everything Kainhofer prepared for him. He was victorious in the Trans-Am, Can-Am and Formula 5000.

In 1969, Penske made good on his promise to Kainhofer nine years earlier as Donohue won rookie of the year honors at Indianapolis. Two years later, Donohue claimed Penske Racing's first Indy Car victory in the inaugural Pocono 500, having started from the pole in his Offy-powered Sunoco McLaren M16A. In 1972 they achieved a long-held goal by winning at Indianapolis with a McLaren-Offy M16B.

For the ambitious Penske-Kainhofer-Donohue combination, a venture into Formula 1 represented the next logical progression. So in 1974 they established Penske Cars Ltd. and bought a race shop in Poole on the south coast of England. The first Penske chassis, the PC1, designed by Geoff Ferris, was ready for competition before the end of the season. Ferris, like Kainhofer, is still with Penske. Having penned an illustrious series of winning chassis through the 1970s and '80s, he is now in charge of transmission design for all Penske cars.

Tragically, in 1975, Donohue lost his life as the result of a crash practicing for the Austrian Grand Prix. His death came as a devastating blow to the entire Penske Racing family. Nevertheless, as Donohue would undoubtedly have insisted, the Formula 1 program continued until the end of the 1976 season, during which John Watson scored an emotional victory in the Austrian GP – almost exactly one year after Donohue's accident.

Since then Penske Cars has been devoted solely to designing and manufacturing chassis for Indy Car competition, and the United States base for Penske Racing, which in 1973 moved to a new facility in Reading, Pennsylvania, has concentrated on running and developing them.

Combined, the two companies have been a formidable force on the Indy Car circuit for more than two decades, with Penske Racing scoring at least one Indy Car victory every year since 1977. Still, 1994 has been an extraordinary year by any standard, and certainly the most successful season for any team in Indy Car history.

The highlight was undoubtedly Unser Jr.'s victory at Indianapolis, which vindicated Penske's risky but inspired decision to field an all-new Mercedes-Benz 500 I V8 engine in the most important event of the year. Unser Jr.'s triumph also secured a remarkable trifecta for the Unser family, since his father, Al, and uncle Bobby had previously won the Indy 500 for the Penske team.

'This is a very special day,' said Unser Jr. 'I want to thank Roger Penske and everyone at Marlboro Team Penske. They won this race today. Roger loves this place as much as I do; and it shows. He just gave me a pretty special car.'

Unser, gracious in victory, just as he always is even on less auspicious occasions, did not miss the opportunity to heap praise on all those who helped make his victory possible. Unser, as much as anyone, appreci-

ates the importance of teamwork in the sport of auto racing.

'It's just a pleasure working with the entire team,' he declares. 'We do a lot of testing. All the engineering staff, they do a super job. I've been watching Penske Racing from the outside the last 10 years, and the moment a car comes into the pits, a mob of engineers just surround the car. Now I'm on the inside and they're all around me, and it's just great. Everybody has lots of ideas and Terry Satchell, my personal engineer, has been doing a great job. It's a real pleasure to work with so many good guys.'

One of the keys to the success of Penske is undoubtedly the strength in depth of its personnel – allied to the way those people are focused on the same goal: winning. The loyalty of the work-force, too, provides a stabilizing effect, since it allows relationships to blossom and ideas to be

formulated and brought to fruition.

The positive forces apply with equal benefit in the day-to-day operation of the team as much as they do in the design and build process of the Penske chassis.

The cars themselves are designed and built in Poole. The current shop facility (actually the third occupied by Penske in the town over the past 20 years) now comprises 17,500 square feet of working space. In 1995, a new 8,000 square-foot design center and composite shop is due to be completed next door to the main production base on the Upton Industrial Estate.

Nick Goozee, managing director of Penske Cars since 1989, is responsible for the staff of 80. Goozee, too, has followed the Penske tradition, progressing through the ranks at Poole after joining the team as a fabricator on the Formula 1 program. He knows every detail of the company intimately.

A typical year at Penske Cars is split into three distinct parts. Starting in May or June, chief designer Nigel Bennett begins to formulate plans and ideas for the car to be raced the following season. By July the 10-man design office is operating at maximum capacity, utilizing the latest CAD/CAM technology from Computervision and Sun Microsystems, and by mid-August is produc-

ing detailed drawings so the manufacturing process can begin.

The work-load gradually increases during the first couple of months, and for the following six months it's all hands on deck to complete the scheduled order. The finished race cars are then shipped to the United States, usually directly to the Penske Racing shop in Reading, Pennsylvania. The first car is generally ready during December, with subsequent chassis delivered every three weeks.

'By the time the people in Poole finally come up for air, we're starting practice for the Indy 500,' asserts Penske Racing Team Manager Chuck Sprague. 'They're completely flat-out from October to May to get the job done.'

The end of the production run provides the only real opportunity to catch up on regular maintenance and perhaps some re-organization. Then the whole procedure begins again.

During the peak production period, Goozee tries to keep the shop hours to within reasonable limits.

'We're much better than we used to be,' he says. 'A few years ago we thought nothing of running 14-hour days for three or four months solid; but now we start at 7.30 a.m. and generally close at 6.30 p.m. Apart from Saturday mornings, we try to keep the weekends sacred. It gives

Clockwise from top: John Youngman fine-tunes a 40 percent scale model in preparation for the latest round of wind-tunnel testing; cleanliness and attention to detail are hallmarks of the entire organization; chief designer Nigel Bennett gathers information at the race track; the fruit of all the labor – Paul Tracy and Al Unser Jr. running in tight formation.

Left: The proud Penske Cars family gathers as the prototype 1994 chassis is ready for shipment to Reading.
Inset left: The engineers and build team confer during final assembly.

everyone something to look forward to, and we hardly ever work late at night any more.'

The operation is divided into seven separate departments, each with its own supervisor. Most have been with Penske Cars for many years – 'lifers,' as Goozee calls them. The largest department, the composite shop, employs 20 people and is responsible for producing the entire monocoque chassis and all of the bodywork components. It actually has two chiefs: Don Beresford, who handles development and is, says Goozee, 'the main troubleshooter,' and Kevin Emmet, who oversees day-to-day operations.

Other senior personnel include John Youngman, whose group produces the intricate scale models for use in the team's continual wind-tunnel development program; Barry Sweetland, who heads the pattern shop; Steve Lockyer, who supervises fabrication; Phil Jones, in charge of the machine shop; Mark Grimes, who is responsible for the actual car-building process; plus production manager Colin Heard, works manager Martin Webster and office manager/accountant Anita Cole.

The weekly routine is well-established. The managers and department heads meet with Goozee and Bennett every Wednesday morning to discuss the on-going program and any potential problems. A schedule is then drawn up for the following week. Each Monday the department heads provide Goozee with a worklist outlining specific deadlines for the week. The same list is resubmitted to Goozee on Friday confirming that all the deadlines were met – or stating reasons why not!

'Unfortunately,' reflects Goozee, 'it's a very regimented society here, but that's the only way we can produce the amount of stuff we have to and still have an outside life.'

Indeed, there are very few complaints. The system seems to work extraordinarily well, and Goozee proudly points out that Penske Cars has never missed a completion date: 'If we say in June that the first car's going to be ready on December 9th, on December 9th the car is finished. We do whatever we need to get it done.

'We try to adopt a policy, as Roger does throughout the corporation, to make everyone feel involved and that it's a democratic society,' explains Goozee. 'Everybody is involved in his own work environment and is encouraged to express thoughts on how the company is run; and we always keep them appraised, as far as possible, as to what's happening and why. And of course they can see their product performing on a regular basis. We very rarely have anybody leave.'

The actual design process is an on-going operation directed by Bennett, who joined Penske in 1987 after four years as chief designer at Penske's main rival, Lola. Bennett attends most of the races, gathering information himself and gleaning input from both the drivers and the race engineers.

Bennett begins by formulating a design for the road course version of the new car – primarily because the first race of the season is usually held on a street circuit. Then he turns his mind to the Speedway derivative, which will incorporate an entirely separate aerodynamic package to maximize the car's effectiveness on the high-speed ovals. Throughout this process, chief aerodynamicist David Johnson-Newell operates a continual program of wind-tunnel testing at Southampton University, also on the south coast of England.

In preparing for the 1994 season, Bennett had a hard act to follow. His 1993 chassis, the PC22, had earned an impressive eight race wins – exactly half of the 16-race season – with Emerson Fittipaldi only narrowly failing to claim the PPG Cup title. But, he says, there is always room for improvement.

'As you run the car during the year you find out more and more about it,' says Bennett.

For example, in 1993, Bennett found through extensive experimentation that the car's performance was improved by a slightly revised weight distribution: 'So that's one area where you can change: the dimensions of the car – where you put the heavy lumps, such as the engine and the wheels, in order to affect the weight distribution.' Small gains were also found in the aerodynamic and suspension packages through constant development.

Bennett continually tries to incorporate more advanced safety features, including additional protection for the driver in the event of an accident and, for the 1995 car, removing all sharp protrusions from the cockpit and improving the layout of the controls. In short, he says: 'Lots of little changes which we hope will lead to a better car.'

Bennett also has to consider input from the engine supplier, Ilmor Engineering, based at Brixworth, Northamptonshire, England. Ilmor and Penske Cars are entirely independent, yet they liaise closely in terms of items such as mounting points for the engine, transmission requirements, cooling and other plumbing details. And of course, in recent years, finding space to house and wire the electronic systems required for engine management has become a distinct challenge.

Left: Geoff Oliver, one of the charter members of the Ilmor design team, gets down to basics.
Right: A hive of activity – the main production shop at Ilmor Engineering.
Inset: Paul Morgan (left) and Mario Illien, originators of the Ilmor Indy V8.
Below: A Mercedes-Benz 500 I V8 engine is put through its paces on the dynamometer at Brixworth.

I lmor Engineering was formed in 1984 by two ex-Cosworth engineers, Mario Illien and Paul Morgan, in collaboration with Roger Penske. Later that same year General Motors joined forces on the project, and indeed the first three Ilmor Indy Car race engines carried the Chevrolet nameplate. The very first engine, the 265A, made its race debut in 1986. Rick Mears showed the potency of the package by claiming two poles, at Sanair and Michigan, during the first season in which the engine was run exclusively by Penske Racing, while the following year Mario Andretti recorded Ilmor's first victory on the streets of Long Beach, California.

By the beginning of 1988, the Chevrolet/Ilmor combination had become the dominant force, winning all but one of the 15 PPG Cup Indy Car races that season. Between September 1989 and June 1992 it recorded a sensational streak of 42 consecutive victories. During that time a satellite operation, Ilmor Engineering, Inc., was established at a base in Detroit. Paul Ray heads the nine-man team which provides field service for the entire Indy Car program.

For 1992, Ilmor developed an updated, more compact version of its Indy engine, the 265B, in response to a concerted attack from Cosworth Engineering, which had introduced an all-new, slimline challenger. Honors were shared evenly over the ensuing two seasons. Ilmor and Chevrolet claimed the seasonal honors in 1992, when Bobby Rahal triumphed with the older 265A motor, while in '93, ex-Formula 1 World Champion Nigel Mansell evened the score by taking the PPG Cup title for Ford and Cosworth, despite the advent of the new Chevrolet/Ilmor 265C. In both years, however, Ilmor took the spoils in the Indianapolis 500.

For the 1994 season, Ilmor produced yet another iteration on the theme. The resultant Ilmor Indy V8 represented the very latest thought processes and utilized technology derived from the Ilmor V10 Formula 1 engine.

By the end of the season, the 'D', as it was also known, had recorded 11 wins in concert with Bennett's Penske PC23 chassis. Seven of those victories were claimed by Unser Jr., three by Paul Tracy and one by Fittipaldi. In addition, the triumvirate filled the top three point-scoring positions in the PPG Indy Car World Series. The successes in 1994 bring

to 97 the total number of Indy Car victories earned so far by Ilmor Engineering.

Toward the end of the 1993 season, it became apparent that Chevrolet would cease its involvement in Indy Car racing. In the meantime, serious discussion had begun on a project which resulted in the headline-grabbing success story of the 1994 Indianapolis 500.

In late June, Mario Illien set to work on the design of a totally new engine intended specifically for Indianapolis. Unlike all other events on the PPG Indy Car World Series schedule, the Indy 500 is governed by the United States Auto Club. For years there have been subtle differences in the regulations at Indianapolis, mostly aimed at luring more of the major automobile manufacturers into the sport.

In particular, the rules at Indy allowed slightly more turbocharger boost pressure for production-based 'stock-block' engines, which also were permitted a larger displacement – 209 cubic inches as opposed to 161 cubic inches for four-cam racing engines such as the latest Ilmor Indy V8/D. But when it became apparent that no one wanted to build an engine to those regulations, USAC and the Indianapolis Motor Speedway decided in 1992, for the first time, to open up the equivalency formula by permitting any two-valve pushrod engines – whether or

not they were derived from production-based engines. Thus, significantly, pure-bred racing engines were allowed to take advantage of the increased boost and greater capacity.

Illien had considered the possibility of developing this type of engine when the new rule was first promulgated. At the time, however, he concluded he was too busy with his parallel projects on the 'B' and 'C' programs as well as in Formula 1. The notion was put on the back burner.

'I realized even in those days there was an advantage to be gained – or there should be an advantage, but I wasn't quite ready to do it,' explains the Swiss engineer. 'I must say, too, that I didn't like the idea of making a racing engine out of a pushrod engine. I was not really in favor of the equivalency formula and I felt that would not be the thing to do.'

After witnessing the 1993 Indianapolis 500, however, Illien was convinced the 209 engine would be a winner.

'Indy confirmed our belief that we absolutely needed to do a pushrod project,' says Morgan. 'We wanted to be ahead of Honda and Ford, and we felt it was really important to get involved in a pushrod so that we would be at least among the first, if not the first, to do so.'

Penske quickly agreed with the principle, and right away the wheels

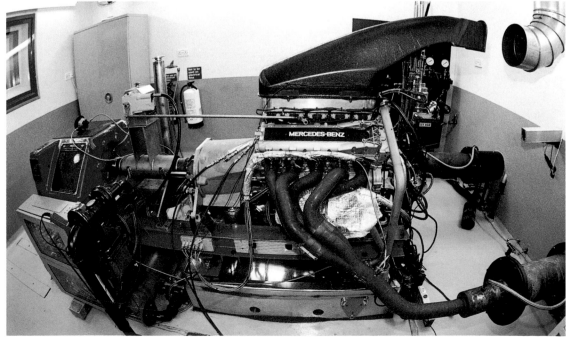

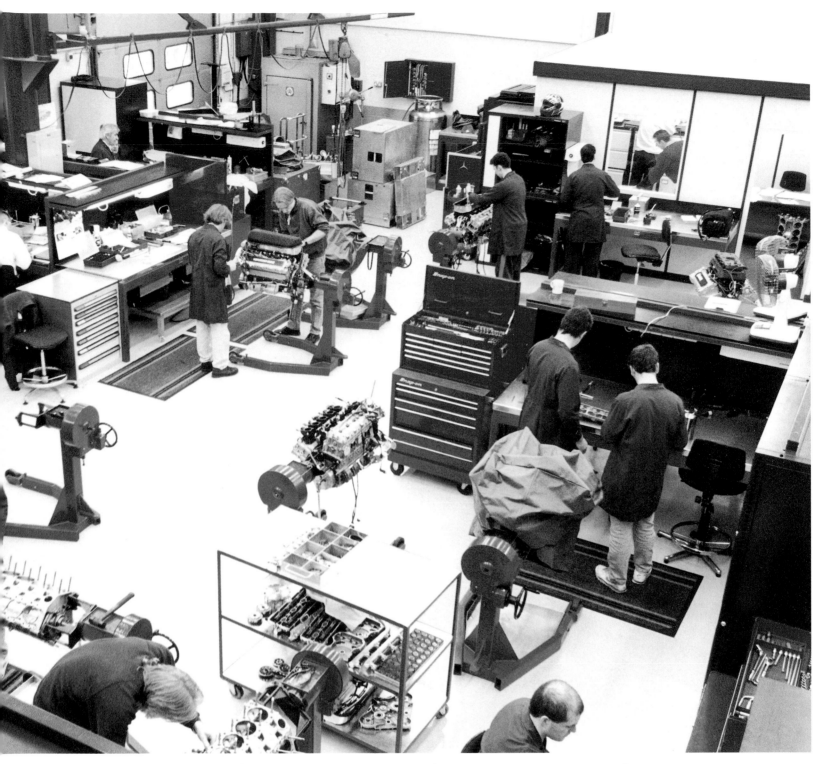

were put in motion to study the feasibility of such a project. And, make no mistake, it represented a major commitment. At that stage, no firm backer for the project was on the horizon. On top of that, all three Ilmor partners realized that if they did go ahead and build a pushrod engine, the chances were high that it would be eligible for just one race: the 1994 Indianapolis 500.

'The pushrod program was the fastest and most intense we've ever done,' declares Morgan, 'because it captured everybody's imagination here at Ilmor. It was a unique opportunity – almost do-or-die, if you like. It was quite likely that the engine would be eligible for only one race – the 1994 Indianapolis 500. We rather expected the equivalency formula to be banned immediately after that race. Therefore it was absolutely essential that it worked correctly the first time.'

Ilmor's first priority, however, was to proceed with production of its 'conventional' Ilmor Indy V8 engine,

the 'D', which, of course, would provide the impetus to Penske's challenge for the 1994 PPG Cup title.

In fact, the two programs dovetailed conveniently. Through prior experience, Morgan, who is responsible for administering the company while Illien concentrates on design, knew that from initial concept to having a new engine ready to run on the dynamometer would take around 35 weeks. And as planned, the four-cam 'D' motor was ready for bench-testing by mid-November. The prototype 'D' was shipped across to Penske Cars, then given its first shakedown run, in Al Unser Jr.'s hands, at Nazareth on December 7.

Meanwhile, and with the utmost secrecy, design on the pushrod Indy engine was proceeding rapidly.

'It was a big challenge from an engineering point of view,' admits Illien. 'Obviously, there were a lot of difficulties in making the whole valve-train survive at relatively high rpm. That in itself was quite a task.'

Neither Illien, nor any of his

design staff, had worked on a pushrod, two-valve engine before. They learned quickly. Alan Cook assisted Illien in scheming the engine, while Philip Le Roux concentrated on development of the likely-to-be-troublesome valve-train. Ilmor's Indy Car project engineer Andrew Hurley also was heavily involved, along with five other detail designers.

A dedicated test rig for the valve-train was built, then run 'day and night' to evaluate a large number of different versions before the design was finalized.

One of the primary requirements (and challenges) for Illien was to retain as near as possible the same mounting points, plumbing and location of ancillaries as on the 'D', in order to minimize the myriad problems associated with switching from one engine to the other for Indianapolis – and then back again once the month of May was over.

Once more, co-operation between the Ilmor designers and the Penske

Cars drawing office was crucial. Chuck Sprague and the engineers in Reading also were kept apprised of progress. Early on, due to the anticipated extra torque of the pushrod engine, it was realized a revised transmission would be required, featuring stronger gears, larger bearings and a stiffer case. Several other new components also would be required, including a discrete aerodynamic package to accommodate the slightly taller and wider engine, as well as a completely different underbody.

'The whole program was extremely well-orchestrated,' praises Nick Goozee from Penske Cars. 'Because it was such a major undertaking, and the two projects had to run in parallel with neither affecting the other, we had to spend a lot of time working out exactly how we were going to do it.'

One of the biggest difficulties for Goozee was to anticipate how many of the pushrod-engined cars would run at Indianapolis. Initially,

94 MARLBORO PENSKE MERCEDES-BENZ

Al Unser Jr. and Emerson Fittipaldi compare notes.

Penske Racing Team Manager Chuck Sprague *(right)* **confers with his chief lieutenant, Clive Howell.**

Mum's the word

The entire Mercedes-Benz/Ilmor pushrod engine project, geared solely toward winning the 78th Indianapolis 500, highlighted not only the engineering excellence of the entire Penske auto racing organization but also its dedication and tenacity. All told, it is a remarkable story centered upon teamwork, co-operation and commitment.

One of the most interesting aspects of the program was the cloak of secrecy under which it was conducted, for fear a rival engine manufacturer might learn of the project and embark upon a similar development. In the early stages, only those key personnel who were directly involved knew about it, and indeed the majority of Penske Racing employees remained in the dark until shortly before it was formally announced to the press on Wednesday April 13 – just over three weeks before the Indianapolis Motor Speedway opened for official practice.

The fact that no news leaked out was impressive in itself. 'To me, that was very satisfying,' says Ilmor's Paul Morgan, 'because Northampton is an absolute hotbed of racing, and within two or three months of getting started, a lot of the rest of the work-force had to get involved. We prefer to operate on a basis of trust, so we got everyone together and said, look guys, this is what we're doing and it is very, very important that it's kept secret. We explained that to the whole work-force – 150 people - and I have to say we're really proud of the fact that the word never leaked.'

Morgan and his crew resorted to some ingenious tactics to keep news from spreading. For example, when larger than usual valves were required from an outside supplier, the order was placed using the Penske Racing South NASCAR team as a cover by labelling the valves as 'Pontiac' components.

'I think there were some fairly deep suspicions, but fortunately nobody said anything,' says Morgan with a smile. Amazingly, the first engine ran on the dynamometer just 26 weeks after Mario Illien began work on the design, and once the prototype engine had been despatched to Reading, talented young engineer Kevin Walter played a major role in development and acted as the primary liaison between Penske Racing and Ilmor.

Walter's first responsibility was to set up an 'under-cover' workshop, separate from the main facility, where he could build and strip down the engines before and after each test. There was also room (just) for the designated Indy project test car, run by Guy Oder. It was a spartan establishment that quickly earned the somewhat sarcastic sobriquet 'Taj Mahal'.

'Really, it was kind of a throwback to the small-team racing days,' says Walter. 'It was quite a change from our regular environment.'

Nevertheless, it was home to Walter, Oder and their small group for weeks on end, usually working long into the night and incorporating frequent trips to Nazareth Speedway and then later to Michigan International Speedway, for on-track testing. (Initial tests at Nazareth took place, incidentally, only after record-breaking snow drifts had been cleared from the track.) All dyno testing was carried out overnight, away from prying eyes (and ears) at Penske Racing.

'Basically our job was to build the engine for the tests, support the tests at the track, then evaluate everything and report back to Ilmor to let them know, well, this is good, this is not good,' says Walter, 'and at times, scream for help!'

The group encountered many pitfalls along the way in terms of reliability. Frequently, new parts were designed and manufactured in a matter of days, then flown across the Atlantic on Concorde. On one memorable occasion, with time running especially short, airplane aficionado Morgan was obliged to 'run up the road' to his local airfield, climb aboard his vintage P51 Mustang and ferry some new parts to another airfield close to Heathrow, whereupon a waiting car whisked the consignment to the waiting Concorde! Sometimes the gestation period from drawing board to on-track testing was as little as 36 hours.

The engine never actually completed a full 500-mile test at Michigan until Sunday, May 8 – the day after official practice began at Indianapolis. Only then could the engineers finalize the race specification. Ultimately, however, the engines ran flawlessly, without a single failure during the entire month of May at Indy; and the Mercedes engines actually exceeded Mario Illien's estimated power output by around 3.5 percent.

And finally on race day, when the chips were down, Al Unser Jr. and Emerson Fittipaldi led all but seven of the 200 laps en route to one of the most extraordinary victories of all time.

Left: **Mission accomplished. Al Unser Jr. pulls into Victory Lane after scoring his second and Penske Racing's 10th Indianapolis 500 triumph.**

Right: **Kevin Walter assembles one of the Ilmor Indy V8s.**

Far right: **Karl Kainhofer has dyno-tested every Indy Car engine assembled at Reading over the past 19 years.**

Below right: **In the main race shop, poster portraits of Penske Racing's ten Indianapolis 500 champions provide a constant reminder of the ultimate goal.**

Bottom: **Richard Buck (kneeling) and crew prepare Unser's car for action.**

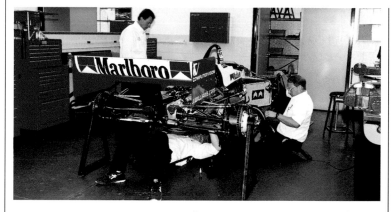

thought had been given to splitting the program, with only one or two of the three drivers making the switch. But once the Ilmor engineers were convinced the engine was capable of running 500 miles – and then, particularly because Mercedes-Benz agreed to back the entire program – the decision was made to run all three drivers at Indy with Mercedes-powered cars.

'It was controlled mayhem,' admits Goozee. 'We were geared for it, but with only a month before Indianapolis opened for practice, it was the one decision we didn't want to hear – for obvious reasons. Still, once we got under way it was fine because by then we realized what a huge advantage the engine was going to give us, and that fueled our enthusiasm.'

While work continued behind closed doors on the Mercedes 'E' project (code-named using Ilmor's alphabetical designation), development on the regular PC23-Ilmor/D combination also had to proceed. Once the first production car and engine had been delivered, the emphasis switched over to Penske Racing in Pennsylvania. A concerted test program had already been conceived by Sprague and assistant team manager/chief mechanic Clive Howell (or 'chief cook and bottle-washer' as he terms himself). In all, the cars completed almost 4500 miles of testing even before the first race in Australia.

One of the major gains this season by comparison with years past came from the fact that all of the new cars arrived from Poole in turn-key condition, rather than in kit form.

'It had developed into a major logistical problem,' says Goozee. 'I guess we were getting a bit lazy because we had a habit of air-freighting the chassis and bodywork one week, a majority of the components the following week and then any remaining bits in the third week. It meant we had problems keeping track of what had been sent, and of course it increased our shipping bills unnecessarily.'

The new procedure of assembling the entire car in Poole is overseen by former race mechanic Mark Grimes.

'It helped a ton,' says Sprague, 'on both sides of "the pond." They learned a lot and now we know that when a car arrives, it has to be complete or it wouldn't be sitting on all four wheels. It allows Penske Cars to co-ordinate so many of the details. Now they see all the little brackets and widgets and routing problems

with lines and things, which, before, you couldn't visualize, no matter how good your design system.'

At Penske Racing, the planning process begins for both tests and races in much the same way. Clive Howell is responsible for organizing preparation of the cars, and along with Sprague schedules the travel arrangements for the entire crew. Team logistics co-ordinator Tim Lombardi then takes care of all the specific details.

At the shop itself, which has been expanded twice from its original 10,000 square-foot area and now comprises almost 33,000 square feet, everything is neatly compartmentalized. Each of the six race cars (one for each of the three drivers, plus two spare cars that travel to all of the

races and a designated test car) has its own separate bay, with the name of each crew chief and his two assistants displayed on a neat plaque on the partition wall. At the end of each working day, the cars are covered and everything is packed neatly away. Not a hair is left out of place.

The same attention to detail dictated by Kainhofer, who is general manager of Penske Racing and also runs the engine rebuild shop, is prevalent throughout the practical but certainly not overwhelming facility. The individual departments are headed by Grant Newbury (engineering), John Faivre (electronics), Jerry Breon (fabrication), Earle MacMullan (sub-assembly), Tim Raiskup (shock absorbers), Dave Eisenhofer (paint shop), Bill White (transporters) and

Jean MacMullan (office manager).

The engineering and electronics departments have grown substantially over recent seasons and are involved in several interesting projects, including development of tire pressure sensors in conjunction with an outside specialist company, Epic. The idea for the system, which is designed to transmit an alarm if the pressure on any tire drops below a designated limit, came after the race at Phoenix in 1993. On that occasion, during a full-course caution shortly before the end of the race, Fittipaldi was unsure whether to make a pit stop to check for damage after running over debris – ironically from team-mate Tracy's crash. Fittipaldi, leading by more than a lap, decided to remain on the track and unfortunately just one lap after the restart he crashed – due to a puncture.

'The cost of a failure in a race is just too high to nickel-and-dime anything,' says Sprague. 'It's false economy to use one component which is $10 cheaper than another. If anything fails while you're leading a race, first it's going to cause perhaps $100,000 worth of damage to the equipment and then it's going to throw away $100,000 of prize money.

'Several projects that we have initiated, including the tire sensors, are real expensive from top-to-bottom development, but the first time they work, they've more than paid

for themselves.'

The sensors were used for the first time during the Marlboro 500 at Michigan International Speedway, where any tire problem has the potential to cause a serious accident. Subsequently, at Nazareth, again following an accident, the sensors confirmed that despite running over some debris, all four Goodyear Eagle tires remained properly inflated, thus saving the need for an exploratory pit stop.

Another feature of the Penske cars this season has been the distinctive fin atop the engine cover, which aroused considerable interest from rivals teams – especially after Fittipaldi and Unser sped to a clear 1-2

finish when it first appeared at Phoenix. In typical Penske fashion, the fins had not been run at the first race of the season, in Australia, since the circuit is comprised mainly of slow-speed corners – and also because the team did not want to give away what it perceived as a small but appreciable benefit.

'The gain would have been minimal in Australia, but we particularly wanted to have the fins for Phoenix, where there is quite an advantage and where we had tested them,' says Nigel Bennett mischievously. 'In fact we tested something similar a year ago, and it alerted us to the possibilities. We introduced the fin at Phoenix, and sure enough, people

had copied it by Indy – whether they knew what it did or not!'

Indeed, the fins stabilize the rear of the car, especially in high-speed corners when the car is yawed. Bennett is convinced that the fins also act as a safety feature, helping to deter the car from spinning, and he was therefore extremely miffed when the USAC technical inspectors insisted the fins be trimmed so that they should not extend beyond the center-line of the rear axle.

The fins are just one small example of how Penske Racing works hard to maximize the resources at its disposal. Sure, the team is adequately funded, but there is no fat, and absolutely no wastage. The budget is generally spent wisely and effectively.

There is no doubt, too, that the Penske team has benefited from running three cars. Roger Penske took the decision to trim back from three cars to two in 1990, but this season the team showed it had learned from previous experiences.

'You always learn from what you've done before,' declares Rick Mears, who has acted as coach/adviser/technical guru for Marlboro Team Penske since retiring at the end of the 1992 season.

'Everybody sat down and studied what we had done in the past with a three-car team – what our weak

points were and how to shore them up – and that just made everything a little bit stronger, a little bit better.'

Once again, attention to detail. The phrase crops up again and again, in all aspects of the racing operation, be it at Penske Cars, Penske Racing or Ilmor Engineering. Every little detail is continually under the microscope during the race weekends, and the diligence pays off.

Once the team arrives at the race track, chief engineer Grant Newbury effectively takes charge of the operation, at least in terms of co-ordinating how the cars are run. Interestingly, however, his role in 1994 turned out to be rather different to that which had been originally envisaged.

'I wasn't supposed to go to all the races,' reveals Newbury, whose previous responsibilities as race engineer for Fittipaldi were assumed by Tom Brown. 'Instead I was going to concentrate on R & D projects – take the next step technologically, if you like.'

But the pressure of running three cars eventually led to Newbury co-ordinating the engineering team at the races. The switch allowed him to keep a firm grasp on what was being tried on each of the cars.

'Looking back, it was a good move,' he says. 'As long as we could keep each of the drivers communicating his thoughts, ideas and experiences

Far left: (l to r) Chief engineer Grant Newbury takes overall charge of the engineering team, while John Faivre heads electronics. Nigel Beresford works with Paul Tracy at the races and Tom Brown liaises with Emerson Fittipaldi.
Main picture: Fittipaldi is stationary in the pits for around 14 seconds while his crew adds a full load of fuel and four fresh tires.
Bottom left: Teddy Mayer and Rick Mears confer over race strategy.
Right: (l to r) Crew chiefs Rick Rinaman (Fittipaldi), Jon Bouslog (Tracy) and Richard Buck (Unser). Unser led the way with eight victories during the 1994 season with his distinctive Marlboro Penske PC23. *Inset:* Unser and race engineer Terry Satchell discuss some of the finer details of the car's set-up.

to the other two, it benefited the team as a whole. I think each of them realized that, hey, I might tell this guy something and he might go as fast or quicker than me, but there's two of them helping me the same way, so I think all three of them realized the advantage of doing that. We learned much more that way and we did manage to get all three cars pretty much on a par with each other by race day, which was one of our goals.'

On a typical race weekend, all three cars would be set up identically at the start of first practice – except for the fact Unser preferred a firmer brake pedal, so different master cylinders always were fitted to his PC23. After that, each driver would go in different directions in terms of the set-up, searching for the optimum handling characteristics. All the drivers and engineers were in radio contact, with Sprague and Newbury overseeing the carefully planned operation from the pits. The system allowed a large number of variables to be tested in a minimum amount of time and enabled the team to make enormous strides.

Thus, if one driver had gone in the wrong direction with his set-up, the pooling of information allowed significant changes to be made, if necessary, even on race morning without taking any undue risk.

That particular spirit of teamwork was undoubtedly a major factor in ensuring the team's success this year. The wealth of experience and knowledge imparted by Mears also proved to be a major benefit.

'Having Rick around is such a huge plus,' says Sprague. 'The technical benefits are obvious, but unless you work with him, you cannot appreciate how good he is for the entire team – just his outlook, his attitude. When he walks in, the place lights up.

'He's worked primarily with Paul Tracy this year, but Al insisted on having him at most of the tests. In fact, Al credited Rick with helping him find three miles an hour around Phoenix. After his first test there in January, Junior was quicker than he'd ever been before.'

The highlights this season have been numerous. Indianapolis, of course, is memorable for the huge effort and co-operation that went into ensuring success. Also the fact that Marlboro Team Penske scored 12 wins in 16 races – and with its drivers claiming the top three posi-

tions in the PPG Indy Car World Series. Indeed, on no fewer than five occasions Unser, Fittipaldi and Tracy, clad in their distinctive red-and-white Marlboro uniforms, stood together on the victory podium. For many people, however, the 1-2-3 at Milwaukee – just one week after Indianapolis – stands out above the rest. Especially for Karl Kainhofer.

'There was a lot of talk about how "easy" we had things at Indy, because we had an advantage with the engine, but I don't know if those people would have said the same

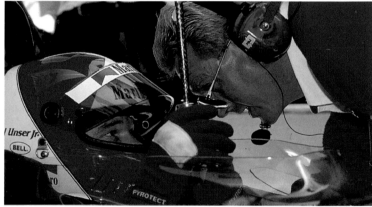

thing if they'd come into the shop during the winter and seen us all working at two, three or four o'clock in the morning, day after day,' says Kainhofer. 'For me, Milwaukee provided a perfect example of what this team is capable of achieving. We had only three days after Indianapolis to change all the cars over from the Mercedes engine to the Ilmor/D; we had to turn the whole program around – and showing that strength just one week later, I thought, was incredible. You can't knock performance like that.'

HOLD YOUR HORSEPOWER, DON'T BLAME THE WINNER
by JIM MURRAY

One of the aftermaths of the 78th Indianapolis 500 is something I find distressing and can only refer to as "Roger bashing."

It goes like this: Break up Roger Penske or his team. Hogtie him with rules. Make him tee it up next year in a stock '54 DeSoto. Ban him. Exile him. Get a restraining order against his getting within 25 miles of Indianapolis in May. Hold him in custody.

What did he do? He won his 10th Indy 500 in 26 years and his third in the last four. He got the best drivers in the world and put them in the best cars.

Wait a minute! Isn't that what you're supposed to do? I thought that was the whole idea of the race. I thought that was the whole idea of sport.

So, why should we send Penske to Elba?

They say he has an unfair advantage. Well, what?

Well, he hooked up with Mercedes-Benz and Ilmor Engineering and produced an engine that was clearly faster than the competition.

Well, so he did. So he has always done. So what?

He did that as far back as 1972 with a four-cylinder Offenhauser engine. He did that several times subsequently with Cosworth Fords. Then he did it with V-8 Chevies. Now, he does it with Mercedes.

Well, in the news conferences after the race you would have thought he had performed grand larceny.

"What about Michael Andretti saying your cars had 200 more horsepower in the straights?" he was asked accusingly in tones usually reserved for kidnapping suspects. An "All right, Joe, what did you do with the baby?" tone of voice.

So? Whose fault is it he had more horsepower? Well, they said resentfully, he took advantage of a loophole in the rules.

Hey! Why didn't those other guys? Penske didn't write the rules. He simply read them.

Well, he had the might of Mercedes behind him. Well, OK. But, if it was that easy, why didn't Rolls-Royce do it? Honda did try it. It not only couldn't get a car on the pole or in Victory Lane, it couldn't get one in the race.

Let me tell you something about Roger Penske: In the preparation for the Gulf War three years ago, Gen. Norman Schwarzkopf consulted him on vehicular problems for Operation Desert Storm. Does that tell you something about him?

Many years ago when Ben Hogan was dominating the game of golf, a rival, Mike Souchak, once observed ruefully, "Ben Hogan just knows something about hitting a golf ball the rest of us don't know." Same with Roger Penske and automobiles.

Consider his record. If you check the accomplishments of a lot of guys in Penske's position – which essentially is that of coach or manager – you find that they had the advantage of a field leader. You will note the former Pittsburgh Steeler coach, Chuck Noll, got to four Super Bowls – all with the same quarterback, Terry Bradshaw. Tom Landry was most successful when he had Roger Staubach, Bill Walsh with Joe Montana. John McGraw was a great manager – when he had Christy Mathewson. Miller Huggins had Ruth *and* Gehrig.

When the constant is the coach, you know you are dealing with genius. When Roger Penske first went to the Speedway, he had Mark Donohue, a sports car driver. On their fourth try, they won. Penske later hooked up with Rick Mears. And he won four times at Indy with him.

Roger won with Bobby Unser. Then, Danny Sullivan. Then Al Unser. Then Emerson Fittipaldi. Last Sunday, he won with Al Unser Jr. Four different engines, seven different drivers. Two generations of Unsers.

That is awesome. Dynasty stuff. The chauffeurs didn't seem to make all that difference. When Fittipaldi crashed last Sunday with 15 laps to go, his teammate, Little Al, was running right behind him.

Years ago, the carpers used to shout, "Break up the Yankees!" They didn't. They copied them.

They complained about Rockne and Notre Dame. In horse racing, they picked on Calumet Farms.

What were the Yankees supposed to do? Swap franchises with the St. Louis Browns? What was Notre Dame supposed to do? Get in the Mid-American Conference?

That's not the American way. You don't penalize excellence, you emulate it.

It's expensive? Hey! Where could Mercedes get that kind of publicity, advertising? How many millions of dollars would it have to spend to get the kind of exposure winning the world's most important race brings it?

Detroit turned its back on Indy racing years ago. The activists – who would be the only ones having any fun if they were able to remake the world the way they want it – had bullied them into thinking any association with speed would detract from their campaign for safety.

As if safety ever sold a single car. "My air bags are better than your air bags," is not the stuff of legend. "My car won Indianapolis," is.

In the military, a guy with this much edge in smarts over his adversary is known as "the Swamp Fox," or "the Desert Fox" or "the Iron Chancellor" or some such.

At Indy, Penske is peerless. But they call him to task. They mutter darkly about changing the rules. He beats them at their own game. He should be "the Wizard of the Wabash."

It didn't used to be a sin to win in this country.

There is no single reason why Marlboro Team Penske swept all before it during the 1994 PPG Indy Car World Series season. Rather it was the cumulative effect of a number of factors, not least of which was the manner in which Al Unser Jr., Emerson Fittipaldi and Paul Tracy worked together for the common good. The trio displayed entirely differing approaches to their tasks, and indeed it is interesting to note the comments of chief engineer Grant Newbury, who is responsible for correlating the information gained from each of the three Penske drivers.

'Al concentrates on preparing for the race the whole time,' says Newbury. 'He generally uses only one set of tires for qualifying on Friday, knowing that he will go faster on Saturday; and that way he can keep an extra fresh set for the race. He definitely doesn't like the car to be loose at all. Emerson, through the years, has had the most problems dealing with the ride of the car. He's always been more sensitive to variations in aerodynamics and ride-height and how the car handles over the bumps. Paul, meanwhile, basically just goes as fast as he can all the time. He just drives through whatever the car is doing. You always know he's driving flat-out.'

The differing techniques and nuances add spice to Newbury's job. More pieces of the puzzle are supplied by the race engineers, Terry Satchell, Tom Brown and Nigel Beresford, and from close liaison with crew chiefs Richard Buck, Rick Rinaman and Jon Bouslog.

Valuable assistance, too, comes from Rick Mears, who retired from driving at the end of the 1992 season after winning four Indianapolis 500s and three PPG Cup titles for Penske Racing. Mears, indeed, remains as closely involved as ever, particularly in helping to disseminate the information from the drivers.

'Mainly this year I worked with Paul,' says Mears, 'but I did work with all three from time to time. The main thing is that they worked well together, and they seemed to be pretty close in terms of what they wanted from the car. Their driving styles are all very different, but setup-wise, what they want from the car, they're all pretty close.

'Tracy is certainly more impetuous than the other two and tends to run every lap as if it's a qualifying lap. Al is kind of the opposite. He only runs as hard as he needs to get a feel for the car and then he turns it on when it's time to qualify. And Emerson is kind of in between. He's kind of Steady-Eddie. So we really have the spectrum covered.'

Penske Racing Highlights

1994 – Al Unser Jr. won the Indianapolis 500 plus seven other races and the PPG Indy Car World Series; Paul Tracy won three races; Emerson Fittipaldi won one race; Rusty Wallace won eight NASCAR races.

1993 – Fittipaldi won the Indianapolis 500 and two more PPG Cup races; Tracy won five PPG Cup races; Wallace won 10 NASCAR races.

1992 – Fittipaldi won four PPG Cup races.

1991 – Rick Mears won the Indianapolis 500 and one more Indy Car PPG Cup race; Fittipaldi won one PPG Cup race.

1990 – Danny Sullivan won two PPG Cup races; Mears and Fittipaldi won one PPG Cup race each.

1989 – Sullivan won the Pocono 500 and one more PPG Cup race; Mears won three PPG Cup races.

1988 – Mears won the Indianapolis 500 and another Indy Car race; Sullivan won four races and the PPG Indy Car World Series.

1987 – Al Unser Sr. won the Indianapolis 500; Mears won the Pocono 500.

1986 – Sullivan won two PPG Cup races.

1985 – Sullivan won the Indianapolis 500 plus another PPG Cup race; Unser Sr. won the PPG Indy Car World Series and one race; Mears won one race.

1984 – Mears won the Indianapolis 500.

1983 – Unser Sr. won the PPG Indy Car World Series championship and one race; Mears won one Indy Car race.

1982 – Mears won the PPG Indy Car World Series and four races.

1981 – Bobby Unser won the Indianapolis 500; Mears won the PPG Indy Car World Series and six races.

1980 – Bobby Unser won four PPG Cup races; Mears and Mario Andretti each won one PPG Cup race.

1979 – Mears won the Indianapolis 500, the inaugural PPG Indy Car World Series and three races; Bobby Unser won six PPG Cup races.

1978 – Tom Sneva won the USAC Championship; Mears was co-Rookie of the Year at Indianapolis and won three races; Andretti also won one race.

1977 – Sneva won the USAC Championship and two races; recorded first ever 200 mph lap in claiming pole at Indianapolis.

1976 – John Watson won Austrian Grand Prix (F1).

1975 – Sneva won Michigan 150 Indy Car race; Bobby Allison won three NASCAR races.

1974 – Allison won NASCAR Ontario 500.

1973 – Mark Donohue won the Can-Am Championship and NASCAR Riverside 500; Gary Bettenhausen won one Indy Car race.

1972 – Donohue won the Indianapolis 500; George Follmer won the Can-Am Championship; Bettenhausen won one Indy Car race.

1971 – Donohue won the Trans-Am Championship and the inaugural Pocono 500 Indy Car race.

1970 – Donohue won three Can-Am and two Formula 5000 races and finished second at Indianapolis.

1969 – Donohue finished seventh in Indianapolis 500; was Rookie of the Year and won the Daytona 24 Hours with Chuck Parsons; Donohue won the Trans-Am Championship.

1968 – Donohue won the Trans-Am Championship and the United States Road Racing Championship (USRRC).

1967 – Donohue won six of seven USRRC races and Penske Racing's first championship.

1966 – Donohue won one race in the USRRC.

spirit

power

victory

legend.

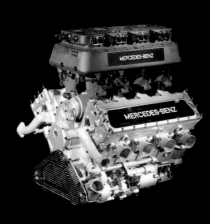

We're going ahead
with this one

A-class study

▶ It's no mere coincidence that our A-class study turned out the way it did. After all, we were out to design a car primarily geared to urban driving. Since road space in city traffic is valuable – and parking space even more so – every centimetre counts. The new car thus had to get by with the dimensions of a hatch. But to provide the right degree of comfort for a longer stay on board we had to fit the generous passenger compartment of a midrange saloon into this limited space. And all without compromising on the traditional safety of a Mercedes.

▶ At first it was far from clear whether we weren't setting out in pursuit of the impossible. But then our engineers came up with a solution as surprising as it is sophisticated: To make room for a top quality Mercedes-Benz safety cell and keep dimensions to a minimum, they hid the engine and transmission safely out of the way – under the floor level of the passenger compartment. This has the additional advantage that in the event of an accident, all the underfloor engineering cannot be pushed into the survival space.

▶ Although some people feel that it is in cars like this that the future lies, this won't be the only car we build in future. Because people's requirements and expectations they place in the car they drive will still be too varied for us to meet them all with only a single model.

We're staying ahead with this one

The S-class

▶ It's no mere coincidence that our S-class turned out the way it did. After all, we build it for people whose above-average professional commitment means they take more passengers than average on longer than average trips. And they all need to arrive in good shape for a hard day's work.

▶ Such people rightly expect their car to go easy on their own personal energy reserves. Which is why, over more than 30 years now. We have constantly re-turned to thinking of new ways in which the S-class can help them. The result of our efforts to date is a whole spectrum of inventions that make the S-class a paragon of auto-motive engineering in so many areas. From comfort to safety.

▶ The fact that we're on the right road is constantly reconfirm-ed when many of the aspects we first introduced in the S-class begin, just a few years later, to ap-pear on a broad front – like the airbag is doing right now. In the meantime, today's S-class has, of course, moved further ahead – and that is where it will stay.

▶ Of course, not everyone needs a car like this. But on the other hand, are many people who need such a car more than ever. And will need one in future, too.

Mercedes-Benz
Engineered like no other car in the world

Here's

1

Marlboro Team Penske
Paul Tracy
3rd in the PPG Cup standings.
Oil: Mobil 1

IndyCar record they'll be chasing forever.

Marlboro Team Penske
Emerson Fittipaldi
2nd in the PPG Cup standings.
Oil: Mobil 1

Marlboro Team Penske
Al Unser Jr.
Winner of the 1994 PPG Cup.
Oil: Mobil 1

This year was really one for the record books. It was the first time in IndyCar history that a single team, and a single oil, came in first, second and third in the PPG Cup standings. So congratulations to Al Unser, Jr., Emerson Fittipaldi, Paul Tracy and the entire Marlboro Penske team. You made it look as easy as 1-2-3.

It keeps your engine running like new.

by Jeremy Shaw

Michael C. Brown

first

IMPRESSIONS

IT is safe to say that even toward the end of the 1993 PPG Cup season the mention of Andrew Craig would have elicited barely a flicker of recognition from anybody involved in Indy Car racing.

At the time, the IndyCar board of directors was searching for a successor to Bill Stokkan, who had tendered his resignation as chairman and chief executive officer following less than three years on the job. Craig was among many who filed an application, although during the initial phases his name was discarded virtually out of hand. Instead, most insiders felt the vacant post would be filled either by Sports Car Club of America President Nick Craw, retiring Ford motor sports manager Michael Kranefuss, or highly respected race track promoter/lawyer Cary Agajanian.

But the board failed to reach a unanimous agreement, whereupon a fresh ballot brought Craig's name to the surface. His resume was impressive. It showed he had gained an intimate knowledge of the business of sports marketing and management through his experience as Executive Vice-President and Deputy Chief Executive Officer of Swiss-based ISL Marketing AG. Among other projects, Craig had been responsible for the development and management of the International Olympic Committee's vast world-wide sponsorship program.

Eventually, Craig was invited to make a presentation to the search committee entrusted with locating a new chief executive, although even that decision, frankly, was met with a degree of incredulity from several board members who had not been involved in the selection process. For a start, he was an Englishman, which did not go down well in some quarters. What could he possibly know about Indy Car racing – apart, perhaps, from being

21

a member of recently crowned PPG Cup champion Nigel Mansell's cheering section?

Well, it turns out Craig knew a great deal about the sport. Apart from being an avid auto racing enthusiast who had himself competed at a modest level, Craig had made a point of carrying out an in-depth study to determine what was really needed from the sport's new head honcho. The board was impressed. It was quickly agreed that he was amply qualified as a dedicated professional with an impressive knowledge not only of Indy Car racing but also of the inner dealings of sports management and sponsorships. The cry went up: 'He's our man!'

Nevertheless, Craig had other hurdles to overcome. For a start, so far as everybody else involved in the sport was concerned, apart from the team owners, he remained an unknown quantity. As such, his appointment was treated with skepticism. But less than nine months after being appointed President and Chief Executive Officer of Championship Auto Racing Teams, Inc., Craig had won over many doubters.

He has impressed everyone with his willingness to talk – and, perhaps even more importantly, to listen. He has worked diligently to review the strengths and weaknesses of the organization. He has solidified a firm plan of action and already has cemented a strong base for the future, which includes an expanded and improved television package as well as a healthy calendar of events which is locked in virtually through until the turn of the century.

Craig, however, readily acknowledges that the television package was almost completely in place when he took charge of CART/IndyCar on March 31. Indeed, he says, the sport already was in good health.

'There were a few organizational difficulties and obviously some things that needed to be sorted out,' he says, 'but basically I took over something that was remarkably strong. It's very encouraging to come into a series where in every single race this year we've had a record number of spectators and in every single race this year we've had full grids. So there was obviously a very solid base on which to build.'

Craig has now worked through virtually an entire season of PPG Cup competition, having officially started work just one week after the opening race at Surfers Paradise, Australia. Being able to join the organization at

that juncture, he reflects, brought both benefits and disadvantages.

'In some ways it was difficult joining just as the season was beginning, because the train had already left the station, so to speak, and quite clearly it would have been inappropriate to make any major changes right away. But also, of course, I needed a period of time to understand the business. It was very important to get to know the directors, the teams, the drivers, my staff and the race promoters, and to understand what their individual needs were.

'I think my prime objective coming in was to make sure we had a properly organized business that could meet the needs of our public and our race promoters – and, of course, the needs of our owners; and that reorganization is still taking place. It's a very broadly based re-organization, covering everything from operations, office administration, right the way through to TV and marketing.

'I would hasten to add that when I came into the company, things were in no way disastrous from an organizational point of view; but it just wasn't the organization I felt we needed to take us forward. Now I know exactly what sort of organization I want to have, so I'm actually looking for people. Now we're moving into a positive phase of the whole thing.

'My strategic goals, quite simply, are to boost levels of interest in the sport and thus to generate more revenue flowing throughout the industry; and I also want to introduce people to the product effectively, and to make sure their experience is an enjoyable one, both on television and

for the live audience. In order to achieve that we need to get better promotion of the sport on TV and, in particular, in the press, where we're particularly weak – outside of the specialist press, there's very little coverage of IndyCar racing.'

In effect, of course, Craig is trying to please everyone, from the fans to the sponsors, the officials, the drivers, the car owners and the promoters. It is not an easy task, but it's one he appears to undertake with relish. Craig, clearly, has a good way with people. He is able to make himself understood and has already established a solid rapport with most groups.

On the whole, too, he has found a favorable response from the vast majority of individuals with whom he has come into contact. And some of the horror stories he had been led to expect have simply not materialized. At least, not yet!

'I was pleasantly surprised at how absolutely committed our board of directors are to motor racing,' he declares. 'I'd been given the impression coming in, from the press or whatever, that somehow this was an avaricious group, merely there to line their own pockets. I had been given the impression that perhaps this wasn't the most friendly group of people; but actually what I found was a group of people who, first of all, made me feel extremely welcome and, secondly, care passionately about motor racing. Passionately about it. Which I guess is kind of obvious, otherwise they wouldn't be doing it . . .

'Thirdly, actually, I have found them to be remarkably uncomplicated. The whole political bit, I think, is

grossly overplayed. When I arrived here I was told this is political and that is political. I can only say, from my experiences in sport in the past, I have often heard things being described as "political." In truth, I find half the time that "political" means, "Well, we don't really understand it;" or "Mr. A doesn't like Mr. B," or "Mr. B is frightened of Mr. A," or whatever. But it's not political. This is the normal cut and thrust of any organization where human beings have to inter-react.

'I think "political" is a wonderful smoke-screen for hiding behind. I think "politics" is the most over-used word in sport. Really, it's not politics, it's business – a business in which the teams come together and they're very, very united in the board room; and then they come out of the board room and become archrivals on the track. I think that's thoroughly healthy.'

Also in contrast with what he had been led to expect, Craig has been able to establish a sound dialogue with the officials at the United States Auto Club and with Tony George, President of the Indianapolis Motor Speedway.

'I think as far as USAC is concerned, on a day-to-day basis, we have an extremely good relationship,' he says. 'They are responsible for sanctioning the Indy 500 and that requires a lot of liaison between our two organizations; and I think that's been done in a very co-operative, businesslike manner, even though obviously during the course of this year, potentially [with the advent of the controversial Indy Racing League], that could have become difficult. But quite the opposite. I found that my opposite numbers, [USAC President] Richard King and [Director of Competition] Johnny Capels and [Technical Director] Mike Devin, have been extremely open and supportive and basically very anxious that we continue to get the job done and to make sure that when it comes to the inter-relationships between our two organizations, as far as the PPG Indy Car World Series is concerned, we work smoothly and effectively regardless of the current gap between ourselves and The Speedway.

'With regard to the relationship with Tony George at The Speedway, I must say at all times it's been extremely cordial. I met with Tony very early on and he very clearly set out his concerns about the direction in which he saw IndyCar heading.

Nigel Mansell has contributed substantially to the growth of Indy Car racing during his two-year stint with Newman-Haas Racing.

We've talked about various topics, ranging from Tony's views regarding the number of oval tracks in our series to the lack of American drivers and, of course, the basic philosophical point that the series is being run by the team owners as opposed to being run by the sanctioning body. I don't necessarily share his views, in fact in many areas I don't share his views, but I do understand his position and I think he has a very clear view.'

And on the subject of the IRL?

'That has obviously been a difficult topic throughout the year,' he agrees. 'Our objective remains that we would like to find a way to bring the whole thing back together. We do not believe that it is in either party's interest that there are two series. We think it will damage both. We do not in any way accept the view that without the Indy 500 Championship Auto Racing Teams would go away. I'm very confident that we can develop a highly effective race schedule on our own; but we don't want to do that. I think we would be weakened and I think The Speedway would be as well. I hope we can find a way to come back together.'

Another potentially prickly subject for Craig was to re-establish a working relationship with the FIA, the governing body of world motor sport.

'We've spent a fair amount of effort on rebuilding the relationship with the FIA,' he says. 'We have made it very clear, both through ACCUS, our governing body in North America, and directly to the FIA, that we are a team player, part of the broader community of motor sport, and I would like to think that the relationship with the FIA is now as it should be.

'We're part of the world of motor sport. I, probably more than most people, do understand how fragile international sport and its structures are, and I think that it's terribly important that you recognize that somebody has to run these things and it's important that you support them and not work against them. And we certainly support the FIA fully.'

To that end, Craig confirms that while he does intend to continue the PPG Cup series' tradition of supporting a few overseas races, such events will only be undertaken under ideal circumstances.

'I think that in the last few years we've sent out a few wrong signals about what we want to be,' says Craig. 'IndyCar is and will remain essentially a North American race series. We have a group of teams that are all North American in orientation, our sponsor-base is essentially North American and, quite frankly, that's where we want to remain strong: in North America. Having said that, we will take the series overseas where it meets two clear goals. Firstly, it's obviously got to be very financially attractive to us. There's a lot of down-time involved for us in loading up the cars, shipping them and coming back. It's got to be a very attractive deal. Secondly, it's got to be more than just money. It only makes sense to take the series to markets where I could showcase our products, so as to heighten sponsor interest in those countries and then bring those sponsors back to the USA; and the two markets we would be interested in are Japan and Europe.

'Also I should point out that, whatever we do overseas, it's going to have to be on an oval, in compliance with our agreement with the FIA.'

Craig's overriding goal, of course, is to continue the growth of Indy Car racing – a trend that has benefited over the last couple of years from the involvement of Nigel Mansell.

'I think Nigel's made an enormous contribution to Indy Car,' says Craig. 'He's boosted awareness of the sport outside of the US dramatically, and that's been a major factor in improving our worldwide TV audiences. I think it's also fair to say he brought a new level of interest in the championship to the US as well. The good news is that his departure doesn't mean we necessarily lose all the interest he created, because basically what he did was open people's eyes to the sport. I think we will retain those viewers and their interest with or without Nigel.

'He made a great contribution – we'd much rather have him in the series than see him go – but I don't think his departure is going to cause any decline in Indy Car, because I think he acted as the catalyst to introduce a new group of potential fans to the sport; and I believe we'll keep those fans.'

In speaking with Craig, his enthusiasm for the sport is conveyed immediately. The switch to IndyCar obviously represented a major upheaval, and since moving from Switzerland to the organization's base in Bloomfield Hills, Michigan, in April, he has been effectively separated from his American wife, Virginia, and their two young sons, Alexander and Christopher. But Craig stands by his decision. He remains proud of his accomplishments during 11 years with ISL, a very successful family-owned business, but, by his own admission, his ambitions had begun to exceed his expectations.

'It really was time to move on and do something new and something which I really enjoyed,' he says. 'And the challenge of IndyCar was something that appealed to me enormously.'

So far, and in a relatively short space of time, Craig has earned a great deal of respect from within the Indy Car community. Virtually everyone with a firm grasp of the sport is full of praise for what he has accomplished thus far.

'I think he's doing a hell of a job,' declares three-time PPG Cup champion and four-time Indianapolis 500 winner Rick Mears, who certainly keeps his finger on the auto racing pulse. 'He's making things happen. It's not taken him a year and a half to figure out which way to go. He got in there and he started doing things – and good things. I'm very impressed. Like everyone else, I'm looking forward to a long relationship between him and Indy Car racing.'

Michael C. Brown

The R1100GS: a motorcycle that doesn't promise anything it can't deliver. Shown in its true light, it is, without a shadow of a doubt, an awesome proposition. Consider its wealth of mid-range torque, its impressive 80bhp at only 6,750rpm, and the security of ABS II braking.

Couple that with BMW's Telelever and Paralever suspension systems and a very imposing motorcycle becomes a pleasure to ride.

APPEARANCES CAN BE DECEPTIVE.
SOMETIMES.

Suddenly, a journey to the Alps is something to savour, and the R1100GS is just the motorcycle to get you there. With its adjustable windshield and seat height, and a carrying capacity that can take the full complement of BMW luggage, two people can travel in comfort.

So, in the case of the R1100GS, the camera doesn't lie. It really is a motorcycle to overshadow everything else on the road.

THE NEW BMW R1100GS

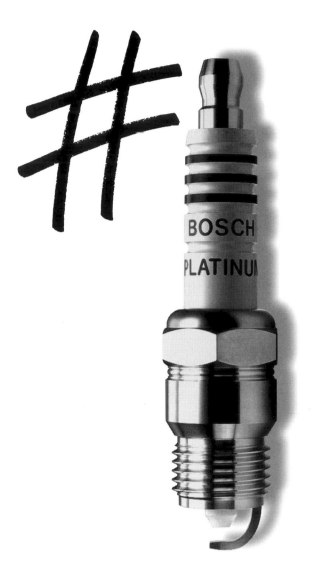

We'd like to thank Al Unser, Jr. and Team Penske for putting us in our place.

World Series winner, Al Unser, Jr.'s victory makes seven straight Indy Car championships for Bosch.

It takes something very special to win the PPG Indy Car World Series. That's why the last seven winners have insisted on nothing less than the power of Bosch spark plugs. And you can get that same winning performance for your car or truck with Bosch Platinum spark plugs.

Because for quicker starts, smoother acceleration and improved fuel efficiency, Bosch Platinum spark plugs truly are number one.

For a Bosch retailer near you, call 1-800-882-8101.

BOSCH®
The Ultimate Spark Plug

PPG INDY CAR WORLD SERIES 1994

TOP TEN DRIVERS

Chosen by the Editor, taking into account their racing performances and the equipment at their disposal

Photographs by Michael C. Brown

1

Roger Penske knew what he was getting when he signed Al Unser Jr. at the end of the 1993 season. Unser, after all, was a seasoned professional who had already won both the Indianapolis 500 and the PPG Cup championship. He was experienced and ultra-reliable. He made precious few mistakes.

Unser, meanwhile, saw the switch to Penske Racing as the opportunity of a lifetime. And also as a lifeline. Over the course of the previous few seasons he had grown increasingly frustrated with Rick Galles, a long-time friend who had given Unser his start in the Indy Car ranks in 1984 (following a championship-winning graduation through Super Vee and Can-Am). Unser, basically, wanted more than Galles was able to offer. Specifically in terms of testing. Unser, by his own admission, struggled to retain his motivation. His learning curve had dipped. His career was in danger of stagnation. And his disillusionment was heightened by the fact he had been shunned by a couple of top Formula 1 teams following some initial signs of encouragement.

All along, Unser had been aware that Penske habitually provided the best of everything: equipment, testing, personnel and commitment. He had learned that from the experiences of his father, Al, and uncle Bobby, both of whom won at Indianapolis for Penske. So when he, in turn, was offered the chance to drive for Penske, he jumped. It has proved a perfect marriage. Unser has maximized the resources at his disposal. He worked tirelessly in testing. He also came on strong as a qualifier, the only previously perceived flaw in his all-round ability. He is a worthy champion.

Al Unser Jr.

Date of birth: April 19, 1962
Residence: Albuquerque, New Mexico
Indy Car starts in 1994: 16
PPG Cup ranking: 1st
Wins: 8; Poles: 4; Points: 225

al UNSER jr

2

The early part of the season brought little except disappointment and frustration for Paul Tracy. At Surfers Paradise he was knocked off-course on the opening lap, and later retired due to gearbox failure. Next he was involved in a huge accident, not of his making, while leading comfortably at Phoenix. One week later in Long Beach he was hobbled by more gearbox woes, again while in the lead. Thus after four races he could boast a meager two PPG Cup points, both gained from pole positions.

Worse was to come at Indianapolis, where he crashed during practice and so was unable to maximize the benefits of the Mercedes-Benz/Ilmor engine. Nothing was going right. Even in Detroit, when Tracy finally found his way to Victory Lane, his success was tarnished after having inadvertently punted his own team-mate, Unser, out of the lead.

Soon after that, Tracy began to realize his services might not be retained for 1995, despite the fact he still had one year remaining on his contract with Roger Penske. He began to explore other opportunities.

Throughout all the dramas, Tracy never lost his will to win. He undertook an exhaustive test program over the winter months, especially, later, in developing the Indy engine. The entire Penske team was able to benefit from Tracy's excellent rapport with both race engineer Nigel Beresford and team 'guru' Rick Mears; and the technical information gleaned from Tracy was frequently applied, with equally good results, to the team's other two drivers. He was very much a team player. And toward the end of the season he began to reap some reward, notably with a pair of dominant performances in the final two races.

Paul Tracy

Date of birth: December 17, 1968
Residence: West Hill, Ontario, Canada
Indy Car starts in 1994: 16
PPG Cup ranking: 3rd
Wins: 3; Poles: 4; Points: 152

paul TRACY

3

The French-Canadian was the find of the season. His performance at Indianapolis, where he finished a game second, was sensational, while at Road America he joined Nigel Mansell in becoming only the second driver in the past ten years to win a race in his rookie campaign.

Villeneuve looks to possess a more well-rounded ability than his late, lamented father, Gilles, whose legendary car control and will to win captivated Formula Atlantic and, especially, Formula 1 audiences in the 1970s and early '80s. Jacques' laid-back approach is entirely reminiscent of his father, and he, too, is consumed by the notion of success; yet rather than mask any inherent handling deficiencies in the chassis with his own God-given ability, he is intent upon solving them. His technical feedback, says Forsythe-Green race engineer Tony Cicale, is awesome. Adds team co-owner Barry Green: 'I think the kid's getting better and better. If I had a choice to pick anyone to drive for me for the next three years, my first choice would be Jacques.'

He certainly made a few rookie mistakes early in the year, notably at Surfers Paradise, where he attempted an ambitious overtaking maneuver around the outside of Stefan Johansson, who is noted as a difficult man to pass at the best of times, while at Phoenix he was slow to react to a full-course yellow and was extremely fortunate that no serious injuries resulted from him slamming into the stationary car of Hiro Matsushita. Nevertheless, Villeneuve belied his level of experience by being frequently the fastest Reynard qualifier. He will surely develop into a legitimate championship contender within a year or two.

Jacques Villeneuve

Date of birth: April 9, 1971
Residence: Indianapolis, Indiana
Indy Car starts in 1994: 15
PPG Cup ranking: 6th
Wins: 1; Poles: 0; Points: 94

jacques
VILLENEUVE

4

The manner in which Andretti bounced back into the Indy Car limelight at Surfers Paradise led everyone to believe he would be a serious contender for the PPG Cup crown. But he was unable to repeat that performance on a regular basis. Quite why is hard to fathom. Certainly, the Reynard 94I's tendency toward understeer did not complement Andretti's forceful driving style, especially in terms of ultimate speed. Hence he was often to be found languishing farther down the starting grid than one would have expected, since Andretti is famed for his all-out laps. It came as a surprise to note that several other Reynard drivers were able to extract more, consistently, from their steed than he.

In the races, however, more often than not, Andretti charged quickly toward the front, usually displaying the same uncompromising style that has been a hallmark of his career. In terms of pure racing ability, Andretti has few equals. Prime examples came at Milwaukee, where his car was clearly no match for Nigel Mansell's Lola. But no one told Andretti. He kept himself in contention, then pounced in the closing stages when Mansell was momentarily delayed in traffic. Andretti finished fourth that day, beaten only by the three Penskes.

He went on to score a second victory, in Toronto, where he has now been beaten only once in his last five visits. He also played a starring role in the other Canadian street race, in Vancouver, twice rising from the back of the pack after making unscheduled pit stops. At the same time, his forceful tactics raised the ire of several rivals and ultimately earned him a $10,000 fine for 'unsportsmanlike driving.'

Michael Andretti

Date of birth: October 5, 1962
Residence: Nazareth, Pennsylvania
Indy Car starts in 1994: 16
PPG Cup ranking: 4th
Wins: 2; Poles: 0; Points: 118

michael
ANDRETTI

5

On the face of it, the 47-year-old Brazilian enjoyed yet another very successful season with Marlboro Team Penske. He usually qualified among the top two rows of the grid and in every race he finished, bar one, he was on the victory podium. The only exception was in the season finale, at Laguna Seca, where he was muscled back to fourth in the closing stages. Statistically, that's pretty impressive. He also uncorked two sensational pole-winning efforts at Loudon and Nazareth – incredibly, the first short-oval poles of his career. For the most part, Fittipaldi was his usual paradigm of efficiency and consistency. His only real mistake, however, was a costly one, when he crashed at Indianapolis while boldly attempting to put Unser, in second place, a lap down just 15 laps shy of the finish. Ouch!

Paul Tracy will tell you that he fears Fittipaldi, along with Mansell, above all other rivals on the Indy Car circuit. Fittipaldi, he says, despite his advancing years, is capable of being the fastest driver on any given day. Fortunately, adds Tracy, Emmo doesn't always fulfill that potential.

In a straight fight, Fittipaldi never once beat Unser, although he was on course to do so at Indy and was a little unlucky at Loudon, where he fell behind only when obliged to take on a splash of fuel shortly before the finish. Usually, too, he was out-raced by Tracy, with the notable exceptions of Milwaukee and Portland, where the old magic was in full bloom. On the ovals, Fittipaldi continued to be a true force to be reckoned with; on the road courses, however, perhaps we have seen the best of this remarkable man, whose appetite and enthusiasm for the sport remain undimmed.

Emerson Fittipaldi

Date of birth: December 12, 1946
Residence: Key Biscayne, Florida
Indy Car starts in 1994: 16
PPG Cup ranking: 2nd
Wins: 1; *Poles:* 2; *Points:* 178

emerson
FITTIPALDI

6

Robby Gordon's season did not begin well. First of all he crashed heavily during testing at Phoenix, then he went off again on only the second lap of the very first practice session at Surfers Paradise. Gordon also crashed early in the race, shortly after being passed by Mansell. It was an inauspicious start; and the financial implications were not lost on team owner Derrick Walker.

Against all expectations, and thanks in no small part to Walker's expert guidance and calming influence, Gordon proceeded to string together a sequence of eight point-scoring finishes, including a pair of thirds at Long Beach and Detroit. It seemed only a matter of time before he would claim his first victory. Along the way, Gordon executed some breathtaking outside-line passes at Indianapolis, where, incidentally, he was hindered by the fact his seat-belts had become unfastened. 'He didn't tell us because he didn't want to worry us,' commented Gordon's incredulous race engineer, Tim Wardrop.

Gordon is immensely talented, as shown by his poles at Toronto and Vancouver, and totally fearless, but he has much to learn about car set-up and communication. He needs to adopt a more focused approach. Gordon remains prone to his own animal instincts, as evidenced by his refusal to pay heed to either the blue or yellow flags at Mid-Ohio, and a couple of spectacular but ill-advised tire burn-outs following separate spins at Laguna Seca. The ability is there. The question is, can Walker (or anyone else) harness that genius and transform Gordon into a consistent race winner. Next year will be a vital one for this exciting young talent.

Robby Gordon

Date of birth: *January 2, 1969*
Residence: *Orange, California*
Indy Car starts in 1994: *16*
PPG Cup ranking: *5th*
Wins: *0; Poles: 2; Points: 104*

robby
GORDON

7

Dick Simon's small but dedicated team continued to perform wonders on occasion, despite a tight budget. On the ovals, especially, Boesel was always a serious contender. He mirrored his accomplishments in 1993 by qualifying on the front row at Indianapolis and then a week later taking the pole at Milwaukee. He also followed home the Penske phalanx as 'best of the rest' at both Loudon and Nazareth.

It was on the road circuits, however, that the lack of money – and therefore testing – really hurt. This year's Lola was not an easy car to manage, and frequently Boesel was to be found farther down the grid than expected. Boesel, though, like Simon, is a fighter, and he was generally able to move up during the races.

A case in point was at Laguna Seca, where Boesel finally displayed the aggression required of an all-round champion. Toward the end of the race, while running in fifth, he watched Villeneuve dive-bomb his way past Fittipaldi. Two corners later, despite Fittipaldi earnestly protecting his line from further attack, Boesel pulled off a similar maneuver. Thus, when Unser dropped out of second place and Villeneuve made a slip while trying to lap a slower car, Boesel suddenly was elevated into the runner-up position, claiming his best finish of the season.

It was no more than he deserved. Next year Boesel will move across to Rahal/Hogan Racing. If he can recapture the form he showed at Laguna, hone his skills and understanding of the car with adequate testing, and earn just a little bit of luck, surely he will be rewarded with a victory.

Raul Boesel

Date of birth: December 4, 1957
Residence: Key Biscayne, Florida
Indy Car starts in 1994: 16
PPG Cup ranking: 7th
Wins: 0; Poles: 1; Points: 90

raul BOESEL

8

More than half of Bobby Rahal's total points for the season were collected from just two races. Nevertheless, his second-place finish at Toronto with the recalcitrant Lola-Honda ranks as one of the very best drives of the season. His pass of Fittipaldi was of the highest caliber and, despite the Brazilian's noticeable power advantage, Rahal was able to pull out enough breathing space on the twisty portions of the track to remain out of reach on the longest straightaway.

Rahal and his team worked tirelessly on development of their customer Lolas, to the extent they often looked among the best-handling cars in the field; and while there were no commensurate gains from the Honda engines, Rahal drove his heart out on several occasions. His rise to seventh place at Milwaukee, after starting 19th, was another tribute to his resolve, as was his subsequent sixth at Detroit.

Rahal posted another excellent effort at Indianapolis, where he was obliged to take over a rented, year-old Penske-Ilmor/D during the second week of practice. Inside a day, Rahal had coaxed more speed out of the hastily rebuilt car than his own Lola-Honda, and in the race he moved up steadily and surely from 28th on the grid to claim third-place points.

After two dreadful weekends at MIS and, more embarrassingly, at his home track, Mid-Ohio, Rahal confirmed he would be switching to Mercedes-Benz/Ilmor power for next season. In truth, he was surprisingly undiplomatic in making his announcement but, as one who is ranked among the more professional drivers, that only goes to show how frustrated he had become during the year.

Bobby Rahal

Date of birth: January 10, 1953
Residence: Dublin, Ohio
Indy Car starts in 1994: 16
PPG Cup ranking: 10th
Wins: 0; Poles: 0; Points: 59

bobby
RAHAL

9

Three pole positions turned out to be the highlights of the defending PPG Cup champion's season. The enigmatic Englishman began the year strongly and was expected to put up a spirited defence of his crown. He ran second in Australia until spinning off the road in the wet, then finished third at Phoenix behind a pair of Penskes. He was second, too, at Long Beach, beaten only by Unser's Penske. But his hard-working Newman-Haas team had precious little else to cheer about.

'I've resigned myself this year that it's going to be an uphill battle,' said Mansell at Portland in June. Perhaps that comment set the tone. Indeed, after a typically gutsy performance which brought him a runner-up finish next time out in Cleveland, Mansell scored a meager sum of 16 points – equivalent to one second-place finish – from the final eight races of the year.

After his supposed one-off return to Formula 1 at the French Grand Prix, Mansell's heart seemed not to be in it. On a couple of occasions, at Toronto and Loudon, he pulled into the pits and simply stepped away from the car. His crew, however, remained loyal to the last, despite Mansell's refusal to test in the second half of the season.

Mansell rankled the usually unflappable Fittipaldi with an outrageous 'last of the late-brakers' bid to take fourth place on the final corner at Vancouver, but that maneuver was born more out of frustration than design. Mansell, indeed, had looked to be sitting pretty until the yellow flags conspired against him. He was unlucky, too, at MIS, where he was in control until his engine blew, while at Indy he could not conceal his anger at being involved in a ludicrous accident in pit lane ... during a full-course caution. That rather summed up his year. It was one to forget.

Nigel Mansell

Date of birth: August 8, 1953
Residence: Clearwater, Florida
Indy Car starts in 1994: 16
PPG Cup ranking: 8th
Wins: 0; Poles: 3; Points: 79

nigel
MANSELL

10

Almost always the fastest of those running year-old equipment, Stefan Johansson claimed one fourth and three fifth-place finishes with Tony Bettenhausen's Alumax Penske PC22-Ilmor/D. He qualified as often as not among the top ten, which represented no mean feat in itself, and with a little luck on his side he could have recorded several other strong results. At Toronto, for example, he was running fourth until his gear linkage came apart with less than ten laps remaining. In Vancouver, for the other Canadian street race, the Swede ran a strong fourth in the early stages, despite a last-minute switch to his back-up car following an incident in the morning warm-up, only to make a mistake and clip one of the omnipresent cement walls. At Loudon, having qualified eighth, he was eliminated following an early altercation with Eddie Cheever.

Another highlight came at MIS, where he out-qualified all the factory Penskes to secure sixth on the grid.

A laid-back, amiable character out of the car, Johansson remained susceptible to the occasional 'red mist.' At Portland, he had to be physically restrained from striking Hiro Matsushita, whom he accused of deliberately blocking him in the closing stages, while in the season finale at Laguna Seca his impatience in pit lane earned him a $10,000 fine and an eight-race suspension for a needless incident during which he nudged his car's front wing into a Galles crew member who was changing a tire in the adjacent pit.

Stefan Johansson

Date of birth: September 8, 1956
Residence: Indianapolis, Indiana, and Monte Carlo
Indy Car starts in 1994: 16
PPG Cup ranking: 11th
Wins: 0; Poles: 0; Points: 57

stefan

JOHANSSON

CLOSE, BUT . . .

Compiling a top-ten list is always a difficult and, usually, thankless task. Inevitably, some drivers (or their car owners, wives, mothers, whomever) feel slighted if they are not included. This year will be no different. The intention of the list, however, is to reflect not only the results achieved during the season but also the equipment at each driver's disposal, his level of experience and the relative merits of the team for which he drives. The positioning is entirely subjective.

Hence, for example, Mansell's relatively low ranking.

Clearly, Mansell possesses enormous talent and capability. He showed it in 1993, when he sped to five wins and the PPG Cup title while driving a car that most people felt was slightly inferior to the Penske. But this year, while fast in qualifying, he was unable to translate that speed into solid results.

A couple of drivers, Adrian Fernandez and Teo Fabi, came very close to making the top echelon. Fernandez, particularly, was extremely impressive toward the end of the season, although a couple of mishaps (not of his instigation) were costly, most obviously at Michigan, where a miscommunication caused by a redeployment of the crew due to the absence of a couple of key players led to a potentially disastrous pit fire. There was a problem, too, at Vancouver, where the telemetry system misled the team into asking Fernandez to go one lap too far on the available fuel. Then again, everyone else had already made their stops . . .

Typically, Fernandez took the disappointments in his stride.

He also refused to place the blame on Villeneuve following their 'racing accident' on the oval at Nazareth. Fernandez had driven superbly until their contretemps.

'The good thing is that we were competitive,' says Fernandez. 'I proved I can run with these guys and I learned a lot. We should be in good shape next year.'

Fabi, too, drove some strong races – as befits a man of his talent and experience. Ninth place in the PPG Cup table represented an entirely respectable result. But, curiously, he often complained of not being able to utilize full boost on his Ilmor motors. Most crucially, Fabi was only rarely able to extract the full potential from his Pennzoil Reynard, despite having undertaken more testing than most.

From among the younger group of drivers, the up-and-comers, Bryan Herta shone brightly in his sadly foreshortened season. He achieved some superb results in A.J. Foyt's Copenhagen Lola, without the benefit of a single test day. Foyt promised to make a car available for Herta as soon as he was recovered from the broken leg and pelvis sustained in his crash at Toronto, but Herta declined the offer of a full-time drive for 1995 when it became apparent Foyt was not able to offer him a concerted test program. Instead his services were snapped up by Chip Ganassi as a replacement for the departing (to Newman-Haas) Michael Andretti. Those are some big shoes to fill, but Herta is confident he can make the grade.

Jimmy Vasser posted some good drives in Jim Hayhoe's car, although his progress, too, was hindered by a lack of testing. Fellow Californian Mike Groff, meanwhile, was fighting an uphill battle with his equipment. Falling out of nine races helped him not one iota.

Scott Sharp is another talented young American who showed good pace from time to time in his first full season with the PacWest team. Next year will determine how far the very likable two-time Trans-Am champion is likely to progress.

Europeans Andrea Montermini, Franck Freon, who graduated from Indy Lights, and Alessandro Zampedri, from Formula 3000, surely would have achieved more with representative budgets.

Among the ranks of the more experienced drivers, Scott Goodyear endured a thoroughly frustrating time with Kenny Bernstein's team, having entered the program with high expectations. His victory at Michigan was handed to him on a silver platter when all the quicker cars fell by the wayside. Aside from that, the team was only rarely able to maximize the capabilities of its well-funded Lola-Ford.

Arie Luyendyk and Dominic Dobson drove well to secure the other podium placings at MIS, the highlights of their year, while Mauricio Gugelmin demonstrated the reason why he was so highly rated by (current Williams-Renault F1 race engineer/aerodynamicist) Adrian Newey when they worked together with the Leyton House/March team in Formula 1. The Brazilian displayed a good feel for the car and was able to provide excellent technical feedback. This year he gained valuable experience. With a good test program, he could be a real dark horse in 1995.

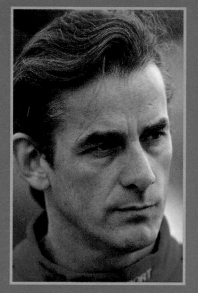

ARIE LUYENDYK

ADRIAN FERNANDEZ

MAURICIO GUGELMIN

MARK SMITH

BRYAN HERTA

SCOTT SHARP

SCOTT GOODYEAR

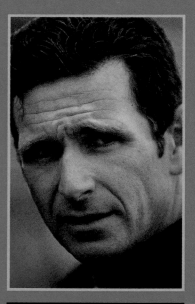

DOMINIC DOBSON

1994
A Good Year
for the rec

GOOD YEAR

ord

Al Unser Jr. racing to victory in the 1994 PPG Indy Car World Series
The Goodyear-equipped Marlboro Team Penske PC23s won 12 out of 16 races
and finished 1-2-3 in the championship

#1 in Racing

1994

Left; A Goodyear engineer checks racing slicks in the pit lane. Note the wet weather treaded tires in the background. *Below:* The field streams past the pit lane at the Indy 500 on their Goodyear Eagles. The winner averaged over 160 miles per hour. *Right:* Goodyear's 300th Grand Prix win: Damon Hill races to victory at the Spanish Grand Prix in May 1994. *Far right:* Jeff Gordon takes the flag at the inaugural Brickyard 400.

world of auto racing. Goodyear Eagles have won virtually every motorsports series in the world – from Formula 1 and international sports cars to the U.S. Winston Cup stock car series, Indy Car, drag and dirt racing.

In addition, mid-June marked the production milestone of the one millionth Eagle *radial* race tire in the Akron Technical Center since that tire construction's introduction in 1982. All the racing radials used worldwide by Goodyear are built in the Akron facility.

In 1994, Goodyear has once again proved it is No. 1 in racing, in spite of competition from 13 other race tire

A Milestone Year

Spanning a 96-year history, The Goodyear Tire & Rubber Company has a legion of firsts, facts and figures that reveal a company determined to continue leading in a competitive market.

Today, still headquartered in Akron, Ohio, Goodyear boasts 91,000 associates worldwide with manufacturing operations in 27 countries. The company's tires are supplied to the world's major auto manufacturers, including the makers of the top luxury and performance cars. In 1993, sales for the company totaled $11.6 billion.

In the replacement market, tires are sold through more than 25,000 retail outlets around the globe. More than 4,000 independent dealers, 800 franchise tire centers and 900 company-owned and operated stores supply the U.S. market with Goodyear brand tires, including the popular Eagles and Wranglers.

Goodyear's technological leadership is exemplified in the continued dominance of Goodyear Eagle tires in the

1994 marked milestones for Goodyear in all forms of racing. At the end of May, Damon Hill rolled into Victory Lane in Barcelona, Spain, on his yellow-lettered Eagle radials marking the 300th Formula 1 win for Goodyear. In September, Al Unser Jr. drove to victory in Vancouver, B.C., Canada, as Goodyear celebrated its 300th consecutive win in Indy Car racing. On the NASCAR Winston Cup front, 23-year-old Jeff Gordon made history on his Goodyears, becoming the winner of the inaugural Brickyard 400 – the first non-Indy Car auto race ever held at the famed Indianapolis Motor Speedway.

manufacturers worldwide. Hoosier Racing Tire announced in 1993 it would return to the NASCAR Winston Cup series in '94. It did, and won a handful of pole positions and a few races, and initiated a 'tire war' in Winston Cup that pushed Goodyear to design and develop a different tire for every track on the 31-race circuit. Goodyear handily won the championship.

That tire skirmish continues, but it has helped prepare Goodyear for a tire war brewing with Firestone in Indy Car competition in 1995. Tire tests are ongoing, new technology is being explored and top teams are working closely with Goodyear to prepare for

the '95 season opener at a new course in Miami, Florida.

Perhaps the most important internal event for Goodyear's racing organization in 1994 was its establishment as a broadened, self-contained racing group, led by longtime director of racing worldwide, H. Leo Mehl. Under the new title of General Manager, Mehl will direct race tire sales and marketing, development and production of race tires and other facets of the operation.

Becoming a semi-autonomous group within the corporate business structure is the first major organization change for Goodyear racing in 30 years. Among key members of the business unit are Stu Grant, director of race tire sales and marketing; Don Vera, manager of product development, and Pat Jodon, business center manager of race tire manufacturing.

Over three decades, Goodyear has parlayed its racing involvement into high-performance tire marketing and technological leadership. This move is expected to solidify Goodyear's global racing leadership well into the next century.

Historically, Goodyear's growth has come from its innovative spirit. In 1899, when it was less than a year old, its crystal ball focused far beyond the current products of bicycle and carriage tires, horseshoe pads and poker chips to reveal introduction that year of its first pneumatic tire for automobiles.

In 1916, Goodyear launched into racing and soon its cord tires were dominating U.S. racing circuits and, in 1919, won every important race in the country.

At the Indianapolis 500 that year, qualifying speeds jumped over the 100 mph mark. During the race, 27 of 33 starters were on Goodyears, including winner Howdy Wilcox. In fact, two of Wilcox's tires made it the entire distance. Two other cars, finishing eighth and ninth, covered the 500 miles without a single tire change – an unbelievable feat at that time.

After proving the technological leadership of its cord race tires and faced with a national economic depression, Goodyear began reducing its involvement in racing and finally withdrew in 1922.

Re-entry into racing was triggered in the late 1950s when marketing surveys revealed Goodyear had a 'stodgy' public image.

To begin a turnaround, the company approached stock car driver Lee Petty in 1957 to do some tire testing, and the relationship with the Petty family that ensued continues today. It also began what was later to be termed 'tire wars' between Goodyear and Firestone.

By 1963, successes began in international sports car racing, at the Bonneville Salt Flats for land speed records, and in stock car racing. But, in May of that year, Goodyear forever altered the face of racing when it rolled into the Indianapolis Motor Speedway.

A young Texan named A.J. Foyt persuaded Goodyear's chairman to

Al Unser Jr.'s Goodyear-tired Penske carries him to victory at the 1994 Indy 500. *Far left:* On the right the new H-rated and V-rated Eagle Aquatred, to the left the T-rated Aquatred, of which more than half a million have been sold in Europe during its first year. Sales in the U.S. have neared the three-million mark since the tire's introduction.
Below left: A jubilant Al Unser Jr. wears the winner's wreath after his Indy 500 victory. The legendary Borg Warner trophy stands behind him.
Below: A new set of Goodyears and a fresh load of fuel for Brian Herta, who drove for A.J.Foyt's Copenhagen Racing.
Right: Lifesavers: Robby Gordon's helmet rests on top of one of his Goodyear Eagles.

authorize a development program for the Indy 500, which had been virtually the sole domain of Firestone for about 44 years.

The obvious importance of the Indy 500 and its physical demands launched a tire war between the two companies that accelerated race tire technology through several decades in just 10 short years. After Goodyear won the Indy 500 for three straight years, Firestone withdrew at the end of 1974.

Paced by its Eagle tires, Goodyear today dominates the world of auto racing. And interest in racing continues to skyrocket. According to Goodyear's 1993 race attendance figures, more than 13.6 million people attended the

nel Eagle Aquatred is the latest passenger tire product to emerge in the marketplace with roots from rain tires used in Formula 1 racing. Perhaps most famous is the unidirectional 'gatorback' design that was introduced on the 1984 Corvette and remains popular to this day.

With the milestones reached in 1994, Goodyear looks ahead to gaining more ground in innovative passenger tire construction in the years to come.

major racing events in North America alone. Indy Car racing topped the three million attendance milestone, and Winston Cup crossed the four million mark.

Those years of racing success have paid off for Goodyear in what it calls 'transfer of technology' from track to street. It is a key to passenger tire development that has made the Eagle name the top high-performance passenger tire brand in the world.

'The track-to-street connection is stronger than you might think,' said Stu Grant. 'Much of what we learn with race tires in terms of handling, cornering and overall tire response can be transferred to the design of tires that operate at lower speeds and with less strenuous maneuvers.' The dual-chan-

Today, on the threshold of a new century and nearing its centennial, Goodyear stands alone as the only major publicly-held tire and rubber company in the United States. Its flexibility and competitive spirit throughout its nearly 100-year history permit it to adapt quickly to a changing world and to remain a leader.

The quality of its tire developments is proved publicly to millions each year as yellow-lettered Goodyear Eagle race tires carry drivers to championships in virtually all of the world's major racing series.

And for good reason.

AL UNSER JR.
LEADING TEAM PENSKE

*A profile of the
1994 PPG Indy Car
World Series champion*

by Gordon Kirby

ANY Indy Car fans have long believed that Al Unser Jr. is the finest racer in Indy cars. Some say he is America's greatest driver, ahead even of seven-time NASCAR champion Dale Earnhardt, who is widely considered to be the USA's toughest, most relentless racer. Unser has repeatedly beaten Earnhardt and the other stars of NASCAR in the IROC series, the only Indy Car driver to do so in recent years. As a result he's earned a powerful reputation across the heartland of the USA and in 1994, his first year with Roger Penske's operation, Unser finally began to show the world the vast depth of his talent and commitment.

Al took control of the PPG Indy Car World Series by winning three races in a row from Long Beach in April through Indianapolis in May to Milwaukee in June. He scored two more wins in June and July and put the championship on ice with another trio of successive wins in August and September. Unser scored his eighth win of the year in the streets of Vancouver on the first Sunday in September and wrapped up the title by finishing a strong second to debutant winner Jacques Villeneuve on the 4.0-mile Elkhart Lake road course the following week.

Unser's seasonal statistics are quite impressive: eight wins, four poles and 677 laps led. The Penske team record from 1994 is even more impressive, with Emerson Fittipaldi and Paul Tracy finishing second and third in the championship to complete a clean-sweep for the team. Unser, Fittipaldi and Tracy won 12 races, a record for a team in Indy Car racing, and took ten poles in '94 as well as nine seconds and eight third places. Five times they finished 1-2-3 and in total they led 1584 of the year's 2083 laps.

As strong as Roger Penske's team has been for many years, winning seven of the last eleven Indy 500s, for example, the PPG Cup title had somehow eluded Penske since Danny Sullivan took the championship for the team in 1988. In order to repair that shortcoming Penske decided in the summer of '93 that he had to hire Al Jr., who was at the end of a three-year contract with Rick Galles. The difficult proposition of running three cars in 1994 did not deter Penske in his desire to hire Unser.

'Last year,' commented Penske, 'I said that if Emerson decides to retire I'm sitting with Tracy, who can absolutely race with the best of them but hasn't had nine or ten years' experience, hasn't won the Indy 500 and hasn't won the championship. At that point you have to say I'm going to have to have what you might call a center- or a quarterback that's had the experience.

'So I had to make the move on Al to hire him because he'd been in this business for ten years, he'd won Indy and won the championship and was a very consistent driver. I took my hat off to Galles because Al was on a roll with those guys. He finished every race and he was strong.

'I didn't quite understand why he didn't qualify better. I never did understand that and I'm thrilled that we can give him the kind of equipment so that we've got him to the point where he can get through all the things he wants to try and still be able to run as hard as he wants in qualifying.'

Even Penske has been surprised with Unser's shrewdness and commitment. 'He is an amazing young driver,' noted Penske. 'He's very focused. He's committed to racing. He's a racer. He's a lot like [Rick] Mears was. I mean his life revolves around racing. His family, his dad, his uncle. Racing is everything for them. It's like a golfer. You've got to have that club in your hand every single day if you're gonna be successful and that's what Al's doing.

'He's a shrewd race driver. He really is shrewd. He knows what he wants. He's always putting money in the bank for the race during practice and qualifying, instead of taking it all out. He doesn't use up his tires. He knows the set-up. You can see when he goes out. He's the kind of guy that knows when it's time to go. He's not just out there running ten- or eleven-tenths all the time. He settles down and then he goes.'

For his part, Al Jr. has been amazed by the depth and capabilities of Penske's team. Penske is certainly the strongest team in Indy cars, the only operation which builds its own cars for the category, and Unser was delighted with Nigel Bennett's 1994 chassis, the PC23.

'The car is a great race car,' declared Unser. 'Nigel Bennett and all of the design staff at Penske Cars have done a fantastic job of understanding today's Indy car. They're producing real good cars. That's the main reason for our success this year.

'The car's been right from day one,' continued Unser. 'I drove the PC22 [at the end of last year] and the first time I drove it, it was a beautiful race car. And now the PC23 is enhanced a little bit from the '22. What Nigel does is he keeps turning the page. He doesn't go off on big, different revolutionary paths. He takes what he's got and tries to enhance it. He stays with the same basic ball and just makes it a little bit more round, a little bit more aerodynamic, a little bit more of everything.'

Unser also tips his hat to Penske's Reading, Pennsylvania-based race team. 'What enhances immensely that great car is the great people at the Penske race shop in Reading. They prepare the cars better than any team I've worked for.'

Al didn't take home any points from the season-opener in Surfers Paradise. He and Tracy had problems all weekend in Australia with an electronic speed-shifter and Al had to pit for repairs after the first lap and never finished the race's final lap. He began to gather momentum, however, when he finished second to team-mate Fittipaldi at Phoenix in April.

His roll to the championship began the following weekend at Long Beach, a race he won for the fifth time in 1994. Unser came back from a stop-and-go penalty for speeding in the pit lane to win after team-mates Tracy and Fittipaldi hit trouble.

'Even though I was making my mistakes,' noted Al, 'Roger was saying it was OK, not to worry about it, we were going to come on. For a man in his position with all the drivers that he's had in the past, he can have the best in the world work for him. And there I was making all these little mistakes. Yet afterward he was still saying it was OK, which gave me confidence within the organization.'

At Indianapolis the Penske team ran the 3.4-liter, single-cam Mercedes-Benz 500I V8, taking advantage of USAC's rules to out-power the rest of the field. Unser was outpaced in practice by team-mate Fittipaldi but a quirk of the Indianapolis qualifying rules, and hot, windy weather on the Sunday, allowed Al to take the pole, the first time he's done so at Indianapolis.

'I didn't have the car exactly the way that I wanted it at Indianapolis. But the only one that was really outrunning me was Emerson, who had been with the team for quite a while. I was still learning to work with the engineers and it still wasn't right.

But then we drew an early number and we qualified on Saturday.

'And Emerson had to qualify on Sunday because he drew a late number. He was the faster guy but then Sunday was a totally different day and he couldn't get the speed in those conditions to take the pole away from me. It was then that I started to feel that the good Lord is smiling on me, that we were having good fortune with the win at Long Beach and now the pole at Indy.'

In the race, Fittipaldi and Unser ran away from the field although Al stalled when trying to leave the pits, losing time during his first stop.

With less than fifty miles to go Fittipaldi lapped Unser but Al repassed in traffic and then Fittipaldi lost it and hit the wall while running hard in Unser's slipstream. He remembers that victory as proof of the strength of the Penske team.

'That's when I knew for sure this is the strongest team I've ever been with. I was still making mistakes 'cause I messed up that first pit stop again. My third race in a row that I can't get out of the pits on the first stop but we still came out winners.'

At Milwaukee the next weekend Al was superb, soundly beating Fittipaldi and Tracy, who finished second and third for the team's first of five sweeps of the top three places. Al says his car handled better at Milwaukee than in any other race in 1994.

'The next few races I had the confidence in myself and in the team and the team started to have confidence in me, that I could get it out of the pits. Milwaukee was the first race where I got it out of the pits on the first pit stop. I told 'em, "If I can get out of the pits on the first pit stop, there ain't gonna be no looking back." I had the car working the best there it's ever been. We had a good race with Emerson but we had him covered. It was wonderful.

'That was where [engineer] Terry Satchell and I started working pretty good with each other. I was starting to mix in with the team, with the mechanics, really well, and starting to have confidence within myself on this race team. I think that was kind of like the turning point in the year where I knew I had a legitimate shot at the championship. I had Lady Luck helping me out and as long as Lady Luck kept helping me out we were for sure going to do it because I've got the strongest team.

'From there we were just kinda riding the wave. We were building confidence in ourselves. The team

knows it's not easy at any time, that was a heck of a compliment.'

Al says unwaveringly, incidentally, that his father was the greatest driver ever on dirt. Al Sr. and A.J. Foyt share the Indy Car record of ten wins in a season, with Unser Sr. winning ten races in 1970 and Foyt doing so in '64. In those days more than half the Indy Car series took place on one-mile dirt tracks and in 1970 Al Sr. was unbeaten on the dirt, winning all six dirt-track races. 'He was just awesome, beautiful to watch,' recalls Jr. warmly.

Al expects to be as strong next year as this past year. 'Next year we're gonna keep working hard. We've got a new car coming in January. I don't think we're going to have the same horsepower advantage at The Speedway [Indianapolis] in '95 that we had in '94, but we've got a great team and

we've got a great car that really shines on race day. If we can keep shining with it then we're going to be OK. And try to do it all again. I think we'll have a head start on it when we start at Miami next March. We will have a head start on it because I'll have a year with the team.'

He says he hopes to continue with Penske for many years to come. 'I hope my future with Penske Racing goes for quite a long time. As long as we keep doing what we're doing, Roger, I think, is going to be happy with us. And that's really all I want, to make Roger and the guys happy. Whatever I can do to make that happen is what I'm going to do.'

Al Jr.'s partnership with Penske has only just begun. With a little luck, it could turn out to be one of the most profitable relationships in modern motor racing.

had confidence in me. They knew we had definitely arrived as the driver that I guess Team Penske thought was there – which is why I got hired, because of all I'd done in the past. And it wasn't being shown in those first few races. You know, the experience. I was like a new kid, a rookie.

'But as soon as I settled down and started doing what I've always been doing, it just snowballed. So we just started knocking the race weekends over like a domino effect. We started sittin' on pole and really working it to a very good outcome. That led us to sewing it up early.'

Al's win streak was broken in Detroit when team-mate Tracy hit him in the tail. Al spun and recovered to finish tenth while Tracy went on to win. He then won the Portland road race and Cleveland airport race, both times leading all the way from pole. Mid-July, halfway through the season, and he already had his hands, if not his arms, around the PPG Cup trophy.

'One of the best compliments I ever had from my father,' declared Junior, 'was when I talked to him on the phone after Cleveland. He said I had really done good, that I made it look easy. Coming from my dad, who

ANY
COLOR
YOU LIKE . . .

by Jeremy Shaw

Industries, the Pittsburgh-based global producer of automotive and industrial coatings, glass, fiber glass, chemicals and bio-medical systems, has been involved in Indy Car racing since 1975, when it began supplying its durable urethane paints to cars entered in the Indianapolis 500. Five years later PPG became the title sponsor of North America's premier category of open-wheel racing.

It has been an extraordinarily successful relationship. During the past 15 years, the PPG Indy Car World Series has grown to become recognized as one of the world's most successful forms of auto racing. It is also one of the richest. In 1994, more than $24 million in prize money has been distributed.

Unlike some companies involved in sports sponsorship, PPG has pursued an aggressive marketing program centered upon the Indy Car circuit, notably in development of the PPG Pace Car Team.

The pace car concept was first introduced for the inaugural Indianapolis 500-mile race in 1911. Local car dealer Carl Fisher, who devised the Memorial Day event, decided that instead of the traditional 'standing start,' where the race would begin with all cars in a stationary position, he would employ a 'rolling start' whereby the competitors would parade at a sedate pace behind his Stoddard Dayton – driven by himself, of course. Then, once the field was in order (and the vast crowd had been afforded a clear view of his fine automobile), the signal to start the race was given.

Pace cars have been used ever since to ensure a safe and equitable starting procedure. Over the years their role has evolved to serve also as a safety vehicle, specifically in the event of any incidents on the race track. In such an instance, yellow flags are waved (and/or warning lights will flash) to signify danger, whereupon the pace car is dispatched and the competitors are required to hold station, at reduced speed, behind the pace car until the all-clear (green flag) is displayed.

For years, standard production cars were chosen to perform these duties. The involvement of PPG, however, led to the introduction of a range of far more technically advanced vehicles – concept cars – several of which cost well over $1 million to produce.

The idea was to have PPG working with the engineers and designers at the automotive companies to display the finest products of the American automobile industry. Later, as PPG expanded its horizons, the theme was augmented by the introduction of more cars representing overseas manufacturers.

The PPG technicians worked directly with the various manufacturers, and the fruit of their labor resulted in a dazzling array of cars finished in stunning liveries – using PPG Automotive Finishes.

Before long, PPG began to exploit the pace car program by inviting its employees, executives, customers and other corporate guests to the races. The visitors would be entertained in PPG's own hospitality area, and many were afforded an opportunity to ride around the track in one of the pace cars.

Former Indy car driver Tom Bagley was employed as the first official PPG pace car pilot. Before long the duties were assumed by a select group of well-known women race car drivers. The first PPG Pace Car Team comprised Lyn St. James, who went on to win Rookie of the Year honors at Indianapolis in 1992, Margie Smith-Haas and Kathy Rude, two very experienced sports car racers who remain on the team to this day.

Since then the group has grown to a total of 14, including Desiré Wilson, who, at Brands Hatch, England, in 1980, earned the distinction of becoming the only woman ever to win a race for Formula 1 cars. The other team members are Laura Barnes, Terry MacDonald-Cadieux, Robin McCall-Dallenbach, Margy Eatwell, Kellie Ann La Follette, Kim Gillette, Trisha Hessinger, Rhonda Regnier, Alice Ridpath, Janey Smith and Gail Truess.

The entire pace car program, managed by Ken Lowe, is now multifaceted, with the pace car drivers and the cars attending not only all the PPG Cup Indy Car events but also a multitude of car shows and other functions throughout the year.

TEAM-BY-TEAM

review

A total of 64 drivers attempted to qualify for at least one race in the 1994 PPG Indy Car World Series, of whom 33, representing 18 different teams, earned points. In the following pages, Editor Jeremy Shaw assesses some of the strengths and weaknesses of each team.

> **Penske Racing**
>
> Base: Reading, Pennsylvania
> Drivers: Al Unser Jr., Emerson Fittipaldi, Paul Tracy
> Sponsor: Marlboro
> Chassis: Penske PC23
> Engines: Ilmor Indy V8/D and Mercedes-Benz V8
> Wins: 12 (Unser 8, Tracy 3, Fittipaldi 1)
> Poles: 10 (Unser and Tracy 4, Fittipaldi 2)
> PPG Cup points: 555
> Unser 225 (1st), Fittipaldi 178 (2nd), Tracy 152 (3rd)

Having narrowly missed out on the PPG Cup title in 1993, Penske Racing left nothing to chance this time around. Team stalwart Fittipaldi and young charger Tracy were joined by Unser, a seasoned veteran and proven winner, who added depth to the team and was able to take full advantage of Nigel Bennett's excellent PC23 chassis and Mario Illien's powerful Ilmor/D engines. The package was almost unbeatable.

The team had undertaken almost 4500 miles of testing prior to the season-opener, and although niggling problems prevented Unser or Tracy from finishing in Australia,

Fittipaldi emerged in a solid second place. From then on, Penske enjoyed a dream season with its so-called 'super team,' winning a record 12 times in 16 races. Unser, in particular, thrived on the intra-team rivalry. He also took full advantage of the technical benefits of being able to share set-up information with his two team-mates and their impressively qualified engineering staff.

Placing Grant Newbury in overall charge of the engineering team was an inspired decision, since it allowed him to co-ordinate the efforts of Terry Satchell (who worked with Unser), Nigel Beresford (Tracy) and

Tom Brown (Fittipaldi) to ensure maximum benefit from the available time and resources. Team Manager Chuck Sprague oversaw the entire race/test program, while Clive Howell took charge of the crew and Tim Lombardi (somehow) managed all the logistics. This was a magnificent example of true teamwork.

'It's a first-class operation,' praised 1993 PPG Cup champion Nigel Mansell. 'They are as good as any Formula 1 team. Motor racing isn't magic; they've worked hard for their success. The Penske team had the edge this season and they deserved it. My hat's off to them.'

Commitment and co-operation were the keys to success for Marlboro Team Penske. Emerson Fittipaldi *(top left)* was the early pace-setter for the team, while Paul Tracy *(far left)* was a dominant force at the end of the season. Assisted by several inspired strategic calls from Roger Penske *(bottom left)* and excellent pit work *(below)*, Al Unser Jr. *(left)* scored eight victories within the space of 11 races to clinch the PPG Cup title. Team manager Chuck Sprague *(above center)* oversaw the entire operation, with Richard Buck *(middle center)* looking after the car of long-time friend Unser and Jon Bouslog *(left center)* responsible for Tracy's PC23. The knowledge and experience of Rick Mears *(top center)* added greatly to the depth of the engineering staff.

Chip Ganassi Racing Teams

Base: Indianapolis, Indiana
Drivers: Michael Andretti, Mauricio Gugelmin
Sponsors: Target, Scotch Video, Hollywood
Chassis: Reynard 94I
Engines: Ford/Cosworth XB
Wins: 2 (Andretti)
Poles: 0
PPG Cup points: 157
Michael Andretti 118 (4th), Gugelmin 39 (16th)

When Chip Ganassi signed Andretti to lead his team for the 1994 season, after agreeing to be the front man for Reynard Racing Cars' latest and most ambitious foray in the world of auto racing, it was a mark of how serious he was about moving up among the top echelon within the PPG Cup series. Justifiably, Ganassi was ecstatic when Andretti repaid the compliment by earning a sensational first-time-out victory in Surfers Paradise.

Rather more difficult to understand was Ganassi's decision to conclude a separate arrangement with Gugelmin – especially since Andretti's deal was based upon total commitment to a one-car effort. In reality, perhaps the 'blue team,' as it became known, didn't detract from Andretti's 'red team' because it was run from separate premises (sharing space with Reynard North America) and with its own crew; but then again, its mere existence rankled the major players on Andretti's car. At least in the early part of the year there was virtually no contact between the two . . . until Gugelmin, despite a minimalist crew (and budget), led by the immensely practical

John Bright and Grant Weaver, outqualified Andretti in three successive races. Then the information began to flow more freely.

Gugelmin displayed his talents on several occasions, despite a difficult year in which he had to cope with the loss of one of his closest friends, Ayrton Senna. Andretti, meanwhile, was strangely inconsistent, especially in qualifying, although, as ever, he charged hard in the races. Andretti is a man who can never be faulted in the effort department, as evidenced when he scored a second victory for the team in Toronto.

Top left: **Chip Ganassi, with two wins in 1994, courtesy of Michael Andretti** *(above left),* **was the most successful team owner aside from Roger Penske. Mauricio Gugelmin** *(top and center right),* **in partnership with engineer John Bright** *(above),* **made good progress on the ovals.**

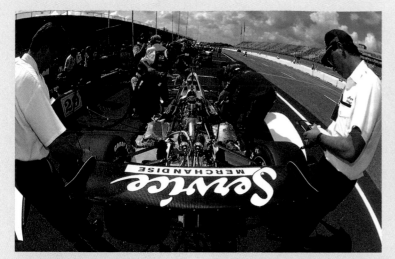

Robby Gordon *(bottom)* began to throw off his 'Brash Gordon' image under the calming influence of team owner Derrick Walker *(left)*. A seventh-place finish at MIS represented the best finish of the season for Willy T. Ribbs *(top and center left)*. Also at Michigan, Mark Smith *(center right and below left)* claimed a career-best fifth.

Walker Racing

Base: Indianapolis, Indiana
Drivers: Robby Gordon, Mark Smith, Willy T. Ribbs
Sponsors: Valvoline, Cummins, Craftsman, Service Merchandise
Chassis: Lola T94/00
Engines: Ford/Cosworth XB
Wins: 0
Poles: 2 (Gordon)
PPG Cup points: 133
Gordon 104 (5th), Smith 17 (19th), Ribbs 12 (22nd)

The season did not start well for Derrick Walker. Gordon demolished one car in testing, then ended the first race with his Lola's rear end crumpled against a concrete wall. Smith also hit the barriers – on his way out of the pits – and Ribbs was taken out in an over-zealous move by Fernandez. It was an expensive weekend.

Thankfully, the team's fortunes improved rapidly, at least so far as Gordon was concerned. The young-ster made excellent progress as the year unfolded, thanks to Walker's strong hand and the technical and interpretive skills of race engineer Tim Wardrop. Gordon was unlucky not to emerge a winner in either Toronto or Vancouver, having start-ed from the pole in both races.

Walker later confessed to spend-ing perhaps too much of his time with Gordon – 'That was a full-time job in itself' – to the obvious detri-ment of his two other drivers, Smith and Ribbs, who struggled for most of the season and especially at Indy, where they failed to muster enough speed to make the field. Their confidence was badly eroded, although both managed to post sev-eral solid performances at some later races.

RESET FUEL
Valvoline
Cummins

Photos: Michael C. Brown

Newman-Haas Racing

Base: Lincolnshire, Illinois
Drivers: Nigel Mansell, Mario Andretti
Sponsors: Kmart, Texaco Havoline
Chassis: Lola T94/00
Engines: Ford/Cosworth XB
Wins: 0
Poles: 3 (Mansell)
PPG Cup points: 133
Mansell 88 (8th), Andretti 45 (14th)

One of the biggest surprises of the season was the conspicuous lack of success for the team owned by Carl Haas and Paul Newman. The year began promisingly, as both Mansell and Andretti were delighted with their new Lolas in pre-season testing. And in the first race at Surfers Paradise, even though Mansell fell back following a spin, an inspired drive from Andretti netted a place on the podium. Mansell added a third and second in the two subsequent races. But then his slide into oblivion began with the bizarre and widely publicized accident at Indianapolis.

Mansell's attention seemed to be at first distracted by the lure of a return to Formula 1, then diverted by what he (quite rightly) perceived as an overwhelming dominance by the Penske juggernaut. The second half of the season brought no tangible reward at all, although it would certainly be true to say Mansell was unlucky on several occasions, notably at Michigan, Loudon and Vancouver.

One of the team's problems was highlighted when Mansell declined to take part in any testing after it became apparent he would not succeed in defending his title. Mario was obliged to take over the chores although, frankly, his pace – at least on the road courses – was not sufficiently competitive to ensure any real gains.

Photos: Michael C. Brown

Top left: Nigel Mansell and Mario Andretti never really saw eye to eye. For the first time since combining forces and moving into the PPG Cup series in 1983, Paul Newman *(above left)* and Carl Haas *(above center)* emerged winless from the season, despite the best efforts of team manager Jim McGee *(above)* and the entire crew.

DYMAG

ENJOY THE PRIVILEGE

Dymag Racing has emerged as the dominant wheel supplier for the 1995 Indy Car season.

Following the initial move by Lola and Reynard to choose Dymag as the preferred supplier of high performance racing wheels, over 80% of the cars built will be racing on Dymag wheels in the 1995 season.

Coveted by many, the Dymag reputation for design and performance has been available only to the privileged few, like Nigel Mansell and his co-competitors. Until now!

For Dymag is making the move from race track to the open road with the launch of an exclusive range of high performance road wheels for discerning drivers.

So now that you have the opportunity, we invite you, like Nigel, to enjoy the privilege.

DYMAG
HIGH PERFORMANCE RACING WHEELS

FOR FULL DETAILS OF DISTRIBUTORS PLEASE CONTACT:
DYMAG RACING U.K. LIMITED., BUMPERS WAY, BRISTOL ROAD, CHIPPENHAM, WILTSHIRE SN14 6LH, ENGLAND. TEL: +44(0)1249 460848. FAX: +44(0)1249 460833.

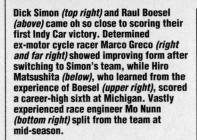

Dick Simon Racing

Base: Indianapolis, Indiana
Drivers: Raul Boesel,
Hiro Matsushita, Marco Greco,
Lyn St. James, Hideshi Matsuda,
Dennis Vitolo
Sponsors: Duracell, Sadia, Fuji,
Mobil 1, Panasonic, Duskin, Bordon,
JCPenney, Reebok, Lee,
Carlo Environmental,
Charter America, Hooligan's
Chassis: Lola T94/00 and T93/00
Engines: Ford/Cosworth XB
Wins: 0
Poles: 1 (Boesel)
PPG Cup points: 100
Boesel 90 (7th), Matsushita 8 (26th),
Greco 2 (29th)

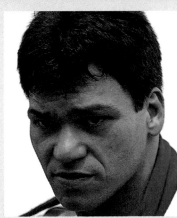

The raw enthusiasm of teams such as Dick Simon Racing cannot make up for a lack of financial resources, especially in today's increasingly competitive environment. As ever, Simon achieved much with little, although Boesel had a disastrous time in mid-season, especially after the departure of race engineer Morris Nunn following a difference of opinion with the team's new Director of Racing, Emory Donaldson. Nevertheless, Boesel rebounded strongly in later races (ironically after he had made up his mind to switch teams for 1995), culminating in an aggressive drive to second at Laguna Seca. Excellent pit work also worked in Boesel's favor at several races.

Matsushita endured another disappointing year without ever displaying the kind of pace which enabled him to win a Toyota Atlantic Championship in 1989. Greco, on the other hand, while horribly inconsistent, did show flashes of inspiration, notably at Long Beach, where he ran tenth until his first pit stop. He also endured more than his share of mechanical problems, although perhaps he needs to take a touch more care with his equipment.

St. James starred in qualifying at Indianapolis, out-qualifying many more illustrious names, including Mansell, while Matsuda drove sensationally in the race before he crashed. The amiable Vitolo, sadly, ruined his Indianapolis debut by almost decapitating none other than Mansell following a moment's inattentiveness.

Dick Simon *(top right)* and **Raul Boesel** *(above)* came oh so close to scoring their first Indy Car victory. Determined ex-motor cycle racer **Marco Greco** *(right and far right)* showed improving form after switching to Simon's team, while **Hiro Matsushita** *(below)*, who learned from the experience of **Boesel** *(upper right)*, scored a career-high sixth at Michigan. Vastly experienced race engineer **Mo Nunn** *(bottom right)* split from the team at mid-season.

Forsythe-Green Racing

Base: Indianapolis, Indiana
Driver: Jacques Villeneuve
Sponsors: Player's Ltd., Indeck
Chassis: Reynard 94I
Engines: Ford/Cosworth XB
Wins: 1
Poles: 0
PPG Cup points: 94 (6th)

Top: The relationship between Jacques Villeneuve and race engineer Tony Cicale translated into a marvelous win at Road America for the team part-owned and managed by Barry Green *(above).*

Both team and driver were a credit to the PPG Cup series. Gerry Forsythe and Barry Green, of course, had combined successfully at this level before, and indeed they started out by graduating from the Can-Am and winning four races with rookie Teo Fabi in 1983. Villeneuve's performance this year, against far stiffer competition, was perhaps even more impressive. Unfortunately, Forsythe and Green faced some 'philosophical differences' and agreed to part before the season's end, fortunately without imparting any untoward interference on the running of one of the slickest and most orderly teams along pit lane.

As Villeneuve put it, the 'chemistry' between himself, Green, race engineer Tony Cicale, crew chief Kyle Moyer and the rest of the gang was first-rate. Having worked together the previous year in Toyota Atlantic also helped immeasurably.

Hall Racing

Base: Midland, Texas
Driver: Teo Fabi
Sponsor: Pennzoil
Chassis: Reynard 94I
Engines: Ilmor Indy V8/D
Wins: 0
Poles: 0
PPG Cup points: 79 (9th)

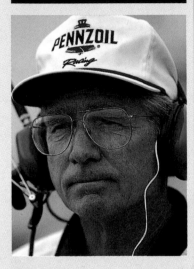

With long-time friend and partner Franz Weis electing this year to concentrate on his core business, VDS Engines, Jim Hall carried on alone with his Pennzoil-backed team. Teo Fabi was retained but, once again, by Hall's exacting standards, results were disappointing. Nevertheless, there were clear signs of improvement toward the end of the year . . . whereupon the cynics pointed out that the diminutive Italian always shows strongly at the end of the season – contract time. Indeed, coincidentally, five of his last six (out of nine) Indy Car poles, and all three of his F1 poles, have come in August, September or October!

Seriously, Fabi did show some of the old speed at Nazareth, where he finished a strong fourth, matching his results earlier in the season at Detroit and Michigan. He also drove well at Laguna Seca, where he had a legitimate shot at finishing second until being delayed by a couple of slow pit stops.

Top: **Teo Fabi worked with Reynard Chief Designer Malcolm Oastler in developing the Pennzoil Reynard-Ilmor owned by Jim Hall** *(above).*

A promising start to the Rahal-Hogan/Honda marriage ended in premature divorce *(bottom left)*, despite which three-time champion Bobby Rahal *(left and below left)* posted several strong performances. At Indianapolis, for example, Rahal and partner Carl Hogan *(below)* overcame their tribulations by leasing a pair of Penske-Ilmors. Mike Groff *(lower middle left and bottom right)* always tried hard in his Motorola Lola-Honda.

Rahal/Hogan Racing

Base: Columbus, Ohio
Drivers: Bobby Rahal, Mike Groff
Sponsors: Miller Genuine Draft, Motorola
Chassis: Lola T94/00, T93/00 and Penske PC22
Engines: Honda V8 and
Ilmor Indy V8/C-D
Wins: 0
Poles: 0
PPG Cup points: 75
Rahal 59 (10th), Groff 17 (20th)

The disappointing performance of the Honda V8 was almost as surprising as the lack of results gained by Newman-Haas. Winter testing had shown that the Japanese motors were no match for the ever-improving Ford/Cosworths and Ilmors, but that notion didn't sink in with the Honda folks until well after the abysmal showing at Indianapolis, where it had become almost immediately apparent that neither Rahal nor Groff would make the field. They simply didn't have enough power. And believe this if you will: one of the Honda engineers reportedly asked Rahal's partner, Carl Hogan, if he wouldn't mind asking his drivers to try a little harder! Needless to say, that didn't sit too well, especially as Groff already had survived a solid meeting with the Turn One wall after suffering a major engine meltdown.

Perhaps the writing had been on the wall even before that: on the way to Indianapolis, one engine had broken loose from its mountings, and, as the Honda transporter negotiated a sharpish turn on the freeway, it burst free, crashed through the side of the truck and then rolled down the road. True story!

The team salvaged its pride when Rahal drove a leased Penske-Ilmor beautifully in the race to finish third, while his performance in Toronto was even more impressive. Groff, too, showed well from time to time, although only rarely was he supplied with equal equipment. Having borne the brunt of the testing chores, he deserved better.

Photos: Michael C. Brown

65

Budweiser King Racing

Base: Indianapolis, Indiana
Drivers: Scott Goodyear, Andrea Montermini
Sponsor: Budweiser
Chassis: Lola T94/00
Engines: Ford/Cosworth XB
Wins: 1 (Goodyear)
Poles: 0
PPG Cup points: 61 – Goodyear 55 (12th), Montermini 6 (of 10, 24th)

Goodyear's victory at Michigan, where all the other top contenders fell by the wayside, was the only high spot in an otherwise disastrous year for a team which had promised to achieve so much more. The partnership between Goodyear and race engineer Dave Benbow began well, with the Canadian posting some excellent times during testing, but their confidence was sapped by a series of curious decisions by higher authorities on the team.

Goodyear qualified among the top ten only three times all season, although he did run strongly in Vancouver, where he started and finished fourth. It was his best overall performance.

Highly rated Italian Andrea Montermini joined the team for two races in mid-season and, despite the fact he was still suffering noticeably from the effects of a bad F1 crash, he drove well to finish seventh in Toronto.

Despite the best efforts of new team manager John Dick, the team sadly folded at the end of the year.

Drag racing star Kenny Bernstein *(top left)* crowned an otherwise disappointing season with a victory at Michigan, where Scott Goodyear *(left)* drove faultlessly and took advantage of the mechanical carnage. Andrea Montermini *(top right)* ran strongly in a couple of guest appearances.

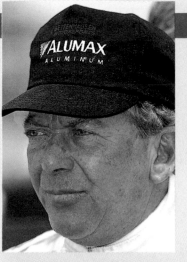

Bettenhausen Motorsports

Base: Indianapolis, Indiana
Drivers: Stefan Johansson, Gary Brabham, Robbie Groff, Gary Bettenhausen
Sponsors: Alumax, Split-Cycle Technology, Condor
Chassis: Penske PC22
Engines: Ilmor Indy V8/C-D
Wins: 0
Poles: 0
PPG Cup points: 57 Johansson (11th)

Photos: Michael C. Brown

A quartet of top-five finishes represented a solid achievement for Tony Bettenhausen's team, which continued to rely on its 1993 Penske PC22 chassis, albeit with the updated Ilmor/D engines. Johansson and race engineer Ken Anderson make a good combination, although their progress, as ever, was hindered by the lack of adequate resources to fund a proper test program.

Nevertheless, Anderson injected some interest by continuing to develop his springless Quantum shock absorbers, which brought promising results on the street and road circuits.

Brabham and Groff (younger brother of Mike) ran respectably, making the most of their rare opportunities, with Groff only just missing out on scoring a point as he finished 13th at both Long Beach and Portland. Gary (older brother of Tony) Bettenhausen struggled dreadfully at Indy, where he eventually crashed in a vain attempt to make the show. The team really should have concentrated its efforts on Johansson.

The future looks bright with Johansson, Anderson and loyal sponsors Alumax having signed long-term contracts to remain with the enthusiastic and hard-trying Bettenhausen. For next season they can hardly wait to get their hands on a pair of the all-conquering Penske PC23 chassis.

There were mixed fortunes for the Bettenhausen brothers, Tony *(top right)* and Gary *(top center)*. Stefan Johansson *(top left and above right)* was delighted to out-qualify the 'factory' Penskes at Michigan. The popular Swede's tally of four top-five finishes with his year-old PC22 represented a fine effort.

Below: Rick Galles regarded 1994 as a learning year with new driver Adrian Fernandez *(lower center)* and his colorful Tecate/Quaker State Reynard *(right)*. PacWest co-owners Tom Armstrong *(top center left)* and Bruce McCaw *(top center right)* created an excellent impression in their first full season, during which Scott Sharp and Dominic Dobson combined to good effect *(right center)* under the expert technical guidance of Alan Mertens *(lower right)*.

Galles Racing International

Base: Albuquerque, New Mexico
Driver: Adrian Fernandez
Sponsors: Tecate, Quaker State
Chassis: Reynard 94I
Engines: Ilmor Indy V8/D
Wins: 0
Poles: 0
PPG Cup points: 46 (13th)

Rick Galles started from scratch this year. He had lost Unser Jr. to Penske, while his plans to continue with Danny Sullivan foundered through lack of adequate financing. But Galles is no quitter. He reluctantly, and amid some acrimony, left Sullivan (whose services do not come cheaply) high and dry. Instead he regrouped, gathered what resources he could, bought a pair of new Reynards, and started afresh with the very promising Adrian Fernandez, a former stand-out in Indy Lights. Indeed the personable Mexican can consider himself unlucky to have missed out on our Top Ten rankings. He made excellent progress this year, working well with engineer Ed Nathman and learning, too, from the considerable experience of crew chief-turned-team manager Owen Snyder, who appeared far more relaxed than in years past.

Fernandez started astonishingly well by earning fourth on the grid at Surfers Paradise, although it wasn't until later in the season that he began to show any consistency. If he can sustain the improvement into next year, he could be challenging for a win or two.

PacWest Racing Group

Base: Indianapolis, Indiana
Drivers: Dominic Dobson,
Scott Sharp
Sponsors: PacWest, Vancouver Grizzlies, Bank of America
Chassis: Lola T94/00
Engines: Ford/Cosworth XB
Wins: 0
Poles: 0
PPG Cup points: 44
Dobson 30 (18th), Sharp 14 (21st)

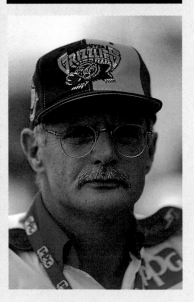

Hayhoe Racing

Base: Indianapolis, Indiana
Driver: Jimmy Vasser
Sponsors: Conseco, STP
Chassis: Reynard 94I
Engines: Ford/Cosworth XB
Wins: 0
Poles: 0
PPG Cup points: 42 (15th)

Indy Regency Racing

Base: Indianapolis, Indiana
Drivers: Arie Luyendyk, Franck Freon
Sponsors: Eurosport, Boost Monaco, Autosport Specialists
Chassis: Lola T94/00
Engines: Ilmor Indy V8/D
Wins: 0
Poles: 0
PPG Cup points: 34 Luyendyk (17th)

Formed by prominent Pacific Northwest businessmen Bruce McCaw, Tom Armstrong and Wes Lematta, in association with Dominic Dobson, the PacWest team, like Forsythe-Green, made an excellent impression in its first full season. The cars were always immaculately presented and on occasion they showed good pace. The crew is top-notch, led by experienced team manager John Anderson and with a solid engineering crew headed by Alan Mertens. The two drivers tended to be closely matched, with Dobson usually the faster in qualifying and the less experienced Sharp often a little quicker in the races. Quite frequently they could be found in close proximity on the race track.

Dobson, appropriately, supplied the best finish, a career-best third at Michigan, although some idea of the team's potential was shown in a late-season test at Mid-Ohio, where the under-utilized (and highly motivated) Danny Sullivan posted some very impressive times.

The 1994 season was a case of so near and yet so far for Jim Hayhoe's team. The talented Vasser came out swinging with a fourth at Surfers and a fifth at Phoenix, despite the entire operation having been put together in something of a rush by team manager/race engineer David Cripps.

Randy Bain came on board later to help ease the load, but after posting several strong efforts in qualifying, Vasser suffered a string of bad luck in mid-season. At Portland, for example, he was punted off by Michael Andretti, while at Cleveland and Michigan he was put out in the early going by a broken fuel pump mount and a failed wheel bearing. A couple of spins didn't help, and nor did a budget that could not be stretched to allow any testing.

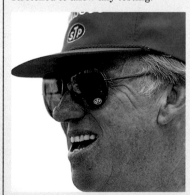

Sal Incandela's group boosted its image by buying new equipment and hiring former Indianapolis 500 champion Arie Luyendyk. It was a bold step which led to the team continuing to make progress, despite the lack of a major sponsor.

The highlight, of course, was a fine run to second place in the Marlboro 500 at Michigan. Luyendyk had struggled with his car's handling throughout practice, then qualified without any boost whatsoever, but in the race he found the car transformed after seeking some set-up advice from former employer Dick Simon. The Dutchman also enjoyed a strong race at Laguna Seca, where he finished sixth.

The team entered its spare chassis for Freon at the season finale, with preparation entrusted to Greg Beck and Steve Erickson. Freon ran well in midfield until misjudging an overtaking maneuver, spinning and causing himself to lose a couple of laps.

The small team owned by Jim Hayhoe *(left center)* produced some solid results with Jimmy Vasser *(top center and left)*. *Above center:* Arie Luyendyk worked hard to overcome the handicap of a minimalist budget with the Indy Regency Lola of Sal Incandela *(top right)*. Frenchman Franck Freon *(above)* also displayed promise during his debut for the team in the season finale.

69

Davy Jones *(below)* scored one point during three races for A.J. Foyt *(lower middle)*, whereupon Bryan Herta *(right and below right)* brought a new lease of life to the team with some inspired performances which belied his rookie status.
Below middle: Dale Coyne installed a variety of drivers in his Mi-Jack Lola, with Alessandro Zampedri *(upper middle right)* showing best of all. Ross Bentley *(lower middle right)* always remained optimistic, while Mauro Baldi thoroughly enjoyed his one-off drive at Mid-Ohio *(center far right)*. Johnny Unser *(lower right)* gained some valuable oval experience in finishing 15th at New Hampshire.

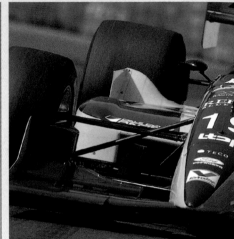

Photos: Michael C. Brown

A.J. Foyt Enterprises

Base: Houston, Texas
Drivers: Davy Jones, Bryan Herta, John Andretti, Eddie Cheever
Sponsors: Copenhagen, Bryant Heating & Cooling, Jonathan Byrd's Cafeteria
Chassis: Lola T94/00
Engines: Ford/Cosworth XB
Wins: 0
Poles: 0
PPG Cup points: 15
Herta 11 (23rd), Andretti 3 (28th)
Jones 1 (31st)

Dale Coyne Racing

Base: Plainfield, Illinois
Drivers: Robbie Buhl, Brian Till, Alessandro Zampedri, Johnny Unser, Mauro Baldi, Ross Bentley
Sponsors: Mi-Jack, Ruger Firearms, Agfa, Hankook
Chassis: Lola T93/00 and T92/00
Engines: Ford/Cosworth XB and Ilmor Indy V8/A
Wins: 0
Poles: 0
PPG Cup points: 10
Zampedri 9 (25th), Till 1 (33rd)

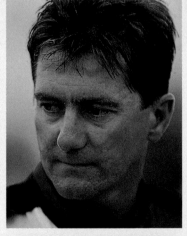

With Robby Gordon having departed for pastures new, A.J. Foyt signed on Davy Jones to drive his familiar black Copenhagen car. But the partnership quickly soured and, despite scoring a point at Phoenix (after crashing his primary car in testing), Jones left by mutual consent after just three races. Then Foyt made an inspired decision by hiring Herta, a runaway winner of the 1993 Firestone Indy Lights Championship.

Up until that time, the young Californian had been unable to secure a drive, despite carrying the promise of a new Lola chassis as part of his prize for winning in Indy Lights. Herta was thrown in at the deep end at Indy. He not only survived but thrived, finishing a strong ninth, one place higher than his vastly more experienced team-mate, John Andretti. Herta was equally impressive in the next four races, claiming two more top-ten finishes before, sadly, his rookie campaign was halted by a bad crash in practice at

Toronto. Herta, though, had made his mark.

Foyt's small team was devastated by the accident, and in the final seven races replacement Eddie Cheever scored not a single point. Cheever, though, could consider himself unlucky on a couple of occasions, his flashes of speed negated by mechanical woes.

That perennial hard-trier, Dale Coyne, scored one point more than in 1993, thanks primarily to a couple of strong mid-season performances by Zampedri. The personable Italian, a graduate of Formula 3000 who had switched from Antonio Ferrari's camp after a couple of fruitless outings, was particularly impressive at Portland, where he qualified an excellent ninth on the first day with a year-old Lola-Ford, then overcame a mechanical problem during Saturday qualifying to finish seventh. He also claimed tenth in Cleveland, only to suffer a painful pelvic injury in a crash (caused, most probably, by a tire failure) during practice at Michigan.

Earlier, both Buhl and Till, who drove well to score a point for 12th at Indy, had decided they needed more competitive equipment if they were to further their careers. Sadly, neither was seen again. Baldi enjoyed his first single-seater race in ten years and drove respectably while subbing for Zampedri at Mid-

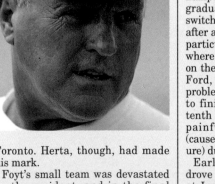

Ohio, while Bentley struggled on gamely with the hopelessly outclassed '92 Lola-Ilmor/A. 'You kind of hope you can pull off a miracle some time,' commented Bentley with a smile after failing to make the field at Laguna Seca.

Andrea Montermini *(left)* started and finished the season in Project Indy's '93 Lola-Ford. Domenico Schiattarella *(far left)* impressed on his debut in Canada, and team part-owner Christian Danner *(lower left)* scored PPG Cup points in each of his two races. Eddie Cheever *(below)* and Scott Brayton *(far below)* qualified with ease at Indianapolis, repaying John Menard's faith in the Buick V6 concept.

Project Indy

Base: Brownsburg, Indiana
Drivers: Andrea Montermini, Franck Freon, Didier Theys, Christian Danner, Mimmo Schiattarella
Sponsors: No Touch, Van Dyne, Marcelo Group
Chassis: Lola T93/00
Engines: Ford/Cosworth XB
Wins: 0
Poles: 0
PPG Cup points: 7
Montermini 4 (of 10, 24th), Danner 2 (30th), Freon 1 (32nd)

Team Menard

Base: Indianapolis, Indiana
Drivers: Eddie Cheever, Scott Brayton, Geoff Brabham
Sponsors: Glidden Paints, Quaker State
Chassis: Lola T93/00
Engines: Menard/Buick V6
Wins: 0
Poles: 0
PPG Cup points: 5
Cheever (27th)

The small team owned by Christian Danner, Rainer Buchmann and Andreas Leberle actually achieved more than their original expectations by contesting nine (rather than eight) races with an ex-Matsushita '93 Lola-Ford. A variety of drivers took it in turns behind the wheel, and all showed they can cut the mustard, so to speak, at this level. The same goes for the team.

Indy Lights graduate Franck Freon scored the first PPG Cup point with a promising run to 12th at Long Beach, while Danner, whose primary thrust was aimed at the thriving German Touring Car Championship, in which he competes for Alfa Romeo, took points at Detroit and Road America. Italian Formula 3 grad Schiattarella looked good in two races, before Montermini capped the year with a solid run to ninth at Laguna.

Genial lumber/hardware store mogul John Menard made his usual foray to Indianapolis with his fleet of specially commissioned '93 Lolas, powered by uprated Menard/Buick V6 engines. The cars were quick, with both Cheever and Brayton running handily inside the top five or six, although only Cheever made it to the finish line. It was the team's only appearance of the year. Unfortunately, having been loyal to Tony George's controversial 'stock-block' concept by committing himself to development of a new 209 c.i. V8 pushrod engine, Menard now finds himself out on a limb for 1995 with the decision by USAC to restrict those engines to a mere 48 inches of boost.

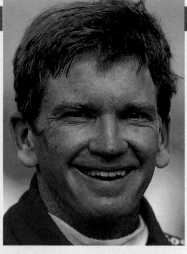

Left and far left: Parker Johnstone and Comptech proved themselves worthy additions to the PPG Cup scene. Antonio Ferrari *(bottom left)* fielded cars for a variety of drivers, including Jeff Wood *(below)* and Giovanni Lavaggi *(center)*. Fredrik Ekblom *(below left)*, Claude Bourbonnais *(lower center)* and Buddy Lazier *(bottom center)* are among the younger guard beginning to make their presence felt in Indy Car racing.

No points but trying. . .
THE REST

Managing to finish within the top 12 represents a notable achievement in these days of ever-improving competition within the PPG Cup series. Several other teams tried during the year. The most notable, perhaps, was Comptech Racing, run by former IMSA stalwarts Doug Peterson and Don Erb. The ambitious and very well presented team, which had swept to three straight Camel Lights division titles with Acura and Parker Johnstone, dipped its toes in the Indy Car waters and was far from out of its depth, despite Johnstone's lack of recent single-seater experience and the handicap of a year-old Lola chassis and old-spec Honda engines.

Ralph Wilke's once-famous Leader Card Racers team, run these days by the resourceful Paul Diatlovich, struggled to find a good set-up on the road courses with its ex-King Racing Lola T93/00-Ilmor/C, although Buddy Lazier did post several strong efforts on the short ovals. On a couple of occasions, notably at Phoenix, he was *en route* to a points-paying finish until losing out in the closing stages. Former sports car racer Giovanni Lavaggi also took a couple of runs in the car.

Swede Fredrik Ekblom looked highly promising in a one-off drive at Detroit with Dennis McCormack's tidy but unreliable (and equally under-financed) Lola T93/00-Ilmor/C, which even the vastly experienced Pancho Carter couldn't hustle into the field at Indy. Claude Bourbonnais also impressed the crew in a

couple of unfulfilling road course outings in the same car. Bourbonnais, who shone brightly alongside Forsythe-Green team-mate Jacques Villeneuve in Toyota Atlantic during 1993, left a similarly good impression on Tim Duke's Pro Formance Motorsports team, which was forced to close after being unable to raise a representative budget.

Finally, Antonio Ferrari's franchise-holding Euromotorsport team somehow made it to all but two races (Indianapolis and Milwaukee), although more often than not its '93 Lola-Ilmor/C was left tucked away in the transporter due to a lack of finance. Jeff Wood instead battled the odds with an ancient, poorly prepared '92 Lola-Ilmor/A, which never once made it to the finish line.

The usual group of hopefuls appeared at Indy for the month of May, with by far the most successful (apart from Menard) being Hemelgarn Racing. The team arrived, late, with a hastily prepped new Reynard, which veteran Stan Fox had absolutely no trouble in getting up to speed despite a bare minimum of laps. The midget star also ran well in the race, until, unfortunately, he crashed out of tenth place with less than a handful of laps remaining.

The underrated Roberto Guerrero also hustled Pagan Racing's two-year-old Lola-Buick into the field before finding the concrete, while one of the more interesting entries saw Johnny Parsons at the wheel of an ex-Fabi '93 Lola, into which had been fitted an ambitious home-built 209 c.i. pushrod motor designed and built by Peter and Michael (father and son) Greenfield. Not surprisingly, a variety of teething gremlins prevented them from making a qualifying run, but that certainly wasn't for a lack of trying.

Photos: Michael C. Brown

Penske

Production base: Poole, England
Number of cars built in 1994: 8
Wins: 12
Poles: 10

Chief designer Nigel Bennett and the staff at Penske Cars are renowned for their methodical, analytical approach. This year's PC23 reflected a logical progression from the successful 1993 chassis with very few major modifications. Nevertheless, Bennett was able to draw on the experience of a dozen design engineers based either at Poole or at the race shop in Reading, Pennsylvania. The team estimated more than 15,000 man-hours were involved in finalizing the PC23's concept, including extensive wind-tunnel development at Southampton University, England.

The primary focus was aimed at gaining aerodynamic efficiency for the short ovals, since new regulations introduced over the winter had placed a severe restriction on rear wing sizes in a bid to control escalating speeds. Prior to the final short-oval race of the season, at Nazareth Speedway, Penske had tried and tested as many as 17 variations on the original theme. No wonder the team romped away to a clear 1-2-3 success.

A revised gearbox was produced during the year, specifically as a result of difficulties experienced during the race at Long Beach. The California street circuit poses a unique problem in that the cars are required to accelerate from a very tight 30 mph hairpin directly onto a long straightaway with speeds in excess of 180 mph. Traditionally, the Penske transverse transmission, which features an F1-style sequential-shift mechanism, has utilized only four forward speeds; at Long Beach, however, the abnormally large differential between the gears led to failures on the cars of both Tracy and Fittipaldi. A new five-speed version was tested in mid-season, and following more development centered upon the need to maintain a usable reverse gear, it was finally raced for the first time at Vancouver.

The Penske team also devoted an enormous effort to developing an Ilmor-designed Mercedes-Benz engine specifically to race at Indianapolis. A new gearbox/transmission was produced to accept the more powerful, torquier engine, as well as a different aerodynamic package. The entire project was shrouded in secrecy but produced the desired results as Al Unser Jr. sped to his second and Penske's tenth victory in the prestigious 500-miler.

Another interesting and time-consuming project, carried out in conjunction with an outside electronics company, Epic, saw the adoption of tire pressure sensors housed within the wheels.

Reynard

Production base: Bicester, England
Number of cars built in 1994: 14
Wins: 3
Poles: 0

Reynard Racing Cars was the new kid on the Indy Car block in 1994. The company had established its reputation producing small-formula cars in England in the middle 1970s. It had also built up a remarkable record of winning its first race in any new category. The trend had been repeated through Formula 3 and Formula 3000 in Europe and, amazingly, it was to continue in Indy Car racing as Michael Andretti rocked the establishment by claiming a debut win at Surfers Paradise.

The design team for the Reynard 94I was headed by Australian Malcolm Oastler, with former Lola chief designer Bruce Ashmore also providing input, especially during the build process. The original design brief was to produce a car that would be, quote, 'Simple but soundly engineered, easy to tune and maintain, and with a highly developed aerodynamic package.'

There was nothing radical about the 94I, although it was easily distinguishable from the rival Penskes and Lolas, especially on the superspeedways, where it ran with anhedral front wings. Reynard departed from the current trend by producing a three-shaft longitudinal gearbox operated by a cable-operated sequential shift system. The 'box proved extremely reliable but heavy. Later in the year, a new 'shortitudinal' version, some 30 lbs lighter, was tested, then given its debut at Laguna Seca.

The Reynards proved extremely competitive on the superspeedways but were difficult to set up on the tighter courses. Andretti, in particular, could not get to grips with the car's inherent tendency toward understeer. It also proved to be more pitch-sensitive than anticipated. As the year progressed, a concerted wind-tunnel program attempted to address the car's shortcomings, for inclusion in the package for the 95I.

Lola

Production base: Huntingdon, England
Number of cars built in 1994: 30
Wins: 1
Poles: 6

A new transverse sequential-shift gearbox was the most significant innovation on the latest Lola T94/00, designed by a team headed by John Travis and Keith Knott. The new gearbox was expected to improve the weight distribution as well as providing aerodynamic advantages. Early testing in Phoenix showed immense promise as Nigel Mansell and Scott Goodyear circulated well underneath the existing track record both on the one-mile PIR oval and on the nearby Firebird road course. Those performances, however, could not be reproduced on a consistent basis, and the regular army of Lola representatives struggled to match not only the resurgent Penskes but also the newcomer Reynards.

Mansell and Robby Gordon, in particular, showed their paces by taking six poles between them, although a succession of niggling problems and plain bad luck precluded either from winning a race. By the end of the season, Lola had scored only one victory – in somewhat fortuitous fashion – at MIS, where Scott Goodyear triumphed after a sequence of mechanical problems or accidents had taken care of the expected front-runners. It was the worst year for Eric Broadley's marque since it re-entered the Indy Car fray in 1983.

Top left: The Penske PC23, a logical development of Nigel Bennett's 1993 car, proved to be a dominant force.

The first Reynard Indy car, the 94I *(above)*, was especially effective on the ovals, yet needed more development to reach full competitiveness on the road courses.

Below: Six poles confirmed the Lola's speed, yet a sequence of problems restricted it to a solitary victory.

Photos: Michael C. Brown

Below: Mario Illien's latest creation, the Ilmor Indy 94, won 11 races in concert with Nigel Bennett's Penske PC23 chassis. Cosworth Engineering, meanwhile, continued development of its 1993 PPG Cup-winning Ford/Cosworth XB *(bottom)*.

Photos: Michael C. Brown

Ilmor
Production base: Brixworth, England
Wins: 12
Poles: 10

The Penske team is convinced the biggest advancement in its package compared to 1993 came in the engine department. Impressively, Mario Illien and Paul Morgan, the driving forces behind Ilmor Engineering, built and developed not only a brand-new Ilmor Indy V8/D engine, which offered substantial gains over last year's 'C' motor, but also the astonishingly successful Mercedes-Benz 500I V8, which swept all before it at Indianapolis, despite only running for the first time in January.

Ilmor and Penske, which has its own engine department in-house at Reading, run by Karl Kainhofer, somehow managed to run parallel development programs through the first few races. Improvements to the 'D' brought a reputed extra 30 horsepower between the first two races, at Surfers and Phoenix, whereupon all efforts were concentrated upon extracting power and reliability from the Mercedes in preparation for Indy. Once that goal had been realized, attention reverted to the conventional 'D' in readiness for the remainder of the PPG Cup season. It was a fine effort.

Ford/Cosworth
Production base: Northampton, England
Wins: 4
Poles: 6

Steve Miller and his crew at Cosworth continued to make some gains with the XB motor, which was once again especially strong on the superspeedways. For top-end power, this was the engine of choice. During the season, however, it became apparent that perhaps the Ilmor was a little more tractable and offered more usable power in the mid-range, which proved invaluable on the majority of circuits.

The success of Mansell & Co. in 1993 had led to a vast increase in orders over the winter, and Cosworth was hard-pressed to keep pace with the demand for rebuilds. Particularly in later races, the Cosworth runners seemed to experience more than their usual share of failures.

Honda
Production base: Santa Clarita, California
Wins: 0
Poles: 0

Honda produced a variety of different engine specifications without ever reaching parity with the opposition. Mostly they featured a distinctive, raspy exhaust note signifying the so-called 'big-bang' configuration pioneered by Honda in Grand Prix motor cycle racing whereby two opposing cylinders are fired simultaneously. Later in the season, on most engines, Honda reverted to a conventional firing order (and a 'regular' engine sound), albeit without any apparently significant boost in performance. In fact, for most of the later races, Rahal and Groff usually were running engines to a different specification, although by then the Rahal/Hogan 'factory' team already had made its decision to switch engine suppliers for the 1995 season.

Certainly, the lack of competitiveness displayed by Honda, allied to some mid-season unreliability and the non-appearance of an oft-promised newer-generation V8, came as a major disappointment – and also something of a surprise.

'It's a matter of hopes and expectations,' said a philosophical Robert Clarke, general manager of Honda Performance Development. 'Our hopes were that we'd be further along than we are. Our expectations, I think, were a little bit behind our hopes. [The Rahal/Hogan team's] expectations were higher than even ours.'

Honda, however, has maintained that it is committed to the Indy Car series and that development will continue.

Nigel Mansell, Newman-Haas Racing, Kmart/Havoline Lola T94/00 Ford-Cosworth

Michael Andretti, Ganassi Target/Scotch Video Reynard 94I Ford-Cosworth

The success of Cosworth engines in international motor racing is legendary.

Continuous research, development and new manufacturing technology form the centre of our race ethic. Our commitment to excellence ensures that Cosworth will continue to achieve the competitive edge vital for tomorrow's success.

Ford-Cosworth XB
Indy Car Engine

Robby Gordon, Walker Valvoline/Cummins Special Lola T94/00 Ford-Cosworth

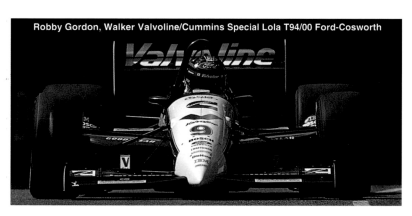

Raul Boesel, Simon Duracell/Fuji Film/ Mobil/Sadia Lola T94/00 Ford-Cosworth

Jacques Villeneuve, Forsythe-Green Player's Ltd. Reynard 94I Ford-Cosworth

COSWORTH®

Cosworth Engineering, St James Mill Road, Northampton NN5 5JJ, UK.
Telephone: (0) 1604 752444/Fax: (0) 1604 580470
Cosworth Engineering Inc., 3031 Fujita Street, Torrance, CA90505-4004, USA.
Telephone: (0) 310 534 1390/Fax: (0) 310 534 2631

A division of Vickers PLC

THE CURTAIN COMES DOWN

A tribute to Mario Andretti

by David Phillips

THIRTY-ONE years ago Mario Andretti made his debut in National Championship competition at Trenton Speedway. Not even the most prescient observer could have foretold that the cocky Italian-American from eastern Pennsylvania was destined to enter no fewer than 407 championship races, let alone win 52 of them on the way to four National Championships as well as the Daytona 500, a half-dozen international sports car races, 12 Formula 1 races and the 1978 World Driving Championship.

Heck, a lot of people didn't expect him to survive long enough to see 1965, let alone 1995. Other drivers in that rough, tumble and all too often tragic era were known to place wagers on whether or not Mario would survive the weekend; Newman-Haas Team Manager Jim McGee used to send him Christmas cards in August because he figured Andretti wouldn't be around for the holidays.

But against all odds Mario Andretti not only survived, he prospered; prospered to race for legends such as Enzo Ferrari, Colin Chapman, Roger Penske, Al Dean, Andy Granatelli, Parnelli Jones, Carl Haas and Paul Newman; to race in cars that changed the sport, like the Lotus 78 and 79, the Porsche 962 and the Lola T87/00-Chevy; to race on tracks from the Nürburgring to Pikes Peak, Daytona to Langhorne, Kyalami to Monza, Watkins Glen to Indianapolis; to race against men like A.J. Foyt, Jackie Stewart, Jud Larson, Niki Lauda, Rick Mears and Richard Petty; to race with team-mates like Ronnie Peterson, Al Unser, Joe Leonard, Nigel Mansell and, most memorably, his son Michael.

And finally, he survived and prospered to bring the curtain down on his Indy Car career after the Bank of America 300 at Laguna Seca Raceway on October 9.

The end of Mario Andretti's Indy Car career came as no surprise, of course. A year earlier he had announced this would be his final season of open-wheel competition, and he pursued what became known as the 'Arrivederci, Mario' season with the same passion and commitment that have marked his racing since he and his twin brother, Aldo, first wheeled their home-built Hudson Hornet onto the dirt at Nazareth Speedway in 1959.

Indeed, though Mario went winless in his final campaign, he takes a great deal of pride from the fact that he never let the attention showered upon him detract from the job at hand.

'This year has just been fabulous. I've felt good, very relaxed,' he says. 'I think I've accomplished what I wanted. We haven't let the retirement stuff interfere with my driving, and I give a lot of the credit for that to the group that organized things for me this year. We held on to a specific routine or plan and it worked.

'The only negative has been some engine failures and other things that cropped up whenever we had an opportunity to finish in the top five. In the past you could walk away from that stuff thinking, "OK, it was a bad weekend, we'll get 'em next time." But in the case of the big races – Indianapolis, Michigan – it leaves me with a sense of unfinished business. I'd have given anything to get to the end of those races. But it's the same old story, that's racing and you have to take it in stride or you'd go mad or you'd never quit.'

As he has for the past 24 Mays, Mario failed to win the Indianapolis 500. Since winning the race in 1969, Andretti has unwittingly found every conceivable way to lose the Indianapolis 500, from suffering a broken valve spring after leading 171 of the first 178 laps in 1987, to finishing second to Bobby Unser in 1981, then being awarded the win after Unser was penalized only to have USAC reverse that decision months later. Together with Raul Boesel, Mario probably had the fastest car in the 1993 race, but a mismatched set of tires were bolted on his car on the final pit stop and he was lucky to salvage sixth place.

To say Mario has a love/hate relationship with the Indianapolis 500 is the height of understatement.

'I think the race has to be put in perspective,' he says. 'It's unfair to the good drivers that have never won it to be judged by the Indianapolis 500.

'I was a young driver, 25, when I came to Indianapolis, won Rookie of the Year and went on and won the National Championship. And to me that was an achievement. So I go on a talk show, Johnny Carson hosted by Joey Bishop, and I'm introduced as the Indianapolis Rookie of the Year; and the National Championship is never mentioned. I thought, "Well, that's bull." If the Rookie of the Year at Indianapolis is more important than the National Championship then something is

Clockwise from top left: Mario shares a Porsche 962 with sons Michael and Jeff in the 1991 Daytona 24 Hours race; his 52nd and final Indy Car victory came at Phoenix in 1993; *en route* to his 1978 Formula 1 World Championship crown with Colin Chapman's sensational Lotus 79; the partnership with Lola, Paul Newman and Carl Haas netted 18 Indy Car wins in 12 seasons; charging on at Detroit in 1990; as Mario reflects on his own career, son Michael looks to the future. The legacy continues.

The final verdict

A.J. Foyt (seven-time Indy Car champion):
'He and I always respected one another because neither one wanted to settle for second. When we first started racin' together it was a Firestone-Goodyear tire war. He was Firestone and I was Goodyear. That was a pretty rough battle, but I think, really, the news media made more out of it than Mario or I. They would call him up and say, "A.J. said so-and-so," and they knew if they would call me and say, "Mario said so-and-so," I'd fire right back. They were the ones stirring it more than Mario and I.'

Richard Petty (seven-time NASCAR Winston Cup stock car champion):
'I think he and I thought about [retirement] alike. We stayed long enough to get it out of our blood – even though it's always gonna be there, at least, in our minds we can tell ourselves we carried it as far as we could. Now it's time to get out!'

'He came to the Daytona 500 in 1967 and won the race. I didn't like him after that because he comes into our territory and wins the biggest race. My car wasn't runnin' good that day, so probably the only time I saw him was when he was passin' me!'

Dan Gurney (owner, All American Racers; former F1 and Indy Car winner):
'What a real champion. Ever since Mario went to Europe and won the Formula 1 Championship I've started calling him "champ." I'd say, "Hello, champ," and I really mean it. He, along with A.J. Foyt, were the stars of the 1960s. Their duels in Indy Car racing have never been beaten. He's made his mark in history and I'm awfully proud to have known him.'

Emerson Fittipaldi (two-time Formula 1 champion and Indianapolis 500 winner):
'Mario has been one of the greatest drivers in history. I have a lot of respect for him. Everything he drove, he won. I think that's amazing.

'The first time I raced with Mario was in the South African Grand Prix [in 1971]. Since then we are good friends. I think he has been an example for a lot of young people, including myself when I started racing, as someone you want to be like. I think there's not many athletes in the world like that.'

Rick Mears (three-time Indy Car champion and four-time Indianapolis 500 winner):
'Mario was a big help to me when I first came to the Penske team [in 1976]. He helped me understand how everything works: testing, racing, whatever. He helped me see the big picture. If I had any questions, I could always go to him.'

Roger Penske (owner, Penske Racing, winner of ten Indianapolis 500s and nine Indy Car championships):
'I've said many times that when Mario drove for me [in 1976-80], he was the most intense and committed driver. A lot of young guys coming up today could learn from him. I wish we had had the opportunity to work together longer, because I feel we would have had significant success.'

Danny Sullivan (1985 Indianapolis 500 winner and 1988 PPG Cup champion):
'I look at Mario as a friend, but also to have raced against him is something I will tell my grandchildren about. He's a special racer. He's one of those guys you can never, never, count out.'

For the record

Full name: Mario Gabriel Andretti
Born: February 28, 1940
Birthplace: Montona, Italy
Status: Married to Dee Ann
Children: Two sons, Michael and Jeff, and one daughter, Barbra Dee
Lives: Nazareth, Pennsylvania
Biggest influence of his career: Alberto Ascari
First race car: 1948 Hudson Hornet
First Indy Car race: Trenton, April 19, 1964 (finished 11th)
First Formula 1 race: United States Grand Prix, Watkins Glen, October 6, 1968 (qualified on pole)

Career highlights

1965	Indianapolis 500 Rookie of the Year
1965	USAC National Champion
1966	USAC National Champion
1967	Daytona 500 winner
1967	Sebring 12 Hours winner
1969	Indianapolis 500 winner
1969	USAC National Champion
1969	ABC 'Wide World of Sports' Athlete of the Year
1974	USAC Silver Crown Champion
1978	World (Formula 1) Driving Champion
1979	International Race of Champions IROC VI series champion
1984	PPG Indy Car World Series champion
1988	Won 50th Indy Car race
1989	Indy Car 'Triple Crown' winner
1992	Named as 'Driver of the Quarter Century' by panel of US journalists
1993	Victory at Phoenix was his 100th major international win, his 52nd in an Indy car; became oldest driver to win an Indy Car race (53 years, 34 days)

wrong. What I'm trying to say is the place is not the ultimate yardstick. You can't tell me that Lloyd Ruby or Tony Bettenhausen, who never won the thing and won everywhere else, they're lesser drivers because they didn't win at Indianapolis.'

Thanks to the fact that Andretti was racing what amounted almost to eight days a week in the 1960s and '70s, however, he won a few other pretty big events . . . like the Daytona 500, the 12 Hours of Sebring, and Formula 1 races from Fuji to Long Beach.

Although A.J. Foyt won more Indy Car races and others more Formula 1 races, no other driver in history can match Mario in terms of the length and breadth of his accomplishments.

'I won in every season of my career since 1959, when I started, until 1988,' he says. 'And the reason that I probably didn't win races from 1988 on was because I stayed primarily in Indy cars. Now that doesn't mean I won a race in Indy cars every year, but when we weren't winning we'd go into Formula 5000, dirt races, sports cars and always come away winning something. In 1972 we didn't have a good season in Indy cars but we helped win the World Sports Car Championship for Ferrari.

'That to me has always been the greatest help, in feeling I'm always going forward. Even though I'm not always going forward in that specific category, I'm always going forward career-wise. That was a great opportunity I gave myself. To be concentrating and specializing in just one area and hope to be a winner every year is almost impossible.

'There was a period in my life, a long period, where I just couldn't get enough. My wife would say, "Geez, can't you take a weekend off?" and if you look back, not for one year or a couple of years, but for many, many years, I just would not. I would run sprint cars, I'd run sports cars. I'd be up and away from Zandvoort to Atlanta and all that sort of thing. But it did catch up to me. I'm pretty sure it was 1980, with five Sundays in May. Imola was one Sunday, Indy qualifying was the second, the third was somewhere else, the fourth was the Indianapolis 500 and the fifth Sunday was Monaco. So you get up in the morning and, honest to God, you just look at the ceiling and say "Where am I? The Speedway Motel or the Hotel de Paris?" '

Quite possibly the *only* classic races

he hasn't won are the Grand Prix of Monaco and the 24 Hours of Le Mans. Although you should never say never when it comes to Mario Andretti, Monaco would seem to be out of the question. Le Mans is very much a possibility, however. Indeed, it might be the perfect venue for a man of Mario's matchless experience.

'I've had some conversations about Le Mans next year,' he says. 'I'd definitely be interested in something like that if it were a factory effort and maybe I could team up with Michael, Jeff or John.'

Clearly, however, the days when Andretti focuses all his energies on driving a racing car are a thing of the past. There has been speculation about him entering the ranks of the Indy Car team owners, but he is playing that one close to the vest.

'We'll have to wait and see,' he says. 'I don't see myself working for somebody, but at the same time I could see myself joining a team as an owner or co-owner. By no means do I think it's a small task to run a race team properly. Most drivers are lousy businessmen. I think the trick is to spend money to hire the right

people to run the show and just be there, give 'em your blessing every morning and that's it. Let them do their job.'

If he does decide to go into competition with Carl Haas, Roger Penske et al, he certainly won't be lacking in role models from his own career.

'I could probably write a book about the great team owners I've driven for,' says Andretti. 'Al Dean, for instance. I mean he was the ultimate sportsman in the '50s and '60s. So I was certainly touched by his life, his presence. Colin Chapman. There's no other man that has ever revolutionized motor racing like Colin Chapman. He was a true maverick. He looked at the construction of cars and exploring all possibilities to achieve that unfair advantage. You always had that extra confidence because you knew he was always looking for that angle.

'Enzo Ferrari was probably the most special individual, because I think it's because of him, because of Ferrari, that I felt the desire to devote my life toward motor racing. As a driver you almost feel like you haven't accomplished anything

unless you drove for him. The one thing that happened to me, that I'll always hold very, very special, is that I always dealt with him direct. Totally. Whether it was on the phone or in person. For me it was joy to do that. I'll tell you, he's a guy that commanded respect.

'Carl and Paul, the fact that I've been with them for so many years tells you it's more than just a business association, but a good solid friendship between us that, hopefully, will continue. There were times that not everybody saw eye to eye, not the most harmonious; but time has a way of just allowing one to mature into situations, and I think Paul and Carl now are finally good friends.'

Likewise, Mario has raced against virtually every great (and not so great) driver in professional racing since the 1960s. A compilation of just his team-mates alone would go a long way toward naming a 'Who's Who of Drivers' in the last four decades. But when Mario reflects on his career, no period of his life is more special than the years he spent racing with his sons, Michael and Jeff.

'To see your kids go from toddlers to the starting grid with you, then run 1-2 and share so many precious moments, from a personal side they have no equal satisfaction,' says Mario. 'Sometimes I have to pinch myself when I realize Michael and I did it over and over, not just one lucky shot. Then there are the weekends when I won in my own Indy car and Jeff won at Milwaukee in Super Vees and at Pocono in ARS. We cleaned up. When you look back at that side of it, that's what's going to be everlasting to me.'

Only time will tell if Mario will eventually make the switch from Michael's former team-mate to his team owner. Whatever Mario does, however, he will do it from Nazareth, Pennsylvania, his home since 1955.

'Nazareth is a great little town; I'm here by choice. It's given me and my family everything we could want from life,' says Mario. 'When I come home from the races I'm just another guy around town. I can go down to the hardware store, to the local diner and I don't get treated any differently than anyone else. There's no pretenses here and I don't think we'd have that somewhere else. It's a great place to call home.'

And a place Mario will be seeing a little more of now that he's brought the curtain down on one of the most remarkable careers in the history of auto racing.

Michael C. Brown

∂P RACING

FIT TO WIN

Check the record books.
No other manufacturer of racing brakes
or clutches even comes close.

AP Lockheed and AP Borg & Beck
components have become a byword for
performance - the standard by which
all others are judged.

AP Racing, Wheler Road,
Seven Stars Industrial Estate,
Coventry CV3 4LB. Tel: 01203 639595
International: +44 1203 639595
Fax: +44 1203 639559

THE SON ALSO RISES

IF there's an ongoing debate over whether the Allisons, Andrettis, Pettys or Unsers are the first family of racing in the United States, there can be no doubting the Villeneuve clan holds that honor in Canada. That was probably true even when 'all' the Villeneuves had to boast about was Gilles, one of the most popular Grand Prix drivers in history, and his brother Jacques, snowmobiler *par excellence* and the first Canadian driver ever to win an Indy Car race.

But the past few seasons have seen Gilles' son, Jacques, rise to prominence among racing's bright new stars, an ascendancy that accelerated in 1994 when he scored his first win in Indy Car competition, finished sixth in the PPG Cup championship and earned both Indy Car and Indianapolis 500 Rookie of the Year honors.

Just 11 years old at the time of his father's fatal accident at Zolder, Belgium, in 1982, Jacques did not come of age at the race track *à la* Davey Allison, Michael Andretti, Kyle Petty or Al Unser Jr. Rather, he lived with his mother in Monaco and attended private school in Switzerland.

Nevertheless, the die had been cast. Young Jacques was attracted to speed sports, be it water skiing, motor cycles or snow skiing, and at age 15 his mother enrolled him in the Jim Russell Racing Drivers School at Mt.

by David Phillips

Tremblant, Quebec. Two years later he was working as a mechanic and racing part-time at the Spenard-David school in Shannonville, Ontario.

In a classic case of jumping off the deep end, Villeneuve made his professional debut in 1989, racing touring cars in Italy in front of some of his father's most devoted fans.

'As soon as I started racing in Italy at age 17 I was under tremendous pressure,' says Jacques. 'I had to mature quickly; if not I wouldn't have lasted very long.'

He continued racing in Italy the following three seasons, competing in the frenetic Italian Formula 3 championship, before moving to the Japanese F3

series and finishing third in the prestigious Macau F3 race at the end of 1992. Last season saw Jacques join Claude Bourbonnais on the new Forsythe-Green Racing team in the Player's Toyota Atlantic series, with Jacques earning seven poles and five wins in 15 races.

Although the Toyota Atlantic title ultimately eluded Forsythe-Green, 1993 laid the groundwork for the team's long-term objective: the PPG Indy Car World Series. Unlike most rookies, Jacques would be undertaking his first season of Indy Car racing in familiar surroundings.

'It's different cars and a different series this year, but it's the same people,' he says. 'So we didn't have to spend half a season learning to work together. That's been a big help. The team is made up of all good people, very focused people.'

People like team owners Gerry Forsythe and Barry Green, engineer Tony Cicale and crew chief Kyle Moyer. Green, for example, was team manager on Galles-Kraco's PPG Cup championship-winning team in 1990, while Cicale is widely recognized as one of the best race engineers in the business.

After qualifying a solid eighth at Surfers Paradise in their Indy Car debut, Villeneuve & Co. put the Player's Reynard-Ford on the front row at Phoenix, then stunned the racing fraternity with a brilliant second place in the Indianapolis 500.

'Indianapolis is the one place where you have to stay concentrated for a long period of time,' says Jacques. 'Not only is it the longest race, it's a whole month from the start of practice till the end of the race. It's easy to lose your focus, to get mad if things aren't going well. We spent the whole month without losing focus; we have a good chemistry on the team and the result was great for us.'

Certainly one thing Villeneuve had going for him at Indianapolis was his driving style. The very antithesis of his father's (and uncle's) 'all arms and elbows' style, Jacques takes an analytical approach that is perfectly suited to today's hyper-sensitive chassis set-ups.

'I never compare myself to my father,' says Jacques. 'The times are so different. Now it is a case of having the car perfectly balanced. Back then you drove sideways to go fast. Who knows? If my father was driving today he'd probably be just as successful but drive differently. Really, there's no one right way and I try not to compare myself to my father. By the same token, I'm proud to be his son and if I end up accomplishing some of the

things he did that will be great. But if not, that's OK too.'

However, 1994 was not without its downsides for Villeneuve. First came a spectacular crash at Phoenix when he center-punched Hiro Matsushita's disabled Lola-Ford after the yellow lights had been on for what seemed an eternity.

'People said I didn't put the brakes on until I was on top of the accident, but I was on the brakes earlier,' he says. 'I was being criticized for being crazy, driving out of my mind, but I was driving very comfortably, in control.'

And after that marvelous month of May and several additional top-ten finishes in June and July, Jacques went into something of a slump in late July and August. By his own admission, the ceaseless round of personal appearances leading up to the Toronto race left him drained before practice even began. Then came crashes at Michigan and New Hampshire in which he was manifestly blameless.

But the team rebounded with a strong (but brief) showing at

Vancouver before Jacques outraced Paul Tracy and Al Unser Jr. to score a brilliant win at Road America. A month later, he scored his third top-three finish of the season at Laguna Seca to clinch sixth place in PPG Cup points, ahead of the likes of Nigel Mansell, Bobby Rahal and Mario Andretti.

'At the start of the season we hoped to be able to finish in the top ten in the championship,' says Jacques. 'I knew the team was ready to win. Many of the guys on the team had won with other drivers, although personally I knew I had a lot to learn. But I think the season turned out better than we could have hoped for. This was my second year with Barry Green and Tony Cicale, and if we do the same thing with the same people next year we should have a good chance to do even better.'

Indeed, with continuing support from Player's Ltd., a fine young team behind him and a cool head to match his heavy right foot, it can truly be said that the sky is the only limit for the son of Gilles Villeneuve.

PPG **POINTS**

1994 PPG INDY CAR WORLD SERIES PERFORMANCE CHART

Position	Driver	Nationality	Car	Surfers Paradise	Phoenix	Long Beach	Indianapolis	Milwaukee	Detroit	Portland	Cleveland	Toronto	Michigan	Mid-Ohio	New Hampshire	Vancouver	Road America	Nazareth	Laguna Seca	Points total
1	Al Unser Jr.	USA	Marlboro Team Penske PC23-Ilmor/D	14	2	*1	–	*1	*10	P*1	P*1	29	8	P1	1	1	2	2	20	225
			Marlboro Team Penske PC23-Mercedes-Benz	–	–	–	P1	–	–	–	–	–	–	–	–	–	–	–	–	
2	Emerson Fittipaldi	BR	Marlboro Team Penske PC23-Ilmor/D	2	*1	21	–	2	2	2	20	3	10	3	P*3	9	3	P3	4	178
			Marlboro Team Penske PC23-Mercedes-Benz	–	–	–	*17	–	–	–	–	–	–	–	–	–	–	–	–	
3	Paul Tracy	CDN	Marlboro Team Penske PC23-Ilmor/D	16	P23	P20	–	3	1	3	3	5	16	*2	2	20	P*18	*1	P*1	152
			Marlboro Team Penske PC23-Mercedes-Benz	–	–	–	23	–	–	–	–	–	–	–	–	–	–	–	–	
4	Michael Andretti	USA	Ganassi Target/Scotch Video Reynard 94I-Ford	*1	20	6	6	4	5	31	18	*1	22	5	5	3	17	9	28	118
5	Robby Gordon	USA	Walker Valvoline/Cummins Special Lola T94/00-Ford	23	7	3	5	6	3	4	11	P6	13	4	13	P2	25	23	13	104
6	Jacques Villeneuve	CDN	Forsythe-Green Player's Ltd. Reynard 94I-Ford	17	25	15	2	9	7	6	4	9	20	9	26	24	1	7	3	94
7	Raul Boesel	BR	Simon Duracell/Fuji Film/Mobil/Sadia Lola T94/00-Ford	27	8	4	21	P8	28	23	6	12	*9	8	4	23	6	4	2	90
8	Nigel Mansell	GB	Newman-Haas Kmart/Texaco Havoline Lola T94/00-Ford	P9	3	2	22	5	P21	5	2	23	P26	7	18	*10	13	22	8	88
9	Teo Fabi	I	Hall Pennzoil Special Reynard 94I-Ilmor/D	7	26	9	7	17	4	26	9	8	4	21	20	18	4	6	5	79
10	Bobby Rahal	USA	Rahal-Hogan Miller Genuine Draft Lola T94/00-Honda	26	14	30	NQ	7	6	12	28	2	28	27	9	7	9	14	29	59
			Rahal-Hogan Miller Genuine Draft Penske PC22-Ilmor/D	–	–	–	3	–	–	–	–	–	–	–	–	–	–	–	–	
11	Stefan Johansson	S	Bettenhausen Alumax Aluminium Penske PC22-Ilmor/D	5	4	10	15	26	22	8	5	14	14	12	23	26	8	5	12	57
12	Scott Goodyear	CDN	Budweiser King Racing Lola T94/00-Ford	10	11	19	30	22	11	28	14	10	1	22	11	4	7	8	27	55
13	Adrian Fernandez	MEX	Galles Tecate/Quaker State Reynard 94I-Ilmor/D	13	10	8	28	16	23	10	7	13	23	6	8	22	5	21	7	46
14	Mario Andretti	USA	Newman-Haas Kmart/Texaco Havoline Lola T94/00-Ford	3	21	5	32	14	18	9	27	4	18	10	19	11	16	25	19	45
15	Jimmy Vasser	USA	Hayhoe Conseco/STP Reynard 94I-Ford	4	5	24	4	11	20	32	31	25	25	14	7	15	28	13	26	42
16	Mauricio Gugelmin	BR	Ganassi Hollywood Reynard 94I-Ford	6	15	7	11	15	8	30	8	20	15	25	14	5	19	10	22	39
17	Arie Luyendyk	NL	Indy Regency Eurosport/Boost Monaco Lola T94/00-Ilmor/D	25	22	11	18	21	19	14	21	31	2	13	27	6	22	26	6	34
18	Dominic Dobson	USA	PacWest Racing Group Lola T94/00-Ford	12	24	17	29	13	25	7	25	11	3	15	6	19	11	19	10	30
19	Mark Smith	USA	Walker Craftsman Tools Lola T94/00-Ford	21	NQ	25	NQ	24	14	16	22	W	5	20	12	8	26	12	14	17
			Walker Craftsman Tools Lola T93/00-Ford	–	–	–	–	–	–	–	–	30	–	–	–	–	–	–	–	
20	Mike Groff	USA	Rahal-Hogan Motorola Lola T93/00-Honda	8	–	–	–	–	–	–	–	–	–	–	–	–	–	–	–	17
			Rahal-Hogan Motorola Lola T94/00-Honda	–	6	27	NQ	19	27	11	19	22	27	26	25	14	20	11	15	
			Rahal-Hogan Motorola Penske PC22-Ilmor/C+	–	–	–	31	–	–	–	–	–	–	–	–	–	–	–	–	
21	Scott Sharp	USA	PacWest Racing Group Lola T94/00-Ford	11	9	28	16	12	13	18	24	16	12	11	24	12	10	15	21	14
22	Willy T. Ribbs	USA	Walker Service Merchandise/Bill Cosby Lola T93/00-Ford	18	28	18	–	–	–	–	–	–	–	–	–	–	–	–	–	12
			Walker Service Merchandise/Bill Cosby Lola T94/00-Ford	–	–	–	NQ	25	16	25	12	21	7	28	10	25	24	18	11	
23	Bryan Herta	USA	A.J. Foyt Copenhagen Racing Lola T94/00-Ford	–	–	–	9	10	9	27	13	NS	–	–	–	–	–	–	–	11
24	Andrea Montermini	I	Coyne Project Indy Lola T93/00-Ford	NS	–	–	–	–	–	–	–	–	–	–	–	–	–	–	–	10
			Budweiser King Racing Lola T94/00-Ford	–	–	–	–	–	–	–	16	7	–	–	–	–	–	–	–	
			Project Indy No Touch/Van Dyne/Marcelo Lola T93/00-Ford	–	–	–	–	–	–	–	–	–	–	–	–	–	–	–	9	
25	Alessandro Zampedri	I	Euromotorsport Agip/Dinema/Fluoril Lola T93/00-Ilmor/C	22	–	22	–	–	–	–	–	–	–	–	–	–	–	–	–	9
			Coyne The Mi-Jack Car Lola T93/00-Ford	–	–	–	–	–	26	7	10	17	NS	–	–	28	23	20	16	
26	Hiro Matsushita	J	Simon Panasonic/Duskin Lola T94/00-Ford	15	27	–	14	23	NQ	21	15	18	6	18	17	NQ	14	16	23	8
			Simon Panasonic/Duskin Lola T93/00-Ford	–	–	NQ	–	–	–	–	–	–	–	–	–	–	–	–	–	
27	Eddie Cheever	USA	Menard Quaker State Special Lola T93/00-Menard	–	–	–	8	–	–	–	–	–	–	–	–	–	–	–	–	5
			A.J. Foyt Copenhagen Racing Lola T94/00-Ford	–	–	–	–	–	–	–	–	–	21	17	21	17	27	24	25	
28	John Andretti	USA	A.J. Foyt Jonathan Byrd/Bryant Lola T94/00-Ford	–	–	–	10	–	–	–	–	–	–	–	–	–	–	–	–	3
29	Marco Greco	BR	Simon Arciero Project Indy Lola T94/00-Ford	NQ	16	23	27	20	24	20	26	15	11	NQ	16	16	21	17	24	2
30	Christian Danner	D	Project Indy No Touch/Marcelo Group Lola T93/00-Ford	–	–	–	–	–	12	–	–	–	–	–	–	–	12	–	–	2
31	Davy Jones	USA	A.J. Foyt Copenhagen Racing Lola T94/00-Ford	W	–	–	–	–	–	–	–	–	–	–	–	–	–	–	–	1
			A.J. Foyt Copenhagen Racing Lola T92/00-Ford	18	–	–	–	–	–	–	–	–	–	–	–	–	–	–	–	
			A.J. Foyt Copenhagen Racing Lola T93/00-Ford	–	12	14	–	–	–	–	–	–	–	–	–	–	–	–	–	
			Budweiser King Racing Lola T94/00-Ford	–	–	–	W	–	–	–	–	–	–	–	–	–	–	–	–	
32	Franck Freon	F	Project Indy No Touch/Marcelo Group Lola T93/00-Ford	–	–	12	–	–	–	15	–	–	–	–	–	–	–	–	–	1
			Euromotorsport Agip/Hawaiian Tropic Lola T92/00-Ilmor/A	–	–	–	–	–	–	–	–	–	–	–	–	NQ	29	–	–	
			Indy Regency/Autosports Specialists Lola T94/00-Ilmor/D	–	–	–	–	–	–	–	–	–	–	–	–	–	–	–	18	
33	Brian Till	USA	Coyne The Mi-Jack Car Lola T93/00-Ford	–	19	–	12	–	–	–	–	–	–	–	–	–	–	–	–	1
	Buddy Lazier	USA	Leader Card Financial World Lola T93/00-Ilmor/C+	NQ	13	29	NQ	18	17	24	–	NS	24	NQ	NS	27	–	NQ	–	
			Leader Card Financial World Lola T92/00-Buick	–	–	–	NQ	–	–	–	–	–	–	–	–	–	–	–	–	
	Robbie Groff	USA	Bettenhausen Condor Penske PC22-Ilmor/C+	–	–	W	–	–	–	13	–	–	–	–	–	–	–	–	–	
			Bettenhausen Condor Penske PC22-Ilmor/D	–	–	13	–	–	–	–	–	–	–	–	–	–	–	–	–	
	Stan Fox	USA	Hemelgarn Delta Faucet/Jack's Tool Reynard 94I-Ford	–	–	–	13	–	–	–	–	–	–	–	–	–	–	–	–	
	Parker Johnstone	USA	Comptech Racing Acura Lola T93/00-Honda	–	–	–	–	–	–	19	17	27	–	23	–	13	–	–	17	
	Johnny Unser	USA	Dale Coyne Racing Lola T92/00-Ilmor/A	–	NQ	NQ	–	–	–	–	–	–	–	–	–	–	–	–	–	
			Coyne The Mi-Jack Car Lola T93/00-Ford	–	–	–	–	NQ	–	–	–	–	–	–	15	–	–	–	–	
	Giovanni Lavaggi	I	Euromotorsport Agip/Hawaiian Tropic Lola T92/00-Ilmor/A	–	–	–	–	–	NQ	–	–	–	–	–	–	–	–	–	–	
			Leader Card Financial World Lola T93/00-Ilmor/C+	–	–	–	–	–	–	–	30	–	–	–	–	–	15	–	NQ	
	Robbie Buhl	USA	Coyne The Mi-Jack Car Lola T93/00-Ford	20	–	16	–	–	–	–	–	–	–	–	–	–	–	–	–	
	Mimmo Schiattarella	I	Project Indy No Touch/Van Dyne/Marcelo Lola T93/00-Ford	–	–	–	–	–	–	–	–	26	–	16	–	–	–	–	–	
	Jeff Andretti	USA	Euromotorsport Agip/Hawaiian Tropic Lola T93/00-Ilmor/C+	–	17	–	–	–	–	–	–	–	–	–	–	–	–	–	–	
			Hemelgarn Gillette Lola T92/00-Buick	–	–	–	NQ	–	–	–	–	–	–	–	–	–	–	–	–	
	Jeff Wood	USA	Euromotorsport Agip/Hawaiian Tropic Lola T92/00-Ilmor/A	–	–	–	–	–	–	29	23	28	17	NQ	NQ	–	–	–	–	
			Euromotorsport Agip/Hawaiian Tropic Lola T93/00-Ilmor/C	–	–	–	–	–	–	–	–	–	–	–	–	–	–	NQ	NQ	
	John Paul Jr.	USA	Pro Formance Motorsports Lola T93/00-Ilmor/C+	–	18	–	25	–	–	–	–	–	–	–	–	–	–	–	–	
	Lyn St. James	USA	Simon JCPenney/Reebok/Lee Lola T94/00-Ford	–	–	–	19	–	–	–	–	–	–	–	–	–	–	–	–	
	Ross Bentley	CDN	Coyne Agfa Film Lola T92/00-Ilmor/A	–	–	–	NQ	NQ	NQ	22	29	19	19	NQ	22	NQ	NS	NQ	NQ	
	Mauro Baldi	I	Coyne The Mi-Jack Car Lola T93/00-Ford	–	–	–	–	–	–	–	–	–	–	19	–	–	–	–	–	
	Scott Brayton	USA	Menard Glidden Paint Special Lola T93/00-Menard	–	–	–	20	–	–	–	–	–	–	–	–	–	–	–	–	
	Claude Bourbonnais	CDN	Pro Formance Player's/Indeck/Losi Lola T93/00-Ilmor/C+	–	–	26	–	–	–	–	–	–	–	–	–	–	–	–	–	
			McCormack Motorsports Player's Ltd. Lola T93/00-Ilmor/C+	–	–	–	–	–	–	–	–	24	–	24	–	21	30	–	–	
	Gary Brabham	AUS	Bettenhausen Split Cycle Penske PC22-Ilmor/C	24	–	–	–	–	–	–	–	–	–	–	–	–	–	–	–	
	Hideshi Matsuda	J	Simon Racing Beck Motorsports Lola T93/00-Ford	–	–	–	24	–	–	–	–	–	–	–	–	–	–	–	–	
	Dennis Vitolo	USA	Simon Hooligan's/Carlo/Charter America Lola T93/00-Ford	–	–	–	26	–	–	–	–	–	–	–	–	–	–	–	–	
	Roberto Guerrero	USA	Pagan Racing Interstate Batteries Lola T92/00-Buick	–	–	–	33	–	–	–	–	–	–	–	–	–	–	–	–	

Bold type indicates car still running at finish

* led most laps   P pole position   W withdrawn   NQ did not qualify   NS did not start

AS SOON AS OUR ENGINES STOP RACING, OUR MINDS START.

A PHILOSOPHY OF CONSTANT IMPROVEMENT. At Toyota, we've won Championships in every racing series in which we've ever competed. But one thing we've never done is become complacent. **TECHNOLOGY ON A FAST TRACK** ││/

Take our engine program for example. Every time a Toyota begins a race, beneath its hood lies an engine that's state of the art. But by the time we cross the finish line – even if the engine carried us to victory – it's no longer good enough for us. Before the next race, we'll improve that engine in at least one of three ways. Sometimes we'll boost the power. Other times we'll increase its strength. Or else we'll make it lighter. There are even times when we'll do all three.

IMAGINE HOW FAR WE GO TO BUILD YOUR TOYOTA.

The same philosophy that drives our motorsports program is evident in every car Toyota builds. And nowhere more so than in the all-new 1994 Toyota Celica. In fact, some of the Celica's components are so advanced they'd be prohibited in many race cars. Because they'd offer an unfair advantage. It's a perfect example of how our minds...are always racing.

⊕ TOYOTA
"I love what you do for me."

Michael C. Brown

SURFERS PARADISE

Photos: Michael C. Brown

He's ba-a-a-ck!

Michael Andretti arrived on the Gold Coast of Queensland, Australia, for the now traditional Indy Car season-opener as a man on a mission. He had a point to prove. And boy, did he prove it.

First of all, Andretti rebounded from his hugely disappointing one-year sabbatical in Formula 1 by qualifying second fastest in Chip Ganassi's Target/Scotch Video Reynard 94I-Ford/Cosworth XB. It was a promising start. Then on race day, following an inordinately long delay caused by a sudden rain squall, he displayed the same aggressive style which characterized his early career and led him to the PPG Cup title in 1991.

Andretti charged from the start, demoting defending series champion Nigel Mansell's pole-winning Kmart/Caltex Havoline Lola-Ford in a typically forthright outside-line pass on the opening lap. Before long he had opened up a substantial margin over his pursuers. Mansell, Emerson Fittipaldi (Marlboro Penske-Ilmor/D) and Robby Gordon (Valvoline/Cummins Lola-Ford) chased hard, but Andretti was not to be denied. Gordon crashed while trying to keep pace. Mansell also made a mistake, caught out by a mid-race shower. The crowd favorite lost more than a lap before his stalled car could be restarted. Fittipaldi, this day at least, simply wasn't fast enough.

So Andretti emerged victorious in the Australian FAI Indy Car Grand Prix, rejoining the PPG Cup circuit in exactly the same manner in which he had departed at Laguna Seca in the final race of the 1992 season.

1st – MICHAEL A.

2nd – FITTIPALDI

3rd – MARIO A.

After an unhappy Grand Prix sojourn in Europe the familiar helmet colors of Michael Andretti returned to the Indy Car scene for 1994.

Left: Michael's style through the chicanes was certainly spectacular as he hurled the new Target/Scotch Video Reynard over the curbs toward a fairytale debut victory.

A proud moment for Chip Ganassi *(below)* as in the dark of the pit lane the overjoyed team owner savors success after a long lean spell out of the Indy Car winner's circle.

QUALIFYING

Surfers Paradise provides a splendid setting for the start of a new season. Accordingly, many drivers grasped the opportunity to spend a few days relaxing in the Queensland sun prior to the start of official practice on Friday morning.

Then it was down to the serious business. As usual, it didn't take long for a familiar pattern to emerge. Paul Tracy was the first to dip below the existing track record of 1m 38.555s in his Marlboro Penske-Ilmor, soon to be followed by Mansell, who was seeking to repeat his sensational debut Indy Car victory of one year ago.

The reigning PPG Cup champion's confidence had been buoyed by some impressive pre-season testing times aboard Newman-Haas Racing's latest Lola T94/00, and it came as no surprise to see car #1 atop the timing sheets in every session.

'Obviously, I'm delighted,' said Mansell. 'The [pole-winning] lap was even better than you think because it was on the second run of the first set of tires, not the second set. We're very, very happy.'

This year, like last, Mansell was awesomely fast through the Powers Chicane on Main Beach Parade. Whereas several other drivers bounced high and not so handsomely over the curbs, most notably Andretti and Gordon, Mansell's style was far more fluid. He was able, seemingly, to finesse his car rather than merely chuck it and rely upon lightning-fast reflexes to sort out the ensuing sideways, speed-sapping slide. In final qualifying, Mansell was visibly fastest through the turn. It showed on the timing monitors.

Andretti annexed the other front row placing, yet he wasn't quite so happy.

'That [final] session was very disjointed for me,' he said after losing a few minutes in the pits following a high-flying excursion at the aforementioned chicane. Incredibly, the only damage to the car upon landing was a broken heat-exchanger.

'I came into the chicane and was going way too fast, so I hit the curb square and went pretty high,' confessed Andretti with admirable understatement. 'I thought my session was over, but I have to take my hat off to [Reynard chief designer] Malcolm [Oastler]. That car is strong! It's built like a tank.'

A pretty quick tank, mind you, as exemplified by the fact all five other Reynard runners were within the top six rows on the grid.

Young Mexican Adrian Fernandez caused something of a surprise by qualifying a fine fourth in Rick Galles' colorful Tecate/Quaker State Reynard-Ilmor, followed by Mauricio Gugelmin (seventh), who came into the race with virtually no testing aboard Chip Ganassi's Hollywood Reynard-Ford. Jacques Villeneuve, eighth in his Player's Reynard-Ford, Jimmy Vasser, tenth in Jim Hayhoe's Conseco/STP version, and Teo Fabi, 11th in Jim Hall's bright-yellow Pennzoil Reynard-Ilmor, were close behind.

The Marlboro Penske team also was in the thick of the action with Fittipaldi on row two, followed by Al Unser Jr. and Tracy, hindered by a persistent electrical malady, one row farther back.

Interestingly, apart from Mansell on the pole, the only other Lola driver among the top 12 was Gordon, who qualified a disappointed ninth after encountering gearbox problems both days.

RACE

A record-sized crowd was attracted by expectations of a classic contest. There were also plenty of intriguing questions. For example, could Mansell maintain his superiority from qualifying and emerge triumphant again? Would Michael Andretti be able to rediscover the form which had made him one of the fiercest competitors on the Indy Car circuit? Which was the best chassis: Lola, Penske or Reynard? Was the new Ilmor Indy V8/D engine a match for the updated Ford/Cosworth XB?

Unfortunately, there was a lengthy delay before any answers became apparent.

The gorgeous weather which had prevailed throughout the previous two days gave way to increasing wind and cloud as the scheduled start time approached. Then, right on cue, just as the 27-car field completed its parade laps, the rain started. It came with a vengeance. Within moments the track was awash. There was no question the start would have to be delayed.

Chief Steward Wally Dallenbach wisely declared it to be a wet race, which meant all cars would be required to start on grooved tires. Fair enough. And while the pit crews leapt into action, the Valvoline truck was dispatched to add a few gallons of fuel to each car in

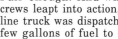

Michael C. Brown

The warm evening sunlight casts deepening shadows on the Surfers Paradise course as Michael Andretti holds off the challenge of Emerson Fittipaldi in the Marlboro Penske.

took advantage of his superior momentum through the Powers Chicane to outbrake Fittipaldi neatly into Conrad Jupiters Corner. Then he set his sights on Andretti.

By lap 19, Mansell had trimmed his deficit to the leader from 7.3 seconds to less than five. But before he could mount a challenge, out came the yellow flags again. Gordon, in trying to keep pace with the leaders, had lost control at the exit of the Powers Chicane and backed hard into the wall.

All the leaders took the opportunity to take on fresh tires and a full load of fuel. While the pace car remained on the track, however, the rain also made a fresh appearance in concert with heavy winds from the south.

The track was treacherously slippery as the pace car pulled off at the completion of lap 25. Even before the green flag could fly, Mansell's challenge ended when he jumped on the power a fraction too early – and spun. Worse, he stalled the engine. Mansell lost more than a lap before he was able to resume.

Andretti also had a major moment. The race leader found out exactly how slippery the track was as he attempted to negotiate the first chicane. His Reynard snapped into a half-spin at the exit and Andretti was fortunate that his car's sideways progress was arrested by a tire wall. Incredibly, Andretti not only regained control, but did so without any damage to his car.

Once more, he was impressed. 'There was no difference to the car after hitting the tires,' related Andretti. 'I couldn't believe it. I don't think it bent one thing. That car is strong, that's all there is to it.'

Several other drivers had moments as the rain increased in intensity, while veteran Mario Andretti revelled in the conditions and moved up from eighth to third in his Kmart/Caltex Lola-Ford before the safety car was scrambled into action again.

The brisk breeze saw to it that only a couple of laps were necessary under caution before the track was dry enough for racing to resume. This time Michael Andretti quickly opened out a two-second advantage over Fittipaldi, who now had the elder Andretti pressing from behind.

Vasser had moved quietly up to fourth, while an attempt by Scott Goodyear (Budweiser Lola-Ford) to take the position ended with the Canadian disappearing down an escape road. Goodyear slipped to 11th, the last man on the lead lap,

order to maintain the mandatory allocation based upon a minimum consumption of 1.8 miles per gallon.

That's when the real problems began. By the time that task had been completed, almost an hour had passed. The track was now dry. So everyone switched back to slicks . . . just in time for more rain! Back to wets again.

The cars ventured out again almost 80 minutes behind schedule, whereupon an incident toward the back of the pack, even before the green flag, brought out the red. Yet more delay followed as the cars were topped off with fuel once more.

Finally, at a little after 4 p.m., with the patience of the crowd sorely tested and the live television broadcast thrown into utter confusion, came the real start. There were sighs of relief all around.

Briefly. For at the very first corner, a concertina incident saw several cars make contact. By the end of an action-packed opening lap, Bobby Rahal's raucous-sounding Miller Genuine Draft Lola-Honda and Raul Boesel's Duracell Lola-Ford were done for the day. Tracy ran down an escape road following an incident with Fernandez, while Davy Jones (Copenhagen Lola-Ford), Dominic Dobson (PacWest Lola-Ford) and Hiro Matsushita (Panasonic Lola-Ford) also were delayed. Then every other car headed directly into the pits, since the entire field had been obliged by the officials to start on wet tires despite the fact the track had long since dried!

It was Andretti who led the charge onto pit lane, having already pulled a typically bold maneuver on Mansell.

'I tried to be aggressive,' confirmed Andretti, 'and he went to block me on the inside, so I passed him on the outside. I think that was the most important move of the race.'

Sure was, Michael. Smart pit work by the Ganassi crew enabled him to maintain his hard-won advantage, and following a handful of laps under caution while the debris was swept up Andretti soon began to edge clear in the lead.

Mansell, meanwhile, had fallen behind Fittipaldi during the pit stops. Then Gordon executed a fine pass under braking to leave Mansell suddenly in fourth place. The Englishman refused to be flustered, however, and after a few laps to catch his breath and let the race order settle down Mansell began to move forward.

On lap 14, Mansell drew alongside Gordon as the pair accelerated onto The Esplanade. Side by side they raced toward the FAI Esses, with Mansell on the inside. He was through. Three laps later, Mansell

Above: A satisfactory start to his final year of racing saw Mario Andretti take third place with the Newman-Haas Lola.

Jimmy Vasser *(far left)* confirmed the promise he had shown during 1993 by bringing the Hayhoe team's Conseco/STP Reynard home in fourth place.

Mike Groff *(left)* again drove well in the Rahal/Hogan Motorola Lola-Honda, taking eighth place with a car which was still some way off the pace of the front-runners.

Despite the absence of significant sponsorship, the PacWest team – running '94 Lola-Fords – were determined not just to make up the numbers. Dominic Dobson *(left)* took the final point on offer with 12th place, while his young team-mate Scott Sharp went one better, taking 11th spot with some exuberant driving *(right)*.

Michael C. Brown

Left: Keeping the customer satisfied. Bruce Ashmore, Adrian Reynard and Rick Gorne wear the contented smiles of men who have just achieved their ambitious goal of winning an Indy Car race at the first attempt with their new car.

Below: The race ended in almost complete darkness with Al Unser Jr. and Paul Tracy *(right)* both out of luck on this occasion.

A winning start for Reynard

Michael Andretti was justifiably elated after winning on his return to the Indy Car arena following a hugely disappointing one-year sabbatical in Formula 1.

'I went through a lot last year and I prayed that things would get better,' said an emotional Andretti after scoring the 28th victory of his Indy Car career. 'I couldn't ask for a better day.'

The triumph was equally satisfying for Chip Ganassi, who was able to celebrate his first-ever victory as a solo team owner.

'This opens a new chapter for me and our racing team,' said Ganassi, a former driver who turned to team ownership by joining forces with long-term car owner Pat Patrick in the late 1980s. 'Since Michael joined our team last year he has given 100 per cent, 24 hours a day.

'When we first tested this car back in November I knew it would be good, but this is something special. Our entire team deserves a big thank-you for all of their hard work during the off-season.'

Nevertheless, perhaps the broadest smile of all was worn by Englishman Adrian Reynard, whose Malcolm Oastler-designed Rey-

nard 94I chassis had succeeded in knocking established Indy car manufacturers Lola and Penske off their perch at the very first attempt. This momentous feat extended a quite extraordinary record which also included debut successes for Reynard in Formula 3 (Andy Wallace at Silverstone, England, in 1985) and Formula 3000 (Johnny Herbert at Jerez, Spain, in 1988).

'It wasn't a shock; it was expected,' revealed Reynard. 'Before the start I had a word with Michael and said, "There's something you should know about the tradition of Reynard Racing Cars . . ." He stopped me right there and said, "I know all about it. I've had it rammed down my throat. I know exactly what's expected of me!"

'Everybody expected us to win, from the guys on the team to the designers to the people who clean the shop floor. You couldn't ever predict [a debut victory] because motor racing always has its elements of good luck and bad luck. [But] just look at our record and we've usually won our first race – at least in the major formulae. Has it been a coincidence? Is it luck? Well, I think there must be some element of method there.'

although he soon moved up two places when Willy T. Ribbs (Service Merchandise Lola T93/00-Ford) was taken out by a wayward Fernandez and then Villeneuve's brave attempt to pass an unwilling Stefan Johansson (Alumax Penske PC22-Ilmor) ended with his Player's Reynard bundled unceremoniously into the wall. Exit one disgruntled French-Canadian.

The leaders made their second scheduled pit stops at around lap 46. By that time all the delays had taken their toll on the available daylight. Evening was closing in. Local residents began to turn on lights in their apartments.

Before long, spectators were treated to the rare sight of red-hot brake rotors and exhausts glowing brightly in the gathering gloom. It was an eerie scene. The street lights afforded some visibility for the drivers, but it soon became apparent the race would not run its full 65-lap distance.

Andretti finally was greeted by the checkered flag after 55 laps, in virtu-

al darkness. He had been especially cautious in the closing laps, anxious not to throw away certain victory, while Fittipaldi gave his all in pursuit. It wasn't quite enough. They were separated by 1.36 seconds at the close.

Mario Andretti took a fine third, absolutely thrilled to join his son on the victory podium. Vasser, troubled by a broken exhaust header which cost valuable power, followed in a distant fourth, with Johansson and Gugelmin the only other unlapped runners. Fabi was next ahead of Mike Groff, who drove a good race in his Motorola Lola T93/00-Honda despite losing a front fin early on. A disgruntled Mansell claimed four PPG Cup points for ninth, his run punctuated by another couple of trips into the escape road, with Goodyear and Scott Sharp (PacWest Lola-Ford) another lap down. Sharp's team-mate, Dobson, completed the point scorers at the end of what Mansell later described as 'the craziest race I've ever been in.'

SNIPPETS

• Australian Gary Brabham *(below)* made his second Indy Car start, this time in a year-old Penske-Ilmor/C run by Bettenhausen Motorsports. Brabham, who had tested only briefly for what was to be his first race since a year earlier at Surfers, drove well in the PC22, which boasted support from Split Cycle Technology, even though he only made the field after Montermini withdrew.

• Lap times were markedly faster than a year before, due primarily to the fact that the inside walls on several corners had been moved back and replaced by curbing. This had the effect not only of vastly improving visibility for the drivers but also of rewarding those with more aggressive styles who crashed headlong over the curbs to find a little extra speed. The top 20 drivers all bettered Mansell's pole time from 1993.

• Qualifying times also were much closer than last year. Whereas, in 1993, first and last on the 26-car grid were separated by 9.513 seconds, this time the entire field, which included an extra starter, was covered by 5.240 seconds. Less than two seconds spanned third (Fittipaldi) to 20th

(Boesel). In addition, four more drivers failed to make the cut, although in the case of Andrea Montermini *(right)* the circumstances were unfortunate. The diminutive Italian had set the fourth-fastest time during practice on Saturday morning before crashing his Project Indy/Dale Coyne Racing Lola-Ford beyond immediate repair.

• The tabloid newspapers considered it manna from heaven when front-row qualifiers Mansell and Michael Andretti squared up to each other following the aborted first start.

Andretti accused the 1993 PPG Cup champion of chopping across before the green flag had been shown, whereupon Mansell, only partly in jest, invited his rival to don his boxing gloves. The offer was declined. Afterward, both drivers were keen to play down the incident.

PPG INDY CAR WORLD SERIES • ROUND 1

AUSTRALIAN FAI INDY CAR GRAND PRIX

SURFERS PARADISE STREET CIRCUIT,
QUEENSLAND, AUSTRALIA

MARCH 20, 55 LAPS – 153.725 MILES

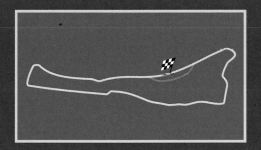

Place	Driver (Nat.)	No.	Team Sponsors Car-Engine	Q Speed (mph)	Q Time	Q Pos.	Laps	Time/Status	Ave. (mph)	Pts.
1	Michael Andretti (USA)	8	Ganassi Target/Scotch Video Reynard 94I-Ford	105.286	1m 35.568s	2	55	1h 53m 52.770s	80.994	21
2	Emerson Fittipaldi (BR)	2	Marlboro Team Penske PC23-Ilmor/D	104.788	1m 36.023s	3	55	1h 53m 54.096s	80.978	16
3	Mario Andretti (USA)	6	Newman-Haas Kmart/Caltex Havoline Lola T94/00-Ford	102.736	1m 37.940s	19	55	1h 54m 00.650s	80.900	14
4	Jimmy Vasser (USA)	18	Hayhoe Conseco/STP Reynard 94I-Ford	103.864	1m 36.877s	10	55	1h 54m 34.577s	80.501	12
5	Stefan Johansson (S)	16	Bettenhausen Alumax Penske PC22-Ilmor/D	103.382	1m 37.328s	12	55	1h 55m 01.217s	80.190	10
6	Mauricio Gugelmin (BR)	88	Ganassi Hollywood Reynard 94I-Ford	104.372	1m 36.405s	7	55	1h 55m 22.328s	79.946	8
7	Teo Fabi (I)	11	Hall Pennzoil Reynard 94I-Ilmor/D	103.812	1m 36.925s	11	54	Running		6
8	Mike Groff (USA)	10	Rahal-Hogan Motorola Lola T93/00-Honda	103.059	1m 37.633s	14	54	Running		5
9	Nigel Mansell (GB)	1	Newman-Haas Kmart/Caltex Havoline Lola T94/00-Ford	106.053	1m 34.877s	1	54	Running		5
10	Scott Goodyear (CDN)	40	Budweiser King Lola T94/00-Ford	102.846	1m 37.835s	17	53	Running		3
11	*Scott Sharp (USA)	71	PacWest Racing Group Lola T94/00-Ford	102.737	1m 37.940s	18	53	Running		2
12	Dominic Dobson (USA)	17	PacWest Racing Group Lola T94/00-Ford	100 843	1m 39.779s	27	52	Running		1
13	Adrian Fernandez (MEX)	7	Galles Tecate/Quaker State Reynard 94I-Ilmor/D	104.713	1m 36.091s	4	52	Running		
14	Al Unser Jr. (USA)	31	Marlboro Team Penske PC23-Ilmor/D	104.384	1m 36.394s	5	51	Engine		
15	Hiro Matsushita (J)	22	Simon Panasonic/Duskin Lola T94/00-Ford	101.545	1m 39.089s	24	48	Running		
16	Paul Tracy (CDN)	3	Marlboro Team Penske PC23-Ilmor/D	104.380	1m 36.398s	6	39	Gearbox		
17	*Jacques Villeneuve (CDN)	12	Forsythe-Green Player's Ltd. Reynard 94I-Ford	104.291	1m 36.480s	8	36	Accident		
18	Willy T. Ribbs (USA)	24	Walker Service Merchandise/Bill Cosby Lola T93/00-Ford	101.690	1m 38.948s	23	34	Accident		
19	Davy Jones (USA)	14	A.J. Foyt Copenhagen Racing Lola T92/00-Ford	100.894	1m 39.729s	26	31	Transmission		
20	Robbie Buhl (USA)	19	Coyne The Mi-Jack Car Lola T93/00-Ford	101.512	1m 39.122s	25	30	Engine		
21	Mark Smith (USA)	15	Walker Craftsman Tools Lola T94/00-Ford	103.225	1m 37.476s	13	19	Accident		
22	*Alessandro Zampedri (I)	50	Euromotorsport Agip/Dinema/Fluoril Lola T93/00-Ilmor/C	101.730	1m 38.909s	22	19	Accident		
23	Robby Gordon (USA)	9	Walker Valvoline/Cummins Special Lola T94/00-Ford	104.077	1m 36.678s	9	16	Accident		
24	*Gary Brabham (AUS)	76	Bettenhausen Split Cycle Penske PC22-Ilmor/D	100.503	1m 40.117s	28	10	Transmission		
25	Arie Luyendyk (NL)	28	Indy Regency Eurosport/Boost Monaco Lola T94/00-Ilmor/D	102.947	1m 37.739s	15	8	Transmission		
26	Bobby Rahal (USA)	4	Rahal-Hogan Miller Genuine Draft Lola T94/00-Honda	102.902	1m 37.783s	16	0	Accident		
27	Raul Boesel (BR)	5	Simon Duracell/Fuji Film/Mobil/Sadia Lola T94/00-Ford	102.672	1m 38.002s	21	0	Accident		
W	Andrea Montermini (I)	39	Coyne Project Indy Lola T93/00-Ford	102.717	1m 37.959s	20	–	Withdrawn/accident		
NQ	Marco Greco (BR)	25	Simon Arciero Project Indy Lola T94/00-Ford	100.042	1m 40.578s	29	–	Did not qualify		
NQ	Buddy Lazier (USA)	23	Leader Card Financial World Lola T93/00-Ilmor/C	99.463	1m 41.164s	30	–	Did not qualify		
NQ	David Kudrave (USA)	55	Euromotorsport Agip/Hawaiian Tropic Lola T92/00-Ilmor/A	No speed	No time	31	–	Did not qualify		

* denotes Rookie driver

Caution flags: Laps 1–5, multi-car accident; laps 18–24, accident/Smith and Zampedri; laps 25–28, tires dislodged at first chicane. Total three for 16 laps.

Lap leaders: Michael Andretti, 1–55 (55 laps).

Fastest race lap: Mansell, 1m 37.487s, 103.213 mph, on lap 15.

Championship positions: **1** Michael Andretti, 21 pts; **2** Fittipaldi, 16; **3** Mario Andretti, 14; **4** Vasser, 12; **5** Johansson, 10; **6** Gugelmin, 8; **7** Fabi, 6; **8** Groff and Mansell, 5; **10** Goodyear, 3; **11** Sharp, 2; **12** Dobson, 1.

PHOENIX

Any doubts about Marlboro Team Penske being a serious contender in this year's PPG Indy Car World Series were well and truly blown away during the Slick-50 200 at Phoenix International Raceway.

Roger Penske's team, which this year added a third string to its bow in the form of 1990 PPG Cup champion Al Unser Jr., had made a disappointing start to the season in Australia with only Emerson Fittipaldi earning a points-paying finish. Nevertheless, on the challenging one-mile oval at PIR, the most successful team in Indy Car history bounced back with a vengeance.

Paul Tracy set the ball rolling with a new track record in qualifying, while Penske PC23-Ilmor/D team-mates Fittipaldi and Al Unser Jr. soon moved up into contention once the race was under way. In reality, only Nigel Mansell (Kmart/Texaco Havoline Lola-Ford/Cosworth) and Robby Gordon (Valvoline/Cummins Lola-Ford) were able to mount a serious challenge to the Penske triumvirate.

After Tracy was taken out of the race in a frightening multi-car crash and both Lola drivers fell off the lead lap due to various miscues, Fittipaldi and Unser Jr. romped home to a decisive 1-2 finish. Fittipaldi emerged the victor by 13.482 seconds, after which he said his only real problems had been caused by the increasingly blustery conditions.

'It was a difficult race,' declared the 47-year-old Brazilian after scoring the 21st win of his Indy Car career. 'The wind was strong, and especially in the last 15 laps it was very gusty in Turn Three.'

Mansell, who lost a lap after stalling in the pits, recovered to claim third place ahead of Stefan Johansson (Alumax Penske PC22-Ilmor/D) and Jimmy Vasser (Conseco/STP Reynard-Ford), who also finished fourth and fifth in Australia, albeit with their positions reversed.

| 1st – FITTIPALDI | 2nd – AL UNSER JR. | 3rd – MANSELL |

Far left: Emerson Fittipaldi led the Marlboro Penske-Ilmor challenge at Phoenix, heading home team-mate Al Unser Jr. for a 1-2 finish which sounded a warning to the opposition that they would face a long, hard struggle in 1994.

A familiar scene from the first oval race of the season, with spectators scattered on the distant srub-covered hillside as Stefan Johansson leads a pack of drivers comprising *(left to right)* Scott Sharp, Marco Greco, John Paul Jr., Raul Boesel and Jimmy Vasser. Just behind this bunch is Davy Jones in A.J. Foyt's Copenhagen Lola.

Photos: Michael C. Brown

QUALIFYING

New rules this year, intended to slow the cars on the short ovals by reducing aerodynamic downforce, ultimately were negated by a new track surface laid since the Indy cars last raced on the Phoenix mile. The result was even faster speeds than before.

During intensive testing over the winter, even with the new two-element rear wing configuration, several drivers recorded laps in the sub-20-second range – at better than 180 mph. Those times, however, were set in ideal weather conditions. By the time practice and qualifying rolled around, the ambient temperature had risen into the 80s, which, as usual, afforded slightly less adhesion.

There was one other variable too: the latest Goodyear tires permitted fractionally less 'stagger' (the difference in rolling circumference of the two rear tires, promoting turn-in capabilities for the left-turn only ovals) than before. Most teams lost some time in dialing in their cars to optimize the new configuration.

Mansell, who had taken full advantage of an additional two days of testing earlier in the week, duly set the pace for Newman-Haas Racing in the opening two practice sessions on Friday. His best was a sub-record 20.699 seconds, although oval specialist Raul Boesel then made his presence felt with a 20.622s in Dick Simon's similar Duracell Lola-Ford. The Penske team, which had opted not to attend the test, preferring instead to concentrate on preparations for Indianapolis, was a little more circumspect at first, although Fittipaldi made a significant improvement in the final session of the day before stopping the clocks at a mere 20.335 seconds. The die was cast.

'All our drivers complained of understeer in the first sessions,' related Penske's chief designer Nigel Bennett. 'Once we realized the cause, we were able to dial it out.'

Tracy also benefited from the subtle suspension changes, as well as from an intensive debriefing with the team's resident guru – and former three-time PPG Cup champion – Rick Mears.

'After talking to Rick, I changed my whole pattern, my line on the race track,' related Tracy. 'He was saying maybe that'll change how the car reacts. And it did. The car just came right into balance.

'I was running in tight and "pinching" the turns. I was picking up understeer, so I couldn't get on the gas, pick up the throttle. With the changes we made, it's much better.'

Tracy displayed the worth of Mears' pep-talk by setting fastest time in the Saturday morning session, then repeating the feat during one-at-a-time qualifying in the heat of the day.

Fellow Canadian Jacques Villeneuve was perhaps even more impressive in qualifying. The rookie driver, in only his second Indy Car start, rocked the establishment by securing the outside front row grid position in Forsythe-Green Racing's Player's Ltd. Reynard-Ford. His lap at 20.442 seconds was more than two-tenths faster than he had managed previously.

'I was honestly surprised,' admitted experienced team manager/co-owner Barry Green. 'I knew he could run fast and I was fairly confident we had improved the car. I couldn't *believe* he could run that fast in so few laps, because Jacques is usually quite conservative. It takes him a few laps to get up to full speed. I'm very pleased.'

Mansell couldn't match the two Canadians, instead sharing row two with Newman-Haas team-mate Mario Andretti. The third rank comprised Boesel and Fittipaldi, a pair of Brazilians who now reside in Key Biscayne, Florida.

RACE

Pole-sitter Tracy set a fast pace toward the green flag and duly led the record-sized 28-car field into Turn One. Behind, Mansell jumped inside rookie Villeneuve for second, while Fittipaldi took the high line around Mario Andretti to emerge in fourth on the exit of Turn Two.

As ever at PIR, the action was fast and furious. Tracy set a torrid pace out front, matching the warm Arizona sunshine, but he couldn't shake Mansell from his mirrors. Villeneuve also held on tightly in third, belying his lack of experience and managing to keep the veteran Fittipaldi at bay.

The first significant place change came on lap 11, by which time the leaders already were beginning to work through the slower traffic. Mansell grasped his opportunity to move around Tracy for the premier position and soon began to work a little breathing space between himself and the Canadian.

On lap 21, Fittipaldi's pressure on Villeneuve also paid off, although even then there was no opportunity for the youngster to relax. Soon his mirrors were being filled by the third Marlboro Penske, with Unser Jr. having worked his way cautiously through from ninth on the grid.

Unser had spent the first 16 laps cooped up behind Scott Goodyear's Budweiser King Lola-Ford in eighth place. Once past, he quickly began to make up ground on the leaders. Mario Andretti and Robby Gordon (Valvoline/Cummins Lola-Ford) proved rather easier to pass, and within five laps he had whittled down the deficit to Villeneuve from almost three seconds to just a couple of car lengths. Unser was on the move.

But then came the first caution of the day. Willy T. Ribbs, on his first outing at Phoenix, had lost control of his Service Merchandise Lola T93/00-Ford in Turn One, apparently due to a cut tire, and backed solidly into the wall. Ribbs, fortunately, was unhurt.

'The car was so loose it was unbelievable,' said Ribbs. 'I just lost it going in [to the corner]. I knew it was loose but it never reacted that way in the corner before.'

As soon as the yellow flashed on, just 29 laps into the 200-lap race, Mansell ducked into the pits for service. Several other cars followed suit. Tracy and Fittipaldi, however, remained out on the track, allowing Tracy to regain the lead. Different strategies already were being played out.

'We had decided beforehand that, whatever happened, we would make it a two-stop race,' revealed Tracy's race engineer Nigel Beresford. 'The timing was just a bit unfortunate. Paul was actually complaining about understeer, so we were going to put a bit of front wing in at the first stop. But [29 laps] was too early for us to two-stop it for sure.'

Mansell's team, by contrast, had opted to take the gamble. 'Nigel had called in [on the radio] a couple of laps earlier to say the car was really loose,' explained Newman-Haas Team Manager Jim McGee, 'so we wanted to take a little [front] wing out.'

The ploy might have worked, except for the fact Mansell killed the engine as he attempted to resume. By the time it had been refired, Mansell had lost a lap to the new leader. Several others who followed the Englishman into the pits, including Villeneuve, Teo Fabi (Pennzoil Reynard-Ilmor), Michael Andretti (Target/Scotch Video Reynard-Ford) and Mario Andretti (Kmart/Havoline Lola-Ford), also lost a lap, due to the fact the Penskes were able to complete one more circuit at speed before being picked up by the pace car.

When racing resumed on lap 42, only nine cars were on the lead lap. Tracy and Fittipaldi took off as one on the restart, chased by Gordon and Unser Jr. Villeneuve and Mansell headed those one lap down.

The two leading Penskes put on quite a show as they battled for the lead. Tracy, despite the understeer, was able to hold on, and in fact, as they encountered a group of slower cars just before the 60-lap mark, the Canadian was able to eke out a more discernible advantage.

But then came disaster. Fabi, running 13th, and Hiro Matsushita, whose Panasonic/Duskin Lola-Ford already had made a long pit stop due to handling problems, tangled as they sped into Turn Three. Poor Tracy was left with absolutely nowhere to go. An instant later he, too, was trapped up against the wall.

That wasn't the worst of it. As both Tracy and Matsushita prepared to exit their stricken steeds, several seconds after the initial impact, Villeneuve arrived on the scene, apparently oblivious to the carnage ahead, and piled heavily into the side of Matsushita's Lola. It was a frightening impact which tore the Japanese driver's car in two.

Dominic Dobson's PacWest Lola also was taken out, ending a promising run which had seen Dobson running as high as fifth. Miraculously, no one was seriously injured, although it took the clean-up crews fully 27 laps to remove the debris.

Tracy's misfortune allowed team-mates Fittipaldi and Unser Jr. to take over in the lead with only Gordon and Stefan Johansson (Alumax Penske PC22-Ilmor) on the same lap. Mansell, still one lap adrift following his earlier error, had risen to fifth ahead of Mike Groff, who had driven a solid race in his underpowered Motorola Lola-Honda. Michael Andretti and Vasser, who had been obliged to make an extra stop when he picked up a puncture from debris, also were one lap down.

By the halfway mark, Fittipaldi had edged away to a two-second lead over Unser Jr., with Gordon more than a half-lap behind. Mansell, meanwhile, had not given up hope. He had chased doggedly after Fittipaldi, and when the Brazilian got caught up in some traffic, which included Johansson, Mansell took the opportunity to nip past both of

Inset right: Race leader Paul Tracy is taken out by Hiro Matsushita in the Panasonic car #22.

The incident soon escalates with frightening ferocity as Jacques Villeneuve's Forsythe-Green Reynard *(below)* explodes through the wreckage.

Left: With his Lola virtually sliced in half, Matsushita is extricated with no more than an injury to his shoulder. Miraculously, all the other drivers involved escaped the carnage unscathed.

Right: Michael Andretti three-wheels back to his pit after losing his front wheel in a coming-together with John Paul Jr.

Just the beginning. Al Unser Jr. *(below)* opened his points account for Penske at Phoenix, finishing a solid second to team-mate Emerson Fittipaldi.

them. At a stroke he was up into fourth place and, more significantly, back on the lead lap.

Alas, Mansell knew he had soon to make a pit stop. He needed a caution if he was to stay in contention. None came. On lap 130, Mansell duly peeled off and headed onto pit lane.

The stop was a good one, under 15 seconds for fresh tires and a full fuel load. Mansell made sure there was no repeat of his earlier mistake, lighting up the rear tires to the delight of the large crowd, but while the rear tires were duly up to temperature, the fronts weren't. When the Englishman scorched around the curving pit exit lane, anxious to get up to speed as fast as possible, his car merely understeered onto the grass. Once more he was in trouble. Mansell managed to keep the car straight, only to slide out onto the track directly in front of Goodyear, who was exiting Turn Two at full

speed. Only some smart evasive action by the Canadian averted potential disaster.

Fittipaldi and Unser Jr. made nice, clean stops on laps 142 and 146 respectively, which elevated the persistent Gordon into the lead. Now it was his turn to pray for a caution. Again, no luck. Sadly, his crew waited for the break they needed just a fraction too long. On lap 155, Gordon slowed dramatically. He was out of gas.

'For some reason, the computer gave us some bad information,' declared race engineer Tim Wardrop. 'According to it, we had four more laps to go.'

Gordon, who lost five laps while he coasted in, remained philosophical: 'We were leading the race. I felt it coming down the front straightaway run out of fuel. But that's what you call racing.'

Ironically, the yellow lights did

flash on just a half-dozen laps later, when Mario Andretti lost control of his ill-handling car and crashed on the entrance to Turn Three. Son Michael also was involved. Unsighted by a cloud of dust, which he thought was caused by the increasing wind, Michael suddenly was confronted by two slow-moving cars. One of them, John Paul Jr.'s Pro Formance Lola, he hit hard, tearing a front wheel from Andretti's Reynard. The errant projectile glanced off Goodyear's car before bouncing high over the debris fence and into a spectator area, miraculously without causing any serious injury. Once again, it had been a lucky escape.

The remaining laps, thankfully, were uneventful. Unser Jr. had chosen to make an extra stop during the ensuing caution, hoping to alleviate a push complaint, but even the fresh tires didn't allow him an opportunity to catch team-mate Fittipaldi.

Mansell followed the Brazilian closely across the finish line, albeit one lap down in third.

'I finished and I'm happy,' summarized Mansell. 'I'd like to congratulate the Penske team. They did a great job all weekend.'

Johansson and Vasser were three laps off the leaders, with Groff another lap back. Gordon deserved far better than seventh, his only solace the fact he had driven another heads-up race.

Boesel overcame severe oversteer in the early stages and a knock on the head from debris in the Andretti crash to claim eighth ahead of Scott Sharp (PacWest Lola), Adrian Fernandez (Tecate/Quaker State Reynard) and Goodyear. Davy Jones completed the point scorers, having driven a sensible race in A.J. Foyt's year-old Copenhagen Lola-Ford following a confidence-sapping crash in midweek.

SNIPPETS

made since the season-opener in Australia on the Ilmor Indy V8/D engines, which reportedly produced an additional 30 horsepower. 'When we tested here [before the season], Mansell was 7 mph slower than us in the corners and 5 mph quicker on the straights,' declared Penske's chief designer, Nigel Bennett *(left)*. 'That shows you how much of an advantage they had. But we've got some more power since then, I have to say. They [Ilmor] are working away and making improvements, and now we're pretty close.'

• The Penskes boasted another surprise innovation in the form of a prominent vertical stabilizer – dubbed a 'shark's fin' – mounted atop the engine cover.

• The three Penske drivers took full advantage of several improvements

• Andrew Craig, the newly appointed president and chief executive officer of Championship Auto Racing Teams, gave his first media briefing in Phoenix, and in conjunction with Steve Bornstein, president and chief executive of ESPN, confirmed a long-term commitment for all Indy Car events to be broadcast on the popular cable TV channel.

• The perennially underfinanced Buddy Lazier *(right)* had a good run going in his ex-Budweiser Lola T93/00-Ilmor/C, having worked up from 25th on the grid to the verge of the top ten before incurring a penalty for inadvertently passing the pace car as he sped out of the pits. Lazier, who finished 13th, just out of the points, also had to contend with a lack of brakes toward the end.

Photos: Michael C. Brown

SLICK-50 200

PHOENIX INTERNATIONAL RACEWAY, PHOENIX, ARIZONA

APRIL 10, 200 LAPS – 200.000 MILES

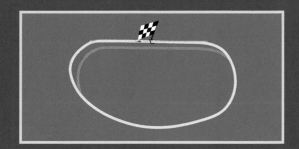

Place	Driver (Nat.)	No.	Team Sponsors Car-Engine	Q Speed (mph)	Q Time	Q Pos.	Laps	Time/Status	Ave. (mph)	Pts.
1	Emerson Fittipaldi (BR)	2	Marlboro Team Penske PC23-Ilmor/D	173.346	20.768s	6	200	1h 51m 41.615s	107.437	21
2	Al Unser Jr. (USA)	31	Marlboro Team Penske PC23-Ilmor/D	172.342	20.889s	9	200	1h 51m 55.097s	107.221	16
3	Nigel Mansell (GB)	1	Newman-Haas Kmart/Texaco Havoline Lola T94/00-Ford	175.478	20.515s	3	199	Running		14
4	Stefan Johansson (S)	16	Bettenhausen Alumax Penske PC22-Ilmor/D	168.330	21.386s	15	197	Running		12
5	Jimmy Vasser (USA)	18	Hayhoe Conseco/STP Reynard 94I-Ford	171.912	20.941s	11	197	Running		10
6	Mike Groff (USA)	10	Rahal-Hogan Motorola Lola T94/00-Honda	164.453	21.891s	20	196	Running		8
7	Robby Gordon (USA)	9	Walker Valvoline/Cummins Special Lola T94/00-Ford	173.113	20.796s	7	195	Running		6
8	Raul Boesel (BR)	5	Simon Duracell/Fuji Film/Mobil/Sadia Lola T94/00-Ford	173.357	20.766s	5	195	Running		5
9	*Scott Sharp (USA)	71	PacWest Racing Group Lola T94/00-Ford	170.240	21.147s	13	194	Running		4
10	Adrian Fernandez (MEX)	7	Galles Tecate/Quaker State Reynard 94I-Ilmor/D	167.820	21.452s	16	194	Running		3
11	Scott Goodyear (CDN)	40	Budweiser King Lola T94/00-Ford	172.303	20.893s	10	192	Running		2
12	Davy Jones (USA)	14	A.J. Foyt Copenhagen Racing Lola T93/00-Ford	165.428	21.762s	17	190	Running		1
13	Buddy Lazier (USA)	23	Leader Card Financial World Lola T93/00-Ilmor/C	159.872	22.518s	25	190	Running		
14	Bobby Rahal (USA)	4	Rahal-Hogan Miller Genuine Draft Lola T94/00-Honda	161.889	22.237s	22	188	Running		
15	Mauricio Gugelmin (BR)	88	Ganassi Hollywood Reynard 94I-Ford	156.431	23.013s	28	187	Running		
16	Marco Greco (BR)	25	Simon Arciero Project Indy Lola T94/00-Ford	165.009	21.817s	18	180	Running		
17	Jeff Andretti (USA)	55	Euromotorsport Agip/Hawaiian Tropic Lola T93/00-Ilmor/C	157.806	22.813s	27	179	Running		
18	John Paul Jr. (USA)	45	Pro Formance Motorsports Lola T93/00-Ilmor/C	161.826	22.246s	25	177	Running		
19	Brian Till (USA)	19	Coyne The Mi-Jack Car Lola T93/00-Ford	158.255	22.748s	26	168	Running		
20	Michael Andretti (USA)	8	Ganassi Target/Scotch Video Reynard 94I-Ford	171.204	21.028s	12	162	Accident		
21	Mario Andretti (USA)	6	Newman-Haas Kmart/Texaco Havoline Lola T94/00-Ford	174.932	20.579s	4	156	Accident		
22	Arie Luyendyk (NL)	28	Indy Regency Eurosport/Boost Monaco Lola T94/00-Ilmor/D	164.552	21.878s	19	146	Electrical		
23	Paul Tracy (CDN)	3	Marlboro Team Penske PC23-Ilmor/D	176.266	20.424s	1	62	Accident		1
24	Dominic Dobson (USA)	17	PacWest Racing Group Lola T94/00-Ford	168.848	21.321s	14	61	Accident		
25	*Jacques Villeneuve (CDN)	12	Forsythe-Green Player's Ltd. Reynard 94I-Ford	176.110	20.442s	2	61	Accident		
26	Teo Fabi (I)	11	Hall Pennzoil Reynard 94I-Ilmor/D	172.355	20.877s	8	60	Accident		
27	Hiro Matsushita (J)	22	Simon Panasonic/Duskin Lola T94/00-Ford	162.440	22.162s	21	44	Accident		
28	Willy T. Ribbs (USA)	24	Walker Service Merchandise/Bill Cosby Lola T93/00-Ford	160.518	22.427s	24	26	Accident		
NQ	David Kudrave (USA)	50	Euromotorsport Agip/Dinema/Fluorin Lola T92/00-Ilmor/A	156.295	23.033s	29	–	Did not qualify		
NQ	Johnny Unser (USA)	39	Dale Coyne Racing Lola T92/00-Ilmor/A	155.576	23.140s	30	–	Did not qualify		
NQ	Mark Smith (USA)	15	Walker Craftsman Tools Lola T94/00-Ford	No speed	No time	31	–	Did not qualify		

* denotes Rookie driver

Caution flags: Laps 28–41, accident/Ribbs; laps 62–88, multi-car accident; laps 165–174, accident, Michael and Mario Andretti. Total three for 41 laps.

Lap leaders: Paul Tracy, 1–10 (10 laps); Nigel Mansell, 11–29 (19 laps); Tracy, 30–62 (33 laps); Robby Gordon, 63 (1 lap); Emerson Fittipaldi, 64–141 (78 laps); Al Unser Jr., 142–146 (5 laps); Gordon, 147–154 (8 laps); Fittipaldi, 155–200 (46 laps). **Totals:** Fittipaldi, 124 laps; Tracy, 43 laps; Mansell, 19 laps; Gordon, 9 laps; Unser Jr., 5 laps.

Fastest race lap: Fittipaldi, 21.530s, 167.212 mph, on lap 122.

Championship positions: 1 Fittipaldi, 37 pts; **2** Vasser and Johansson, 22; **4** Michael Andretti, 21; **5** Mansell, 19; **6** Unser Jr., 16; **7** Mario Andretti, 14; **8** Groff, 13; **9** Gugelmin, 8; **10** Gordon, Fabi and Sharp, 6; **13** Boesel and Goodyear, 5; **15** Fernandez, 3; **16** Dobson, Jones and Tracy, 1.

LONG BEACH

Al Unser Jr. has made the Toyota Grand Prix of Long Beach virtually his own. Five times in the last seven years he has emerged triumphant on the unforgiving streets, and although his latest margin of victory, at 39.107 seconds, might appear to have been overpowering, Unser had to employ all his skills before clinching his first win of the season.

In the early stages, Unser displayed his patience as pole-winning Marlboro Penske team-mate Paul Tracy set a torrid pace at the front of the pack. Later, after Tracy fell out of contention, Unser showed his speed as he outpaced the third Penske PC23-Ilmor of Emerson Fittipaldi. But the greatest tests were still to come. First, Unser remained (relatively) calm after being assessed a stop-and-go penalty for exceeding the 60 mph speed limit on pit lane, and then, mindful of the fact his Penske's transmission was a potential Achilles heel, he resisted the temptation to chase new leader Fittipaldi.

Unser's prudence paid off when Fittipaldi, like Tracy before him, began to suffer gear selection difficulties. Finally, on lap 62, Fittipaldi slowed dramatically. His race was over. Gearbox. Unser Jr. regained the lead and thereafter maintained a steady pace which was fast enough to keep him out of reach of his nearest challenger, Nigel Mansell, and slow enough not to prove too burdensome on his own transmission.

'After I saw Emerson slowing down, Roger [Penske] called in [on the radio] and said, "Watch fourth and fifth [gears]," ' related Unser. 'I had been watching fourth and fifth from the start because I knew that was the weak link.

'On any of these race cars, the transmission is the weak link. When you're up and down [the gears] all the time, any transmission you have to take care of.'

Unser did so admirably.

Mansell was content to take second place in Newman-Haas Racing's Kmart/Texaco Havoline Lola T94/00-Ford/Cosworth, especially after suffering a blown tire just after two-thirds distance. Despite the delay, Mansell finished clear of nearby Orange County resident Robby Gordon, who delighted the California crowd with a strong run to third place in Derrick Walker's Valvoline/Cummins Lola-Ford.

Streetwise: Al Unser Jr. celebrates his fifth win at Long Beach, his Penske-Ilmor having survived while team-mates Tracy and Fittipaldi were both sidelined by transmission failures. Happy to be on the podium are Robby Gordon *(left)* and reigning PPG Cup champion Nigel Mansell.

Even a blown tire failed to prevent Nigel Mansell *(right)* from taking a strong second place in the Kmart/Texaco Havoline Lola-Ford. Nigel and third-placed Gordon (behind) were the only runners not lapped by the winner.

Photos: Michael C. Brown

QUALIFYING

The Lola-Fords of Mansell and Gordon topped the time sheets following the first practice session on Friday morning, whereupon Mansell confirmed his mastery of the street circuits by claiming the provisional pole later in the afternoon.

Mansell, though, was under no illusions.

'Whoever wants the pole tomorrow will have to go at least a half a second faster,' he predicted. 'That's going to be hard to find. I'm sure the Penske team has it up their sleeves, so we as a team are going to have to work extremely hard.'

Mansell showed just how hard he was trying when he nosed off into the tire barriers on the exit of Turn Three on Saturday morning. Damage, fortunately, was minimal, and while Mansell continued to search for speed in his back-up Lola, Tom Wurtz and his crew were able to complete repairs on the primary car well in time for final qualifying. It was to no avail. Mansell duly recorded his fastest lap of the weekend at 52.915 seconds, but it was good for only fourth on the grid behind all three Marlboro Penskes.

'I couldn't do any more. That was it,' stated Mansell. 'I'm very happy with the lap but disappointed with the time. It felt like a 51-second lap.

'We have a balanced car,' he continued. 'It's not as if we have a bad car. The car is good. I have no major complaint. We're just not quick enough. The Penskes are very, very good. The thing is, they have a three-pronged attack. When one [driver] finds something, bang, they all have it.'

Fittipaldi, second fastest to Mansell on Friday, praised Ilmor Engineering for having made substantial improvements on the 'D' motor since its introduction in Australia, and while he improved his time on Saturday it was cohort Tracy who emerged fastest of the impressive Penske contingent.

'I think the reason we're 1-2-3 is because we all work together,' said the bespectacled Canadian. 'That's a big advantage over the other teams.'

Gordon was disappointed after slipping to fifth on the final grid. He had been fastest on Saturday morning, but lost valuable time in qualifying when the entire nose section became detached.

'I really don't know what happened,' said Gordon. 'We didn't hit anything; it just fell off on the straightaway.'

Afterward his progress was hampered by the fact he was unable to find a clear lap during the frenetic final minutes.

Mario Andretti shared row three with Gordon, just 0.002s faster than Raul Boesel's Duracell/Fuji/Mobil/ Sadia Lola. Mauricio Gugelmin proved fastest of the Reynard contingent in his Hollywood car, although what pleased him more was to out-qualify his more illustrious Chip Ganassi Racing team-mate Michael Andretti (Target/Scotch Video Reynard).

Yet another Brazilian, Marco Greco, posted by far his most competitive qualifying effort to date, 13th in Frank Arciero's Dick Simon-run, Bob Sprow-managed '94 Lola-Ford.

Some idea of the intensity of the competition can be gained from the fact Mario Andretti, in sixth, and Davy Jones, 25th in A.J. Foyt's Copenhagen Lola-Ford, were separated by just under nine-tenths of a second!

RACE

A record-sized crowd was on hand for the 1 p.m. start, and Tracy ensured he kept the advantage by accelerating rapidly out of the Turn Nine hairpin prior to the green flag. Behind, under braking for Turn One, Unser withstood a challenge from Fittipaldi for second place as the three red and white Penskes remained out front.

Mansell already was a few car lengths back in fourth at the end of the first lap, while the only change in order among the entire field was for 15th, with Arie Luyendyk's Eurosport/Boost Monaco Lola-Ilmor muscling ahead of Scott Goodyear's Budweiser Lola-Ford. At the tail of the field, Scott Sharp's PacWest Lola-Ford started several laps behind after encountering gearbox problems on the parade lap.

The first retirement was posted by Bobby Rahal. His Honda-powered Miller Genuine Draft Lola had shown signs of increased competitiveness in qualifying, but after only two laps Rahal dropped out of 11th place with a broken gearbox oil line.

The order remained largely unchanged after 20 laps, and sadly, despite the proximity of lap times during qualifying, there was precious little in the way of close racing.

Tracy, Fittipaldi and Unser were all separated by a second or so, with Mansell having dropped back into a lonely fourth. Gordon and Mario

Michael C. Brown

Keeping it in the family

Auto racing's two most famous dynasties, the Andrettis and the Unsers, have always found the streets of Long Beach, California, to provide a happy hunting ground. In 1977, Mario Andretti guided his Formula 1 Lotus 78 to a famous 'home' victory in what was then called the US Grand Prix West, while in 1984, when promoter Chris Pook first switched the attraction into a round of the PPG Indy Car World Series, Andretti claimed both the pole and the race victory *en route* to winning the PPG Cup title for Newman-Haas Racing.

Andretti won twice more in Long Beach, in 1985 and 1987, with only his own son, Michael, breaking the string when he earned his very first Indy Car victory for Kraco Racing in 1986.

Then it was the turn of Al Unser Jr. to take control. 'Little Al' claimed his first Toyota Grand Prix of Long Beach title in 1988, driving the unloved March 88C for Rick Galles, and remained unbeaten on the downtown streets for four straight years. On two occasions, in 1989 and 1990, Unser also claimed the pole – the only two poles of his career up until that point. Moreover, in 1992, the first year in which the shortened 1.59-mile course had been utilized, Unser Jr. seemed set for an unprecedented fifth straight triumph, leading strongly in the Galmer G92 until being inadvertently tapped into a spin by none other than his very own team-mate, Danny Sullivan, with just three laps remaining. An irate Unser had to be content with fourth place as Sullivan sped away to the victory.

A total of 11 Indy Car races have now been staged at Long Beach, and between them the Andrettis and Al Unser Jr. have scored a total of nine wins and seven pole positions.

Andretti also were on their own. The only real battle was being waged over seventh place, with Boesel narrowly holding off Gugelmin and Michael Andretti.

Stefan Johansson rounded out the top ten, his Alumax Penske PC22-Ilmor/D having been repaired following a crash on Saturday, while Greco maintained his strong presence in 11th ahead of Teo Fabi (Pennzoil Reynard-Ilmor) and Jacques Villeneuve (Player's Reynard-Ford).

The first significant change came on lap 21. Tracy was already well among the back-markers, and as he closed on a dicing Mike Groff (Motorola Lola-Honda) and Robbie Buhl (Mi-Jack Lola T93/00-Ford) under braking for Turn One, suddenly the Penske snapped sideways.

'I had axle-hop every time I downshifted from fourth to third [gear],' related Tracy. 'The gearbox would lock up and the car started to shake at the rear. This time I started to slow down a little early but the back end locked up and it came around on me.'

An instant later he was spinning, taking an innocent Groff into the escape road and out of the race. Tracy's car was undamaged but the engine had stalled. He lost several laps, only to retire later on when the gearbox gave up for good.

Tracy's misfortune handed Unser the lead, which he was able to extend to almost five seconds during the course of lapping a group of midfield cars around the 30-lap mark.

Shortly before that, Michael Andretti also had taken advantage of some slower cars to find a way past Gugelmin for what had now become seventh place.

Unser was the first of the leaders to make his first routine pit stop, which came on lap 40. Fittipaldi, Mansell, Gordon et al followed him in next time around.

Unser maintained his advantage after the stop, only to learn he had been penalized for exceeding the speed limit in pit lane.

'I was so excited I thought I was back in an "H" pattern instead of a sequential [gear] shift,' explained Unser. 'When I grabbed a hold of the shifter, I didn't know where it was going. When I pulled out of the pits, the car quickly accelerated and when the tires stopped buzzing I was past the speed limit. As soon as I realized it I tried to stop, but the CART officials were sharp today and they got me.'

On lap 43, Unser was back in the pits. Incredibly, despite the stop-and-go penalty and the speed limit, he lost only one place – to team-mate Fittipaldi. Even better, a handful of laps later, he was able to erase most of the 12-second deficit due to a full-course caution after Greco's day ended with his Lola embedded deep in the tire wall in Turn One.

The restart came at the end of lap 52. At that stage the only other drivers on the same lap as Fittipaldi and Unser were Mansell, Gordon and Boesel. The two Andrettis ran next, Michael ahead of Mario following a lengthy pit stop for the elder statesman, although at the restart Mario reasserted himself by passing his son fairly and squarely on Shoreline Drive.

'My dad was able to get by me because I was in second gear when I should have been in first,' said Michael. 'His car was better than mine, so he would have passed me anyway.'

Unser found himself trapped behind a few slower cars at the restart, and before long Fittipaldi had managed to eke out an advantage of around seven seconds. The gap stayed fairly constant as Fittipaldi circulated consistently in the low 54-second range, but then, quite suddenly, on lap 62, the leading Penske slowed dramatically instead of accelerating hard onto Shoreline Drive.

'My car was flying. It was easy, cruising, and I was expecting to have my first win here at Long Beach,' declared the Brazilian. 'Then I had a problem with fourth gear. I lost third and second and finally fifth.' Fittipaldi crawled round for a couple more laps before calling it a day, by which time Unser had long since swept by to regain the lead. He was never again seriously challenged.

'Emerson and I were close all day,' summarized Unser after claiming the 20th victory of his career and his fifth at Long Beach. 'When I was leading the race, I couldn't really pull away from him unless he got

caught in traffic. It's a shame what happened to him, but his misfortune was my good fortune.'

Mansell inherited second place, almost ten seconds behind, only to endure a lurid moment on Shoreline Drive when a rear tire blew almost at maximum speed.

'The main problem you've got is trying to stop the car on three wheels,' related Mansell. 'It certainly catches your attention.'

Mansell managed to limp back to the pits without losing too much time, and he was fortunate enough to be able to take on sufficient fuel to ensure he wouldn't have to make an extra stop late in the race. Thus he resumed in fifth place on lap 69, but duly moved back up into second when everyone else made their own fuel-and-tire stops, on schedule, around ten laps later.

Gordon led for a couple of laps during the stops, before resuming in third, too far behind Mansell to offer a challenge in the closing stages. 'We thought [the track] would get slick,' explained Gordon, 'so we had a lot of wing in the car. Because of that we were slow on the straights all day. It was almost impossible to pass anyone.'

Boesel ran steadily to fourth, happy to reach the finish line since he was drastically short of fuel in the closing stages, while Mario and Michael Andretti were well spaced out in rounding out the top six. Gugelmin ran next ahead of Adrian Fernandez (Tecate/Quaker State Reynard-Ilmor), who just held off Teo Fabi's similar Pennzoil car in a spirited duel.

A problem changing the right-rear tire on his second stop cost Johansson seventh place, although he did hold on to tenth despite running out of fuel on his last lap.

Luyendyk and Indy Car debutant Franck Freon (Marcelo Group Lola T93/00-Ford) completed the point scorers, the Frenchman emerging ahead after a lengthy scrap with fellow Indy Lights graduate Robbie Groff (Condor Penske PC22-Ilmor/D), who, amazingly, mirrored Bettenhausen Motorsports teammate Johansson by running out of fuel on the last lap. Late retirements also sidelined Robbie Buhl, who ran as high as eighth in Dale Coyne's '93 Mi-Jack Lola before succumbing to gearbox problems, and Willy T. Ribbs, who was poised to move into a points-paying position when his Service Merchandise Lola T93/00 fell out due to a wastegate failure.

Emerson Fittipaldi and Paul Tracy thread their Penskes between back-markers Mark Smith (Craftsman Tools Lola) and Teo Fabi in the distinctive yellow Hall/VDS Pennzoil Reynard. Both the Marlboro cars were out of luck, succumbing to transmission failures.

Michael C. Brown

Above: Despite running short of fuel in the closing stages of the race, Raul Boesel managed to score a fourth-place finish with Dick Simon's Duracell/ Fuji Film/Mobil/Sadia Lola T94/00-Ford.

Below: Franck Freon brought the Marcelo Group's '93 Lola into 12th place and thus scored a PPG Cup point on his Indy Car debut.

After a lively battle with Teo Fabi, the impressive young Mexican driver Adrian Fernandez *(above)* took the brightly colored Tecate/Quaker State Reynard into eighth place.

SNIPPETS

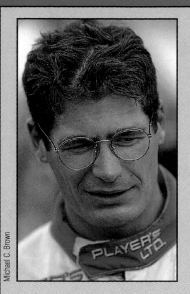

Michael C. Brown

• Toyota Atlantic graduate Claude Bourbonnais *(left)* made his Indy Car debut in Long Beach, driving for Tim Duke's Pro Formance Motorsports team. The tall French-Canadian badly damaged his Player's-backed Lola T93/00-Ilmor/C+ in a crash on Saturday morning, but thanks to the assistance of secondary sponsors Janet, Gil and Jay Losi, who under the Team Losi banner are among the leading producers of radio-controlled cars, Bourbonnais was able to take over a similar back-up Lola.

• Paul Tracy's pole-winning performance was all the more remarkable since his car, Penske PC23 chassis 006, had not been slated to debut until Indianapolis. Following the Canadian's unfortunate crash the previous weekend, however, the Penske team worked around the clock to race-prepare the chassis and deliver it to the West Coast.

• Hiro Matsushita's crew had been faced with an even bigger task. The Japanese driver's Lola had been totally destroyed in the crash at Phoenix, yet by 8.30 the following morning Mark Bridges and the crew had fitted a fresh engine to the team's spare '93 chassis and completely repainted the car in preparation for the filming of a TV commercial on behalf of Panasonic. 'Usually the painting alone would take five days,' marveled team owner Dick Simon.

• Roger Penske caused quite a furor a few days before Long Beach when he called a press conference in Indianapolis to confirm his intention of taking advantage of the unique USAC rules for the Indianapolis 500. Penske duly unveiled a brand-new 209-cubic inch motor, featuring a single in-block camshaft and two valves per cylinder, which would be allowed to run at 55 inches of manifold boost pressure, compared to 45 inches for all 'conventional' four-cam engines. To the surprise of most Indy Car insiders, the Ilmor Engineering-developed engine would carry a Mercedes-Benz name tag.

PPG INDY CAR WORLD SERIES • ROUND 3

TOYOTA GRAND PRIX OF LONG BEACH

LONG BEACH STREET CIRCUIT, CALIFORNIA

APRIL 17, 105 LAPS – 166.950 MILES

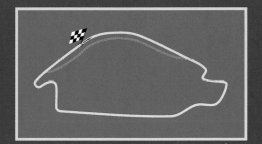

Place	Driver (Nat.)	No.	Team Sponsors Car-Engine	Q Speed (mph)	Q Time	Q Pos.	Laps	Time/Status	Ave. (mph)	Pts.
1	Al Unser Jr. (USA)	31	Marlboro Team Penske PC23-Ilmor/D	108.407	52.801s	2	105	1h 40m 53.582s	99.283	21
2	Nigel Mansell (GB)	1	Newman-Haas Kmart/Texaco Havoline Lola T94/00-Ford	108.173	52.915s	4	105	1h 41m 32.689s	98.646	16
3	Robby Gordon (USA)	9	Walker Valvoline/Cummins Special Lola T94/00-Ford	108.004	52.998s	5	105	1h 41m 39.854s	98.530	14
4	Raul Boesel (BR)	5	Simon Duracell/Fuji Film/Mobil/Sadia Lola T94/00-Ford	106.833	53.579s	7	104	Running		12
5	Mario Andretti (USA)	6	Newman-Haas Kmart/Texaco Havoline Lola T94/00-Ford	106.837	53.577s	6	104	Running		10
6	Michael Andretti (USA)	8	Ganassi Target/Scotch Video Reynard 94I-Ford	106.614	53.689s	9	104	Running		8
7	Mauricio Gugelmin (BR)	88	Ganassi Hollywood Reynard 94I-Ford	106.660	53.666s	8	104	Running		6
8	Adrian Fernandez (MEX)	7	Galles Tecate/Quaker State Reynard 94I-Ilmor/D	105.695	54.156s	19	104	Running		5
9	Teo Fabi (I)	11	Hall Pennzoil Reynard 94I-Ilmor/D	106.408	53.793s	12	104	Running		4
10	Stefan Johansson (S)	16	Bettenhausen Alumax Penske PC22-Ilmor/D	106.480	53.756s	10	102	Out of fuel		3
11	Arie Luyendyk (NL)	28	Indy Regency Eurosport/Boost Monaco Lola T94/00-Ilmor/D	106.014	53.993s	16	102	Running		2
12	*Franck Freon (F)	64	Project Indy Marcelo Group Lola T93/00-Ford	104.085	54.993s	27	101	Running		1
13	*Robbie Groff (USA)	76	Bettenhausen Condor Penske PC22-Ilmor/D	103.769	55.161s	29	100	Out of fuel		
14	Davy Jones (USA)	14	A.J. Foyt Copenhagen Racing Lola T93/00-Ford	105.122	54.451s	25	100	Running		
15	*Jacques Villeneuve (CDN)	12	Forsythe-Green Player's Ltd. Reynard 94I-Ford	106.241	53.877s	14	100	Running		
16	Robbie Buhl (USA)	19	Coyne The Mi-Jack Car Lola T93/00-Ford	104.272	54.895s	26	92	Transmission		
17	Dominic Dobson (USA)	17	PacWest Racing Group Lola T94/00-Ford	105.791	54.107s	17	91	Running		
18	Willy T. Ribbs (USA)	24	Walker Service Merchandise/Bill Cosby Lola T93/00-Ford	105.439	54.287s	22	80	Exhaust header		
19	Scott Goodyear (CDN)	40	Budweiser King Lola T94/00-Ford	106.083	53.958s	15	80	Transmission		
20	Paul Tracy (CDN)	3	Marlboro Team Penske PC23-Ilmor/D	108.450	52.780s	1	75	Transmission		1
21	Emerson Fittipaldi (BR)	2	Marlboro Team Penske PC23-Ilmor/D	108.308	52.849s	3	66	Transmission		
22	*Alessandro Zampedri (I)	50	Euromotorsport Agip/Dinema/Fluoril Lola T93/00-Ilmor/C	105.670	54.169s	20	55	Exhaust header		
23	Marco Greco (BR)	25	Simon Arciero Project Indy Lola T94/00-Ford	106.408	53.793s	13	40	Accident		
24	Jimmy Vasser (USA)	18	Hayhoe Conseco/STP Reynard 94I-Ford	105.421	54.297s	23	36	Accident		
25	Mark Smith (USA)	15	Walker Craftsman Tools Lola T94/00-Ford	105.707	54.150s	18	29	Accident		
26	*Claude Bourbonnais (CDN)	45	Pro Formance Player's/Indeck/Losi Lola T93/00-Ilmor/C	104.058	55.008s	28	24	Exhaust header		
27	Mike Groff (USA)	10	Rahal-Hogan Motorola Lola T94/00-Honda	105.301	54.359s	24	19	Accident		
28	*Scott Sharp (USA)	71	PacWest Racing Group Lola T94/00-Ford	105.471	54.271s	21	11	Engine		
29	Buddy Lazier (USA)	23	Leader Card Financial World Lola T93/00-Ilmor/C	103.288	55.418s	30	6	Exhaust header		
30	Bobby Rahal (USA)	4	Rahal-Hogan Miller Genuine Draft Lola T94/00-Honda	106.445	53.774s	11	3	Gearbox oil line		
NQ	Hiro Matsushita (J)	22	Simon Panasonic/Duskin Lola T93/00-Ford	101.445	56.424s	31	–	Did not qualify		
NQ	David Kudrave (USA)	55	Euromotorsport Agip/Dinema/Fluorin Lola T92/00-Ilmor/A	101.052	56.644s	32	–	Did not qualify		
NQ	Johnny Unser (USA)	39	Dale Coyne Racing Lola T92/00-Ilmor/A	98.727	57.978s	33	–	Did not qualify		

* denotes Rookie driver

Caution flags: Laps 47–51, accident/Greco/Turn One. Total five laps.

Lap leaders: Paul Tracy, 1–20 (20 laps); Al Unser Jr., 21–39 (19 laps); Emerson Fittipaldi, 40–41 (2 laps); Unser Jr., 42 (1 lap); Fittipaldi, 43–62 (20 laps); Unser Jr., 63–80 (18 laps); Robby Gordon, 81–82 (2 laps); Unser Jr., 83–105 (23 laps). **Totals:** Unser Jr., 61 laps; Fittipaldi, 22 laps; Tracy, 20 laps; Gordon, 2 laps.

Fastest race lap: Tracy, 53.562s, 106.868 mph, on lap 8.

Championship positions: **1** Unser Jr. and Fittipaldi, 37 pts; **3** Mansell, 35; **4** Michael Andretti, 29; **5** Johansson, 25; **6** Mario Andretti, 24; **7** Vasser, 22; **8** Gordon, 20; **9** Boesel, 17; **10** Gugelmin, 14; **11** M. Groff, 13; **12** Fabi, 10; **13** Fernandez, 8; **14** Sharp, 6; **15** Goodyear, 5; **16** Luyendyk and Tracy, 2; **18** Dobson, Jones and Freon, 1.

INDY 500

The memory of the 78th Indianapolis 500 is likely to haunt Emerson Fittipaldi for a long time.

With 15 laps to go, the veteran Brazilian appeared to be cruising toward what would have been his third victory in the enormously prestigious 500-mile race. He was under no pressure. At least not physically. The second-place car, team-mate Al Unser Jr.'s identical Marlboro Penske PC23-Mercedes-Benz, was right there ahead of him, a few yards short of being lapped.

Therein lay the problem. The mental pressure was intense, and Fittipaldi could feel it building. Moments before, Unser Jr. had passed him to get back on the lead lap. Fittipaldi knew he would feel far more comfortable with the one-lap cushion restored. So he pressed on.

But then, as he sped through Turn Four for the 185th time, Fittipaldi's car snapped out of control and spun into the wall. It was all over. In a flash, his dream of becoming the first man to win back-to-back Indianapolis 500 titles since Al Unser in 1970-71 was shattered.

Unser, who had tearfully announced his retirement from active driving earlier in the month and now, on his 55th birthday, was watching from the Penske pits, could hardly believe his eyes. So could his 32-year-old son, Al Jr., when he glanced in his mirrors and saw Fittipaldi's hobbled car.

'I felt bad for a second,' confessed Unser Jr., who went on to claim his second '500' triumph, an amazing ninth for the Unser clan and a record-extending tenth for car owner Roger Penske, whose decision to field Ilmor Engineering's unproven 209 cubic inch Mercedes-Benz 500I V8 engine had been thoroughly vindicated.

No one else came close to matching the Mercedes/Ilmor's prodigious power. Nevertheless, there were several other notable cameo performances, particularly from Jacques Villeneuve and Bobby Rahal.

Young Villeneuve displayed great maturity in earning the runner-up spoils with Forsythe-Green Racing's Player's Ltd. Reynard 94I-Ford/Cosworth. Meanwhile, veteran Rahal emerged from a dark cloud caused by Honda's surprising under-estimation of what it takes to be competitive at Indy by leasing a year-old Penske PC22 chassis, fitting an Ilmor Indy V8/D motor and storming through from 28th on the grid to finish a strong third in his Miller Genuine Draft-backed entry.

Photos: Michael C. Brown

Marlboro Team Penske, equipped with a specially developed Mercedes engine, dominated the 78th Indy 500, Al Unser Jr. ultimately triumphing in convincing style in car #31. As a happy Unser family pose with the winning PC23, 'Little Al' indicates his two victories, but dad still leads the way with four.

Emerson Fittipaldi led the race, but crashed out with only 15 of the 200 laps remaining *(left)*.

Right: Mercedes' three-pointed star graced the Penskes' engine covers, courtesy of their partnership with Ilmor Engineering, who had conceived the 500I V8 engine.

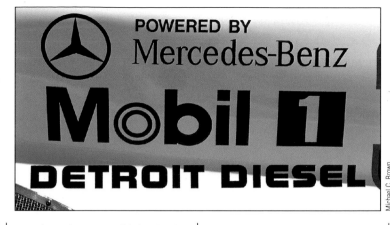

QUALIFYING

Marlboro Team Penske and, particularly, the weather were the big winners during the traditional Pole Day qualifying, which followed a full week of practice at the Indianapolis Motor Speedway.

Conditions were conducive to fast lap times when the track opened for practice at 8 a.m. on Saturday, May 14, with the temperature at around 59 degrees and a southerly breeze not causing many problems. An impressive total of 25 drivers posted their fastest laps of the month to date.

Fittipaldi wasn't among them, having turned the quickest lap of all, at 230.438 mph, two days earlier, but he led the way again with a comfortable best of 229.043 mph. In all, no fewer than 20 cars were faster than the 1993 pole-winning average of 223.967 mph turned by Arie Luyendyk.

One name missing from the line-up was the third member of the Penske 'super-team,' Paul Tracy, who had lost control and crashed on the exit of Turn Three while on a hot lap the previous afternoon. Tracy was kept overnight in Methodist Hospital and wouldn't be released to drive until Sunday.

Nevertheless, few people expected anything other than a Penske-Mercedes/Ilmor to snare the pole. The cars had proven awesomely fast almost from the moment they first took to the track the previous Sunday. Straight-line speeds in excess of 240 mph were commonplace for the finned PC23s, while all of the 'conventional' Ilmor- or Ford-powered cars were struggling to attain more than 235.

Clearly, the new V8 engine enjoyed a distinct power advantage. But who would claim the coveted pole position, Fittipaldi or Unser Jr.?

Even when the gun sounded at 6 p.m. on Saturday evening, no definitive answer could be given. Sure, Unser Jr., 12th in the line of qualifiers, had posted the fastest four-lap average speed at 228.011 mph, but a three-hour delay due to rain meant that several cars remained in line. Under the complicated USAC procedure, any driver who had not yet had an opportunity to run remained classified as a 'first-day' qualifier and would be eligible for the pole when the track opened again on Sunday.

Prime among them was Fittipaldi.

But once again the weather was to play a critical role. A wet track delayed the start of practice, while a strong, blustery wind, emanating now from the west, added a further complication.

'When I was running here, I used to say I could live with any wind if it was coming directly from the north or the south,' declared Bobby Unser, a three-time Indianapolis 500 winner now working as a color commentator for ABC Sports, from his vantage point atop the suites in Turn Two. 'But if it was coming crossways, that was the absolute worst. Number one, you have turbulent air coming over the grandstands on the front stretch, and then, going into Turns Two and Four, the wind would kill you coming off the corners.'

Prophetic words.

Mario Andretti was first in line, seeking to qualify strongly for what would be his 29th and last Indy 500. The deserving veteran received a rapturous ovation from the crowd, but even he was unable to overcome the elements. The best Mario could manage in his Kmart/Texaco Havoline Lola-Ford was a four-lap average of 223.503 mph.

'We were set up for these conditions but we knew we'd struggle,' related Andretti. He did.

So did Fittipaldi, who took to the track a half-hour or so later. The defending Indianapolis champion steeled himself to produce a magnificent first flying lap just shy of 228 mph, which caused a few anxious moments for a spectating Al Unser Jr. and his father, but there was no way he could sustain that pace. Fittipaldi had to be content with third on the grid, the outside of the front row.

'I'm really disappointed because we knew we had a good chance [of the pole],' said Fittipaldi. 'I don't think there was much left. A couple of times I got close to the wall in Turn Two. The wind was blowing hard and making it very difficult in Turns Two and Four. That was all I could do. My concern now is to get ready for the race.'

Raul Boesel was overshadowed by the Penskes but nevertheless had proven consistently fast all month. He secured a berth in the middle of the front row with Dick Simon's Duracell Charger Lola-Ford/Cosworth XB, one place better than in 1993.

Villeneuve served notice of what was to come on race day by annexing not only the inside of row two but also the honor of being fastest of the Reynard contingent. That in itself was something of a surprise, since Michael Andretti, fifth on the grid, had shown consistency and pace throughout the previous week of practice. The cool weather seemed to catch out Chip Ganassi's team. Andretti was able to run absolutely flat out for all four laps, but his car's set-up, or the aerodynamic drag, was such that he wasn't quite fast enough to eclipse Villeneuve.

The outside of row three provided the greatest upset of all, as 1992 Indianapolis Rookie of the Year Lyn St. James upstaged many more illustrious opponents, including her rookie award successor, Nigel Mansell.

'I'm proud of the fact I'm a woman and proud of the fact I'm a race car driver,' said the classy St. James after running four laps at 224.154 mph in Dick and Dianne Simon's JCPenney/Reebok/Lee/'Spirit of the American Woman' Lola-Ford. 'The month of May is like ecstasy for me. I get to come to the race track every day, everybody has a good time, and it just doesn't get any better than that.'

RACE

The traditional Carburetion Day practice session was completed without undue drama on Thursday, May 26, leaving the teams almost three full days in which to prepare for the 500-mile race.

All 33 cars were present and correct well in time for the usual 11 a.m. start and, as ever, a vast crowd had been packed into the 2.5-mile edifice of speed. Happily, too, the weather was altogether more co-operative than it had been for qualifying. Warm temperatures and a clear blue sky provided picture-perfect conditions as Unser Jr. led the field around for the final parade laps behind 1963 '500' winner Parnelli Jones in the Ford Mustang Cobra official pace car.

Boesel's Ford/Cosworth engine was no match for the two Mercedes/Ilmors as the front-row qualifiers accelerated off Turn Four and approached the starter's gantry in front of the packed main grandstands, and for several moments it looked as though USAC Chief Starter Duane Sweeney would not display the green. At the very last instant, however, with the two Penskes virtually beneath him and Boesel lagging behind, Sweeney waved the green flags with his usual flourish. The race was on.

Unser Jr. duly stayed hard on the gas and withstood Fittipaldi's challenge into Turn One. Behind, Michael Andretti swooped to the outside of a frustrated Boesel as they shot past the start/finish line, then tucked in behind the two red and white cars. Third-row starters Arie Luyendyk (Eurosport/Boost Monaco Lola-Ilmor/D) and Mario Andretti also took advantage of Boesel being caught off guard, while Eddie Cheever's Quaker State Special Lola T93/00-Menard/Buick V6 emerged in sixth after starting 11th.

An irate Boesel, who had been well and truly chopped by the Penskes coming off Turn Four prior to the start, completed the first lap in seventh, then lost two more places on the following lap to Villeneuve and Mansell (Kmart/Texaco Havoline Lola-Ford). Already Boesel perceived his engine to be down on power.

Unser Jr. settled into a pace of around 214 mph at the front of the field, comfortably fast enough to hold off Fittipaldi and Andretti.

The first yellow came on lap six, when midfield runner Dennis Vitolo executed a perfect 360-degree spin coming off Turn Four. Miraculously, the Floridian rookie made no contact. Indeed he lost only three places.

The restart came shortly afterward, with the order at the front unchanged. Villeneuve again displayed some inexperience by losing a couple of places, then settled into a comfortable rhythm as he kept pace with Boesel. Farther back, Robby Gordon had chosen to make a pit stop under the first caution. His Valvoline/Cummins Lola had been way too loose for comfort, although a fresh set of tires and a slight rear wing adjustment made all the difference in the world. Soon he was charging through the tail-enders, carving several superb-looking passes around the outside line.

The next interruption came on lap 20, when Roberto Guerrero crashed his Interstate Batteries Lola T92/00-Buick, the oldest car in the race – and, incidentally, the very same chassis with which he established the fastest qualifying run ever at Indianapolis, in 1992, at 232.482 mph.

Guerrero, fortunately, was unhurt in the Turn One mishap, although he, of course, was done for the day. For the second time in three years he was listed as the first retirement.

'It caught me totally by surprise,' admitted the amiable Guerrero. 'Everything was running smoothly. For no reason the back end came around.'

The entire field took the opportunity to make a pit stop under caution, and a mistake by Unser Jr., who stalled his engine as he attempted to leave his pit, enabled Fittipaldi to emerge as the new leader.

Above: Eddie Cheever, out of a regular ride in the PPG Indy Car World Series in 1994, handled one of John Menard's V6-engined machines at the Brickyard. Despite a lack of brakes, Eddie drove an excellent race to take eighth place in his Quaker State Lola.

Right: Mario Andretti prepares for his 29th and final Indianapolis 500. Apart from his win in 1969, 'Lady Luck' has regularly deserted Mario at Indy. And so it was this time round as he posted an early retirement in his Kmart/Texaco Havoline Lola after a lengthy pit stop with a faulty fuel pressure relief valve.

Left: Indy rookie Jacques Villeneuve benefited from the experienced guidance of Tony Cicale and Barry Green.

Below: Once a pole-sitter at the Indy 500, Teo Fabi had to be content with a lowly 24th position on the grid, but made it to a top-ten finish, albeit two laps down.

Nigel Mansell, looking to win the Indy 500 after coming so close in 1993, suffered the 'embarrassment' of being out-qualified by occasional racer Lyn St. James *(bottom left)*, who performed superbly to qualify in sixth place in the Dick Simon '94 Lola backed by JCPenney department stores.

Ever hopeful of success, Nigel's staunchest supporters *(bottom right)* added a touch of patriotic color to the proceedings.

'It was my fault,' admitted Unser. 'I was trying to be easy on the clutch. I just didn't have enough revs.'

Despite the delay, Unser lost only one place, to Michael Andretti, and at the restart on lap 27 he calmly powered past the Reynard to retake second place.

'I couldn't believe it,' said Andretti. 'I couldn't even stay in their tow. Normally you can stay in the tow. They were gone!'

Cheever also moved up a place to fourth at the expense of Mansell, while John Andretti, in A.J. Foyt's Jonathan Byrd's Cafeteria/Bryant Heating & Cooling Lola, got the jump on Boesel for sixth. Jimmy Vasser (Conseco/STP Reynard-Ford) and Stan Fox (Delta Faucet/Jack's Tool Rental Reynard-Ford) also had moved into the top ten ahead of Luyendyk.

Mario Andretti, meanwhile, was already out, victim of a bad fuel pressure relief valve.

'I don't know why things happen like this,' said the bitterly disappointed Andretti. 'It just seems like weird things are always happening to me at this place.'

One lap after the restart, two more cars went crashing out of the race. Mike Groff, already a lap down in his Motorola Penske PC22-Ilmor/C+, and Dominic Dobson (PacWest Lola-Ford) had run either side of Hideshi Matsuda's 1993 Lola-Ford going into Turn One, then, unfortunately, as they converged near the apex from totally different lines, the pair tangled together before careering backward into the wall. Luckily, both men escaped with minor bumps and bruises.

Several drivers were forced to take drastic evasive action, including Rahal, whose quick thinking enabled him to dart sharply to his left, across the grass and onto the pit exit road, a safety feature introduced in time for last year's race. Scott Goodyear (Budweiser Lola-Ford), Adrian Fernandez (Tecate/Quaker State Reynard-Ilmor) and Lyn St. James weren't so lucky. All three cars sustained suspension damage from debris, although St. James, who had slipped back as far as 19th before the incident, was able to resume following a lengthy pit stop for repairs.

This time the caution period was rather longer as the track was cleared. The restart came on lap 41, whereupon Cheever immediately used the power of his Menard V6 to relieve Michael Andretti of third place. Mansell also lost a place to John Andretti.

Caged by the debris fencing, Jacques Villeneuve powers the Forsythe-Green Player's Ltd. Reynard-Ford along the straightaway on his way to a brilliant second place.

Before long, though, all but John A. were to lose valuable time. First into the pits, at the end of that first green-flag lap, was Michael A., who had felt a rear tire going flat. He lost a lap before rejoining. Minutes later, both Cheever and Mansell were bound for the pits after being assessed stop-and-go penalties for illegally passing Boesel in the pit lane during the first round of pit stops.

The alleged infractions took place right at the end of pit lane, just over the so-called 'blend line' which marks the start of the no-passing zone in the pit exit road. At that point, Mansell and Cheever were already up to speed, whereas Boesel, pitted nearest to Turn One, was just beginning to accelerate away from his pit stall. They were needless, but crucial, penalties, which cost Mansell and Cheever a lap apiece. Both men were still fuming once the race was over.

'What did [the officials] want us to do,' raged Mansell, 'brake hard and cause an accident? It was disgraceful, a joke.'

John Andretti thus took up the forlorn chase of the two leading Penskes, although it wasn't long before Gordon and Villeneuve moved up into the picture. Gordon was continuing his impressive charge toward the front. First he passed Boesel around the outside in Turn Four. Then, after Boesel had taken advantage of traffic to regain his position, Gordon pulled off an equally spectacular maneuver around the outside of Turn Two. Amazing.

Villeneuve's progress wasn't quite so daring but it was even more effective as he passed Vasser, Boesel, Gordon and John Andretti on successive laps to move up from seventh to third by lap 59. Make no mistake, Villeneuve was performing like no ordinary rookie!

Two laps later, after Fittipaldi and Unser Jr. had made routine pit stops for fuel and fresh Goodyear tires, Villeneuve suddenly found himself leading his very first Indianapolis 500.

'My car was fantastic,' declared the 23-year-old French-Canadian. 'I was highly confident about the team. I knew they were ready to win and capable of winning. My car was strong all month.'

Unser Jr. lost a few seconds as he almost stalled the engine again during his stop on lap 60, so that by lap 70, with everyone having made their second stops, Fittipaldi led by around 15 seconds. On his own, the race leader was able to turn laps at right around 220 mph. Even in traffic he was circulating at better than 210 mph. The impressive Villeneuve was the only other driver on the lead lap.

A strong run by Rahal had taken him all the way from 28th to fourth, most recently at the expense of Vasser, whom Rahal passed cleanly going into Turn Three on lap 70. Also embroiled in this battle were Scott Brayton, who had moved up stealthily in John Menard's Glidden Paint Lola-Menard, plus the recovering Mansell and Michael Andretti, who was now out of sequence on his pit stops. Michael came in again on lap 74, falling briefly two laps off the front-running pace.

In this middle segment of the race, Mansell was the fastest man on the track. On lap 85 he dispensed with both Rahal and Villeneuve. A handful of laps later, both the defending PPG Cup champion and Villeneuve regained the lead lap when both Penskes stopped for more fuel.

And then, as if answering their prayers, out came the yellow flags to warn of another incident in Turn One. The amazing Mr. Matsuda, after rising as high as seventh, had been caught out by some fluid leaking from Boesel's car, which was running directly in front. Farther around the same lap, after some debris had punctured a rear tire, John Paul Jr. also crashed his Team Losi/Cybergenics Lola T93/00-Ilmor/C+ in Turn Three. Both impacts were heavy but again the drivers escaped injury, yet more testaments to the strength of modern-day Indy cars.

Boesel also retired during the ensuing caution, his engine a victim of rising water temperature, while Tracy, having climbed steadily and sensibly to 12th in the third Penske-Mercedes, despite losing more than a lap when his engine stalled at the first pit stop, succumbed to a broken turbo. Marco Greco had withdrawn a little earlier, too, due to electrical problems.

The caution, of course, would enable Mansell and Villeneuve to stop without being in danger of losing a lap. But Mansell never even made it to his pit.

In a bizarre incident on the pit entry road in Turn Three, the unfortunate Vitolo had misjudged his speed and been launched off the left-rear wheel of John Andretti's car. Vitolo's Lola T93/00-Ford then sailed backward, narrowly missing another couple of cars, before smacking

Photos: Michael C. Brown

A tale of two engines

The Indianapolis 500 is, without a doubt, the most famous and prestigious motor race in the world. Ever since the inaugural event in 1911, many automobile manufacturers have been drawn to the 2.5-mile four-cornered oval, seeking to parlay victory in the annual 500-mile race into increased sales. This year Mercedes-Benz and Honda decided to join the fray.

Their fortunes could hardly have been more disparate. Mercedes-Benz was drawn into the race only at a relatively late stage. Roger Penske, already the most successful car owner in Indianapolis history, decided immediately after the 1993 race that he would take advantage of the unique rules at Indy which permit turbocharged 209 cubic inch (3.43-liter) engines with a single camshaft and two pushrod-operated valves per cylinder to run at 55 inches of mercury manifold boost pressure, compared to 45 inches for all other 'conventional' four-valve motors.

It was a shrewd move. Most engineers reckoned the pushrod option was capable of producing at least 950 horsepower, compared to around 800 hp for the 161.5 cubic inch (2.65-liter) Ford/Cosworths and Ilmor/Ds.

Ilmor Engineering, established almost ten years ago with Penske as a co-founder, was contracted to design the new engine. Mercedes provided the name-brand recognition and the dollars.

Honda, by contrast, had been working on its Indianapolis project for more than three years. All of the conceptual work was carried out in Japan, with development having been continued at the new Honda Performance Development facility in Santa Clarita, California.

Soon after official practice at Indianapolis began, however, it became quite clear that the latest Honda V8 was no match for the 'conventional' Ford-Cosworth or Ilmor Indy V8/D engines, let alone the enormously potent Mercedes-Ilmor.

Rahal/Hogan Racing team-mates Bobby Rahal and Mike Groff did manage to qualify their Honda-powered cars during the first weekend of Time Trials, but it soon became apparent that their speeds of 220.178 mph (Rahal) and 218.808 mph (Groff) would not be good enough to make the 33-car starting field.

'When we came here we did not anticipate we would be in this situation,' said Rahal's partner, Carl Hogan, 'but about the middle of the [first] week [of practice] I think it was obvious that Bobby had got pretty much everything out of the car and it was obvious that we were not happy with those speeds.'

So Hogan went to work on a contingency plan, which was concluded when he leased a couple of Ilmor-powered Penske PC22 chassis from long-time friend and rival team owner Roger Penske. Both Rahal and Groff subsequently re-qualified on the second weekend. Their Lola-Hondas were duly packed away in the transporters.

'Obviously we are disappointed,' said Robert Clarke, General Manager of Honda Performance Development, 'but we understand the Rahal/Hogan team's decision. We have developed an outstanding relationship with the team and will continue to work with Rahal/Hogan Racing in preparation for the remaining events on the PPG Indy Car World Series schedule.'

Mercedes, meanwhile, went from strength to strength. The V8 motors might have owed nothing to the German company's undoubted technical genius, yet they performed magnificently. The famous three-pointed star emblem was much in evidence, and Mercedes backed up its success with an intensive advertising campaign.

The triumph was savored equally by Ilmor Engineering, which now can boast seven straight wins at the Brickyard. The other six wins came with engines carrying the Chevrolet badge. Chief designer Mario Illien was presented with the prestigious 28th annual Louis Schwitzer Award in recognition of his technical excellence and innovation.

For Honda, there is always next year. Its initial foray to Indianapolis – the first ever by a Japanese manufacturer – was an unmitigated disaster, but the Honda engineers will continue their quest. The story in 1995 is likely to be entirely different.

Michael C. Brown

111

Michael C. Brown

Without doubt one of the performances of the race came from Bobby Rahal, who took his hired Penske-Ilmor from a lowly 28th place on the grid to a sensational third at the finish. Here he is shown moving through the midfield runners, passing John Andretti (33) and closing in on Hiro Matsushita (22). In the background are Teo Fabi and Robby Gordon.

heavily into – and onto – the rear of Mansell's Newman-Haas Lola.

Vitolo's car ended up perched precariously, and incongruously, atop Mansell's engine cover, and when hot fluids began to leak out, Mansell was obliged to make a hasty exit. Both men were taken to the infield care center. Again, neither was seriously hurt, although Mansell, in a furious rage due to the manner of his exit from the race, stormed out before the doctors could complete their examinations. Perhaps Vitolo should consider himself lucky!

The green flag flew again as the leaders completed their 100th lap, half-distance. Fittipaldi and Unser Jr. remained to the fore, with the only real question being in relation to the reliability of the Mercedes/Ilmor in its very first race.

Judging by the manner in which Fittipaldi took control of proceedings in mid-race, he had no qualms whatsoever. With a clear road in front of him on lap 118, Fittipaldi averaged 218.066 mph. Next time around was 219.491. As if that wasn't enough, the next two laps remained as the fastest of the race at 220.529 and 220.680. Fittipaldi was flying. And suddenly his lead over Unser had jumped from six seconds to 28 seconds.

Villeneuve held a similarly tight grasp on third place, and even led again for several laps when the fuel-thirsty Penskes stopped earlier than he for service on laps 123 and 124. Behind, though, places were changing constantly. There's no doubt that without the Penskes, this would have been one heck of a race!

Brayton's solid run in fifth place ended on lap 116 when he coasted into the pits, engine dead, although Gordon, Rahal, Vasser and Michael Andretti continued to swap places. All were running to slightly different fuel strategies.

The next major drama came on lap 133, when Fittipaldi pulled down onto pit lane. The stop was unscheduled. He had taken on service just nine laps earlier.

The problem, signified by an overheated engine, was caused by a piece of debris in the left-hand side pod. Fittipaldi was stationary for less than six seconds, enough to remove the errant plastic bag and pump in a few gallons of methanol.

He resumed in second place but regained the point shortly afterward when Unser took advantage of another full-course caution, due to debris on the track in Turn Three, to take regular service.

The race was restarted on lap 140, with Fittipaldi back in control. Unser, who had slipped behind Villeneuve with his latest stop, moved back into second place a couple of laps later. These were still the only cars on the lead lap.

Gordon had by now taken over in fourth, narrowly ahead of Michael Andretti, Rahal and Vasser, with Cheever two laps down in eighth and trailed by Teo Fabi (Pennzoil Reynard-Ilmor) and rookie Bryan Herta. The reigning Indy Lights champion had moved up quietly and impressively in his first-ever Indy Car race, and now was feeling far more confident at the wheel of A.J. Foyt's Copenhagen Lola-Ford.

'He did everything we told him to do,' said team manager Tommy Lamance, A.J.'s nephew. 'He gave us the right information about how the car was handling and we made the right changes.'

Fox and John Andretti, who struggled to maintain a good balance on Foyt's second car, were three laps down, followed by Indy rookies Mauricio Gugelmin (Hollywood Reynard-Ford) and Brian Till (Mi-Jack Lola T93/00-Ford), then veteran Luyendyk, who was also hindered by an ill-handling car. Luyendyk later went out with an engine failure.

On lap 156, Fittipaldi once again put Villeneuve a lap down, and before long, after the two leaders had made yet another fuel stop, Unser, too, came under threat of a

similar fate. That's how much Fittipaldi was in control of this race.

With 20 laps, 50 miles, remaining, Fittipaldi did indeed pass Unser, taking advantage of a slight bobble by the #31 Penske coming off Turn Four. But two tours of the 2.5-mile superspeedway later, when Fittipaldi was slowed momentarily by traffic, Unser returned the favor by sweeping ahead on the outside line into Turn Three. It was a brave pass. But then Unser had nothing to lose. He knew he must be on the lead lap to retain any chance of winning the race.

Now the pressure was back on Fittipaldi, who was faced with a dilemma. Should he seek to ensure himself the protection of a one-lap lead, or should he throttle back and be content to follow Unser? It was a tough call. If he erred on the side of caution, Fittipaldi knew full well that another full-course caution would enable Unser to make up most of that lap and give him one last chance to snatch away the victory.

He decided to press on, and then made the fateful mistake in Turn Four.

'I tried to go a little lower [on the track] than he was,' related Fittipaldi, who had dominated the race for well over two hours, since Unser stalled at his first pit stop. 'I hit the apron – I was about a half a foot too low – and lost the back end. I'm very disappointed. It's a great shame. The car, she was flying.'

So now there was only one Penske. The team's hopes were riding alone with Unser Jr. And he wasn't about to let them down.

Ten laps remained after the wreckage from Fittipaldi's crash had been cleared. Villeneuve was now back on the lead lap but mired deep amidst the pack. Unser quickly pulled out a substantial lead. The yellow had negated any need for a final splash-and-go stop for the new leader, so Villeneuve was quite content to settle for second.

'We figure we're first in Class B,' said team co-owner Barry Green. 'The Penskes are running to different rules than we are, so we're pretty happy.'

There was one final drama when Fox crashed in Turn One with just four laps remaining. The veteran midget racer had been running solidly in tenth, three laps off the pace.

On came the caution lights for the seventh and final time, leaving Unser Jr. to lead the finishers home at little more than a snail's pace. The partisan crowd went wild with delight. Unser Jr.'s father looked on proudly, tears of joy in his eyes.

Michael Andretti crossed the line in third place after a fine recovery drive, only to learn he had been penalized one lap for overtaking Hiro Matsushita's Panasonic Lola-Ford during a late yellow. Andretti thus was demoted to sixth in the final results behind a delighted Rahal, who had driven a superb race, Vasser, who was a factor all day long, and Gordon, who lost time with a bungled final pit stop.

Fabi completed 198 laps, one more than Cheever, who had to overcome a lack of brakes and was delighted to make the finish with Menard's V6 motor.

Herta lost at least one place when, at his final stop, he joined the long list of people to stall on pit road. He still finished ninth, ahead of teammate John Andretti, whose day was far from over. Andretti was promptly whisked away to a waiting helicopter for the first leg of a frantic journey to Charlotte, N.C., where he went on to contest a 600-mile NASCAR race the same evening!

Unser Jr., meanwhile, was left to reflect on a magnificent team effort.

'I want to thank Roger Penske,' he said after wishing his dad a happy birthday in the new Victory Circle. 'He loves this place as much as I do and it shows. He just gave me a pretty special car.'

Al Unser Jr. did the rest.

The bizarre pit lane collision in which Dennis Vitolo *(above)* managed to end up with his '93 Lola atop the Kmart/Texaco Havoline car of Nigel Mansell. It brought to an end yet another brilliant drive by Mansell, but the Brit's histrionics in the aftermath of the incident did little to win sympathy from the home fans.

Below: For the second time in his career Al Unser Jr. turns into Victory Lane.

SNIPPETS

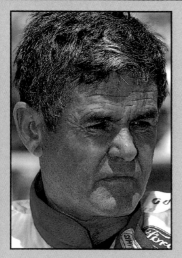

on the straightaways.

• Jacques Villeneuve's Forsythe-Green team, led by crew chief Kyle Moyer, clinched the annual Carburetion Day Miller Genuine Draft Pit Stop Championship by beating Randy Bain's Pro Formance Motorsports crew and driver John Paul Jr. in the final round.

• Question for Fittipaldi: 'Is the Mercedes the fastest engine you have ever driven?' Answer: 'Oh yes. I've never been 245 mph in my life. I don't want to know how many kilometers [per hour] that is. I'll keep it in miles!'

• Dick Simon's fleet of six entries provided several highlights during qualifying. Most of the headlines were claimed by Raul Boesel, second on the grid, and Lyn St. James, sixth. Nevertheless, rookie Hideshi Matsuda *(right)*, who had worked as a pit reporter for Japanese television the previous two years, posted his four fastest laps of the month in becoming the very first qualifier on the opening Saturday, and Dennis Vitolo turned his quickest laps to qualify comfortably. Brazilian Marco Greco also turned up the wick when it mattered to become the 33rd – albeit not the slowest – qualifier on the final day.

• In separate ceremonies during the month, four-time Indianapolis 500 winner Al Unser *(above)* and three-time champion Johnny Rutherford announced their retirement from active driving. Unser came to the realization he would rather cheer on his son, Al Jr., than struggle to compete with the Arizona Motor Sports team's Lola-Ford, while 'Lone Star JR' also reached the conclusion that, at the age of 56, he was unlikely ever to be offered a competitive ride again. Both popular veterans fittingly received a standing ovation from the packed grandstands.

• For the second straight year, Mark Smith was bumped from the field on the final day. Incredibly, no one with America's most prevalent surname has ever started the Indianapolis 500.

• The most under-publicized story at Indy was the huge effort expended during the month by Peter and Michael Greenfield. The father and son team were actually the first to set about building a new engine to meet the USAC's 'pushrod' rules. Sadly, their ingenious Greenfield GC209T V8 suffered a spate of niggling teething problems which necessitated several trips back and forth to their base on Long Island. Driver Johnny Parsons never managed an official qualifying attempt, although the promising engine did run at better than 220 mph

• The Penske team brought six of its Nigel Bennett-designed PC23s *(above)* to Indianapolis. Four had been raced previously this season, so were adapted to take the new-for-Indy Mercedes/Ilmor engine. Changes also included a new, beefier gearbox to cope with the additional power and torque. One car, PC23-004, had been the designated test car for the Indy project, while the other, Unser Jr.'s winning PC23-007, was brand new.

• Al Unser Jr. missed the rain-affected opening day ceremonies and the first full day of practice. Instead he was busy at Michigan International Speedway, continuing tests with the Mercedes/Ilmor engine. They obviously paid off.

• Several cars sprouted dorsal fins atop the engine covers in response to the Penske initiative at Phoenix, although all were required to be shortened by a USAC directive which called for them to terminate at the center line of the rear axle.

• For the second time in three years, Scott Goodyear *(above)* was obliged to take over a car already qualified by another driver. In 1992, of course, running a car qualified by Mike Groff, Goodyear went on to finish second to Unser Jr. in the closest finish in Indianapolis history. This time, following a fraught month with Kenny Bernstein's Budweiser Lola-Ford, Goodyear had to rely on help from Davy Jones *(left)* to make it into the field.

PPG INDY CAR WORLD SERIES • ROUND 4
78TH INDIANAPOLIS 500

INDIANAPOLIS MOTOR SPEEDWAY, SPEEDWAY, INDIANA

MAY 29, 200 LAPS – 500.000 MILES

Place	Driver (Nat.)	No.	Team Sponsors Car-Engine	Q Speed (mph)	Q Time	Q Pos.	Laps	Time/Status	Ave. (mph)	Pts.
1	Al Unser Jr. (USA)	31	Marlboro Team Penske PC23-Mercedes Benz/Ilmor V8	228.011	2m 37.887s	1	200	3h 06m 29.006s	160.872	21
2	*Jacques Villeneuve (CDN)	12	Forsythe-Green Player's Ltd. Reynard 94I-Ford	226.259	2m 39.110s	4	200	3h 06m 37.606s	160.749	16
3	Bobby Rahal (USA)	4	Rahal-Hogan Miller Genuine Draft Penske PC22-Ilmor/D	224.094	2m 40.647s	28	199	Running		14
4	Jimmy Vasser (USA)	18	Hayhoe Conseco/STP Reynard 94I-Ford	222.262	2m 41.971s	16	199	Running		12
5	Robby Gordon (USA)	9	Walker Valvoline/Cummins Special Lola T94/00-Ford	221.293	2m 42.680s	19	199	Running		10
**6	Michael Andretti (USA)	8	Ganassi Target/Scotch Video Reynard 94I-Ford	226.205	2m 39.148s	5	198	Running		8
7	Teo Fabi (I)	11	Hall Pennzoil Special Reynard 94I-Ilmor/D	223.394	2m 41.150s	24	198	Running		6
8	Eddie Cheever (USA)	27	Menard Quaker State Special Lola T93/00-Menard V6	223.163	2m 41.317s	11	197	Running		5
9	*Bryan Herta (USA)	14	A.J. Foyt Copenhagen Racing Lola T94/00-Ford	220.992	2m 42.902s	22	197	Running		4
10	John Andretti (USA)	33	A.J. Foyt Jonathan Byrd/Bryant Lola T94/00-Ford	223.263	2m 41.245s	10	196	Running		3
11	*Mauricio Gugelmin (BR)	88	Ganassi Hollywood Reynard 94I-Ford	223.104	2m 41.360s	29	196	Running		2
12	*Brian Till (USA)	19	Coyne The Mi-Jack Car Lola T93/00-Ford	221.107	2m 42.817s	21	194	Running		1
13	Stan Fox (USA)	91	Hemelgarn Delta Faucet/Jack's Tool Reynard 94I-Ford	222.867	2m 41.531s	13	193	Accident		
14	Hiro Matsushita (J)	22	Simon Panasonic/Duskin Lola T94/00-Ford	221.382	2m 42.615s	18	193	Running		
15	Stefan Johansson (S)	16	Bettenhausen Alumax Aluminum Penske PC22-Ilmor/D	221.518	2m 42.515s	27	192	Running		
16	*Scott Sharp (USA)	71	PacWest Racing Group Lola T94/00-Ford	222.091	2m 42.096s	17	186	Running		
17	Emerson Fittipaldi (BR)	2	Marlboro Team Penske PC23-Mercedes Benz/Ilmor V8	227.303	2m 38.379s	3	184	Accident		1
18	Arie Luyendyk (NL)	28	Indy Regency Eurosport/Boost Monaco Lola T94/00-Ilmor/D	223.673	2m 40.949s	8	179	Engine		
19	Lyn St. James (USA)	90	Simon JCPenney/Reebok/Lee Lola T94/00-Ford	224.154	2m 40.604s	6	170	Running		
20	Scott Brayton (USA)	59	Menard Glidden Paint Special Lola T93/00-Menard V6	223.652	2m 40.964s	23	116	Engine		
21	Raul Boesel (BR)	5	Simon Duracell/Fuji Film/Mobil/Sadia Lola T94/00-Ford	227.618	2m 38.160s	2	100	Water pump		
22	Nigel Mansell (GB)	1	Newman-Haas Kmart/Texaco Havoline Lola T94/00-Ford	224.041	2m 40.685s	7	92	Accident		
23	Paul Tracy (CDN)	3	Marlboro Team Penske PC23-Mercedes Benz/Ilmor V8	222.710	2m 41.645s	25	92	Turbo		
24	*Hideshi Matsuda (J)	99	Simon Racing/Beck Motorsports Lola T93/00-Ford	222.545	2m 41.765s	14	90	Accident		
25	John Paul Jr. (USA)	45	Pro Formance Losi/Cybergenics Lola T93/00-Ilmor/C+	222.500	2m 41.798s	30	89	Accident		
26	*Dennis Vitolo (USA)	79	Simon Hooligan's/Carlo/Charter America Lola T93/00-Ford	222.439	2m 41.842s	15	89	Accident		
27	*Marco Greco (BR)	25	Simon Arciero Project Indy Int. Sports Lola T94/00-Ford	221.216	2m 42.737s	32	53	Electrical		
28	*Adrian Fernandez (MEX)	7	Galles Tecate/Quaker State Reynard 94I-Ilmor/D	222.657	2m 41.684s	26	30	Suspension damage		
29	Dominic Dobson (USA)	17	PacWest Racing Group Lola T94/00-Ford	222.970	2m 41.457s	12	29	Accident		
30	Scott Goodyear (CDN)	40	Budweiser King Racing Lola T94/00-Ford	223.817	2m 40.846s	33	29	Engine		
31	Mike Groff (USA)	10	Rahal-Hogan Motorola Penske PC22-Ilmor/C+	221.355	2m 42.635s	31	28	Accident		
32	Mario Andretti (USA)	6	Newman-Haas Kmart/Texaco Havoline Lola T94/00-Ford	223.503	2m 41.072s	9	23	Fuel system		
33	Roberto Guerrero (USA)	21	Pagan Racing Interstate Batteries Lola T92/00-Buick V6	221.278	2m 42.691s	20	20	Accident		
NQ	*Mark Smith (USA)	15	Walker Craftsman Tools Lola T94/00-Ford	220.683	2m 43.130s	34	–	Bumped		
NS	Davy Jones (USA)	40	Budweiser King Lola T94/00-Ford					Car taken over by Scott Goodyear		
NQ	Willy T. Ribbs (USA)	24	Walker Service Merchandise/Bill Cosby Lola T94/00-Ford					Did not complete qualifying attempt		
NQ	Tero Palmroth (SF)	44	Arizona Motor-Sport Racing Lola T94/00-Ford					Did not complete qualifying attempt		
NQ	Geoff Brabham (AUS)	59T	Menard Glidden Special Lola T93/00-Menard V6					Did not complete qualifying attempt		
NQ	Gary Bettenhausen (USA)	61	Bettenhausen Motorsports Penske PC22-Ilmor/D					Did not complete qualifying attempt		
NQ	Buddy Lazier (USA)	23	Leader Card Financial World Lola T93/00-Ilmor/C+					Did not attempt to qualify		
NQ	Pancho Carter (USA)	30	McCormack Alfa Laval/Cybergenics Lola T93/00-Ilmor/C+					Did not attempt to qualify		
NQ	Stephan Gregoire (F)	30	McCormack Alfa Laval/Cybergenics Lola T93/00-Ilmor/C+					Did not attempt to qualify		
NQ	*Ross Bentley (CDN)	39	Dale Coyne Racing Lola T92/00-Ilmor/A					Did not attempt to qualify		
NQ	Johnny Parsons (USA)	42	Greenfield Industries Lola T93/00-Greenfield GC209T					Did not attempt to qualify		
NQ	Al Unser (USA)	44	Arizona Motor-Sport Racing Lola T94/00-Ford					Did not attempt to qualify		
NQ	Roberto Moreno (BR)	44	Arizona Motor-Sport Racing Lola T94/00-Ford					Did not attempt to qualify		
NQ	Didier Theys (B)	64	Project Indy Marcelo Group Lola T93/00-Ford					Did not attempt to qualify		
NQ	Jim Crawford (GB)	74	Riley & Scott Inc. Lola T91/00-Buick V6					Did not attempt to qualify		
NQ	Jeff Andretti (USA)	94	Hemelgarn Gillette Lola T92/00-Buick V6					Did not attempt to qualify		

*denotes Rookie driver   **including one-lap penalty

Caution flags: Laps 7–9, spin/Vitolo; laps 21–27, accident/Guerrero; laps 30–40, accident/Dobson, Groff; laps 92–100, accident/Matsuda, Paul Jr., Vitolo/Mansell; laps 137–139, debris; laps 185–190, accident/Fittipaldi; laps 197–200, accident/Fox. Total seven for 43 laps.

Lap leaders: Al Unser Jr., 1–23 (23 laps); Emerson Fittipaldi, 24–61 (38 laps); Jacques Villeneuve, 62–63 (2 laps); Fittipaldi, 64–124 (61 laps); Villeneuve, 125–129 (5 laps); Fittipaldi, 130–133 (4 laps); Unser Jr., 134–138 (5 laps); Fittipaldi, 139–164 (26 laps); Unser Jr., 165–168 (4 laps); Fittipaldi, 169–184 (16 laps); Unser Jr., 185–200 (16 laps). **Totals:** Fittipaldi, 145 laps; Unser Jr., 48 laps; Villeneuve, 7 laps.

Fastest race lap: Fittipaldi, 40.783s, 220.680 mph, on lap 121.

Championship positions: 1 Unser Jr., 58 pts; **2** Fittipaldi, 38; **3** Michael Andretti, 37; **4** Mansell, 35; **5** Vasser, 34; **6** Gordon, 30; **7** Johansson, 25; **8** Mario Andretti, 24; **9** Boesel, 17; **10** Villeneuve, Gugelmin and Fabi, 16; **13** Rahal, 14; **14** M. Groff, 13; **15** Fernandez, 8; **16** Sharp, 6; **17** Cheever and Goodyear, 5; **19** Herta, 4; **20** John Andretti, 3; **21** Luyendyk and Tracy, 2; **23** Dobson, Jones, Freon and Till, 1.

MILWAUKEE

Photos: Michael C. Brown

The most surprising aspect of the Miller Genuine Draft 200 was that three sessions of official practice, plus qualifying on Saturday afternoon, gave no real indication of what was to follow on race day.

True enough, Paul Tracy had set the fastest lap in practice, with Emerson Fittipaldi third in his identical Marlboro Penske-Ilmor/D. Al Unser Jr., meanwhile, languished in ninth. After qualifying, the trio lined up second, eighth and 11th on the grid respectively. Nothing special there.

But, oh boy, was it a different story in the race!

Tracy took the lead from pole-sitter Raul Boesel on the opening lap, and pretty soon Fittipaldi, closely followed by Unser, came carving through to the front.

Unser, fresh from victory at Indianapolis just seven days earlier, and powered this time by a 'regular' Ilmor Indy V8/D engine in place of the Mercedes, took over the lead on lap 31. Amazingly, by lap 46, everyone bar his two team-mates was at least one lap down. This was a rout.

Mercifully, a shower of rain brought proceedings to a halt eight laps short of the scheduled 200. By that time Unser and Fittipaldi were two laps clear even of Tracy.

'My third win of the season is just wonderful,' said Unser. 'It really shows the depth of the Penske Indy Car team.'

After almost 160 laps of uninterrupted green-flag racing, a couple of cautions served to liven up the later stages. On what proved to be the final restart, Michael Andretti nosed in front of Nigel Mansell, who had led the pursuit of the Penskes for most of the afternoon. And when the first spots of rain began to fall just a few moments later, any hopes Mansell had of retrieving fourth place were taken away by the yellow flags. It hardly seemed to matter. As eventual sixth-place finisher Robby Gordon pointed out, 'We got beat so bad today it was embarrassing.'

A (3)1-2-3 clean sweep for Marlboro Team Penske at Milwaukee underlined the emerging dominance of the red and white cars with the season only five races old.

Far left: Even the rain fails to dampen the spirits of drivers Emerson, Al Jr. and Paul on the rostrum.

Michael C. Brown

QUALIFYING

Newman-Haas drivers Nigel Mansell and Mario Andretti were first into their stride when the Milwaukee Mile opened for practice on Friday morning. The two Kmart/Texaco Havoline Lola-Ford/Cosworths traded fastest times for the first part of the 90-minute session, with Mansell's level of confidence such that he didn't even bother going out for the final 20 minutes or so.

His best time of 23.162 seconds (155.430 mph) was eclipsed by three other drivers in the closing stages, yet Mansell wasn't unduly concerned. Indeed he was anxious not to use up too many of his mandatory allocation of seven sets of tires.

'After the Speedway, where [with no limitation] you throw tires at the car, you have a tendency to do the same thing here,' explained Mansell. 'Pretty soon you run out of tires.

'I'm happy enough. The car's close.

All the others put new tires on. What's the point in that?'

Mansell went on to set the fastest time of the day, 22.851 seconds (157.544 mph), during the second session later in the afternoon. Again he parked early.

By Saturday, however, the pace had increased dramatically. This time Paul Tracy emerged fastest at 22.376 seconds (160.888 mph).

'The team worked on the car last night and we shared information with Emerson's crew, so I had Emerson's set-up on my car this morning,' revealed Tracy. 'My car was running strong.'

Fittipaldi, having complained of 'understeer, understeer' on Friday, was close behind in third. Both Penskes surely would be contenders for the pole, along with Boesel, a mere 0.001s slower than Tracy in Dick Simon's Duracell Charger Lola-Ford. Robby Gordon, fourth in the morning, was just over a tenth away from the outright pace in Derrick

Walker's Valvoline/Cummins Lola-Ford, with Teo Fabi for once leading the Reynard contingent, fifth in Jim Hall's Pennzoil-liveried, Ilmor/D-powered car.

And so to qualifying.

Jacques Villeneuve was the first to go. Once again, the French-Canadian displayed his talent by producing his fastest lap thus far at 22.597 seconds in the Player's Reynard-Ford.

'The car is great,' he shrilled. 'There was still a little grip left in it. I did a better job in Phoenix. I could've kept more throttle and maybe made a tenth or two. Still, I think it was a good qualifying run.'

Villeneuve's run remained good enough for fourth on the grid.

Pole, however, for the second straight year, was claimed by the amazing Boesel at 22.310 seconds (161.364 mph).

'I was happy with my effort,' said the Brazilian, 'but the car wasn't as good as I would like. Last year I was happy with my car in qualifying. It

was a great lap. My car was on rails. This year, no.'

His comments were echoed by Tracy, whose 22.394 seconds stood as second best on the day.

'I think, aerodynamically, we're close,' he said, 'but mechanically we're just a little bit off.'

Gordon garnered third among the closely matched field, with Scott Goodyear (Budweiser Lola-Ford) and Dominic Dobson (PacWest Lola-Ford) producing by far their best form of the year to date in fifth and sixth. Rookie Bryan Herta also stunned the establishment, seventh in A.J. Foyt's similar Copenhagen car in only his second PPG Cup start. Behind him were many more illustrious names, including Fittipaldi (eighth), Mansell (ninth) and Unser Jr., surprisingly far back in 11th. Nevertheless, a glance at the grid sheet showed the series' true competitiveness. No fewer than 19 cars were within one second of the pole-winner. The race promised to be a cracker.

Michael Andretti, Bryan Herta, Nigel Mansell and Mario Andretti weave their way through a separate battle between the lapped cars of Willy T. Ribbs (24), Mark Smith (15) and Hiro Matsushita (22). The race was remarkable for having only one retirement (Stefan Johansson) from the 26-car field.

RACE

The final practice session Sunday morning was interrupted twice due to single-car incidents, involving Dobson, who spun on cold tires, and Adrian Fernandez, who lost it due to a water leak.

Fernandez had switched back and forth between Rick Galles' pair of Tecate/Quaker State Reynard-Ilmors, due to a variety of problems, but he much preferred the feel of his primary car, 94I-008, to the one he qualified, 003. Thus, despite incurring some minor damage in the warm-up, 008 was the car he would race.

Dobson's car also was repairable, despite damage to both left-side corners.

All 26 qualifiers were ready to go for the relatively late 3 p.m. start, and another record-sized crowd, 45,254-strong, was jammed into the old Wisconsin State Fair Park facility. It made for a fine sight.

The start was clean and fast. Boe-sel and Tracy raced side by side through the south end of the track, whereupon Tracy, on the outside, had a better run on the exit of Turn Two which enabled him to nose ahead on the back stretch. Boesel, though, wasn't about to give up. The Brazilian braked later on the inside to regain the advantage into Turn Three, only for Tracy to make a better exit from Turn Four and take the lead as they sped across the line in front of the packed grandstand to complete lap one.

Gordon also had gotten the better of Villeneuve for third, while up into fifth place, sensationally, came Michael Andretti. From 12th on the grid, Andretti had taken his patented high line through Turns One and Two, already passing almost a half-dozen cars, before sneaking inside an unsuspecting Herta on the entry to Turn Three.

The early laps provided plenty of thrilling action before the order began to settle down. By lap ten,

Tracy had opened up a little breathing space over Boesel. Gordon and Villeneuve were embroiled in a fierce fight for third, while close behind and moving up fast after a cautious start were Fittipaldi and Unser.

Even Michael Andretti could offer no resistance to the Penskes. Nor could Herta, who continued to run impressively ahead of the Newman-Haas pair, Mansell and Mario Andretti.

'When Al Jr. passed me I figured he was going to be the guy to beat,' noted Herta. 'He went past so easily. The Penskes drove right on by. They just blew past.'

Fittipaldi and Unser continued their march forward, breezing past Villeneuve and Gordon in short order, then quickly reeling in Tracy and Boesel. The pole-winner, indeed, already was beginning to experience a push complaint, which was costing him valuable momentum coming off the corners.

By lap 19, the three Penskes were in nose-to-tail formation at the front of the pack. And already they were beginning to carve through slower traffic.

Three tours later, Tracy could hold off the tide no longer. First Fittipaldi then Unser swept past. Soon the Canadian began to fall away in third, although he was never under threat from anyone else.

'My car was loose after about 15 or 20 laps,' related Tracy. 'I was just hanging on.'

On lap 30, as Fittipaldi and Unser encountered a four-car train battling mightily over 11th place, Unser made his move for the front. Initially his challenge was rejected, but next time around he was able to find a clear piece of road in Turn Four. Fittipaldi, boxed in by a slower car, had no choice but to capitulate.

Gordon, who had slipped back to sixth by lap 14, soon was moving forward again. On lap 36 he repassed Villeneuve for fourth place – and, effectively, 'best of the rest,' since the Penskes were long gone. Boesel also remained close behind, along with Mansell and Michael Andretti, who on lap 40 was next to fall a lap down to the race leaders.

Within six laps, Unser had lapped the entire group. Now only Fittipaldi, who was a couple of seconds back, having been unable to deal with the traffic quite so deftly, and Tracy, running a distant third, were left on the lead lap.

On lap 54, just after one-quarter distance, Mansell moved ahead of Gor-

don for fourth place, sliding through on the inside line on the exit of Turn Two. Soon he began to edge clear, leaving Gordon, whose Lola's handling had deteriorated, to come under pressure from Michael Andretti.

Positions were changing almost constantly as drivers fought to keep abreast of the effects of diminishing fuel loads and increasing tire wear. Only now were the drivers beginning to fully appreciate the consequences of off-season rule changes which left them with drastically reduced aerodynamic downforce (see sidebar). Almost everyone commented afterward that their cars would go loose for a while, then revert to a push and so forth. Only the Penskes seemed able to maintain any consistency.

On lap 68, Unser came onto pit road for his first scheduled stop. Significantly, he took on four 'sticker' (brand-new) tires. Fittipaldi followed him in three laps later. Then came Tracy. The pursuing pack, with all but Mansell by now at least two laps in arrears, preferred to wait, hoping – in vain – for a caution.

Fittipaldi's stop was slightly longer than Unser's. Consequently, the gap between them grew to as much as 15 seconds. Little by little, Fittipaldi began to chip away at that deficit. By the halfway point, 100 laps, the margin had been halved.

Tracy and Mansell each were on a lap by themselves in third and fourth, with Michael Andretti's Reynard three laps down. Herta continued to run strongly in sixth, albeit under increasing pressure from Gordon, who lost time by stalling at his first stop, and Boesel. Stefan Johansson also was having a good run in his Alumax Penske PC22-Ilmor/D, with Jimmy Vasser running solidly in tenth with Jim Hayhoe's Conseco/STP Reynard-Ford. Behind him were Bobby Rahal, gradually picking up his pace in the Miller Genuine Draft Lola-Honda, and Villeneuve, who had lost time with severe oversteer toward the end of his first stint.

The hectic pace continued unabated until lap 157 when the first full-course caution was called, due to some debris on the track. Phew! Finally, an opportunity to catch a breath, and take stock of the situation.

The Penskes, of course, were untouchable. Even though all three Marlboro cars had already made their second scheduled stops, they remained well out of reach.

Mansell was unfortunate enough to have made his fuel stop one lap

Bobby Rahal *(left)* **returned to the Honda-powered Miller Genuine Draft Lola for the Milwaukee race, and took seventh place.**

Bottom: **Scott Goodyear's lackluster season in the Budweiser King Racing Lola continued. Fifth place in qualifying promised much but it all went awry in the race, with his car suffering from chronic handling problems.**

On the knife-edge

The historic Milwaukee Mile provided a second opportunity to gauge the effectiveness of last winter's rule changes, which demanded the use of smaller two-plane rear wings on the one-mile ovals. This time, however, unlike at Phoenix, where cars were able to take advantage of a grippier new track surface laid following the race in 1993, lap speeds were significantly slower than before – at least during the race.

Almost all the teams found difficulty in maintaining a consistent balance for their cars under race conditions.

'You've got no rear-end downforce,' said Ken Anderson, race engineer on Stefan Johansson's Alumax Penske. 'You're treading such a fine line here. It's like threading a needle.'

Winner Al Unser Jr.'s fastest race lap, at 24.584 seconds (146.438 mph), was substantially slower than Raul Boesel's best of 23.478 seconds (153.338 mph) one year earlier. The one-second differential seemed to be consistent throughout the field.

In qualifying, however, times were remarkably similar to those of one year ago . . . save for Boesel's sensational 1993 pole-winning track record at 21.719 seconds (165.752 mph), which the Brazilian described later as 'a perfect lap.' Fittipaldi's second-fastest time of 22.352 seconds was considered much more representative. Boesel again was on top this time around, but at a time of 22.310 seconds. The spread behind him was much closer than in 1993.

The reason for the equality in qualifying between 1993 and 1994 can be explained primarily by the effect of fresh Goodyear tires, which enabled drivers to maintain higher cornering speeds.

Under race conditions, however, performance deteriorated quickly as the tires lost their 'edge.' Thus, while straightline speeds were increased by as much as five per cent over 1993, due to the improved acceleration caused by a decrease in drag from the smaller wings, cornering capabilities were dramatically impaired by the cutbacks in downforce and grip. This effect was exacerbated when cars ran in traffic (which was almost continual in race conditions), with turbulent air from the car in front contributing to a further reduction in available downforce.

In years past, teams had been able to compensate for the loss of grip by providing more aerodynamic download – primarily by increasing the wing area, which led to development of the multi-element 'cascade' wings. But not any more. Set-ups for race conditions therefore assumed even greater importance, and Penske Racing clearly proved far superior in overcoming this difficulty to any other team.

before the caution lights flashed on. By the time he was back on the track, he had fallen another lap down and into the clutches of Gordon, Michael Andretti and Rahal, all of whom were able to make their own stops under yellow, without losing a lap.

Prior to the yellow, Fittipaldi had been charging hard. He had reduced Unser's lead to just a few car lengths, and now the caution gave him a fresh opportunity to look for a way past. He tried hard, too, although Unser proved up to the challenge.

Farther back, Andretti sought to pass Gordon as soon as the green flags flew. On lap 165, after a wheel-to-wheel battle through Turns One and Two, then on down the back straightaway, Andretti squeezed through on the inside going into Turn Three. Next in his sights was Mansell.

Incredibly, the only retirement of the day came after the leaders had completed 170 laps, when the Ilmor/D engine let go in Johansson's Penske. The Swede had been running 13th. A huge cloud of smoke as Johansson pulled off to the inside of Turn Two was enough to bring out the yellow flags again.

The next restart came on lap 180. Again, Unser accelerated hard and

early to ensure he was able to withstand any approaches from Fittipaldi. Back in the pack, Andretti was on the move again, taking advantage of heavy traffic to make a move on Mansell for fourth place.

'I passed him on the outside in Turn Three,' related Andretti. 'I knew that's how I was gonna have to do it, and I knew it was gonna be a hard fight holding him back there. Then the rain started and we were OK.'

Sure enough, just a lap or so later, with the first spots of rain starting to fall, out came the yellows one last time. The field continued to circulate behind the pace car for another ten laps, but by then the cause was hopeless. Finally, as the rain intensified, the red and checkered flags were shown together. Andretti's position as first in the non-Penske class was secure.

'It was as good as we could do,' reasoned Andretti. 'I mean, we drove our butts off and we were lucky to get fourth in the end. But I'll take fourth.'

Mansell was unlucky to end up fifth. Both were three laps down to the flying Penskes of Unser and Fittipaldi. So were Gordon and Rahal.

'We passed a lot of cars today,' asserted Rahal after a fine drive from 19th on the grid. 'My car was

handling well but I didn't get a chance to go after Gordon and Mansell. I thought I could have gotten them before the end.

'Our crew gave me a good set-up. I could run almost anywhere on the race track. Handling is so critical at this place.'

Boesel was on a lap by himself in eighth, having battled a severe push all afternoon. Next were rookies Villeneuve, who lost time with a stop-and-go penalty, assessed for passing Vasser under yellow, and Herta, who also fell back after stalling at his final stop. Vasser and Scott Sharp (PacWest Lola-Ford), on his first-ever visit to Milwaukee, drove well to complete the point scorers in what had proved to be an exciting race, even if it was totally dominated by the Penskes.

But one question remained: could Fittipaldi have passed Unser if the race had run its full 200-lap distance?

'I'd have liked to continue [under] green and drive,' said Fittipaldi with his familiar wide smile. 'I think it would be incredible between myself and Junior but, you know, it started raining. It was getting slippery. For sure [the officials] were right to stop the race. They made the right decision.'

We'll never know.

SNIPPETS

• Dale Coyne's team suffered a frustrating weekend when both Johnny Unser (above), entrusted with the Mi-Jack Lola T93/00-Ford for the first time, and Canadian Ross Bentley, still saddled with the engagingly nicknamed 'Agfa-saurus' Lola T92/00-Ilmor/A, crashed in practice. Neither was able to make the 26-car starting field.

• Bobby Rahal's form on race day in his Miller Genuine Draft Lola-Honda was a revelation, especially considering the Japanese engine's embarrassing failure at Indianapolis. Rahal, though, despite qualifying only 19th, had remained optimistic. 'Same old problem,' he lamented. 'Horsepower. You can only go so fast. But I think we'll be in better shape for the race. We'll see.'

• Indy Car Rookie Bryan Herta (below) earned one of the biggest cheers from the always-knowledgeable Milwaukee crowd after qualifying a strong seventh in the ever-popular A.J. Foyt's car. 'Every day in the car I get a little

more comfortable,' said Herta, whose total experience in an Indy car amounted to a test at Sebring the previous winter, the month of May at Indy and a brief shakedown run for Newman-Haas earlier in the year at Milwaukee. 'I think our car should be good for the race. It's very consistent and I can run the high line or the low line. It's very forgiving.' Herta was true to his word in earning his second top-ten finish in as many starts.

• Scott Goodyear was rather more optimistic than of late after qualifying a strong fifth in his Budweiser Lola-Ford. Race day, however, was a disaster. Chronic oversteer left him 22nd at the finish, 14 laps behind the leaders.

Photos: Michael C. Brown

PPG INDY CAR WORLD SERIES • ROUND 5

MILLER GENUINE DRAFT 200

MILWAUKEE MILE, WEST ALLIS, WISCONSIN

JUNE 5, 192 LAPS – 192.000 MILES

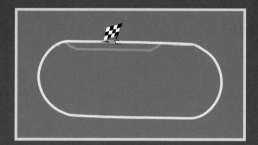

Place	Driver (Nat.)	No.	Team Sponsors Car-Engine	Q Speed (mph)	Q Time	Q Pos.	Laps	Time/Status	Ave. (mph)	Pts.
1	Al Unser Jr. (USA)	31	Marlboro Team Penske PC23-Ilmor/D	157.997	22.785s	11	192	1h 36m 57.964s	118.804	21
2	Emerson Fittipaldi (BR)	2	Marlboro Team Penske PC23-Ilmor/D	158.269	22.746s	8	192	1h 36m 59.458s	118.774	16
3	Paul Tracy (CDN)	3	Marlboro Team Penske PC23-Ilmor/D	160.757	22.394s	2	190	Running		14
4	Michael Andretti (USA)	8	Ganassi Target/Scotch Video Reynard 94I-Ford	157.399	22.872s	12	189	Running		12
5	Nigel Mansell (GB)	1	Newman-Haas Kmart/Texaco Havoline Lola T94/00-Ford	158.224	22.753s	9	189	Running		10
6	Robby Gordon (USA)	9	Walker Valvoline/Cummins Special Lola T94/00-Ford	159.680	22.545s	3	189	Running		8
7	Bobby Rahal (USA)	4	Rahal-Hogan Miller Genuine Draft Lola T94/00-Honda	154.777	23.259s	19	189	Running		6
8	Raul Boesel (BR)	5	Simon Duracell/Fuji Film/Mobil/Sadia Lola T94/00-Ford	161.364	22.310s	1	188	Running		6
9	*Jacques Villeneuve (CDN)	12	Forsythe-Green Player's Ltd. Reynard 94I-Ford	159.317	22.597s	4	187	Running		4
10	*Bryan Herta (USA)	14	A.J. Foyt Copenhagen Racing Lola T94/00-Ford	158.632	22.694s	7	187	Running		3
11	Jimmy Vasser (USA)	18	Hayhoe Conseco/STP Reynard 94I-Ford	155.415	23.164s	16	187	Running		2
12	*Scott Sharp (USA)	71	PacWest Racing Group Lola T94/00-Ford	155.736	23.116s	15	186	Running		1
13	Dominic Dobson (USA)	17	PacWest Racing Group Lola T94/00-Ford	158.732	22.680s	6	185	Running		
14	Mario Andretti (USA)	6	Newman-Haas Kmart/Texaco Havoline Lola T94/00-Ford	157.023	22.927s	13	185	Running		
15	Mauricio Gugelmin (BR)	88	Ganassi Hollywood Reynard 94I-Ford	155.016	23.223s	17	184	Running		
16	Adrian Fernandez (MEX)	7	Galles Tecate/Quaker State Reynard 94I-Ilmor/D	149.982	24.003s	26	184	Running		
17	Teo Fabi (I)	11	Hall Pennzoil Special Reynard 94I-Ilmor/D	158.159	22.762s	10	184	Running		
18	Buddy Lazier (USA)	23	Leader Card Financial World Lola T93/00-Ilmor/C	150.665	23.894s	24	183	Running		
19	Mike Groff (USA)	10	Rahal-Hogan Motorola Lola T94/00-Honda	152.103	23.668s	23	181	Running		
20	Marco Greco (BR)	25	Simon Arciero Project Indy Lola T94/00-Ford	153.005	23.529s	21	181	Running		
21	Arie Luyendyk (NL)	28	Indy Regency Eurosport/Boost Monaco Lola T94/00-Ilmor/D	155.011	23.224s	18	180	Running		
22	Scott Goodyear (CDN)	40	Budweiser King Racing Lola T94/00-Ford	158.748	22.677s	5	178	Running		
23	Hiro Matsushita (J)	22	Simon Panasonic/Duskin Lola T94/00-Ford	150.195	23.969s	25	178	Running		
24	Mark Smith (USA)	15	Walker Craftsman Tools Lola T94/00-Ford	152.476	23.610s	22	177	Running		
25	Willy T. Ribbs (USA)	24	Walker Service Merchandise/Bill Cosby Lola T94/00-Ford	153.617	23.435s	20	174	Running		
26	Stefan Johansson (S)	16	Bettenhausen Alumax Aluminum Penske PC22-Ilmor/D	155.760	23.112s	14	163	Engine		
NQ	Johnny Unser (USA)	19	Coyne The Mi-Jack Car Lola T93/00-Ford	no speed	no time	–	–	Accident/did not qualify		
NQ	Ross Bentley (CDN)	39	Coyne Agfa Film Lola T92/00-Ilmor/A	no speed	no time	–	–	Accident/did not qualify		

denotes Rookie driver

Caution flags: Laps 157–161, debris; laps 170–178, blown engine/Johansson; laps 181–192, rain. Total three for 26 laps.

Lap leaders: Paul Tracy, 1–22 (22 laps); Emerson Fittipaldi, 23–30 (8 laps); Al Unser Jr., 31–68 (38 laps); Fittipaldi, 69–71 (3 laps); Unser Jr., 72–128 (57 laps); Fittipaldi, 129–132 (4 laps); Unser Jr., 133–192 (60 laps). **Totals:** Unser Jr., 155 laps; Tracy, 22 laps; Fittipaldi, 15 laps.

Fastest race lap: Unser Jr., 24.584s, 146.438 mph, on lap 166.

Championship positions: 1 Unser Jr., 79 pts; **2** Fittipaldi, 54; **3** Michael Andretti, 49; **4** Mansell, 45; **5** Gordon, 38; **6** Vasser, 36; **7** Johansson, 25; **8** Mario Andretti, 24; **9** Boesel, 23; **10** Villeneuve and Rahal, 20; **12** Tracy, Gugelmin and Fabi, 16; **15** M. Groff, 13; **16** Fernandez, 8; **17** Herta and Sharp, 7; **19** Cheever and Goodyear, 5; **21** John Andretti, 4; **22** Luyendyk, 2; **23** Dobson, Jones, Freon and Till, 1.

DETROIT

Victory in the ITT Automotive Detroit Grand Prix was just what Paul Tracy needed. The talented Canadian had endured all manner of misfortune in the opening five races of the season, including being involved in someone else's accident while leading at Phoenix and suffering gearbox problems while holding the point at Long Beach. At Indianapolis he made a mistake and crashed on the afternoon before Pole Day qualifying. With four PPG Cup races in the books, his points tally stood at a meager two, courtesy of poles at Phoenix and Long Beach. He had yet to finish a race. Tracy was beginning to think the whole world was conspiring against him.

Milwaukee, at last, had brought his first finish, even though a handling imbalance restricted him to a distant third place. It was a start, something to build from.

He arrived in Detroit confident of a strong showing, and indeed he shadowed series-leading Marlboro Penske Racing team-mate Al Unser Jr. through most of the 77-lap contest. But then, following a full-course caution and pit stops which left several slower cars ahead of the two leaders on the road, Tracy inadvertently nudged Unser smartly from behind under braking for Turn Eight. The impact was enough to send Unser into the tire barrier and out of contention. Tracy, meanwhile, scooted past and went on to victory.

The Canadian's delight at winning was tempered by acute feelings of guilt. He knew he had made a mistake. Unser, the PPG Cup leader, had been robbed of an almost certain 20 points.

'It's happened, it's over,' pronounced a contrite Tracy.

'You can't change the result now. All I can do is offer my hand in apology [to Unser] and hope he accepts it.'

Michael C. Brown

The dice rolled Paul Tracy's way at Detroit as the young Canadian *(left)* finally posted his first win of the 1994 season. It was not achieved without some controversy, however, as in the course of the race he nudged team-mate and race leader Al Unser Jr. into the barrier and out of contention. Note the tire marks on the nose of Tracy's Penske!

QUALIFYING

The talk during practice and qualifying in Belle Isle Park was centered upon the mid-season dominance of Roger Penske's team, which was seeking to win its fifth straight race. Nigel Mansell, however, had other ideas.

'We've put a lot of energy into this weekend,' he said. 'It's been a bit trying following the red and white cars. Hopefully we can play with them this weekend.'

Mansell set the pace from the moment practice began. He was fastest by a full second in the opening session and, although he was narrowly beaten to the provisional pole by Emerson Fittipaldi on Friday, the Englishman bounced back with a sensational lap record to clinch the pole Saturday afternoon.

'We made a few changes to the car and I think we went the right way. I'm very grateful to my mechanics,' said Mansell. 'They worked real hard.'

So did Mansell, who used every inch of the track – as well as a few touches on the cement barriers – to clinch the pole.

'The back end was sliding a bit,' explained Mansell. 'It was just a little soft kiss [on the barrier] and it helped to straighten out the back of the car.'

It was an impressive effort.

'Nigel's car was working well and his driving was excellent,' commented Tracy after qualifying third. 'I couldn't match that pace.'

Tracy was the meat in a Penske sandwich, with team-mates Unser ahead, second on the grid, and Fittipaldi behind, fourth. All were confident of their chances on race day, despite complaints after qualifying of excessive mid-corner understeer. The condition prevented them from applying full throttle as soon as they would have liked on the exits – and therefore challenging Mansell for the pole.

'This track is just a real big compromise,' confided Scotsman Tom Brown, Fittipaldi's race engineer. 'What you gain in one place you lose in another. You've just got to figure out if the gain is worth the loss. Also, on this track, every time you go out, there's more grip. You can really confuse yourself.'

Not so for the Penske team. It remained as focused as ever. 'We're ready to go racing, for sure,' confirmed Unser. 'The Penske's a super race car. We've been working on it vigorously. I'm extremely happy with the race car.'

No one else broke the 1m 11s barrier. Closest, though, was Mauricio Gugelmin, who posted an impressive fifth-best time in Chip Ganassi's low-budget Hollywood Reynard-Ford.

'I was surprised, because it's not an easy circuit,' noted Gugelmin, visiting Belle Isle for the first time. 'The car is good and it's nice to turn left and right again. There are no straights to speak of. Looking at the computer, you're pretty busy most of the time. Here, you have to remember the amount of time you spend in the slow corners. So there's time to be gained in the slow corners.'

The typically pragmatic approach adopted by Gugelmin, race engineer John Bright and crew chief Grant Weaver had paid dividends. Ganassi team-mate Michael Andretti, by contrast, was a disappointed, and disgruntled, 17th on the grid, despite (or perhaps because of) trying a variety of different suspension configurations on his Reynard 94I.

Bobby Rahal also produced a fine effort, sixth in the steadily improving Miller Genuine Draft Lola-Honda.

'We've been working with the chassis and making some gains there,' noted Rahal, who was also using a torquier Honda V8 for the first time.

'It's hard to say how much better it is,' he related. 'From what I understand, there's not much more power but there's better response low down [in the rev range], so I think that's a plus. At least we're up where we belong.'

Jacques Villeneuve and Teo Fabi confirmed the effectiveness of Malcolm Oastler's Reynard design by claiming seventh and eighth on the grid. The pair were powered by Ford and Ilmor engines respectively.

RACE

For the final warm-up session on race morning, Tracy and his race engineer, Nigel Beresford, decided to adopt the chassis set-up preferred by Unser during qualifying. Tracy, who found the car improved in slow corners and 'edgier' in fast corners, responded by establishing the fastest time.

Mansell, though, made full use of his pole to lead the field up toward the starter's stand at a fast clip, leaving outside front row qualifier Unser no hope of posing a challenge into Turn One. Tracy followed dutifully in third ahead of Fittipaldi, Gugelmin and Rahal. Fabi made a forceful start to run around the outside of Villeneuve at the first corner, as Robby Gordon overcame Mario Andretti for ninth.

Farther back, braking problems caused 15th qualifier Mike Groff to embed his Motorola Lola-Honda deep into the tire wall at Turn Three. A separate incident delayed Stefan Johansson's Alumax Penske PC22-Ilmor and the Eurosport Lola-Ilmor of Arie Luyendyk. All three continued with various degrees of delay.

On lap two, Unser gave Mansell a vivid exhibition of the Penske's superb traction capabilities when he drew effortlessly alongside on the exit of the tight Turn 12, then took advantage of his inside line to assume the lead under braking for Turn 13.

'I didn't even have time to move over,' said an incredulous Mansell. 'I came out of the corner flat out, really good, and I looked over and there he was beside me. I couldn't believe it.' Half a lap later, Tracy gave Mansell another dose of the same medicine, when the Canadian's fine exit to the right-left-right complex forming Turns Four, Five and Six assured him of an unassailable position for Turn Seven.

The two Penskes soon began to edge away from Mansell, who instead was intent on staying ahead of Fittipaldi. The order behind remained unchanged as the track lived up to its reputation for allowing precious few overtaking opportunities, despite having been widened slightly in several locations.

Mansell had fallen as much as five seconds in arrears of Tracy after seven laps, although that deficit was swiftly negated next time around when the yellow flags flew to warn of two stricken cars out on the course.

One was Boesel's Duracell Lola, which had fallen victim to a complete electrical failure. The other was Groff's, which had been towed out of the tires after its first-lap incident, only to have the brakes seize up completely. The hydraulic line feeding the rear of the car had been inadvertently pinched when the undertray was attached prior to the start, leaving Groff with absolutely no retardation on the rear end.

Almost immediately after the restart, Adrian Fernandez, having taken over 11th from Boesel, made his way into the pits with a puncture on his Tecate/Quaker State Reynard-Ilmor. The Mexican worsened his plight by stalling the engine. He rejoined at the tail of the field.

The game of high-speed follow-the-leader continued until the end of lap 20 when the yellow flags flew again, this time due to an incident in Turn One involving Dominic Dobson's PacWest Lola-Ford and Alessandro Zampedri's year-old Mi-Jack Lola-Ford. The pair had been disputing 17th.

'I believe I picked up some debris and punctured a rear tire,' explained Dobson. 'The car was getting looser and looser and I think the tire was going down, and I lost it in Turn One.'

A close-following Zampedri was unable to avoid Dobson's car as it slid backward into the wall.

This time all the leaders took the opportunity to make their first scheduled pit stops. Two drivers, however, took a gamble on an alternative

Emerson Fittipaldi *(above)* took second place to keep his PPG Cup hopes very much alive.

The Reynard chassis went well at Detroit and Teo Fabi *(right)* scored his best result of the season to date to take fourth place for the Hall/Pennzoil team.

Mauricio Gugelmin *(left)* put in a very convincing performance in Chip Ganassi's Hollywood Reynard to qualify fifth fastest. In the race Mauricio's chances of a podium finish were blighted by tardy pitwork which saw the unfortunate Brazilian slip back to eighth place.

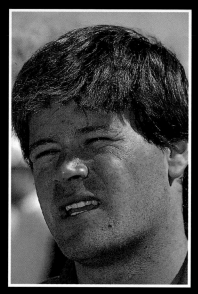

Robby Gordon *(above)* produced another mature performance to bring the Valvoline/Cummins Lola home in third place only yards behind Fittipaldi.

Seventh-placed Jacques Villeneuve showed his undoubted ability on the tricky Belle Isle Park street circuit but, in common with Gugelmin, he suffered through being delayed in the pits.

strategy. Mario Andretti duly moved up from tenth to second, trailing only Unser, while Bryan Herta, after a troubled practice, rose from 12th to fourth. Both had eschewed a stop and were attempting to complete the distance with only one visit to the pits.

Tracy lay between them as the field assembled for the restart. Fittipaldi ran fifth after passing Mansell during the pit stops. Behind, both Villeneuve and Gordon passed Fabi in similar fashion, while dreadfully slow stops by Gugelmin and Rahal saw them fall from fifth and sixth to tenth and 11th respectively. Both men were extremely upset, especially given the physical constraints of the Belle Isle course.

Tracy, anxious not to lose any ground to Unser, immediately out-braked Andretti for second place at Turn Three. A few corners later, Herta also executed a perfect pass on Andretti. The youngster had earlier moved up one position at the expense of Christian Danner, who was otherwise enjoying a fine run in his No Touch/Marcelo Group Lola T93/00-Ford. Herta, incredibly, remained the only driver outside of the Penske team to complete a successful overtaking maneuver within the top 20 positions.

Unser quickly established a comfortable margin of around four seconds over Tracy. At this juncture, the Canadian was content to follow at a respectful distance.

'In the middle of the race I was just pacing myself and hoping for an opportunity,' said Tracy. 'My crew radioed in and they were concerned if I was running too close [to Al] the car might have overheated; so I backed off.'

Herta continued to run strongly in third place. In fact, driving on a partial fuel load, he was able to pull away from Andretti, Fittipaldi and Mansell at almost a second per lap.

'I kept looking in my mirrors because I thought for sure Fittipaldi would be on my ass,' related Herta, 'but we were pulling away from him.'

On lap 37, Herta pitted for what he hoped would be his first and only stop for fuel and fresh tires. Andretti followed him in one lap later. The pair resumed in 13th (Herta) and 17th, although a handful of laps later Andretti slid off into the tire wall under braking for Turn Eight. He lost a couple of laps before he was able to resume.

Otherwise the status quo was maintained. Unser held a lead of 5.2

seconds over Tracy after 40 laps, with Fittipaldi another 16 seconds adrift. Mansell continued to chase the Brazilian, and in doing so had pulled away from a tight group of cars disputing fifth place in the order Villeneuve, Gordon, Fabi, Gugelmin, Rahal, Michael Andretti and Johansson, who had worked his way back to 11th after his early delay. Next in line was Fernandez, also charging along impressively after passing Fredrik Ekblom, Willy T. Ribbs, Jimmy Vasser and Scott Goodyear in quick succession.

On lap 49, however, just a couple of laps after Johansson had peeled off into the pits for service, Fernandez lost control under braking for Turn Three. An instant later he was spinning backward into the tire wall.

'I was just pushing too hard,' admitted Fernandez with refreshing candor.

As soon as the officials called for a full-course caution, Unser dived into the pits for his second stop. Service was completed with typical briskness by the Penske crew, such that his lead was never in jeopardy. Goodyear, Vasser and Ekblom, all running toward the end of the lead lap, followed Unser's example, although, to their chagrin, they were then trapped behind the pace car. Everyone else waited an extra lap before pitting.

Once again, the pit stops were crucial. This time, thanks to excellent work by the Newman-Haas crew, Mansell seemed set to redress the balance with Fittipaldi. Unfortunately, as he accelerated out of his pit stall, he was confronted by an equally eager Villeneuve who was attempting to gain access to the pit directly in front of Mansell's. To the credit of all concerned, there was no contact. But Mansell had lost critical momentum, allowing Fittipaldi to nip past and regain third position. The delay also cost Villeneuve two positions.

Ekblom headed for the pits again prior to the lap 55 restart, victim of a punctured tire, leaving Goodyear and Vasser to lead the field toward the green flag. The true race leaders, Unser and Tracy, followed close behind.

Tracy saw the slower traffic as an opportunity to put the pressure on Unser, perhaps hope for a mistake. Unfortunately, it was Tracy who erred. Approaching the braking zone for Turn Eight, Tracy was tucked in close underneath Unser's rear wing – but when the leader chose to brake slightly early, being

Despite a delay caused by a puncture, Swedish newcomer Fredrik Ekblom, pictured right running ahead of Brazilian Marco Greco's '94 Lola, took things steadily in the Dennis McCormack '93 Lola to finish 15th, one place in front of Willy T. Ribbs *(below right)* in his Service Merchandise/Bill Cosby T94/00.

careful not to be lured into making an injudicious challenge, Tracy was unable to avoid making contact with the rear of Unser's car.

Boom! Unser, brakes locked, was punted into the tire wall.

Tracy was through into the lead.

'I've never taken anybody out on purpose in my life,' declared Tracy, 'and I didn't take Al out on purpose. It's just unfortunate. It's frustrating. I knew I made a mistake. I was thinking, "What's Roger [Penske] going to think?" '

Penske, not surprisingly, wasn't best pleased by the incident. Nevertheless, his focus for the moment was centered upon his prospects of winning the race, which remained good. His drivers still held the first two positions.

A couple of laps later, a remarkably similar incident proved the undoing of Mansell, still looking in vain for a way around Fittipaldi. Once again, the pair had come upon a slower car, Scott Sharp's PacWest Lola-Ford, and Mansell was caught off guard when Fittipaldi braked appreciably earlier than normal for Turn Four. The Englishman locked up his brakes in a desperate attempt to avoid contact, but it was too late for that.

This time Fittipaldi's incredible reflexes enabled him to maintain control of his car. Mansell, meanwhile, brakes locked, skated into the tire wall.

The PPG Cup champion immediately unbuckled his belts, hopped from his car and performed an impressive stepping-stone routine as he made his way across the vertical rows of tires to safety. Damage to his Kmart Lola, however, was minimal, and a minute or so later he was being strapped back in, ready for a tow-start by the ever-efficient IndyCar Safety Team.

Mansell then returned to the pits, where his belts were properly refastened by his crew. He resumed the chase, by now a couple of laps down, only to coast in again shortly afterward with a dead engine. His eventful day was over.

The field regrouped again under the caution caused by Mansell's visit to the scenery, this time with Tracy holding a secure lead over Fittipaldi and Gordon. Next were Fabi, Michael Andretti, Rahal and the delayed Villeneuve. Gugelmin, to his intense annoyance, had fallen back another couple of places following another poor pit stop.

'Ridiculous,' fumed the Brazilian.

'We could have been third today easily. We had some understeer in the car but nothing drastic. I lost all my positions in the pit stops. They were the worst pit stops I've had in my life.'

Herta ran ninth, although team owner A.J. Foyt's one-stop strategy had been ruined by the full-course cautions. Wisely, the team opted to bring in Herta for a quick splash-and-go fuel stop, just to make sure he would have no difficulty in reaching the finish. He didn't even lose a place.

Unser followed in tenth, last on the lead lap and unable to make much of an impression on those in front due to a slightly bent right-front top wishbone.

The final portion of the race was comparatively uneventful. Tracy simply rocketed away in the lead. He left Fittipaldi more than four seconds back after the first lap of green, then extended his margin by more than a second per lap until his cushion stood at better than ten seconds.

'The car was perfect,' reflected Tracy, 'particularly on the last set of tires.'

Tracy finally kicked back into cruise mode the final couple of laps, such that his eventual margin of victory was trimmed to 9.249 seconds. Clearly there were some mixed emotions in the Penske pit, although team owner Roger Penske remained stoical.

'It's unfortunate for Al,' he agreed, 'but, hey, you know, that was tough racing. I guess even Mansell ran into Emerson, so it was awful tight racing.'

Tracy wasn't entirely comfortable with the circumstances of his success, but after stopping to pick up a Canadian flag on his cool-down lap, he steeled himself for the inevitable questions that would follow.

'It's tough to win that way but we were in there battling, I was pacing myself, and with 20 laps to go I knew we had to make a move soon,' said Tracy. 'What happened next was frustrating. I knew I made a mistake but at least we were able to finish 1-2.'

Fittipaldi, after edging clear of Gordon, was content to run in second, secure in the knowledge his points deficit to Unser would be reduced.

'My major concern was not to catch Paul,' confirmed Fittipaldi, 'it was to finish. My mind went back to [the transmission problems in] Long Beach. I was being very easy with the gearbox. I knew I must finish this race.'

Another solid performance by Gordon was rewarded with third place, while Fabi posted his best finish of the year, fourth, for Jim Hall's team.

'With better luck in the pits we might have finished ahead of Gordon,' noted the Italian. 'He beat us on both pit stops. But I can't complain. The car was better today. You're never happy to finish fourth but at least it's a start.'

The remaining positions on the lead lap did not change in the closing stages. Michael Andretti was delighted to take advantage of every opportunity presented to him in rising from 17th on the grid to fifth in his Target/Scotch Video Reynard-Ford, while Rahal, Villeneuve and Gugelmin were left to rue the effect of various mishaps on pit lane.

Unser, too, in tenth, was left to reflect upon what might have been.

The PPG Cup points leader initially refused to comment in public. Later, though, just as had been the case when Galmer team-mate Danny Sullivan robbed him of a win at Long Beach under very similar circumstances in 1992, Unser put on a brave face.

'I'm really happy that Marlboro Team Penske finished one and two,' he said. 'As far as my race is concerned, sometimes you eat the bear and sometimes the bear eats you; and today the bear got us. The good news is that we're still in the lead [of the PPG Cup standings] by 13 points ahead of my team-mate, Emerson Fittipaldi. Now we just have to concentrate on putting my car in Victory Lane for Portland.'

SNIPPETS

• Marlboro Penske Racing added another team member in Detroit, with the delightful Chris Mears (wife of Rick, who acts as a consultant to the team) joining in an official capacity to help out with media relations.

• Christian Danner (right) made amends for a poor first pit stop, which dropped him from 13th to 21st, to earn a creditable 12th-place finish – and one PPG Cup point – in his first Indy Car race of the season with Project Indy's '93 Lola-Ford. 'The speed of the car and the driver was faster than 12th,' concluded Danner, 'but we kept the old lady on the road and got a good finish.'

• Robby Gordon endured all manner of problems on Saturday. First of all, an engine problem severely curtailed his efforts in practice. The team duly set

about fitting a fresh Ford/Cosworth XB, only for a clutch problem to manifest itself. When it became apparent the car would not be ready in time for the final qualifying session,

Michael C. Brown

team owner Derrick Walker initially decided against taking out the team's spare Valvoline/Cummins Lola. But when lap times began tumbling and Gordon faced a distinct

possibility of not making the 28-car field, Walker changed his mind. Gordon – and the crew – rose to the challenge magnificently. Despite the fact he had not yet driven the spare car on the 14-turn circuit, Gordon soon established competitive times and finally earned tenth place on the grid.

• Fredrik Ekblom made his Indy Car debut at the wheel of Dennis McCormack's ex-Galles Lola T93/00-Ilmor/C+. The personable 22-year-old Swede, a graduate of Formula 3, British Formula 2 and Indy Lights, admitted to some nerves the first time he drove the car – 'There are some big names out there' – but quickly settled down to produce a workmanlike drive. He ran as high as 15th in the early stages and, despite a puncture, that is where he finished, one lap behind the leaders.

PPG INDY CAR WORLD SERIES • ROUND 6

ITT AUTOMOTIVE DETROIT GRAND PRIX

BELLE ISLE PARK STREET CIRCUIT, DETROIT, MICHIGAN

JUNE 12, 77 LAPS – 161.700 MILES

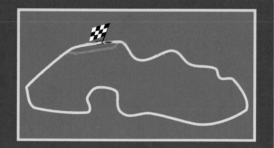

Place	Driver (Nat.)	No.	Team Sponsors Car-Engine	Q Speed (mph)	Q Time	Q Pos.	Laps	Time/Status	Ave. (mph)	Pts.
1	Paul Tracy (CDN)	3	Marlboro Team Penske PC23-Ilmor/D	107.845	1m 10.101s	3	77	1h 52m 29.642s	86.245	20
2	Emerson Fittipaldi (BR)	2	Marlboro Team Penske PC23-Ilmor/D	106.542	1m 10.958s	4	77	1h 52m 38.891s	86.127	16
3	Robby Gordon (USA)	9	Walker Valvoline/Cummins Special Lola T94/00-Ford	105.605	1m 11.588s	10	77	1h 52m 39.929s	86.113	14
4	Teo Fabi (I)	11	Hall Pennzoil Special Reynard 94I-Ilmor/D	105.711	1m 11.516s	8	77	1h 52m 54.175s	85.932	12
5	Michael Andretti (USA)	8	Ganassi Target/Scotch Video Reynard 94I-Ford	103.850	1m 12.797s	17	77	1h 52m 56.035s	85.909	10
6	Bobby Rahal (USA)	4	Rahal-Hogan Miller Genuine Draft Lola T94/00-Honda	106.192	1m 11.192s	6	77	1h 52m 56.783s	85.899	8
7	*Jacques Villeneuve (CDN)	12	Forsythe-Green Player's Ltd. Reynard 94I-Ford	105.984	1m 11.331s	7	77	1h 53m 07.451s	85.764	6
8	Mauricio Gugelmin (BR)	88	Ganassi Hollywood Reynard 94I-Ford	106.300	1m 11.119s	5	77	1h 53m 10.717s	85.597	5
9	*Bryan Herta (USA)	14	A.J. Foyt Copenhagen Racing Lola T94/00-Ford	103.431	1m 13.092s	18	77	1h 53m 11.737s	85.584	4
10	Al Unser Jr. (USA)	31	Marlboro Team Penske PC23-Ilmor/D	107.965	1m 10.023s	2	77	1h 53m 12.171s	85.579	4
11	Scott Goodyear (CDN)	40	Budweiser King Racing Lola T94/00-Ford	103.050	1m 13.362s	21	76	Running		2
12	Christian Danner (D)	64	Project Indy No Touch/Marcelo Group Lola T93/00-Ford	103.906	1m 12.758s	16	76	Running		1
13	*Scott Sharp (USA)	71	PacWest Racing Group Lola T94/00-Ford	102.207	1m 13.968s	26	76	Running		
14	Mark Smith (USA)	15	Walker Craftsman Tools Lola T94/00-Ford	102.741	1m 13.583s	23	76	Running		
15	*Fredrik Ekblom (S)	30	McCormack Motorsports Lola T93/00-Ilmor/C+	103.278	1m 13.201s	20	76	Running		
16	Willy T. Ribbs (USA)	24	Walker Service Merchandise/Bill Cosby Lola T94/00-Ford	101.438	1m 14.528s	28	75	Running		
17	Buddy Lazier (USA)	23	Leader Card Financial World Lola T93/00-Ilmor/C	101.665	1m 14.362s	27	75	Running		
18	Mario Andretti (USA)	6	Newman-Haas Kmart/Texaco Havoline Lola T94/00-Ford	105.700	1m 11.523s	9	75	Running		
19	Arie Luyendyk (NL)	28	Indy Regency Eurosport/Boost Monaco Lola T94/00-Ilmor/D	104.700	1m 12.206s	13	75	Running		
20	Jimmy Vasser (USA)	18	Hayhoe Conseco/STP Reynard 94I-Ford	103.355	1m 13.146s	19	74	Accident		
21	Nigel Mansell (GB)	1	Newman-Haas Kmart/Texaco Havoline Lola T94/00-Ford	108.649	1m 09.582s	1	65	Engine		1
22	Stefan Johansson (S)	16	Bettenhausen Alumax Aluminum Penske PC22-Ilmor/D	105.523	1m 11.643s	11	51	Transmission		
23	Adrian Fernandez (MEX)	7	Galles Tecate/Quaker State Reynard 94I-Ilmor/D	105.512	1m 11.651s	12	48	Accident		
24	Marco Greco (BR)	25	Simon Arciero Project Indy Lola T94/00-Ford	102.901	1m 13.469s	22	30	Driveshaft		
25	Dominic Dobson (USA)	17	PacWest Racing Group Lola T94/00-Ford	102.616	1m 13.673s	24	20	Accident		
26	*Alessandro Zampedri (I)	19	Coyne The Mi-Jack Car Lola T93/00-Ford	102.610	1m 13.677s	25	20	Accident		
27	Mike Groff (USA)	10	Rahal-Hogan Motorola Lola T94/00-Honda	104.317	1m 12.471s	15	7	Suspension damage		
28	Raul Boesel (BR)	5	Simon Duracell/Fuji Film/Mobil/Sadia Lola T94/00-Ford	104.665	1m 12.230s	14	7	Electrical		
NQ	Ross Bentley (CDN)	39	Coyne Agfa Film Lola T92/00-Ilmor/A	100.788	1m 15.009s	29	–	Did not qualify		
NQ	*Giovanni Lavaggi (I)	50	Euromotorsports Agip/Hawaiian Tropic Lola T93/00-Ilmor/C	99.550	1m 15.942s	30	–	Did not qualify		
NQ	Hiro Matsushita (J)	22	Simon Panasonic/Duskin Lola T94/00-Ford	97.345	1m 17.662s	31	–	Did not qualify		

denotes Rookie driver

Caution flags: Laps 8–13, accident/Groff; laps 21–24, accident/Dobson and Zampedri; laps 49–53, tow/Johansson; laps 56–59, accident/Mansell. Total four for 19 laps.

Lap leaders: Nigel Mansell, 1 (1 lap); Al Unser Jr., 2–48 (47 laps); Paul Tracy, 49 (1 lap); Unser Jr., 50–54 (5 laps); Tracy, 55–77 (23 laps). **Totals:** Unser Jr., 52 laps; Tracy, 24 laps; Mansell, 1 lap.

Fastest race lap: Not available.

Championship positions: 1 Unser Jr., 83 pts; **2** Fittipaldi, 70; **3** Michael Andretti, 59; **4** Gordon, 52; **5** Mansell, 46; **6** Tracy and Vasser, 36; **8** Fabi and Rahal, 28; **10** Villeneuve, 26; **11** Johansson, 25; **12** Mario Andretti, 24; **13** Boesel, 23; **14** Gugelmin, 21; **15** M. Groff, 13; **16** Herta, 11; **17** Fernandez, 8; **18** Sharp and Goodyear, 7; **20** Cheever, 5; **21** John Andretti, 4; **22** Luyendyk, 2; **23** Dobson, Jones, Freon, Till and Danner, 1.

PORTLAND

1st – AL UNSER JR.

2nd – FITTIPALDI

3rd – TRACY

The field circulates behind the pace car prior to the start, with Al Unser Jr. leading Nigel Mansell, Emerson Fittipaldi, Paul Tracy, Jacques Villeneuve, Jimmy Vasser, Robby Gordon, Mauricio Gugelmin, Michael Andretti, Teo Fabi, Bryan Herta, Raul Boesel, Stefan Johansson, Adrian Fernandez, Dominic Dobson, Mario Andretti, Bobby Rahal *(behind Andretti)*, Scott Sharp, Andrea Montermini, Mike Groff, Alessandro Zampedri and Willy T. Ribbs.

Al Unser Jr. not only returned to his winning ways in the Budweiser/G.I. Joe's 200 at Portland International Raceway, he did so with a vengeance. In reality, his Marlboro Penske-Ilmor Indy V8/D was never seriously under threat. Unser qualified on the pole – his first-ever on a road course – and was headed only briefly while making his routine pit stops.

'We got through the first couple of turns and after that it was just a matter of being smooth and not making any mistakes,' confirmed Unser after earning his fourth victory of the season.

As had become the norm, Unser's closest challengers turned out to be his own team-mates, Emerson Fittipaldi and Paul Tracy. Indeed, Roger Penske's drivers monopolized the victory podium for the second time in three races.

Fourth place, however, was the subject of a thrilling dispute that was decided by mere inches at the checkered flag.

Nigel Mansell had assumed his customary position as chief Penske-chaser, only to come under increasing pressure in the closing stages from a charging Robby Gordon. Their battle went all the way to the wire. Mansell, having withstood the youngster's determined challenge under braking for the final corner, looked certain to have maintained the upper hand. All he had to do was make a bee-line for the finish line. But as well as having Gordon anxiously looking for a way past, Mansell also had to contend with a group of lapped cars in front of him. Gordon wasn't to be denied. Somehow he coaxed a little extra momentum from his Valvoline/Cummins Lola-Ford/Cosworth XB and, despite Mansell's best efforts, Gordon nosed ahead to claim the position.

'That was one of the best races I've ever had,' said an elated Gordon. 'That was fun.'

The record-sized crowd enjoyed it too, cheering for Gordon on the cool-down lap every bit as loudly as for the dominant Penske team.

Michael C. Brown

Jori Potiker

'Well, we're back to our usual thing – Mansell and the Penskes, then here we are,' noted Gordon after setting fifth-best time during the first session of qualifying on Friday afternoon.

Gordon was moderately content. He would have preferred to be fastest, of course, but he was pleased to be within 0.3 seconds of Mansell's provisional pole time.

'It's good to come to our first road course and see that the Lolas are competitive with the Penskes,' he explained. 'They had us covered on the street circuits, but now that we've come here, we look pretty close. I'm sure tomorrow we'll be quicker.'

True to his word, Gordon did improve on Saturday. Trouble was, so did a whole bunch of others. By a chunk.

An exciting final 30 minutes of qualifying saw Mansell and Unser vying for the honor of pole position. Unser was the first to show his hand, dipping just underneath Fittipaldi's two-year-old track record of 1m 00.658s. Then Mansell responded with what seemed like an unassailable 1m 00.179s. But Unser wasn't finished. His final lap stopped the clocks at 1m 00.071s, more than a half-second better than the old record.

'Little Al did a tremendous job,' praised Mansell, who had to be content with second on the grid in Newman-Haas Racing's Kmart/Texaco Havoline Lola-Ford. 'I did the best lap I could do. We gave them a run

for their money and we're more than a second faster than the next Lola, so we're just not quick enough. Just now I feel the Penskes have the edge.'

In particular, the PC23 chassis displayed its agility through the flowing sequence of corners linking the main front straightaway with the gently curving back section and its majestic view of the snow-capped Mount Hood some 60 miles or so to the east. It was in the transitions from left- to right-hand corners that the Penske stood out from the crowd of Lolas and Reynards. Its traction capabilities, too, were impressive.

Neither Fittipaldi nor Tracy fully optimized their cars in terms of outright speed, yet they were still able to secure third and fourth places on the grid.

'This track really rewards smoothness,' declared Nigel Beresford, Tracy's race engineer, 'which is why Al went so well.'

Jacques Villeneuve, another young driver noted for his fluid style, continued his impressive progress by heading a group of five Reynard drivers among the next six positions, despite the fact he had never been to Portland before.

'I'm absolutely amazed at how quick he can learn the circuits,' commented Player's Ltd./Forsythe-Green team manager Barry Green. 'He did the same last year [in Toyota Atlantic].'

Jimmy Vasser also ran strongly in sixth, his best-ever qualifying effort in the Conseco/STP Reynard-Ford, while Gordon slipped back to seventh. Chip Ganassi's two cars were next

on the grid, with Mauricio Gugelmin once more ahead of Michael Andretti, albeit by less than one tenth of a second. Just behind them in 11th was Bryan Herta in A.J. Foyt's Copenhagen Lola-Ford. The rookie's performance was all the more notable since he missed virtually all of the Friday qualifying session due to a gearbox problem and also sat out the Saturday morning practice when a brand-new engine was hobbled by a faulty fuel injector.

'He did a good job considering what we've been through this weekend,' said team manager Tommy Lamance. 'It's been one of those situations where you get over one problem and another one hits you. You just have to work through it.'

Equally creditable was the effort from Alessandro Zampedri, even though he ended up 21st on the grid due to a broken shift fork in the final session which left him without the use of fifth gear.

The Italian had qualified a fine ninth on Friday in his second outing with the year-old Mi-Jack Lola-Ford, assuring team owner Dale Coyne of a place among the 'fast group' on Saturday for the very first time.

RACE

The lengthy pit lane at PIR ensured enough room for all 32 cars to start the race. The weather on Sunday was cool, with a heavy overcast, but it didn't deter another record-sized crowd from gathering in the grandstands and trackside enclosures.

The start at Portland is always interesting, since the long, wide start/finish straightaway leads into the very tight Festival Curves. It provides an excellent opportunity for overtaking, especially on the opening lap. This time, though, front row starters Unser and Mansell had reached a pact. Unser had won the pole fair and square, and Mansell agreed he wouldn't risk taking both cars out at the first corner.

'We talked about where we were going to stand on the gas [for the start],' related Unser. 'Nigel told me what his plan was and I told him what my plan was, and it went off like clockwork. Nigel was very honorable.'

Just to be sure, Unser jumped hard on the throttle as soon as the pace car peeled off into the pit lane. He was already a car-length clear when Jim Swintal waved the green flag, with the rest of the field spread out behind.

Unser duly maintained his lead under braking for the Festival Curves, with Mansell tucked in behind. Then came the other two Penskes of Fittipaldi and Tracy.

Behind, though, there was plenty of shuffling as drivers sought to grab an early advantage. Gordon, for example, braked deep into the turn, swooped past Vasser on the outside of the first right-hander and then out-muscled Villeneuve as they accelerated out of the ensuing left. Hey presto, he had moved up two places right away.

Gugelmin, meanwhile, was bun-

Switch to Penske helps Unser find qualifying pace

Al Unser Jr. has truly stepped up to the plate this season. In the past, he had been acknowledged as a ruthless racer, one never to be discounted. Paradoxically, though, his ability to piece together the ultimate in quick laps, as demanded in qualifying, has been questioned.

All too often after qualifying, Unser's car could be found mired deep in the pack somewhere, apparently off the pace; but usually he was unconcerned. In the races, one could generally count on him quickly storming to the front.

This year, though, Unser has qualified consistently up toward the front. But that's not due to any change in his own strategy, or priorities.

'I spend the race weekends working on the race set-up,' explains Unser. 'I try to get the car where it's very, very comfortable in the race. I may give up a little in qualifying because I'm always thinking "the race."

'The pole pays one [PPG Cup] point and the race pays 20. So that's what we're concentrating on.'

This year, though, Unser has qualified consistently up toward the front. But that's not due to any change in his own strategy, or priorities.

'It's the team I'm with that has given me the opportunity to do it,' says Unser. 'It's an "A" team and it's what I've wanted for an awfully long time, and it's showing.'

The Penske team has been solidly behind Unser's quest for the 1994 PPG Indy Car World Series championship, and perhaps its biggest strength is its depth of experience and knowledge. That allied to the fact all three drivers and their respective race engineers work together toward a common goal: to win races.

Left: A busy time for the Penske crewmen on lap 33, as Emerson Fittipaldi pits while in the background race leader Al Unser Jr. heads back out onto the track.

Below: Nigel Mansell holds off the challenge of Robby Gordon. The forceful young Californian squeezed past to claim fourth place on the final lap.

dled down to tenth by Michael Andretti, always a force to be reckoned with on the opening turns, and Herta, who also outbraked Teo Fabi's Pennzoil Reynard-Ilmor at the end of the first straightaway.

By the end of lap one, Unser already had pulled out a slight margin over Mansell. Fittipaldi, Tracy, Gordon and Villeneuve filled out the top six, chased by Vasser, Andretti, Herta, Gugelmin and Fabi.

The order quickly settled down, with Unser turning a fast pace and soon beginning to leave Mansell behind. The gap between them grew rapidly, from 1.77 seconds on lap two, to 2.68, 3.48, 4.04, 4.57, 5.47 and up to 6.36 seconds by lap eight. The leader's progress was inexorable.

'The Penskes are in a different class,' reflected Mansell. The Englishman realized there was no catching Unser. Instead he concentrated on keeping the other two Penskes behind him. The first significant change came, predictably, at Festival when, on lap 11, Andretti lunged from several car lengths behind in trying to outbrake Vasser. The move looked to be rather optimistic, even though Andretti had displayed an ability to brake far deeper into the corner. Inevitably, when Andretti

committed himself to the pass and Vasser turned in from a much wider line, they made contact. Vasser's right-rear wheel climbed over Andretti's left-front, pitching both of them out of the race with broken suspension. Predictably, the combatants saw the incident from different perspectives.

'He was really holding me up,' said Andretti. 'I thought there was something wrong [with his car] because he was way over by the wall [on the outside], and I almost thought he was letting me past. If he'd given me two feet of room, we'd both have been all right.'

'I never even saw him,' countered Vasser. 'He was never, ever beside me. I suddenly felt contact and then I was in the air. It's unfortunate.'

Exit two contenders.

The only other changes occurred farther down the field, as Scott Goodyear (Budweiser Lola-Ford) and Zampedri made progress from lowly grid positions. By lap 23 they had risen from 19th and 21st respectively to 13th and 14th.

Unser, who had stretched his lead to almost 13 seconds by lap 22, saw his cushion begin to dwindle as he fought his way through some slower traffic while at the same time seek-

ing to ensure he didn't use up too much precious fuel on a track where excessive consumption has traditionally posed a problem.

Fittipaldi lost a full two seconds to Mansell when he encountered a typically contentious Hiro Matsushita on lap 22, but it wasn't long before he was back on Mansell's tail. Finally, on lap 28, when Mansell's car twitched just a little coming off Turn Nine, the Brazilian saw his opportunity.

'Nigel was driving very hard,' said Fittipaldi. 'It was difficult to pass. I was able to get alongside him on the straight, then pass him under braking for the chicane.'

One lap later, Tracy also found a way around Mansell, albeit after rather more of a battle.

'I saw he was getting a little bit loose coming onto the front straight,' noted Tracy. 'Finally, I was able to get alongside him on the inside line. He put the squeeze on me.'

Mansell nosed ahead once again in the transition from the right-hander and before the left in the Festival Curves, but he left Tracy just enough racing room on the exit. That was all the Canadian required.

'We banged [together] a couple of times going into the kink,' related Tracy, 'and I got past on the inside.'

Even then, Mansell wasn't allowed any respite. Now he had to contend with Gordon, who had gamely kept pace with the battle in front of him. Villeneuve, too, was just a few car lengths back, with Herta also in close attendance.

Gugelmin had slipped back from this dice before being forced out due to gearbox woes after 29 laps. His demise elevated Fabi to eighth, although the Italian remained under pressure from Raul Boesel (Duracell Lola-Ford) and Stefan Johansson (Alumax Penske PC22-Ilmor/D).

Soon, though, it was time for the first round of pit stops. Unser was first onto pit road, on lap 33, followed by Fittipaldi and Mansell. Tracy and Gordon opted to complete one more lap before making their routine stops.

The leading positions didn't change but the gaps between the cars did. Out front, Unser still led Fittipaldi by around nine seconds. Tracy lost some six seconds and Mansell emerged from the pits a further five seconds back. Gordon also fell away slightly.

Herta's stop, meanwhile, was simply disastrous. Foyt had thrown the dice by electing not to fit fresh tires, hoping that by saving a few seconds

Michael C. Brown

Italian rookie Alessandro Zampedri belied his lack of Indy Car experience to bring the Dale Coyne-entered Mi-Jack Lola into the top ten at the finish ahead of some illustrious names.

he might enable his young charger to resume ahead of Villeneuve. It was a curious call. First of all, changing all four tires generally takes less time than filling the 40-gallon fuel cell to capacity. Furthermore, a problem with the refueling nozzle ensured that Herta left the pits with only a partial fuel load. Thus, not only was it a slow stop, but Herta had to contend with well-worn rubber and the knowledge that he would almost certainly have to make a third stop before the end of the race. It was a costly error.

With 51 laps in the books, half-distance, Unser's lead remained fairly static at around nine seconds. Fittipaldi and Tracy were separated by a similar margin, with Mansell a further 5.7 seconds adrift. Gordon, Villeneuve, Herta, Boesel and Johansson also were well spaced out. Everyone else was at least one lap down, with the only real battle being fought out for 16th place between Franck Freon, enjoying his second start in Project Indy's No Touch/Marcelo Lola T93/00-Ford, and fellow Indy Lights graduate Robbie Groff, also making his second Indy Car appearance in Tony Bettenhausen's Condor Penske PC22-Ilmor/C+.

On lap 55, Herta was forced to make his second pit stop for fuel. He rejoined between Mario Andretti, who was enduring a difficult weekend in his Newman-Haas Lola, and Goodyear. Next time around, though, a legitimate attempt by Goodyear to outbrake Herta into Festival ended in almost exactly the same manner as the earlier incident between Vasser and Michael Andretti.

Once again, Herta never saw Goodyear's approach down the inside, due primarily to the fact his right-side mirror had been dislodged earlier when he was forced to bounce high over the curbs in avoidance of Matsushita. Goodyear was out of the race immediately, his car stuck in the gravel trap minus its left-front wheel. Herta was able to resume, only for the engine to cut out abruptly. The crankshaft electrical trigger had been damaged. His race, too, was over.

A full-course caution was necessary while Goodyear's stricken car was removed. Most drivers dived into the pits for their second routine stop. But not the Penskes.

'The yellow came out and I looked at my numbers [on the digital dash] and we had about 15 gallons left,' related Unser. 'Generally, if you're below half-tanks, you come right in [to the pits], but I wasn't going to touch that [radio] button at all.'

Unser had remembered an incident during the race at Phoenix, where, in a similar situation, he and Roger Penske keyed their microphone buttons at the same instant. Neither heard the other's message. This time Unser waited for Penske to make the call. None came. So he stayed out on the track.

'If we'd pitted, we couldn't have made it to the end of the race without stopping again,' explained Unser. 'So it was a good call on Roger's part. He definitely knows a lot about strategy and it's great to have him on my radio.'

Fittipaldi and Tracy followed suit. Gordon's crew also eschewed a pit stop, while Boesel wisely waited until the pack had formed up behind the pace car before making his stop.

Thus, for the restart on lap 64, the three Penskes and Gordon held a clear lead. Mansell and Boesel were the only others on the same lap. Many teams had been caught out by Penske's strategy, including Forsythe-Green. Villeneuve lost a lap by stopping before he had been able to pack up behind the pace car.

Unser and Fittipaldi made full use of a clear track and low fuel load to scorch away after the restart. Even after stopping for service, on laps 69 (Unser) and 70 (Fittipaldi), they maintained their lead over Mansell, who had moved up to third.

A particularly fast stop by Rick Rinaman's crew enabled Fittipaldi to rejoin fractionally ahead of Unser, although his advantage was short-lived. Unser's tires were already up to full working temperature, the championship leader having stopped a lap earlier, so as Fittipaldi slithered through the Festival Curves, desperately trying to warm up his own Goodyears, Unser was able to sneak past and regain the lead.

Unser maintained a cushion of a little less than two seconds over his team-mate, although each time they encountered some traffic, the Brazilian would close in again.

'Emerson definitely kept me hon-

est,' said Unser. 'I knew I was in a dog-fight. It was tough. I was drivin' for all I was worth. It was fun racin'.'

Again, with a clear road, Unser managed to claw back his original advantage.

'He drove fast,' praised Fittipaldi. 'The last ten laps there was a lot of pressure and he made no mistakes. Two or three times under braking I attempted to pass Junior, but I wasn't close enough; I couldn't get side by side with him. He drove a great race.'

The margin between them was just 1.83 seconds at the checkered flag but it was enough. Unser's fourth win was assured, along with a healthy 19-point lead in the PPG Cup standings.

'We still have a long way to go in front of us,' cautioned Unser, 'and anything can happen. We're still taking it race by race. Now we're off to Cleveland and we'll try to get 20 points there on race day.'

Tracy completed the Penske sweep in third, 30 seconds back, having lost some time in traffic during the closing stages.

But all eyes were on the battle for fourth. Gordon had made his second stop, on schedule, after 71 laps. Unfortunately, a problem during the refueling process saw him stationary at least 20 seconds longer than usual. He rejoined a distant sixth.

Gordon moved up one place when the unlucky Boesel suffered a gear linkage failure on lap 84. Boesel had been running strongly in fifth, safe in the knowledge that he had enough fuel to make it to the finish and that Mansell had yet to stop. Then, suddenly, the shift lever mounting broke. A long stop dropped the Brazilian to the tail of the field, although it was a measure of his professionalism that he continued gamely to the finish.

When Mansell stopped on lap 95, with seven to go, he rejoined still with an appreciable lead over Gordon. The youngster, however, was charging. Gradually the gap came down. As they started the last lap, the pair were virtually nose to tail. And right up ahead were a gaggle of slower cars, including the omnipresent Matsushita, plus Zampedri and Johansson, who were also battling for position.

Zampedri had been short-shifting for many laps, trying desperately to make it without an extra stop, while Johansson was flying, anxious to gain back seventh, the place he had lost when he pitted for the third and final time on lap 92. Zampedri made a smart move as he contrived to place Matsushita between them on the back straightaway, then held on doggedly in the dash for the finish line. He took the place by a scant 0.062 seconds.

Immediately behind them, Gordon was looking for a way past Mansell. There seemed to be none, but the manner in which Gordon lit up his rear tires coming off the final corner left no doubt as to his intention. Mansell kept to his line, distracted by the dicing in front of him, and was unable to prevent Gordon drawing up alongside, then snatching fourth place by 0.030s.

'Coming onto the last straight, I saw it happening,' said Gordon. 'He got right up on somebody, so I laid back and went wide [on the entry to Turn Nine], and dove to the inside [on the exit]. He stepped sideways, I stepped sideways. That's what racing's all about. It was a good time.'

'I never drove so hard for a fifth-place finish,' declared Mansell. 'It was a good, hard race. I thought I was OK for fourth but I got boxed in. Robby did a good job.'

Villeneuve drove steadily to sixth, one lap down. Zampedri's fine effort was rewarded with a career-best seventh.

'I think it shows qualifying ninth on Friday was no fluke,' said a broadly smiling Zampedri. 'I overtook people like Mario Andretti and Bobby Rahal, and I'm so happy, because, for me, these are legends of racing.'

Johansson, eighth, was irate at the blocking tactics of Matsushita, five laps behind, who, he said, cost him a chance at seventh. Afterward the Swede had to be physically restrained from telling the Japanese driver what he really thought!

Fabi had been running in between this pair until the Ilmor engine in his Reynard expired after 85 laps.

Mario Andretti coped with inconsistent handling to finish ninth, two laps off the ultimate pace, followed at a distance by Adrian Fernandez. The Honda-engined cars of Mike Groff and Bobby Rahal completed the point scorers. The pair had run in close company for most of the race, with Rahal to the fore until losing time with a puncture before half-distance.

SNIPPETS

• Al Unser Jr. received a $150,000 check from Marlboro for winning from the pole. The bonus had not been claimed since Paul Tracy achieved the feat at Road America last season, although it was withheld at Nazareth last year due to the fact that, after qualifying had been rained out, Mansell's pole was allocated according to championship positions. Also, the Indianapolis 500 is not included in the Marlboro Pole Award scheme.

• Asked to reflect on the altercation between himself and team-mate Paul Tracy in Detroit, Unser made it clear he harbored no grudge. 'Paul and I talked and that was it,' he said. 'It's over and it's water under the bridge. That was Detroit and this is Portland.'

Incidentally, Unser's latest win came ten years and nine days after his very first Indy Car victory, also at Portland.

• Comptech Racing made a quiet Indy Car debut with Parker Johnstone *(shown above leading Marco Greco)*

at the wheel of its ex-Rahal/Hogan 1993 Lola-Honda. The Acura-liveried car was clearly no match for the latest equipment, although Johnstone, a three-time IMSA Camel Lights champion, managed to record a 19th-place finish, despite stopping, out of fuel, within a few yards of the checkered flag.

• European Formula 3000 Championship stand-out Gil de Ferran drove Jim Hall's Pennzoil Reynard in a test at Big Spring, Texas, the weekend before Portland. The outing was arranged by Reynard's Rick Gorne, a long-time supporter of the highly rated Brazilian. Regular driver Teo Fabi was prevented from making the test due to other business commitments.

Michael C. Brown

PPG INDY CAR WORLD SERIES • ROUND 7

BUDWEISER/G.I. JOE'S 200

PORTLAND INTERNATIONAL RACEWAY, PORTLAND, OREGON

JUNE 26, 102 LAPS – 198.900 MILES

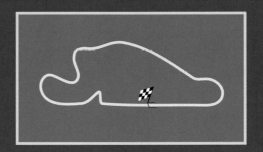

Place	Driver (Nat.)	No.	Team Sponsors Car-Engine	Q Speed (mph)	Q Time	Q Pos.	Laps	Time/Status	Ave. (mph)	Pts.
1	Al Unser Jr. (USA)	31	Marlboro Team Penske PC23-Ilmor/D	116.861	1m 00.071s	1	102	1h 50m 43.706s	107.777	22
2	Emerson Fittipaldi (BR)	2	Marlboro Team Penske PC23-Ilmor/D	116.101	1m 00.465s	3	102	1h 50m 45.536s	107.748	16
3	Paul Tracy (CDN)	3	Marlboro Team Penske PC23-Ilmor/D	115.685	1m 00.682s	4	102	1h 51m 16.162s	107.253	14
4	Robby Gordon (USA)	9	Walker Valvoline/Cummins Special Lola T94/00-Ford	114.849	1m 01.124s	7	102	1h 51m 40.032s	106.871	12
5	Nigel Mansell (GB)	1	Newman-Haas Kmart/Texaco Havoline Lola T94/00-Ford	116.651	1m 00.180s	2	102	1h 51m 40.062s	106.871	10
6	*Jacques Villeneuve (CDN)	12	Forsythe-Green Player's Ltd. Reynard 94I-Ford	115.604	1m 00.724s	5	101	Running		8
7	*Alessandro Zampedri (I)	19	Coyne The Mi-Jack Car Lola T93/00-Ford	112.948	1m 02.152s	21	101	Running		6
8	Stefan Johansson (S)	16	Bettenhausen Alumax Aluminum Penske PC22-Ilmor/D	114.193	1m 01.475s	13	101	Running		5
9	Mario Andretti (USA)	6	Newman-Haas Kmart/Texaco Havoline Lola T94/00-Ford	113.774	1m 01.701s	16	100	Running		4
10	Adrian Fernandez (MEX)	7	Galles Tecate/Quaker State Reynard 94I-Ilmor/D	114.178	1m 01.483s	14	100	Running		3
11	Mike Groff (USA)	10	Rahal-Hogan Motorola Lola T94/00-Honda	112.976	1m 02.137s	20	99	Running		2
12	Bobby Rahal (USA)	4	Rahal-Hogan Miller Genuine Draft Lola T94/00-Honda	113.509	1m 01.845s	17	99	Running		1
13	*Robbie Groff (USA)	76	Bettenhausen Condor Penske PC22-Ilmor/C+	112.369	1m 02.473s	24	99	Running		
14	Arie Luyendyk (NL)	28	Indy Regency Eurosport/Boost Monaco Lola T94/00-Ilmor/D	112.133	1m 02.604s	25	99	Running		
15	*Franck Freon (F)	64	Project Indy No Touch/Marcelo Group Lola T93/00-Ford	110.842	1m 03.333s	28	99	Running		
16	Mark Smith (USA)	15	Walker Craftsman Tools Lola T94/00-Ford	112.916	1m 02.170s	22	99	Running		
17	Dominic Dobson (USA)	17	PacWest Racing Group Lola T94/00-Ford	114.132	1m 01.508s	15	99	Running		
18	*Scott Sharp (USA)	71	PacWest Racing Group Lola T94/00-Ford	113.322	1m 01.947s	18	98	Running		
19	*Parker Johnstone (USA)	49	Comptech Racing Acura Lola T93/00-Honda	111.016	1m 03.234s	27	97	Running		
20	Marco Greco (BR)	25	Simon Arciero Project Indy Lola T94/00-Ford	111.787	1m 02.798s	26	97	Out of fuel		
21	Hiro Matsushita (J)	22	Simon Panasonic/Duskin Lola T94/00-Ford	110.317	1m 03.635s	30	97	Running		
22	Ross Bentley (CDN)	39	Coyne Agfa Film Lola T92/00-Ilmor/A	108.026	1m 04.984s	31	95	Running		
23	Raul Boesel (BR)	5	Simon Duracell/Fuji Film/Mobil/Sadia Lola T94/00-Ford	114.211	1m 01.465s	12	94	Running		
24	Buddy Lazier (USA)	23	Leader Card Financial World Lola T93/00-Ilmor/C	110.433	1m 03.568s	29	91	Out of fuel		
25	Willy T. Ribbs (USA)	24	Walker Service Merchandise/Bill Cosby Lola T94/00-Ford	112.903	1m 02.177s	23	91	Running		
26	Teo Fabi (I)	11	Hall Pennzoil Special Reynard 94I-Ilmor/D	114.645	1m 01.232s	10	85	Engine		
27	*Bryan Herta (USA)	14	A.J. Foyt Copenhagen Racing Lola T94/00-Ford	114.393	1m 01.367s	11	62	Engine		
28	Scott Goodyear (CDN)	40	Budweiser King Racing Lola T94/00-Ford	113.295	1m 01.962s	19	56	Accident		
29	Jeff Wood (USA)	50	Euromotorsport Agip/Hawaiian Tropic Lola T92/00-Ilmor/A	106.146	1m 06.135s	32	52	Transmission		
30	Mauricio Gugelmin (BR)	88	Ganassi Hollywood Reynard 94I-Ford	114.849	1m 01.124s	8	29	Transmission		
31	Michael Andretti (USA)	8	Ganassi Target/Scotch Video Reynard 94I-Ford	114.700	1m 01.203s	9	11	Accident		
32	Jimmy Vasser (USA)	18	Hayhoe Conseco/STP Reynard 94I-Ford	115.370	1m 00.848s	6	10	Accident		

* denotes Rookie driver

Caution flags: Laps 58–62, tow, Goodyear. Total, one for five laps.

Lap leaders: Al Unser Jr., 1–32 (32 laps); Paul Tracy, 33–34 (2 laps); Unser Jr., 35–68 (34 laps); Emerson Fittipaldi, 69–70 (2 laps); Tracy, 71–72 (2 laps); Unser Jr., 73–102 (30 laps). **Totals:** Unser Jr., 96 laps; Tracy, 4 laps; Fittipaldi, 2 laps.

Fastest race lap: Unser Jr., 1m 01.106s, 114.883 mph, on lap 67.

Championship positions: 1 Unser Jr., 105 pts; **2** Fittipaldi, 86; **3** Gordon, 64; **4** Michael Andretti, 59; **5** Mansell, 56; **6** Tracy, 50; **7** Vasser, 36; **8** Villeneuve, 34; **9** Johansson, 30; **10** Rahal, 29; **11** Mario Andretti and Fabi, 28; **13** Boesel, 23; **14** Gugelmin, 21; **15** M. Groff, 15; **16** Fernandez and Herta, 11; **18** Sharp and Goodyear, 7; **20** Zampedri, 6; **21** Cheever, 5; **22** John Andretti, 4; **23** Luyendyk, 2; **24** Dobson, Jones, Freon, Till and Danner, 1.

CLEVELAND

Can *anybody* beat Al Unser Jr. and, particularly, Marlboro Team Penske? That was the question being posed after the Budweiser Grand Prix of Cleveland, presented by Dairy Mart, with Unser having romped to another dominant victory, his fifth of the season and the seventh in a row for Roger Penske's all-conquering *équipe*. Not even a typically spirited drive from defending PPG Cup champion Nigel Mansell could prevent Unser from continuing the streak.

'It was a pretty good run,' summarized Unser, who extended his lead in the PPG Cup standings to 41 points. 'I was very fortunate to get a good start and to get away a little bit, so there was no real pressure coming from behind me.'

Unser took the checkered flag a comfortable 22.950 seconds clear of Mansell's Kmart/Texaco Havoline Lola-Ford/Cosworth XB, taking advantage of a complete lack of caution periods to win the 85-lap race at a new record average speed of 138.026 mph.

Mansell, though, was more than content with his day's work. After all, he had managed to split the Penske team, passing Paul Tracy and maintaining position ahead of Emerson Fittipaldi until the Brazilian retired with a broken exhaust.

'I feel very satisfied because the team did a brilliant job,' affirmed Mansell. 'The pit stops were fabulous. I know I drove as hard as I could and we were beaten by the best car, team and driver. That's what this game is all about. Let the best car, best team and best driver win on the day.

'I had reliability and my second place today almost feels like a win. I'm very comfortable with it. We've just got to work a bit harder and try to be a bit more competitive at the next race. All credit to the Penske team.'

Canadians Tracy and Jacques Villeneuve (Player's Reynard-Ford) were the only other unlapped finishers.

1st – AL UNSER JR.

2nd – MANSELL

3rd – TRACY

QUALIFYING

The oftentimes prickly topic of team orders came to the surface during practice and qualifying on the Burke Lakefront Airport temporary circuit. The opening sessions boiled down to the usual confrontation between the three Penske drivers, with Mansell once again proving the only serious thorn in their side. For Tracy, however, there was much at stake.

Following his controversial victory in Detroit, at a record average speed, Tracy remained eligible for a $1 million bonus if he could capture both the pole and the win at Cleveland. The award was posted by Mark McCormack's International Management Group, promoters of the races at Detroit and Cleveland.

'It's a great incentive and it would be great to win it, but the main thing for me is to get some points this weekend,' said Tracy, unconvincingly, after claiming the provisional pole on Friday evening. His true feelings surfaced a few minutes later when he admitted: 'I'm going to do a rain dance tonight – all night.'

The Canadian's power of mental persuasion didn't prove up to the task as Saturday dawned bright and clear.

Happily, his physical efforts were rather more fruitful. Tracy topped the time sheets again in the opening practice. His time of 59.177 seconds was fractionally slower than his own track record, set in 1993, but faster than his Friday best of 59.513s. No one else lapped within two-tenths. His prospects looked good for at least achieving the first stepping-stone toward the big-money payday.

So, were there any team orders?

'Put it this way, Roger [Penske] has issued no team orders to the drivers,' stated Penske Team Manager Chuck Sprague. 'That doesn't mean the rest of the team hasn't'. Or, as Richard Nixon once said: "We could do that . . . but it would be wrong!" '

Riddles apart, the answer became apparent during a thrilling final half-hour of qualifying on Saturday afternoon. First, Tracy put a dent in his own aspirations by running off course early in the session and making contact with a tire barrier erected around one of the runway marker lights. He claimed to have been caught out by a slight camber change in the front suspension.

Damage to his Ilmor/D-powered PC23 was limited to the intricate aerodynamic appendage along the lower outside edge of the front wing and a bent track rod. His crew soon put that right. In the meantime, Mansell had bettered Tracy's quick time from Friday.

There was a brief respite when the session was stopped due to Michael Andretti's car being stranded by a broken water fitting. Six minutes remained when final qualifying resumed, whereupon first Unser, then Fittipaldi launched themselves to the top of the time sheets. What team orders? Mansell and Tracy also were pitching desperately for the pole.

With less than a minute remaining, Unser ripped off a scintillating 59.232 seconds to retake top time. Fittipaldi couldn't match that. Nor could Mansell. Tracy, though, remained out on the course, with enough time for one more lap. It was quick, on the ragged edge, but at 59.342 seconds it wasn't quite enough to topple Unser.

'We were able to make some changes to the car,' said Unser. 'Once I got the car where I wanted it, the time came.'

A disappointed Tracy ended up second on the grid, his $1 million dream in tatters.

'My crew did a good job to get me going again,' related Tracy. 'It was a good pit stop under the circumstances. I finally got some hot laps in the last five minutes of the session, but traffic was a factor and we came up second best.'

Fittipaldi was a further tenth away, third on the grid, with Mansell next in the fastest Lola.

'I wrung the car's neck,' declared the Briton. 'We changed a lot of things but I don't think there's much left. I couldn't have gone any quicker.'

Villeneuve drove well on his first

Main photo: Nigel Mansell once again provided the main threat to the all-conquering Marlboro Penskes, but the Englishman was powerless to halt the majestic progress of Al Unser Jr. *(inset far left).*

Alessandro Zampedri *(above)* again made a good impression in Dale Coyne's year-old Mi-Jack car to record his second successive top-ten finish, while Willy T. Ribbs *(below left)* enjoyed one of his strongest races of the season and was delighted to score a PPG Cup point.

visit to Cleveland, fifth on the grid and fastest Reynard, while Robby Gordon jumped up to sixth from 19th on Friday, having been hindered by a gearbox lubrication problem which permitted him very few laps in Derrick Walker's Valvoline/Cummins Lola-Ford.

Mauricio Gugelmin never got out on Friday afternoon due to an engine problem in the Hollywood Reynard, although he improved in leaps and bounds on Saturday to annex seventh on the grid ahead of Stefan Johansson's Alumax Penske PC22-Ilmor/D.

RACE

Instead of the hot, muggy conditions generally associated with Cleveland in July, the weather was pleasantly cool as the huge 31-car field assembled in front of the packed grandstands in time for the 1.40 p.m. start.

The drag race to the first corner on this fast temporary circuit is always fraught with danger as the combatants are required to brake hard on the super-wide runway, then funnel down into a very tight right-hand corner. As at Portland, some kind of commotion is almost expected.

Once again, though, Unser realized that a fast start would minimize the risks. Thus, he jumped hard on the gas as he led the field through the right-left Turn Nine/Ten complex leading onto the start/finish straightaway, ensuring that most of the leaders were already beginning to spread out as they swept past Jim Swintal's waving green flags. The race was on.

Tracy briefly looked to the inside of Unser as they approached the braking area for Turn One, but his only sensible option was to tuck in behind the leader. Meanwhile, on the exit, Mansell found a little better traction to usurp Fittipaldi from third. Gordon, too, had found a way past Villeneuve at the start.

Farther back, the seemingly inevitable incident came as Michael Andretti, who started inordinately far back, 17th, following a veritable litany of problems in qualifying, misjudged his braking and struck the rear end of Scott Goodyear's Budweiser Lola-Ford. Both cars spun. Andretti lost more than a lap before he could be tow-started, while Goodyear made a pit stop to check for damage, then was obliged to stop again after being caught exceeding the 80 mph speed limit in pit lane. By then he was almost two laps adrift of the leaders.

The opening segment of the race saw Unser once again assume control. Inch by inch he edged clear of the battling Tracy and Mansell, while Fittipaldi struggled to keep in touch. Gordon and Villeneuve also were running on their own, although Gugelmin, in seventh, came under increasing pressure from an on-form Mario Andretti (Kmart/Texaco Havoline Lola-Ford) and Johansson.

On lap 17, the elder Andretti showed his raciness by nipping alongside Gugelmin on the exit of Turn One, then surging ahead as the pair sped along adjacent to the shoreline of Lake Erie. The Brazilian tried to redress the balance under braking for Turn Three but to no avail. Indeed, Gugelmin succeeded only in scrubbing off some speed, which gave Johansson the opportunity to nip inside under braking for Turn Six. Nice move.

Gugelmin then came under siege from Bobby Rahal's Miller Genuine Draft Lola-Honda, albeit only for a couple of laps before Rahal's engine gave up the struggle. Rahal thus joined early sparring partner Jimmy Vasser on the sidelines, the Californian's Conseco/STP Reynard having been hobbled by fuel pump failure.

On lap 20, Mansell finally saw a chance to go past Tracy when the Canadian was inadvertently held up just a little on the east end of the race track. Mansell assured himself of a quick exit to the double-apex right-hand turn, enabling him to surge alongside Tracy and then assume the optimum inside line under braking for Turn Nine. Again, it was a beautifully executed pass.

'I got kind of boxed in,' said Tracy. 'I was able to go quicker than him on some parts of the track, but he was better in other parts. It was kind of give and take.'

Once into second place, Mansell soon put some distance between himself and the #3 Penske-Ilmor. At the same time he began to creep slightly closer to Unser, reducing the deficit from almost seven seconds to nearer five.

'As soon as Nigel got past Paul, I couldn't open up any more,' admitted Unser. 'In fact, [the gap] started to close a little bit, so I just started trying a little bit harder. I was about to my limit when I started maintaining a pace in front of Nigel.'

Unser turned his fastest laps of the race, dipping below the one minute barrier, just prior to his first scheduled pit stop. He was actually the first of the leaders to pit, after 26 laps,

although Gordon had been in to serve a stop-and-wait (for five seconds) penalty shortly before after being adjudged to have passed a slower car under a local yellow caution flag.

Unser maintained his lead over Mansell during the pit stops, while Fittipaldi emerged in third place ahead of a disgruntled Tracy. Villeneuve ran next, followed by Johansson. Gugelmin, troubled by fading brakes, held seventh, only to fall behind Adrian Fernandez, who was charging hard in the Tecate/Quaker State Reynard-Ilmor. Raul Boesel (Duracell Lola-Ford) and Arie Luyendyk (Eurosport/Boost Monaco Lola-Ilmor) also were running well, although both were a lap down to Unser by lap 34.

Gordon, meanwhile, hadn't been allowed to take on service while serving his penalty, and after pitting again just four laps later he was obliged to make yet another stop due to a suspected puncture. To make matters worse, the third stop was hindered by a recalcitrant wheel. By now he was two laps down in 24th place. And not happy! To his credit, Gordon wasted no time in trying to regain some of his lost ground, despite the fact his hopes of a high placing had been dashed.

Mario Andretti, too, was out of the running. Andretti had been another to fall foul of the pit lane speed limit and, soon after rejoining, on lap 31 he was involved in a contretemps with another car at the chicane in front of the pits. Andretti skated across the grass and then, as he regained control of the car on the edge of the track, his left-front suspension was broken following contact with the right-rear wheel of none other than his passing team-mate, Mansell.

Sadly, there is no love lost between these two great drivers and, predictably, they saw the incident rather differently.

'Car #1 just miscued there a little bit,' recounted Andretti, 'and hit me on the left-front and broke the wishbone. I'm sure he didn't wanna do it but he coulda been more careful!'

'I don't know quite what happened,' said Mansell. 'There were three or four cars going into the chicane and I was the last one. I think Mario got chopped by a back-marker, so he went over some dirt coming out and went wide. So I turned up on the inside and the next thing I know, we touched. I think he had a bit of dirt on his tires coming out and the car just moved a little. I'm not used to being up in the air at 160 mph!'

Above: Penske drivers Al Unser Jr. and Paul Tracy head the field into the first corner. While Unser went on to record his fifth win in six races, the Canadian had to settle for a distant third place.

Ride-height settings are rendered irrelevant as Michael Andretti *(right)* wrestles with the Target/Scotch Video Reynard.

Photos: Michael C. Brown.

Nigel Snowdon

Just an ordinary day at the office. Stefan Johansson *(bottom)* **enjoyed a trouble-free run in the Alumax Penske PC22 to pick up fifth place and a useful haul of points for Tony Bettenhausen's team.**

The incident cost Mansell some time and allowed Fittipaldi to close up from behind. Soon, though, after realizing there was no serious damage, Mansell began to edge away again.

The second round of pit stops were largely uneventful. Unser relinquished the lead briefly when he stopped on lap 57, then resumed with a comfortable cushion of around 20 seconds over Mansell. Unser was able to sustain that margin without overtaxing either himself or his Penske-Ilmor/D.

'The whole team has been super,' commented Unser. 'What can I say? I'm driving a great car. The ball's bouncing my way.'

Unser's only minor inconvenience was a sore back, apparently caused by an improperly fitted seat. Nevertheless, a couple of visits to Don Andrews at Tony Lama's sports therapists eased his predicament considerably: 'It really helped me a lot,' said Unser.

Mansell chased as hard as he could, even catching a piece of the wall one time after understeering slightly wide on the exit of Turn Eight. The left-side tires on Mansell's Lola were 'white-walled' but otherwise undamaged. Unser, meanwhile, was long gone.

'He didn't put a foot wrong. He drove a great race,' praised Mansell. 'I had a lot of excitement and he just had a nice quiet race.'

Fittipaldi briefly snared second

place as he emerged from the pits after making his second stop, but he wasn't able to maintain that position. Mansell, his tires already up to full working temperature after stopping one lap earlier, was able to nip back ahead on the entry to Turn Three. Fittipaldi nevertheless remained well clear of Tracy, only to over-shoot his approach to Turn One on lap 66. An exhaust header had broken. Worse, the hot gases quickly burned through a brake line; hence his problem at Turn One. Fittipaldi was able to maintain control but his day was done.

'It's disappointing,' said Fittipaldi. 'The car was very strong when I was alone. Sometimes I was unlucky in traffic, getting stuck behind slower cars. That is where Al and Nigel were able to pull away from me.'

Tracy and Villeneuve, the only other drivers still on the lead lap, duly moved up one place each, elevating Johansson to a solid fifth.

'It really wasn't a very eventful race for us,' summarized the Swede. 'Overall, the car was very consistent throughout the race and, of course, it's nice to score the points.'

Two excellent pit stops from Dick Simon's crew enabled Boesel to make up several positions, including two at the expense of Gugelmin and Fernandez on the second go-round. Boesel took full advantage and was rewarded with a fine sixth place.

'It's like a victory for us,' said a delighted Boesel, who started a

Turning back the clock

Nigel Mansell was, as usual, the focal point of discussion during the Cleveland weekend. One week earlier, the Englishman had taken a brief respite from his defence of the PPG Cup title and instead returned to the scene of his former glories by contesting the French Grand Prix at Magny-Cours for the Williams-Renault team. Incidentally, if the reports were to be believed, Mansell was paid as much as $1.5 million for his efforts.

'It was a marvelous, exciting weekend,' said Mansell. 'What you've got to understand is that I basically had a half a day [testing prior to the race] at Brands Hatch [England] and then I got thrown right in at the deep end. So my comfort zone was probably a one or a two [out of a scale of ten]. My comfort zone over here [in Indy Car racing] is probably an eight.

'I would say the [Formula 1] car was probably "more lively" [than an Indy car]. The biggest single difference was the braking points. In a Formula 1 car you can brake so much later, because of the carbon brakes.

Acceleration from a standing start is much better, too, because a Formula 1 car is a lot lighter. But a race car is a race car and it just depends on your inherent ability as to what you can do and what you can't do.

'Because it was a one-off guest appearance, everything that happened I enjoyed. It was a wonderful, challenging experience. The first day I was struggling. It took me a little bit of time to get up to speed.

'In some ways it was a breath of fresh air, there's no question about it. If you look at a few things they do over there [in Formula 1] and a few things over here, and combine them, you'd have a great series. But that's the old saying: the grass is always greener on the other side. But it was a great experience.

'I think Indy Car racing is a well-kept secret. The potential for the series to grow is fantastic. But in order for it to grow, you've got to have some better circuits and better opportunities for the sponsors to protect their investment.'

lowly 19th following a dismal time in practice and qualifying. On race day, the Duracell Lola was transformed. 'The car was perfect, the engine was perfect. We turned consistent laps quicker than we qualified.'

Fernandez lost a little ground following his second stop but came back to pass the troubled Gugelmin and then close right up on Boesel at the finish. Seventh place matched his career best since graduating from Indy Lights on a part-time basis in 1993.

'The car was strong all the way,'

commented the Mexican. 'It made my job a little bit easier and it gave me the confidence to push a bit harder.'

'I'm really proud of Adrian and the guys on our crew,' added team owner Rick Galles. 'This is a highly competitive series. Adrian and the team came out and gave us 100 per cent effort this weekend.'

Gugelmin was disappointed with eighth, having struggled throughout with overheating brakes, while Teo Fabi (Pennzoil Reynard-Ilmor) drove steadily to ninth ahead of fellow Italian Alessandro Zampedri, who was delighted with his second straight top-ten finish in Dale Coyne's year-old Mi-Jack Lola.

'It proves Portland wasn't just a single case,' declared Zampedri. 'We struggled in qualifying because of the bumps. We worked hard and we found the right set-up and the car was very good in the race. I'm tired but I'm very happy.'

Luyendyk's hopes of a top-ten finish ended with a turbo failure, while Michael Andretti had worked his way back to 11th before the engine broke in his Target/Scotch Video Reynard. Thus, Gordon salvaged a couple of points from his disappointing afternoon, while Walker Racing stablemate Willy T. Ribbs was delighted to pick up the final PPG Cup point after a solid run in his Service Merchandise Lola-Ford.

'My engineer, Rob Edwards, really pulled out a good set-up for me,' praised Ribbs. 'It was a great race for me because we ran a whole second faster than when we qualified.'

Michael C. Brown

SNIPPETS

• Late on Friday afternoon, on the first day of practice at Cleveland, Indianapolis Motor Speedway President Tony George made an announcement in his home town to the effect he intended to establish a rival series, based around the Indianapolis 500, in 1996. Very few details of the so-called Indy Racing League were given, save the nomination of a five-man board of directors to oversee its development. Reaction to the news was muted. 'It's inappropriate to comment on part of a proposal,' said IndyCar President Andrew Craig. 'We would rather wait to see all of Tony's proposal.' Added series points leader Unser: 'I'm in Cleveland. I'm going to worry about Indy when we get there next year. I just hope everything will get worked out so I can be there every year with my Marlboro car.'

• In an attempt to woo Budweiser into extending its sponsorship for 1995, Kenny Bernstein's team farmed out team leader Scott Goodyear's regular spare car to the impressive Andrea Montermini *(below)*. The Italian acquitted himself well, despite still recuperating from injuries suffered in a bad Formula 1 crash, although both men were out of luck on race day. Goodyear finished 14th, Montermini 16th.

Photos: Michael C. Brown

• Imressive young rookie driver Bryan Herta *(above, right)* again rocked the establishment by setting the fourth-fastest time in the first session with A.J. Foyt's Copenhagen Lola-Ford. Sadly, a contretemps with Giovanni Lavaggi right at the end of the Saturday morning practice saw Herta obliged to switch across to Foyt's spare car, which was then blighted by all manner of electrical problems.

PPG INDY CAR WORLD SERIES • ROUND 8

BUDWEISER GRAND PRIX OF CLEVELAND

BURKE LAKEFRONT AIRPORT CIRCUIT, CLEVELAND, OHIO

JULY 10, 85 LAPS – 201.365 MILES

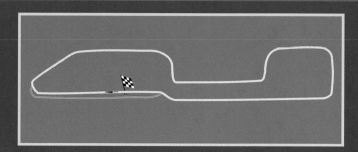

Place	Driver (Nat.)	No.	Team Sponsors Car-Engine	Q Speed (mph)	Q Time	Q Pos.	Laps	Time/Status	Ave. (mph)	Pts.
1	Al Unser Jr. (USA)	31	Marlboro Team Penske PC23-Ilmor/D	143.983	59.232s	1	85	1h 27m 32.000s	138.026	22
2	Nigel Mansell (GB)	1	Newman-Haas Kmart/Texaco Havoline Lola T94/00-Ford	143.354	59.492s	4	85	1h 27m 54.950s	137.426	16
3	Paul Tracy (CDN)	3	Marlboro Team Penske PC23-Ilmor/D	143.716	59.342s	2	85	Running		14
4	*Jacques Villeneuve (CDN)	12	Forsythe-Green Player's Ltd. Reynard 94I-Ford	143.092	59.601s	5	85	Running		12
5	Stefan Johansson (S)	16	Bettenhausen Alumax Aluminum Penske PC22-Ilmor/D	141.318	1m 00.349s	8	84	Running		10
6	Raul Boesel (BR)	5	Simon Duracell/Fuji Film/Mobil/Sadia Lola T94/00-Ford	139.645	1m 01.072s	19	84	Running		8
7	Adrian Fernandez (MEX)	7	Galles Tecate/Quaker State Reynard 94I-Ilmor/D	140.304	1m 00.785s	14	84	Running		6
8	Mauricio Gugelmin (BR)	88	Ganassi Hollywood Reynard 94I-Ford	141.423	1m 00.304s	7	84	Running		5
9	Teo Fabi (I)	11	Hall Pennzoil Special Reynard 94I-Ilmor/D	140.323	1m 00.677s	13	83	Running		4
10	*Alessandro Zampedri (I)	19	Coyne The Mi-Jack Car Lola T93/00-Ford	138.714	1m 01.482s	23	83	Running		3
11	Robby Gordon (USA)	9	Walker Valvoline/Cummins Special Lola T94/00-Ford	141.741	1m 00.169s	6	82	Running		2
12	Willy T. Ribbs (USA)	24	Walker Service Merchandise/Bill Cosby Lola T94/00-Ford	136.636	1m 02.417s	27	82	Running		1
13	*Bryan Herta (USA)	14	A.J. Foyt Copenhagen Racing Lola T94/00-Ford	140.122	1m 00.864s	16	82	Running		
14	Scott Goodyear (CDN)	40	Budweiser King Racing Lola T94/00-Ford	140.210	1m 00.826s	15	81	Running		
15	Hiro Matsushita (J)	22	Simon Panasonic/Duskin Lola T94/00-Ford	137.486	1m 02.031s	25	81	Running		
16	Andrea Montermini (I)	60	Budweiser King Racing Lola T94/00-Ford	138.192	1m 01.714s	24	80	Running		
17	*Parker Johnstone (USA)	49	Comptech Racing Acura Lola T93/00-Honda	135.003	1m 03.172s	28	80	Running		
18	Michael Andretti (USA)	8	Ganassi Target/Scotch Video Reynard 94I-Ford	139.943	1m 00.942s	17	77	Engine		
19	Mike Groff (USA)	10	Rahal-Hogan Motorola Lola T94/00-Honda	139.353	1m 01.200s	21	72	Fuel pump		
20	Emerson Fittipaldi (BR)	2	Marlboro Team Penske PC23-Ilmor/D	143.387	59.478s	3	65	Exhaust header		
21	Arie Luyendyk (NL)	28	Indy Regency Eurosport/Boost Monaco Lola T94/00-Ilmor/D	138.847	1m 01.423s	22	61	Turbo		
22	Mark Smith (USA)	15	Walker Craftsman Tools Lola T94/00-Ford	140.466	1m 00.715s	12	61	Engine		
23	Jeff Wood (USA)	50	Euromotorsport Agip/Hawaiian Tropic Lola T92/00-Ilmor/A	130.862	1m 05.171s	31	53	Exhaust header		
24	*Scott Sharp (USA)	71	PacWest Racing Group Lola T94/00-Ford	139.357	1m 01.198s	20	48	Suspension		
25	Dominic Dobson (USA)	17	PacWest Racing Group Lola T94/00-Ford	139.865	1m 00.976s	18	48	Engine		
26	Marco Greco (BR)	25	Simon Arciero Project Indy Lola T94/00-Ford	137.090	1m 02.210s	26	46	Suspension		
27	Mario Andretti (USA)	6	Newman-Haas Kmart/Texaco Havoline Lola T94/00-Ford	141.143	1m 00.424s	9	31	Suspension		
28	Bobby Rahal (USA)	4	Rahal-Hogan Miller Genuine Draft Lola T94/00-Honda	141.138	1m 00.426s	10	19	Engine		
29	Ross Bentley (CDN)	39	Coyne Agfa Film Lola T92/00-Ilmor/A	133.787	1m 03.746s	30	19	Suspension		
30	*Giovanni Lavaggi (I)	23	Leader Card Financial World Lola T93/00-Ilmor/C	134.770	1m 03.281s	29	12	Exhaust header		
31	Jimmy Vasser (USA)	18	Hayhoe Conseco/STP Reynard 94I-Ford	140.900	1m 00.528s	11	6	Fuel pump mount		

denotes Rookie driver

Caution flags: None.

Lap leaders: Al Unser Jr., 1–28 (28 laps); Emerson Fittipaldi, 29 (1 lap); Unser Jr., 30–57 (28 laps); Nigel Mansell, 58 (1 lap); Fittipaldi, 59 (1 lap); Unser Jr., 60–85 (26 laps). **Totals:** Unser Jr., 82 laps; Fittipaldi, 2 laps; Mansell, 1 lap.

Fastest race lap: Not available.

Championship positions: 1 Unser Jr., 127 pts; **2** Fittipaldi, 86; **3** Mansell, 72; **4** Gordon, 66; **5** Tracy, 64; **6** Michael Andretti, 59; **7** Villeneuve, 46; **8** Johansson, 40; **9** Vasser, 36; **10** Fabi, 32; **11** Boesel, 31; **12** Rahal, 29; **13** Mario Andretti, 28; **14** Gugelmin, 26; **15** Fernandez, 17; **16** M. Groff, 15; **17** Herta, 11; **18** Zampedri, 9; **19** Sharp and Goodyear, 7; **21** Cheever, 5; **22** John Andretti, 4; **23** Luyendyk, 2; **24** Dobson, Jones, Freon, Till, Danner and Ribbs, 1.

TORONTO

1st – MICHAEL A.

2nd – RAHAL

3rd – FITTIPALDI

The Molson Indy Toronto was full of surprises. Not the least of them was the fact that, for the first time since the season-opener in Australia, one of Roger Penske's drivers was not atop the victory podium. The streak was finally over.

After qualifying, a pair of Lola-Ford/Cosworth drivers had looked best placed to bring the Penske charge to an end. Nigel Mansell, of course, was one of them, having hustled Newman-Haas Racing's Kmart/Texaco Havoline car to characteristically good effect on the challenging street course set within Toronto's Exhibition Place fairgrounds complex. But, surprisingly, Mansell wasn't quite fast enough to snare the pole. That honor was taken – for the first time in his career – by Robby Gordon at the wheel of Derrick Walker's Valvoline/Cummins Lola.

Gordon and Mansell ran strongly in the early stages of the 98-lap race, before, coincidentally, both were delayed by punctures. The Penske team also was out of luck. Instead, through into the lead came a typically hard-charging Michael Andretti, running at the front for the first time since his stunning debut victory in Surfers Paradise with Chip Ganassi's Target/Scotch Video Reynard-Ford.

For a while, Andretti's strongest challenge came from another unlikely source, Bobby Rahal's Miller Genuine Draft Lola-Honda, which hitherto had been rarely competitive with the true front-runners. Andretti, though, had matters under control, holding on to score the 29th victory of his Indy Car career.

'It seems like a long time since Australia,' declared Andretti. 'This year's been a strange one. We've been fighting to make the car competitive. To come back here and win at this point in the season is just fantastic.'

Rahal, in second, rewarded his team with its best finish since Vancouver in 1993. His drive included an opportunist pass of Emerson Fittipaldi, who had to be content with third in his Marlboro Penske-Ilmor/D.

Since his sensational season-opening win at Surfers Paradise, Michael Andretti *(left)* had spent most of the year searching for a set-up for his Target/Scotch Video Reynard that would enable him to compete with the front-runners. His unexpected Toronto triumph was a welcome boost for the Ganassi team, which had worked hard to remedy their car's lack of speed.

Emerson Fittipaldi *(top, leading Stefan Johansson)* had an eventful race, much of it locked in combat with Bobby Rahal. The Brazilian veteran eventually had to concede second place to Rahal's Honda-powered Lola.

QUALIFYING

As expected, Mansell and hometown favorite Paul Tracy (Marlboro Penske) were the early pace-setters when the track opened for practice on Friday. The two traded fastest times through much of the 90-minute session before Mansell emerged on top with a best lap in 58.720 seconds. Tracy ended up only fractionally slower, while Andretti ensured all three chassis manufacturers (Lola, Penske and Reynard) were represented among the top three positions. Gordon also was close behind. Then, in afternoon qualifying, in entirely appropriate celebration of Walker's 50th race as a team owner, the young Californian charged to the top of the time sheets to claim his first-ever provisional pole. Gordon's time of 58.154 seconds (110.191 mph) eclipsed Fittipaldi's existing track record by just over one-tenth of a second.

'It's a credit to Derrick's team,' announced Gordon. 'We've been working hard and little by little we've been closing the gap. The car's been so good that I haven't had to go over my head to keep up with the other guys. The Walker crew has given me a great car and it makes my job easier.'

Mansell once again was pressing Gordon for the honor of quickest time when he misjudged his braking for Turn Eight.

'It's a big struggle,' said Mansell. 'This track has just got a little less grip than you anticipate. It's very slippery. I was on a quick lap. On the computer, up until the last couple of corners, I was on a 57-something-second lap; but it doesn't count if you don't finish the lap. I braked a little late. I got round about 90 per cent of the corner, maybe 95 per cent, and then the tire [barrier] just grabbed the left-front [wheel]. Then [the car] stopped real quick.'

Mansell tweaked both wrists in the impact. Fortunately, X-rays revealed no more serious damage. The following morning he was back in action, aided by plenty of heavy strapping.

Series leader Al Unser Jr. improved by almost a second on Friday afternoon to annex third position ahead of Penske team-mates Fittipaldi and Tracy. Michael Andretti also was in close contention.

To everyone's surprise, the track proved slightly slower on Saturday. Unser, following in the wheel tracks of Mansell right at the end of final qualifying, did manage to clip a few fractions from his earlier best, but not enough to improve his grid position. So the order from Friday stood. Gordon's first pole was assured.

'Robby did an exceptional job,' praised team owner Walker. 'He has a competitive background on street courses, so it doesn't surprise me his first pole is at a street course.'

Nevertheless, Gordon's day wasn't without its dramas. First of all, after clipping the wall on the exit of Turn 11 in front of the pits, Gordon suffered a blown rear tire. The youngster did well to maintain control of the car. Then, later, when he ventured out again, Gordon was hit by gearchange difficulties.

'Fortunately, nobody got anywhere near our time from yesterday,' noted race engineer Tim Wardrop.

Indeed, apart from Unser, only two other drivers among the top 20 improved their times from Friday. Both were Canadians. Jacques Villeneuve, who was curiously off the pace all weekend in his Player's Reynard-Ford, overcame an accident on Friday to improve from 24th to 16th, while Scott Goodyear moved from 25th to 19th in his Budweiser Lola-Ford.

RACE

The Lolas of Gordon and Mansell remained atop the time sheets in the final warm-up practice on Sunday morning. Both were looking good for the race, although Mansell gave himself and his team a scare by clipping the inside wall at Turn Three and bending the right-hand steering arm. Contrastingly, farther down the order, Mark Smith was forced to switch to his back-up '93 Lola, following a gearbox failure on his primary Craftsman Tools car.

Another record-sized crowd, packing the grandstands on either side of the start/finish area, ensured a superb spectacle as the 31 cars assembled on the grid. A fascinating race was in prospect.

The field was inordinately strung out as Gordon and Mansell headed the colorful train of cars toward the official starter's gantry, so Jim Swintal had no hesitation in showing the yellow flag. The order wasn't much better next time around but, even so, the front-row starters were greeted by the green. The race was on.

Gordon, Mansell and Unser maintained their grid order through the tight right-hander at Turn One. Behind, Tracy took the opportunity to nip past Fittipaldi. A half-mile or

so later, at the end of the long Lakeshore Boulevard straightaway, Michael Andretti also decided to outbrake the Brazilian. The initial move was clean enough, but then Andretti, on the brakes as late as he dared, came into contact with Tracy.

'It was a real mess down there,' acknowledged Andretti. 'There seemed to be orange and white [Penskes] everywhere.'

Tracy, who was forced to head for the pits, seeking attention to a broken tie-rod on the front suspension, didn't quite see the incident that way.

'I was right there in the pack going into the hairpin,' he related. 'I felt someone hit me from behind and then Michael came past and hit my right-front as well.'

'If I did hit him, I didn't do it on purpose,' responded Andretti. 'It's just one of those things on these race tracks. It's really tight out there.'

A few moments later, Unser's car emitted a huge plume of smoke. The PPG Cup points leader immediately pulled to one side, then coasted into the pits. He remained in the car while his crew took off the bodywork to gain a closer look, but there was nothing to be done. The engine had broken. Unser was out.

And still the opening-lap drama wasn't over. Back in Turn Three there had been an incident involving the '93 Lola-Fords of fellow Italians Alessandro Zampedri and debutant Mimmo Schiattarella. The cars ended up broadside across the road. Then local driver Claude Bourbonnais stalled his engine in attempting to avoid the melee. The track was completely blocked.

Commendably, word of the incident was passed back instantly to race control, whereupon a full-course caution averted any further carnage. Amid the confusion, Arie Luyendyk's Lola-Ilmor was sidelined with electrical problems, while Mark Smith's awful weekend, which included a spectacular slow-motion roll following contact with a tire wall on Friday, also came to a premature end due to an engine failure.

The race was restarted after three laps under yellow. Gordon accelerated early to ensure he was able to maintain his advantage over Mansell, leaving the Briton to come under pressure from a typically aggressive Andretti.

The 1991 PPG Cup champion drew alongside the defending champion under braking for Turn Three but wasn't able to complete the pass. Indeed, having been forced by Mansell onto the outside line, Andretti lost a place as Fittipaldi ducked past.

Gordon took advantage of the dicing behind him to pull out more than five seconds inside a couple of laps. Soon, though, Mansell began to make inroads into that lead. By lap nine the gap was down to 4.03 seconds. Three laps later, Gordon's margin had shrunk to just 2.09 seconds. Mansell was on a charge.

At the same time, Mansell was edging away from Fittipaldi, who had his mirrors full of Andretti's Target Reynard. Behind them was Stefan Johansson, driving strongly in Tony Bettenhausen's year-old Alumax Penske PC22-Ilmor/D. Also in close attendance were Mario Andretti, who was happy with his Kmart/Texaco Havoline Lola-Ford after experiencing gearbox problems in the morning, and Rahal, who looked particularly good through the corners.

As Gordon sped across the start/finish line to complete lap 12, suddenly a puff of smoke emanated from the left-rear corner of his car. An instant later the tire exploded and Gordon was fighting to retain control. He did so, magnificently, but not before sliding down into the escape road in Turn One.

Gordon, who steadfastly maintained he hadn't hit anything untoward to cause the puncture, compounded his problems by stalling the engine. He lost a lap before being push-started by the corner workers. Only then could he return to the pits for a fresh set of tires.

'I want to thank the guys down in Turn One,' said Gordon. 'I don't know how they managed to push-start me with that flat tire.'

In the meantime, the pace car had been sent out again, this time to allow the entire tread of Gordon's tire to be removed safely from the race track.

The next restart came on lap 19. Once again Andretti was on the charge early, this time scorching past Fittipaldi in a bold out-braking maneuver into Turn One. Soon Andretti was on Mansell's tail, anxiously seeking a way past. On lap 26, he made a move under braking at the end of Lakeshore Boulevard. Mansell locked up his brakes in a desperate bid to maintain his lead and, after sliding a little sideways at the apex, the Englishman lost momentum and was clipped by the close-following Andretti. The contact was minimal – so light, in fact, that Mansell didn't realize the two cars

Bobby Rahal *(left)* showed he had lost none of his racing skills. He took advantage of a minor mistake from Emerson Fittipaldi to grab second place and then defended it to the finish. It was the Rahal/Hogan team's best result of the season.

Bottom: Pole-sitter Robby Gordon and Nigel Mansell head Michael Andretti and the rest of the field early in the race. Punctures blunted the challenge of both Lola drivers, but Gordon brought Derrick Walker's Valvoline/Cummins car into sixth place after yet another impressive drive.

stops began on lap 38, when Johansson pulled off into pit lane. It was a lengthy stop, during which the disgruntled Swede fell from third to seventh.

Both Andrettis and Fittipaldi stopped next time around, allowing Rahal – and Honda – the opportunity to lead for two laps before also taking service. It was an historic moment, the very first time a Honda engine had led in Indy Car competition.

Once the stops had been completed, Andretti resumed with a slightly increased lead over Fittipaldi and Rahal, who was still charging along and looking to take over second place. His chance came a few laps later, when Fittipaldi received a call over his radio from team manager Chuck Sprague, beseeching him to lean down the fuel mixture a tad.

'When I was changing it, I hit a bump and [accidentally] switched off the engine,' related Fittipaldi. 'I didn't know what happened. I thought it was [a broken] ignition. Then I saw the ignition was in the wrong position and I switched it on.'

The miscue cost Fittipaldi only a second or two, but it was enough to kill his momentum as he swept past the pits. Rahal grasped his opportunity and dived expertly to the inside under braking for Turn One.

The gap between Andretti and Rahal, now in second, stabilized at around 15 seconds through the middle of the race. Fittipaldi remained within striking distance but never really looked like challenging. Next, now, was Adrian Fernandez, driving well in his Tecate/Quaker State Reynard-Ilmor despite intense pressure from the Hollywood Reynard-Ford of Mauricio Gugelmin. Then came Mario Andretti, after a slow stop, and the delayed Johansson.

A little farther back, Ross Bentley enjoyed a rare taste of glory by moving into the top ten briefly with Dale Coyne's trusty Agfa Lola T92/00. The Canadian had taken advantage of the early yellows to take on service. He was planning to complete the race on only one stop. Sadly, after 81 laps, his Ilmor/A engine succumbed, effectively, to old age.

On lap 62, as the dicing Rahal and Fittipaldi encountered a bunch of slower traffic, Fittipaldi's crew tried to steal an advantage by calling him in early for his second pit stop. The idea was for Fittipaldi to resume on fresh tires and, with luck, make up enough time so that he would remain ahead when Rahal, in turn, made his own second stop. The gamble didn't pay off.

Seven laps later, an even bigger traffic jam converged on Turn Three – this time with disastrous results for Fernandez and Gugelmin, whose protracted duel was now for third place. With no fewer than three slower cars in front, Fernandez dived to the inside of Willy T. Ribbs under braking. At the same time, Gugelmin lunged to the outside. Right behind, Tracy, who was still a lap down but making up ground rapidly, could sense what was to come.

'I saw it was getting real crowded,' said Tracy, 'so I braked early and left them all some room.' Smart move.

Poor Ribbs, of course, was caught between a rock (Fernandez on the inside) and a hard place (Gugelmin to his left). Contact, somewhere, was inevitable, and indeed all three cars became entangled. Tracy and Gordon had to come to a complete halt, while an innocent Mike Groff (Motorola Lola-Honda) was embroiled in the mess, retiring there and then when the transmission locked up.

The incident almost spelled disaster for the race leader, too, since a miscommunication among the officials

had touched – but it was enough to puncture Nigel's right-rear tire.

'I just tapped him a little bit,' admitted Andretti. 'A few corners later I noticed all of a sudden there was something wrong [with Mansell's car], and that's how I was able to get by.'

The Newman-Haas Lola snaked under acceleration through the sweeping Turns Six and Seven, allowing Andretti to pass, and yet still Mansell didn't realize he was in trouble. Instead of pulling into the pits, he struggled onward. He was forced to do a complete extra lap, by which time the tire had completely disintegrated. Mansell, like Tracy and Gordon before him, lost a lap before rejoining. Afterward he ran quickly for a while, before slowing dramatically. Mansell eventually pulled into the pits after 66 laps, alighted briskly, and declared the car 'undrivable.'

Michael Andretti, meanwhile, was left holding a clear lead over Fittipaldi, who was troubled by oversteer. Johansson continued impressively in third, driving his spare PC22 following gearbox problems in the primary car on Friday, while Mario Andretti and Rahal vigorously disputed fourth place.

The first round of scheduled pit

Mario Andretti *(bottom)* could not improve upon tenth-fastest time in qualifying, but in a race of attrition and incident the veteran salvaged fourth place for Newman-Haas after team-mate Nigel Mansell had given up, claiming handling problems made the sister car 'undrivable.'

led to the pace car being scrambled onto the race track in error. Andretti slowed as soon as he saw the flashing lights. He, like pace car driver Johnny Rutherford, was confused by the fact the marshals were not displaying the usual crossed yellow flags. Was there a full-course caution or not?

In fact, there wasn't supposed to be, but the officials had been encountering radio problems all weekend. As soon as the correct information had been relayed to Rutherford, he switched off the lights and signalled the race cars to pass before making his way quickly (and less conspicuously) back to the pits.

The incident cost Andretti around 20 seconds, although that wasn't immediately apparent because Rahal wisely had chosen those few minutes of confusion to duck into the pits for his own second stop. He resumed in third, briefly behind Johansson until the Swede stopped for service.

Mario Andretti also pitted, but promptly lost more valuable time when he inadvertently killed the engine. This just wasn't turning out to be Mario's day.

At least his son was enjoying better fortune, although Michael's own second stop on lap 75 went awry due to a

Nunn the wiser

Since his triumph at Surfers Paradise, Michael Andretti had grown increasingly exasperated by the fact that several other Reynard runners had fared rather better than he on a consistent basis. In consecutive races at Detroit, Portland and Cleveland, for example, Michael was out-qualified by team-mate Mauricio Gugelmin, whose 94I was being run on a fraction of the budget of Andretti's car. More embarrassingly, the underrated Gugelmin had tested not a single day since the start of the season, and his car boasted none of the development pieces that had been tried on Andretti's 'factory' car.

The primary concern, according to Andretti, was the Reynard chassis's tendency toward understeer.

'For my driving style, that's the worst thing I can have,' he said. 'The harder I try, the slower I go.'

A barrage of engineers, led by Reynard's Malcolm Oastler and Bruce Ashmore, working with Ganassi's technical chief, Julian Robertson, had struggled to alleviate the problem. They were joined in early July by veteran

British race engineer (and former car owner) Morris Nunn, who had recently departed from Dick Simon Racing following a less than amicable verbal exchange with the team's new Director of Racing, Emory Donaldson.

Nunn *(seen above with Andretti)* was no stranger to the Ganassi operation, having worked with the team in 1993. True, the season with Arie Luyendyk was largely disappointing, but there were several notable highlights, among them pole at Indianapolis and some strong showings on road courses toward the end of the year.

'I think the combination of Mo and Julian is a good one,' reflected Andretti. 'They worked together last year and they get along well. It's one of those deals where you come in from the outside and you see things slightly differently. I feel a little more confident in the car.

'We started off the weekend fairly good and stayed with it. In the race I had a good, consistent car. At the end, when I needed to, I was able to do some quick times when Bobby [Rahal] was leaning on me. I think that says a lot about the car.'

problem in activating the air jacks. Fortunately, his crew remained relatively calm and only a little time was lost. It could have been much worse. Nevertheless, his advantage already eroded by the delay caused by the pace car mishap, Michael resumed

with a slender four-second lead over the on-form Rahal.

'I thought, oh boy, here we go,' said Andretti. 'Now we've got to fight. From there on I just drove as hard as I could.'

Rahal can attest to that.

'Michael was running some very fast laps at the end and I just couldn't catch him,' said the three-time champion. 'We ran 59-second laps and that's close to where we qualified.'

The gap back to Fittipaldi fluctuated according to the traffic. Sometimes they were separated by as much as four seconds; other times it was just a few car lengths. Rahal, though, kept his cool and his hard-won second place.

'It's definitely a morale boost for the crew,' concluded Rahal, who overcame the fact his Honda motor still was some 7–8 mph slower on top-end speed in comparison to the Ilmors and Fords. 'I had enough speed through the twisty bits to hold off Emerson on the straightaways.'

Fittipaldi was duly impressed.

'Bobby was very good today,' praised the 47-year-old Brazilian. 'He was driving very quick.'

Johansson looked set for a fourth-place finish until just 13 laps to go, when his Penske was stricken by gearchange difficulties. Johansson, reduced to a virtual crawl, undeservedly finished just out of the points.

Mario Andretti thus inherited fourth after his eventful day, earning a solid round of applause from the appreciative crowd. The biggest cheer of all, however, was reserved for Tracy, who, despite the early delay, charged hard throughout the race. His reward was fifth place and ten PPG Cup points.

'It was a tough race,' said Tracy, who overtook Gordon with just five laps remaining. 'The main thing I thought about was points, points, points. I was chasing Robby at the end and they told me over the radio it was for fifth place, so I just kept on driving as hard as I could. I felt it was one of my best races of the year so far.'

Gordon drove equally well for sixth, having gambled on his final stop, on lap 87, by not taking on fresh tires. The time saved in the pits enabled him to slip ahead of Tracy; but that wasn't enough. Tracy, on fresh rubber, was able to run him down, taking the place for good when Gordon's car slithered under heavy braking in Turn Three.

The young chargers of the Indy Car circuit had provided most of the excitement, with Andrea Montermini also driving well to a season-high seventh for Kenny Bernstein's team. Stablemate Goodyear claimed tenth after losing time at his first pit stop.

SNIPPETS

• Bryan Herta's impressive rookie season was sadly truncated when the 24-year-old suffered a frightening crash on Saturday morning. Herta was hustling A.J. Foyt's Copenhagen Lola-Ford with his customary verve when, apparently, the car bottomed over one of the bumps and crashed at the very fast left-hander in front of the pits. The car slammed into the outside wall, whereupon the right-front wheel was punched through the side of the composite monocoque. Herta had to be cut out of the mangled remains of his car, suffering from a broken pelvis, a broken right femur and some internal injuries.

• Mauricio Gugelmin became a proud father for the first time when wife Stella

gave birth to a baby boy, Bernardo, just before midnight on the Wednesday prior to Toronto. A half-hour or so later, but now on Thursday, the Gugelmin household increased

still further with the arrival of a twin brother, Giuliano.

• Mimmo Schiattarella (below) made a promising Indy Car debut at the wheel

of Project Indy's ex-Matsushita '93 Lola-Ford. The veteran of Italian Formula 3, who contested a few Player's Toyota Atlantic Championship races in Canada in 1993, had gained his first taste of Indy Car power during a brief test at Putnam Park earlier in the week.

• Teo Fabi continued to struggle with Jim Hall's Pennzoil Reynard-Ilmor. After practice on Friday, the crew, led by Alex Hering, stripped the car down to its bare tub and made wholesale changes. 'When you're this far back,' commented Hall, 'there's no point in just changing the shock absorbers.' It didn't seem to make much difference. Fabi, who had been 12th on Friday, was 12th again on Saturday morning and remained 12th on the grid.

Michael C. Brown

PPG INDY CAR WORLD SERIES • ROUND 9

MOLSON INDY TORONTO

EXHIBITION PLACE CIRCUIT, TORONTO, ONTARIO, CANADA

JULY 17, 98 LAPS – 174.44 MILES

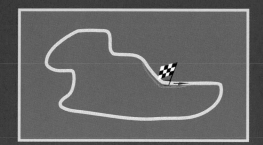

Place	Driver (Nat.)	No.	Team Sponsors Car-Engine	Q Speed (mph)	Q Time	Q Pos.	Laps	Time/Status	Ave. (mph)	Pts.
1	**Michael Andretti (USA)**	8	**Ganassi Target/Scotch Video Reynard 94I-Ford**	109.027	58.775s	6	98	1h48m 15.978s	96.673	21
2	**Bobby Rahal (USA)**	4	**Rahal-Hogan Miller Genuine Draft Lola T94/00-Honda**	108.209	59.219s	9	98	1h 48m 22.779s	96.572	16
3	**Emerson Fittipaldi (BR)**	2	**Marlboro Team Penske PC23-Ilmor/D**	109.136	58.715s	4	98	1h 48m 23.527s	96.561	14
4	**Mario Andretti (USA)**	6	**Newman-Haas Kmart/Texaco Havoline Lola T94/00-Ford**	108.036	59.314s	10	98	1h 49m 18.393s	95.753	12
5	**Paul Tracy (CDN)**	3	**Marlboro Team Penske PC23-Ilmor/D**	109.094	58.738s	5	97	Running		10
6	**Robby Gordon (USA)**	9	**Walker Valvoline/Cummins Special Lola T94/00-Ford**	110.191	58.154s	1	97	Running		9
7	**Andrea Montermini (I)**	60	**Budweiser King Racing Lola T94/00-Ford**	107.657	59.522s	13	97	Running		6
8	**Teo Fabi (I)**	11	**Hall Pennzoil Special Reynard 94I-Ilmor/D**	107.885	59.397s	12	97	Running		5
9	***Jacques Villeneuve (CDN)**	12	**Forsythe-Green Player's Ltd. Reynard 94I-Ford**	107.571	59.570s	15	97	Running		4
10	**Scott Goodyear (CDN)**	40	**Budweiser King Racing Lola T94/00-Ford**	107.208	59.772s	18	97	Running		3
11	**Dominic Dobson (USA)**	17	**PacWest Racing Group Lola T94/00-Ford**	107.440	59.643s	16	97	Engine		2
12	**Raul Boesel (BR)**	5	**Simon Duracell/Fuji Film/Mobil/Sadia Lola T94/00-Ford**	107.348	59.694s	17	97	Running		1
13	Adrian Fernandez (MEX)	7	Galles Tecate/Quaker State Reynard 94I-Ilmor/D	108.002	59.332s	11	97	Running		
14	Stefan Johansson (S)	16	Bettenhausen Alumax Aluminum Penske PC22-Ilmor/D	108.372	59.130s	7	97	Running		
15	Marco Greco (BR)	25	Simon Arciero Project Indy Lola T94/00-Ford	107.015	59.879s	21	96	Running		
16	*Scott Sharp (USA)	71	PacWest Racing Group Lola T94/00-Ford	107.055	59.857s	20	94	Exhaust header		
17	*Alessandro Zampedri (I)	19	Coyne The Mi-Jack Car Lola T93/00-Ford	106.223	1m 00.326s	25	93	Spin/stalled		
18	Hiro Matsushita (J)	22	Simon Panasonic/Duskin Lola T94/00-Ford	103.683	1m 01.804s	29	85	Running		
19	Ross Bentley (CDN)	39	Coyne Agfa Film Lola T92/00-Ilmor/A	102.976	1m 02.228s	30	81	Oil pressure		
20	Mauricio Gugelmin (BR)	88	Ganassi Hollywood Reynard 94I-Ford	107.606	59.551s	14	69	Suspension		
21	Willy T. Ribbs (USA)	24	Walker Service Merchandise/Bill Cosby Lola T94/00-Ford	105.271	1m 00.871s	27	66	Accident		
22	Mike Groff (USA)	10	Rahal-Hogan Motorola Lola T94/00-Honda	107.105	59.829s	19	66	Transmission		
23	Nigel Mansell (GB)	1	Newman-Haas Kmart/Texaco Havoline Lola T94/00-Ford	109.924	58.295s	2	66	Handling		
24	*Claude Bourbonnnais (CDN)	30	McCormack Motorsports Player's Ltd. Lola T93/00-Ilmor/C	105.427	1m 00.782s	26	57	Accident		
25	Jimmy Vasser (USA)	18	Hayhoe Conseco/STP Reynard 94I-Ford	108.351	59.141s	8	43	Spin/stalled		
26	*Mimmo Schiattarella (I)	64	Project Indy No Touch/Van Dyne/Marcelo Lola T93/00-Ford	106.607	1m 00.109s	23	31	Transmission		
27	*Parker Johnstone (USA)	49	Comptech Racing Acura Lola T93/00-Honda	104.829	1m 01.128s	28	30	Transmission		
28	Jeff Wood (USA)	50	Euromotorsport Agip/Hawaiian Tropic Lola T92/00-Ilmor/A	94.506	1m 07.805s	31	12	Electrical		
29	Al Unser Jr. (USA)	31	Marlboro Team Penske PC23-Ilmor/D	109.565	58.486s	3	2	Engine		
30	Mark Smith (USA)	15	Walker Craftsman Tools Lola T93/00-Ford	106.686	1m 00.064s	22	2	Engine		
31	Arie Luyendyk (NL)	28	Indy Regency Eurosport/Boost Monaco Lola T94/00-Ilmor/D	106.447	1m 00.199s	24	1	Electrical		
NS	*Bryan Herta (USA)	14	A.J. Foyt Copenhagen Racing Lola T94/00-Ford	107.735	59.479s	–	–	Withdrawn/accident		
NS	Buddy Lazier (USA)	23	Leader Card Financial World Lola T93/00-Ilmor/C	96.947	1m 06.098s	–	–	Withdrawn/engine		

denotes Rookie driver

Caution flags: Lap 1, no start; laps 2–4, accident/Smith & Luyendyk; laps 13–17, flat tire, debris/Gordon. Total three for nine laps.

Lap leaders: Robby Gordon, 1–12 (12 laps); Nigel Mansell, 13–25 (13 laps); Michael Andretti, 26–38 (13 laps); Bobby Rahal, 39–40 (2 laps); Andretti, 41–98 (58 laps). **Totals:** Andretti, 71 laps; Mansell, 13 laps; Gordon, 12 laps; Rahal, 2 laps.

Fastest race lap: Michael Andretti, 59.153s, 108.329 mph, on lap 86.

Championship positions: 1 Unser Jr., 127 pts; **2** Fittipaldi, 100; **3** Michael Andretti, 80; **4** Gordon, 75; **5** Tracy, 74; **6** Mansell, 72; **7** Villeneuve, 50; **8** Rahal, 45; **9** Mario Andretti and Johansson, 40; **11** Fabi, 37; **12** Vasser, 36; **13** Boesel, 32; **14** Gugelmin, 26; **15** Fernandez, 17; **16** M. Groff, 15; **17** Herta, 11; **18** Goodyear, 10; **19** Zampedri, 9; **20** Sharp, 7; **21** Montermini, 6; **22** Cheever, 5; **23** John Andretti and Dobson, 3; **25** Luyendyk, 2; **26** Jones, Freon, Till, Danner and Ribbs, 1.

MICHIGAN

1st – GOODYEAR	
2nd – LUYENDYK	
3rd – DOBSON	

Prior to the Marlboro 500 at Michigan International Speedway, the 1994 PPG Cup season had not been kind to Budweiser King Racing. The previous Monday, with only a pair of tenth-place finishes to show from nine races, team owner Kenny Bernstein had informed his crew that major sponsor Budweiser would be withdrawing its support at the end of the season. Driver Scott Goodyear already had given notice he wouldn't be taking up the option for a second year on his contract. The team's future was in serious jeopardy.

As a result, Goodyear arrived at MIS knowing his team would not spend the money to procure the latest developments for its Ford/Cosworth XB engines. He would have to make do with the standard package, and as such was not expecting to be on the ultimate front-running pace.

It didn't matter. By the end of a dramatic, exciting and sometimes positively frightening 250-lap race, all of the more fancied contenders had fallen by the wayside, mostly as a result of engine failures or accidents – or, in the case of Adrian Fernandez, a brief but explosive pit fire. Fortunately, no one was seriously injured in any of the incidents.

And through it all came Goodyear, who survived one fright when he ran out of fuel while leading on lap 170. Again, it was of little consequence. Goodyear was still running strongly at the finish, heading just eight survivors from a starting field of 28.

'It's a great feeling,' said the popular Canadian after earning the second victory of his Indy Car career. 'We played it smart and ran as strong as we could.'

Superspeedway specialist Arie Luyendyk (Eurosport/Boost Monaco Lola-Ilmor) and MIS rookie Dominic Dobson (PacWest Racing Group Lola-Ford) joined Goodyear on the victory podium in what also represented their best finishes of the year.

Below left: Budweiser King Racing's largely moribund season was lifted by Scott Goodyear's unexpected triumph in the Marlboro 500. Goodyear *(inset)* was still running strongly at the finish as other more fancied runners fell by the wayside.

Left: Dominic Dobson's first visit to MIS was rewarded with a third-place finish. The result was another boost to the credibility of the ambitious PacWest Racing Group in its first season of Indy Car racing.

QUALIFYING

Shortly after the start of practice, the official timing monitors began to display evidence to suggest Mario Andretti's year-old qualifying lap record of 234.275 mph – a world closed-course record – was in serious jeopardy. Indeed, within 45 minutes, Mario himself had become the first driver above 230 mph. By the end of the first session, six drivers had topped that mark, with Raul Boesel fleetest of all at 233.866 mph in Dick Simon's Duracell/Sadia Lola-Ford/Cosworth.

The afternoon session was interrupted once because of a rain shower, which served to wash away some of the rubber laid down in the morning, and then again when rookie Alessandro Zampedri crashed Dale Coyne's Mi-Jack Lola T93/00-Ford in Turn Four. The impact was massive, and the likable Italian, who had already topped an impressive 224 mph in his first run ever on an oval, was trapped in the car.

The accident occurred after his right-front tire exploded, most likely after picking up some debris. Zampedri's injuries were initially reported as being slight, although it later transpired he had sustained a cracked pelvis following an almost identical impact – albeit at greater speed – to that experienced by Bryan Herta in Toronto.

Another rookie, Scott Sharp, hit the wall later in the day, fortunately sustaining nothing worse than a few bruises, while both Michael Andretti and Jimmy Vasser had near-misses in their Reynards. Close inspection revealed that a mounting bracket for the left-rear lower wishbone had cracked on both cars. By the following morning, every Reynard had been fitted with specially strengthened parts manufactured overnight at the nearby shop of Roush Racing.

Near-perfect conditions on Saturday morning saw speeds continue to rise. Three drivers – Mansell and the two Andrettis, Mario and Michael – bettered the track record. Mansell led the way on 235.639 mph. Boesel and Robby Gordon also were above 232 mph, emphasizing the prodigious top-end power of the Ford/Cosworth XB engines. Emerson Fittipaldi was fastest of the Ilmor contingent, sixth at 231.224 mph.

Official qualifying was similarly conclusive, with the only surprise being that Mansell, on pole, fell shy of the track record.

A test of endurance

Michigan International Speedway poses the season's sternest test of man and machine. The D-shaped two-mile oval's 18-degree banking imposes tremendous lateral G-forces, which, on their own, are hard enough to bear for a full 500-mile distance. Add in the ripple effect of hundreds of small asphalt patches all around the track, a legacy of the harsh Michigan winters, together with awesomely fast speeds, and the loadings on both car and driver reach almost unimaginable levels.

In 1993, after winning the Marlboro 500, Mansell had to be helped from his car. He had been unwell in the days leading up to the race, and the constant pounding over the bumps, combined with the intense level of concentration required by the unrelenting speeds, had left him totally drained by the finish. Afterward he described the race as the toughest of his entire career.

The track, of course, is just as hard on the cars. This year both Reynard and Lola were obliged to supply quick-fixes after experiencing suspension breakages on their cars during practice. Penske, too, had rushed to produce stronger steel engine mountings just a few days earlier, after detecting a potential problem with its aluminum brackets.

'The most important thing in this race is that you're there at the end,' confirmed Scott Goodyear, whose only previous Indy Car victory came at MIS in 1992. 'You have to keep up the pace and keep out of trouble. It's difficult, but you're always looking for the smoother parts of the race track. It all comes down to endurance.'

And perhaps a slice of good fortune . . .

'We'll take [the win] any way it comes,' says Goodyear. 'I'd take five or six of these "lucky" wins every year if I could, because it's a great boost for myself and the team. But the biggest key is you've got to keep on pushing and never stop.'

'We were flat out,' said Mansell. 'I think the track was a little bit slower than this morning. It was warmer out there and the car wasn't moving as well with the same set-up.

'This is the most significant pole I think I've ever had in my career,' he continued, 'and the reason is that this is the fastest circuit in the world. It's a wild race track. It's one of the most challenging race tracks in the world, simply because to average over 230 mph is quite daunting.'

Boesel and Michael Andretti shared the front row with Mansell. Mario Andretti, who complained his car felt 'a bit sluggish,' was disappointed to qualify only fifth, behind Gordon.

Stefan Johansson drove impressively to take sixth on the grid, fastest of the Penske-Ilmor brigade in Tony Bettenhausen's year-old Alumax PC22 chassis. Dobson also posted a fine effort, recording his fastest lap of the weekend to secure a starting position on row three.

RACE

Further evidence of the rigors of racing at MIS came shortly after the morning warm-up session when Walker Racing undertook some pit stop practice with Mark Smith's Craftsman Lola. A loud 'crack!' was heard during the routine, although no one paid much attention until afterward, when the car was rolled onto the set-up pad and it was discovered to have excessive cross-weight on one front wheel. Further investigation revealed a fracture in the machined lower beam that provides primary support for the front suspension. Team-mate Robby Gordon's car was found to have an identical problem.

Time, of course, was short but, after consultation with the Lola engineers, the team decided to add support on either side of the beam. Most other Lola teams adopted similar strengthening.

All cars were ready in time for the traditional pre-race ceremonies, and the largest field at MIS in five years was enough for IndyCar to implement its first three-abreast start since 1990. The action was intense from the moment the green flag waved. Mansell took advantage of his pole position to take the lead

into Turn One, but Boesel and Michael Andretti ensured a superb spectacle as they maintained side-by-side formation.

Boesel wisely chose to back off just a fraction, leaving Andretti to chase Mansell in the opening stages. Behind them was Mario Andretti, then Fittipaldi, who was passed on lap two by a charging Gordon. Paul Tracy, Johansson, Jacques Villeneuve (Player's Reynard) and Goodyear completed the top ten.

Mansell quickly pulled away at the front of the field. By lap eight, he had stretched his advantage to four seconds over the younger Andretti.

Gordon, too, was running well. He passed Mario Andretti early, and on lap 15 moved by Boesel into third place. By lap 23 he was right on the tail of Michael Andretti, although a split second later he was fighting for his life after his right-front tire literally exploded at maximum speed.

Fortunately, the failure occurred on the tri-oval section of the track rather than under maximum G-loading in the corners. Gordon was able to bring the car under control and make it safely back to the pits.

The yellow lights flashed on instantly to warn other drivers of the debris from Gordon's blown tire. Then, after everyone had made their first pit stop of the day, it became apparent Gordon wasn't the only one in trouble. A few laps earlier, as Mansell sped into Turn One at well over 230 mph, his throttle had stuck wide open.

Mansell, like Gordon, was lucky. He, too, was able to make it safely onto pit lane. But after several stops while his crew isolated the problem, it became apparent no cure would be possible. A butterfly valve inside the plenum had failed. He was done for the day.

'That's the scariest moment I've had in my whole career,' said a white-faced Mansell. 'The throttle stuck wide open like a switch. You just can't drive the car that way. You need the throttle control in the corners to balance the car.'

Gordon, meanwhile, was able to resume, albeit a lap down after his crew changed a bent steering arm.

Michael Andretti took over in the lead, and after fending off a challenge from Boesel at the restart he began to move clear. Andretti's car

was handling perfectly following a slight wing change at his first stop.

By lap 58, when he recorded his fastest lap at 228.451 mph, Andretti had stretched his lead to nine seconds over a dicing Boesel and Mario Andretti. Al Unser Jr. had moved stealthily up to fourth, a considerable distance behind, while Adrian Fernandez also was running well, fifth in the Tecate/Quaker State Reynard-Ilmor after disposing of Fittipaldi.

On lap 64, Unser and Fernandez both pitted for service. But while Unser was on his way with a minimum of delay, a miscue over signals saw Fernandez attempt to resume before refueling was complete – with disastrous consequences, as a fire immediately erupted in the Galles pit.

Thankfully, a major catastrophe was averted by some prompt reflex action from the pit marshals and the Galles team, as well as the adjacent Newman-Haas crew, who quelled the flames with remarkable rapidity. Apart from some minor scalding, no one was seriously hurt. It could have been so much worse.

But, once again, that wasn't the only drama. As the caution lights flashed on a second time, Michael Andretti was busily negotiating a group of back-markers, and as he sped into Turn One he didn't notice the yellows. The drivers in front of him, however, did, and suddenly Andretti was confronted by a couple of slowing cars. He locked his carbon front brakes momentarily on instinct, then dodged high on the banking to avoid contact with the rear end of Tracy's Penske, which, incidentally, had been delayed earlier by a mix-up over tires in the pits.

'If the track had been a couple of feet wider at that point, I wouldn't have tagged the wall,' reflected Andretti. Unfortunately, it wasn't, so he did. For the second time inside 67 laps, the fastest car was out.

Shortly after the restart, second-placed Villeneuve also came to grief when an unexplained failure on the right-rear of his car sent him crashing into the wall in Turn Three. It was a severe impact. Once again, the driver escaped serious injury, although Villeneuve was briefly trapped in his car.

The attrition was building. Both Lola-Hondas had gone out of the race early. In fact, following three engine failures during practice, the team had decided not to chance another major problem which, conceivably, might have put Bobby Rahal and Mike Groff at risk. Both cars were

Running side by side on Michigan's testing 18-degree banking are Mauricio Gugelmin *(left)* and Arie Luyendyk, who survived a gruelling race to claim second place in the Indy Regency team's Eurosport/Boost Monaco Lola.

withdrawn as a precautionary measure, although as a public relations gesture the official reasons for retirement were stated as fuel pump (Rahal) and clutch (Groff).

Eddie Cheever, invited by A.J. Foyt to stand in for the injured Bryan Herta, and Buddy Lazier also were out, along with Jimmy Vasser, who had run comfortably inside the top ten.

There was a lengthy caution while the wreckage from Villeneuve's accident was cleared, and shortly afterward there was a shorter delay to inspect the track for more debris after both Jeff Wood and Johansson suffered punctured left-rear tires.

When the green flag waved again, with 96 laps in the books, Boesel took advantage of a clear track to pull out more than six seconds over Mario. But soon Mario began to close again. On lap 111 he circulated at better than 228 mph. By lap 118 the gap between the two leaders had shrunk to 1.83 seconds.

That, sadly, was as close as they came. Andretti made a scheduled pit stop next time around, but then, after just one more lap, his engine let go. There had been no warning.

'I don't think I've ever had a car working so good here,' lamented Andretti. 'The engine was working great. I thought I had a definite shot at Raul.'

Clearly he did. Andretti's demise came as a disappointment not only for himself but also to his countless fans. Even many rivals on pit lane conceded they would have relished the prospect of Indy Car racing's Grand Old Man winning his 67th and final 500-mile race. Sadly, it was not to be.

Boesel was completing his own pit stop just as Mario slowed on the back stretch, thus promoting Unser into the lead for the first time. The Brazilian's stop also enabled Gordon and Goodyear to move back onto the lead lap. Soon, though, the yellows were out again, this time to enable Mario's stricken car to be moved.

Boesel regained the point when everyone else pitted under caution. Unser continued in second ahead of Fittipaldi, while Goodyear motored past Gordon immediately after the restart on lap 132. The race was still only just over halfway through. Dobson, who was committed to making a pit stop just as the yellow lights came on, was now two laps behind and being chased by Johansson.

The middle part of the race was the least dramatic. It also saw the

Inches apart at around 200 mph, young lions Robby Gordon *(top)* and Paul Tracy battle for position.

Nigel Mansell *(below)* was glad to emerge intact after suffering a throttle linkage failure on his Kmart/Texaco Havoline Lola.

longest uninterrupted running under green flag conditions. Boesel's Duracell Lola continued in front, although Unser never lost touch. Indeed, on lap 159, after Boesel began to experience increasing understeer, the series leader swept ahead coming off Turn Two.

Boesel made a bee-line for the pit road after 164 laps, enabling his crew to make a slight change to the front wings. Both Penskes were in next time around. Goodyear was elevated into the lead, still with Gordon glued to his gearbox, until the Californian pitted on lap 168.

The Budweiser car continued to run in front, its driver and crew having kept a close eye on the telemetry, which confirmed they could run another couple of laps before stopping for fuel. But there was some kind of glitch in the electronics. On lap 170, as Goodyear came out of Turn Two, the car suddenly slowed. Its fuel tank was dry.

Looking on the bright side, the problem highlighted the efficiency of modern fuel systems: 'The engine didn't even cough,' said Goodyear, 'it just died.' But the Canadian's mishap also showed just how much reliance is placed these days on computers and electronics. One error can be crucial.

But Goodyear was lucky. He was able to coast around to his pit. The hot engine refired almost immediately. Two laps, however, had been lost.

'You talk about a pit in your stomach,' said Goodyear. 'It was the worst feeling I've ever had in my life.'

At least he was able to continue. Mauricio Gugelmin, meanwhile, was out of the race, having crashed in the pit lane after making a routine

stop. A failure of some sort was suspected, although quite what let go remained a mystery due to the damage inflicted by the Reynard's impact against the wall.

Tracy was also gone by this stage (fuel pressure), and a little while later Johansson coasted in, his engine broken. These dramas aside, the race continued to run under green until lap 184, when Gordon's engine blew spectacularly between Turns Three and Four. Exit another top contender.

'It just popped,' declared Gordon, who had been dicing for third place with Fittipaldi prior to his untimely demise. 'We were running pretty conservative all day in sixth gear. I think we definitely had a shot at winning it.'

Now just three cars remained on the lead lap: Unser, Boesel and Fittipaldi. All three made routine stops under the yellow caused by Gordon's oil-down. Goodyear, elevated to fourth, was able to claim back one of his lost laps by eschewing a pit stop.

Soon after the restart, on lap 192, Boesel showed his hand by using the draft perfectly to slip past Unser into Turn One. Dobson, meanwhile, had incurred the officials' wrath for allegedly passing the pace car. He was assessed a 30-second stop-and-wait penalty which left him still in fifth position but now three laps off the ultimate pace.

Moments later came even worse news for the PacWest team when the sister car of Scott Sharp ground to a halt in the tri-oval due to a drive-line failure. Out came the pace car again.

Despite all the action, three cars remained in contention for the win . . . until lap 209, when Fittipaldi pulled off abruptly. 'It's just a shame,' said Fittipaldi. 'The car was running strong the whole race. Then the engine blew.'

Now just two cars were on the lead lap. But, as has been proven at Michigan before, it only takes two cars to ensure an exciting race. Boesel and Unser were putting on quite a contest. Indeed, as the race entered its final 100-mile phase, the pace was quickening.

The gap between the two leaders fluctuated between one and two seconds, according to traffic conditions – although, admittedly, that was becoming less of a factor as cars fell by the wayside. On lap 222, Boesel turned his fastest lap of the race at 228.172 mph. Unser more than matched that with an overall best of 229.199 mph.

Six laps later, Boesel's dreams of a long overdue maiden Indy Car victory were cruelly dashed. Engine.

'When I came out of [Turn] Two, there was no power,' said a bitterly disappointed Boesel. 'I thought, *#@! [expletive deleted], what are you gonna do?

'I try to see the positive side. I was comfortable and I think I drove very well. I drove the wheels off the thing but I was keeping calm under the circumstances, especially when Al Jr. overtook me. I was checking the temperatures and the revs.

'At least it shows I'm there, I can win.'

Boesel gained solace afterward in the team's motorhome, accompanied only by his family.

'I had tears,' he admitted. 'My kids [Raul Jr. and Gabriela] were there and [wife] Vera. I just wanted to stay with them a little bit, to enjoy the good things in life.'

Unser was left holding a one-lap advantage, his sixth win of the year seemingly assured. But even Unser said he was sorry to see Boesel go.

'I felt sorry for the fans, because me and Raul were gonna have a super race,' said Unser. 'We were pretty even in [Turns] Three and Four, and I could catch him a little in One and Two.'

Now, it seemed, no one would catch Unser. Unless . . . Indeed, the drama wasn't over yet. Six laps later, having made his own final fuel stop, Unser suddenly slowed, a tell-tale plume of smoke emanating from the back of his car.

'We were just cruising, really,' he said, philosophical as ever. 'I turned the boost down. There was really no reason for it to go. We gave it our best effort. We just came up short today.'

What else could happen? That's what Goodyear was thinking as he

took over in the lead. Eighteen laps remained. Thirty-six miles. Anything could happen.

A final caution, to deal with oil from Unser's Ilmor/D, once again proved ill-timed for Dobson, who at that very moment was slowing down on pit lane, ready for his final splash of fuel. Luyendyk, meanwhile, far happier in the race than in practice following a consultation with Dick Simon, who recommended an entirely different set-up on his Lola, was able to complete one extra lap before stopping under green. He, unlike Dobson, did not lose a lap, and therefore took over in second place.

The final cards had been played. Goodyear duly reeled off the remaining laps, although they couldn't go by fast enough.

'Those last 15 laps, it just seemed like such a long time,' he said. 'You just had to keep the pace up and keep out of trouble.'

Which he did admirably.

'I'm just so happy for my guys,' said an emotional Goodyear. 'They did a great job today, especially in the pit stops. We knew, if we ran consistent, we'd be there at the end.'

The same could be said of any of the remaining seven finishers. The last of them, Marco Greco, earned a couple of points, his first of the season, after his crew replaced a broken water hose. Luyendyk, Dobson, Smith, who overcame the morning suspension scare, Hiro Matsushita (Panasonic/Duskin Lola-Ford) and Willy T. Ribbs (Service Merchandise Lola-Ford) all earned by far their best finishes of the season, albeit through consistency rather than pace. Fabi equaled his best result after what he regarded as a disappointing run in the Pennzoil Reynard-Ilmor.

'It's a good thing I finished fourth,' quipped Fabi. 'I would have been embarrassed to go to the press conference.' Luyendyk, though, after claiming second in Sal Incandela's Indy Regency Lola-Ilmor, was rather more pragmatic: 'I just needed one more to go out [of the race] today,' he reflected, a gleam in his eye.

Photos: Michael C. Brown

SNIPPETS

• 'There's one thing I've learned about the ovals,' said Mansell as he waited to learn whether his qualifying speed would stand up for the pole. 'If there's cloud cover, it's cooler. You get more grip, you don't slide so much and you get more power. That's 2 mph. And that's down to luck.'

• A section of track in Turn Three was repaved for the second time this year after it had broken up during the NASCAR Winston Cup race in June. This time the asphalt caused no further problems. MIS owner Roger Penske is contemplating a complete resurfacing prior to the 1995 season.

• Scott Goodyear's wife, Leslie, is a keen horsewoman with a particular knack for the skills of dressage. Leslie's coach, Daphne Edwards, a

top-flight Grand Prix dressage contestant, and her husband, Peter, were present at Michigan as guests of the Goodyears. Their only other visit to an Indy Car race was at Michigan in 1992, when Scott also won!

• Al Unser Jr. was out of luck on race day, like many others, but he did salvage something from the weekend by scoring a brilliant victory in the previous day's final round of the Dodge International Race of Champions (IROC XVIII) series.

• Michael Andretti *(right)* was wide-eyed after the first day of practice. 'The steering is *so* heavy,' he said. 'Unbelievable. It, like, locks up in the corners. I don't know if it's the

Reynard or the speed or the fact I wasn't here last year or

what, but as soon as you get over 230 [mph], Jiminy Criminy! You really have to commit yourself to it.'

Michael C. Brown

MARLBORO 500

MICHIGAN INTERNATIONAL SPEEDWAY, BROOKLYN, MICHIGAN

JULY 31, 250 LAPS – 500.000 MILES

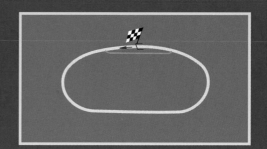

Place	Driver (Nat.)	No.	Team Sponsors Car-Engine	Q Speed (mph)	Q Time	Q Pos.	Laps	Time/Status	Ave. (mph)	Pts.
1	**Scott Goodyear (CDN)**	40	Budweiser King Racing Lola T94/00-Ford	226.641	31.768s	12	250	3h 07m 44.099s	159.800	20
2	**Arie Luyendyk (NL)**	28	Indy Regency Eurosport/Boost Monaco Lola T94/00-Ilmor/D	218.077	33.016s	26	249	Running		16
3	**Dominic Dobson (USA)**	17	PacWest Racing Group Lola T94/00-Ford	228.197	31.552s	9	248	Running		14
4	**Teo Fabi (I)**	11	Hall Pennzoil Special Reynard 94I-Ilmor/D	228.645	31.490s	8	246	Running		12
5	**Mark Smith (USA)**	15	Walker Craftsman Tools Lola T94/00-Ford	220.160	32.703s	25	240	Running		10
6	**Hiro Matsushita (J)**	22	Simon Panasonic/Duskin Lola T94/00-Ford	222.805	32.315s	20	239	Running		8
7	**Willy T. Ribbs (USA)**	24	Walker Service Merchandise/Bill Cosby Lola T94/00-Ford	220.858	32.600s	23	236	Running		6
8	**Al Unser Jr. (USA)**	31	Marlboro Team Penske PC23-Ilmor/D	226.376	31.806s	14	231	Engine		5
9	**Raul Boesel (BR)**	5	Simon Duracell/Fuji Film/Mobil/Sadia Lola T94/00-Ford	232.672	30.945s	2	225	Engine		5
10	**Emerson Fittipaldi (BR)**	2	Marlboro Team Penske PC23-Ilmor/D	228.710	31.481s	7	209	Engine		3
11	**Marco Greco (BR)**	25	Simon Arciero Project Indy Lola T94/00-Ford	226.241	31.825s	15	195	Running		2
12	***Scott Sharp (USA)**	71	PacWest Racing Group Lola T94/00-Ford	223.725	32.182s	18	185	Engine		1
13	Robby Gordon (USA)	9	Walker Valvoline/Cummins Special Lola T94/00-Ford	230.649	31.216s	4	182	Engine		
14	Stefan Johansson (S)	16	Bettenhausen Alumax Aluminum Penske PC22-Ilmor/D	228.771	31.472s	6	176	Engine		
15	Mauricio Gugelmin (BR)	88	Ganassi Hollywood Reynard 94I-Ford	225.965	31.863s	16	160	Accident		
16	Paul Tracy (CDN)	3	Marlboro Team Penske PC23-Ilmor/D	226.825	31.743s	11	150	Fuel pressure		
17	Jeff Wood (USA)	50	Euromotorsport Agip/Hawaiian Tropic Lola T92/00-Ilmor/A	211.656	34.017s	28	138	Overheating		
18	Mario Andretti (USA)	6	Newman-Haas Kmart/Texaco Havoline Lola T94/00-Ford	230.345	31.257s	5	121	Engine		
19	Ross Bentley (CDN)	39	Coyne Agfa Film Lola T92/00-Ilmor/A	210.031	34.281s	27	116	Exhaust manifold		
20	*Jacques Villeneuve (CDN)	12	Forsythe-Green Player's Ltd. Reynard 94I-Ford	227.821	31.604s	10	76	Accident		
21	Eddie Cheever (USA)	14	A.J. Foyt Copenhagen Racing Lola T94/00-Ford	223.239	32.252s	19	67	Electrical		
22	Michael Andretti (USA)	8	Ganassi Target/Scotch Video Reynard 94I-Ford	232.543	30.962s	3	66	Accident		
23	Adrian Fernandez (MEX)	7	Galles Tecate/Quaker State Reynard 94I-Ilmor/D	226.411	31.801s	13	64	Pit fire		
24	Buddy Lazier (USA)	23	Leader Card Financial World Lola T93/00-Ilmor/C	222.263	32.394s	21	55	Electrical		
25	Jimmy Vasser (USA)	18	Hayhoe Conseco/STP Reynard 94I-Ford	224.807	32.028s	17	48	Wheel bearing		
26	Nigel Mansell (GB)	1	Newman-Haas Kmart/Texaco Havoline Lola T94/00-Ford	233.738	30.804s	1	35	Throttle linkage		1
27	Mike Groff (USA)	10	Rahal-Hogan Motorola Lola T94/00-Honda	222.245	32.397s	22	24	Withdrawn		
28	Bobby Rahal (USA)	4	Rahal-Hogan Miller Genuine Draft Lola T94/00-Honda	220.550	32.646s	24	9	Withdrawn		
NS	*Alessandro Zampedri (I)	19	Coyne The Mi-Jack Car Lola T93/00-Ford	no time	no speed	–	–	Withdrawn/accident		

denotes Rookie driver

Caution flags: Laps 23–29, debris/flat tire/Gordon; laps 66–74, pit fire/Fernandez; laps 76–88, accident/Villeneuve; laps 92–95, debris; laps 124–130, tow/Mario Andretti; laps 182–189, blown engine/Gordon; laps 195–202, tow/Sharp; laps 230–233, blown engine/Unser Jr. Total: eight for 60 laps.

Lap leaders: Nigel Mansell, 1–26 (26 laps); Michael Andretti, 27–66 (40 laps); Scott Goodyear, 67 (1 lap); Raul Boesel, 68–120 (53 laps); Al Unser Jr., 121–124 (4 laps); Boesel, 125–158 (34 laps); Unser Jr., 159–164 (6 laps); Goodyear, 165–169 (5 laps); Unser Jr., 170–191 (22 laps); Boesel, 192–224 (33 laps); Unser Jr., 225–230 (6 laps); Goodyear, 231–250 (20 laps). *Totals:* Boesel, 120 laps; Andretti, 40 laps; Unser Jr., 38 laps; Mansell and Goodyear, 26 laps.

Fastest race lap: Al Unser Jr., 31.414s, 229.199 mph, on lap 222.

Championship positions: 1 Unser Jr., 132 pts; **2** Fittipaldi, 103; **3** Michael Andretti, 80; **4** Gordon, 75; **5** Tracy, 74; **6** Mansell, 73; **7** Villeneuve, 50; **8** Fabi, 49; **9** Rahal, 45; **10** Mario Andretti and Johansson, 40; **12** Boesel, 37; **13** Vasser, 36; **14** Goodyear, 30; **15** Gugelmin, 26; **16** Luyendyk, 18; **17** Dobson and Fernandez, 17; **19** M. Groff, 15; **20** Herta, 11; **21** Smith, 10; **22** Zampedri, 9; **23** Matsushita and Sharp, 8; **25** Ribbs, 7; **26** Montermini, 6; **27** Cheever, 5; **28** John Andretti, 3; **29** Greco, 2; **30** Jones, Freon, Till and Danner, 1.

MID-OHIO

1st – AL UNSER JR.

2nd – TRACY

3rd – FITTIPALDI

Michael C. Brown

Following consecutive disappointments at Toronto and Michigan, Marlboro Team Penske bounced back with a vengeance in the Miller Genuine Draft 200. The triumvirate of Al Unser Jr., Paul Tracy and Emerson Fittipaldi filled the top three places in qualifying and the race. Indeed they were never seriously challenged. Their Penske PC23-Ilmor/Ds were in a class by themselves.

Unser ultimately scored his sixth win of the season, but it was Tracy who led the majority of the 83-lap contest around the Trueman family's magnificent 2.25-mile road course. The Canadian had taken the lead in a typically bold maneuver at the first corner, mirroring the pass in which he grasped the lead from pole-winner Nigel Mansell a year ago. Tracy continued to hold the upper hand until he was penalized for passing another car in the vicinity of a waving yellow caution flag. In Tracy's defense, there were mitigating circumstances. But his protestations fell on deaf ears. The stop-and-go procedure cost him any chance of victory and allowed Unser a clear path to the checkered flag.

'I was on his tail, but passing him would have been a total other issue,' admitted Unser. 'We were pretty equal. I could run with him, but I don't know if I had enough car to pass him.'

While most of the attention was focused on the battle for the lead, fourth place, too, was the subject of a protracted dispute. By the close, Robby Gordon had asserted Walker Racing's Valvoline/Cummins Lola-Ford/Cosworth as best of the chasing group after another strong performance. Nigel Mansell, after starting fourth, slipped back to a disappointed seventh, complaining of inconsistent handling on his Kmart/Texaco Havoline Lola-Ford.

Left: **Paul Tracy was undoubtedly the star of the race but the Canadian, here leading team-mate Al Unser Jr., received a harsh stop-and-go penalty which dropped him behind Unser at the finish.**

QUALIFYING

A visit to the Mid-Ohio Sports Car Course is always a treat. Set amid rolling countryside midway between the major cities of Columbus and Cleveland, the undulating circuit provides unparalleled viewing opportunities for spectators. It also ensures a true test of the capabilities of both cars and drivers.

The circuit itself is demanding, with a wide variety of corners. At the same time it represents a stern challenge for the engineers, since nimbleness and good traction must be combined with a quest for outright speed in order to take advantage of the best opportunity for overtaking at the end of the main straightaway.

Mansell's Lola-Ford was among the pace-setters from the start, yet even his renowned road racing skills weren't enough to overcome the superiority of the Penske-Ilmor combination. Paul Tracy proved fastest in the opening practice session, taking full advantage of a productive test at Mid-Ohio less than two weeks earlier, although it was Unser who moved ahead in the afternoon's pivotal half-hour of qualifying.

'Paul did a great job in getting the car set up,' acknowledged Unser after emerging with a new track record, almost seven-tenths faster than Mansell's 1993 pole-winning standard.

Fittipaldi, the winner at Mid-Ohio for the past two years, traded times with Unser before narrowly missing out on the pole, while Tracy, despite suffering from a heavy cold, also squeaked ahead of the Brazilian in the closing moments. Incredibly, all three Penskes were covered by a scant 0.043 seconds.

'When Emmo outran me, it got my blood going,' said Unser, 'and I was thinking, man, where did he come from? But I knew Emerson and Paul were going to be up there because the cars are very, very equal.'

Mansell hustled as hard as ever and expressed hopes of finding some more speed on Saturday. Unfortunately, heavy rain prior to qualifying put paid to that. He had to make do with the fourth-fastest time.

'I did the best I could,' said the Briton. 'We have the three Penskes in front of us and I think I'm a full second faster than the next Lola. I'm pleased.'

Bobby Rahal's Miller Genuine Draft car, with Honda motivation, was actually the next-fastest Lola, almost 1.2 seconds adrift of Mansell's best.

In between them on the grid were the two Reynard-Fords of Mauricio Gugelmin, who equaled his strongest qualifying effort on the first anniversary of his Indy Car debut, and Jacques Villeneuve, shrugging off the effects of a heavy crash two weeks earlier at Michigan.

Rahal's team-mate, Mike Groff, ninth on the grid, also posted a strong effort in his Motorola Lola-Honda, matching his previous best performance, while Michael Andretti, eighth, continued to complain about excessive understeer on his Target/Scotch Video Reynard-Ford, especially through the Carousel.

'If we could get rid of the push, we'd be two seconds quicker,' declared Andretti. 'That's how I got the pole here three years in a row [1991–93]: I had the least amount of understeer. Now I've got the most; at least, that's what it seems like.'

Gordon, meanwhile, after trying differing set-ups on his pair of Lolas, slid off into a sand trap midway through the first qualifying session, primarily as a result of a wrongly adjusted brake balance. Tenth fastest was not a true representation of his competitiveness.

RACE

The rain showers moved away to the east on Saturday evening, and by race morning the clouds had begun to clear. The track was dry for the usual warm-up session. Tracy maintained the Penske form, his #3 Marlboro car quickest of all, while Gordon underlined his intentions by setting second-fastest time, a half-second shy of Tracy's best. Unser, meanwhile, had encountered a problem with his engine. Just to be safe, Richard Buck and the crew installed a fresh Ilmor/D for the race.

A huge crowd gathered in the trackside enclosures, greeted by very pleasant conditions with mainly sunny skies and a temperature of around 70 degrees. Perfect racing weather.

The start was fast and clean, as Unser capitalized on his pole by jumping into a slight but immediate lead over his Penske colleagues as the green flag waved.

'We had talked about it before the start,' explained Unser. 'We didn't want Nigel getting up there and mixing it up with us.'

Sure enough, Fittipaldi and Tracy positioned themselves on either side of – and slightly behind – Unser on the long downhill run toward Turn Five. But Tracy, after lagging momen-

tarily, drew up alongside the leader before reaching his braking point for the following right-hand corner. He then drove calmly around the outside of Unser to assume the lead.

'There's no disadvantage to starting second on this track,' related Tracy, 'because you can go two abreast in the first turn. I hit every [gear] shift perfect and Al backed off a little early, so I went around the outside of him, just like I did Mansell last year.'

Unser, at this early juncture, wasn't prepared to force the issue.

'On cold tires, I didn't want to take any chance of doing anything stupid,' he said, 'so I just backed out a little early and Paul had a lot of momentum and he went right on by. I thought, wow! All I can say is I learned, and next year if we're in the same position, we'll go in a little deeper.'

Tracy, take note.

Paul, though, was through into the lead and soon set about making the most of his opportunity by pulling out a little breathing space over the #31 car of Unser.

Mansell tried to follow Tracy on the outside line at the first corner. He nosed alongside Fittipaldi, but the Brazilian doggedly held his line over the crest at Turn Six and was able to assert himself in third place at the next right-hander. Mansell, therefore, remained in fourth, followed by Gugelmin and Michael Andretti, who had moved up two positions already. Rahal and Gordon were close behind at the completion of lap one, although Gordon took advantage of his superior straightline speed by moving ahead of Rahal on the next go-round. Villeneuve, meanwhile, had found himself muscled back from sixth to ninth in the opening exchanges.

The race order soon settled down. Tracy pulled out a three-second lead over Unser inside the first four laps, as Fittipaldi chased for all he was worth. The deficit to Unser remained at under three seconds for the first nine laps, before, slowly but surely, the Brazilian began to fall farther behind.

Even so, Fittipaldi was under no threat. Mansell had stayed in touch

for the first two or three laps, then began to slip inexorably backward at a rate of close to two seconds per lap.

By lap 14, Mansell was fully 20 seconds adrift of Fittipaldi. Instead, filling his mirrors was a closely matched group comprising Gugelmin, Andretti and Gordon. Mansell, troubled by inconsistent handling, was clearly holding them up, although no one could get close enough to effect a pass. Stalemate.

On lap 16, Gordon saw an opportunity to draw alongside Andretti on the exit of Turn Ten, but after almost banging wheels on the climb up Thunder Valley he opted to tuck back in line. Wise man.

This battle proved the focal point through the early stages, as Mansell clung tenaciously to fourth place. Farther back, Rahal and Villeneuve joined the back of the line, while Jimmy Vasser (Conseco/STP Reynard-Ford) and Teo Fabi (Pennzoil Reynard-Ilmor) became embroiled in a battle of their own over tenth place.

Groff ran just outside the top ten in the early laps, until Scott Goodyear misjudged his braking and punted both of them into the gravel trap at the Keyhole on lap ten. Both lost several laps before rejoining.

The two leaders, Tracy and Unser, made their first routine pit stops, in tandem, after 28 laps. The status quo remained. Fittipaldi enjoyed a lap in the lead before making his own stop, rejoining almost 20 seconds behind his colleagues.

This day he simply wasn't able to keep pace. 'We had a team debriefing before the race,' said Fittipaldi, 'and I don't think these guys listened. Roger [Penske] said, "Take it easy, we want to finish the race" – and they took off!'

Gugelmin, like Fittipaldi, made his first pit stop on lap 30, and when he exited the pit lane he was actually ahead of Mansell. But the Englishman, having pitted a lap earlier, took advantage of his warmer tires to move back into fourth place almost right away. The only problem was that he was already nearly 30 seconds behind Fittipaldi.

The pit stops also were responsible for a few other changes in the order.

New Indy engine formula encourages optimism

Controversial plans to establish a new Indy Racing League, a rival Indy Car series based around the Indianapolis 500, had been announced earlier in the summer by Indianapolis Motor Speedway President Tony George. On the Wednesday prior to the IndyCar-sanctioned PPG Cup race at Mid-Ohio, the saga took a new twist when IRL official Jerry Hauer announced the engine rules package for the United States Auto Club-sanctioned series, which is set to start in 1996.

It came as quite a shock. While most Indy Car insiders had expected the IRL to persevere with George's unpopular formula based upon pushrod-operated engines of 209 cubic inch capacity (despite the recommendations of all the engine manufacturers currently involved in the sport), Hauer and USAC Vice-President/Director of Competition Johnny Capels instead confirmed it would exclusively feature turbocharged, overhead camshaft V8s running at 45 inches of manifold boost pressure – almost identical to the current breed of engines, except for a down-sizing from 2.65 liters to 2.2 liters.

Also, with the current engine equivalency formula due to be superseded, USAC's

Capels confirmed that, for the transitional 1995 Indianapolis 500, instead of reducing the boost of 209-inch motors to 52 inches, from 55, as had originally been stated, engines such as the Mercedes-Benz, which dominated this year's '500', would instead be limited to 48 inches.

Prior to that change, it seemed as though any teams wishing to be fully competitive at Indy in 1995 would have had little alternative but to ditch their 'conventional' overhead-cam engines for the month of May, and instead invest in expensive pushrod engines for that race alone. The new restriction, however, was expected to minimize the pushrod motors' advantage.

The new proposals succeeded in generating a much more optimistic outlook for the future. Now, suddenly, there appeared to be some common ground between IMS/USAC and CART/IndyCar.

'We're pleased that after the process of due diligence and a lot of hard work by the Speedway, the two parties do agree on the right way to go Indy Car racing,' commented Championship Auto Racing Teams President Andrew Craig, 'at least with regard to engines. It's good for the sport.'

Robby Gordon *(left)* again emerged as Lola's strongest challenger, taking fourth place (first in the non-Penske class!) in the Valvoline/Cummins entry.

After qualifying strongly in fourth place, Nigel Mansell once again found himself beset with handling problems during the race. This time the increasingly disaffected 1993 PPG Cup champion persevered with the car to finish seventh.

Rahal, for example, moved up from eighth to sixth, while poor stops by Gordon and, especially, Michael Andretti cost them valuable ground. Adrian Fernandez made the sharpest gain, leaping from 12th to eighth after some fine work by Owen Snyder's Galles Racing International crew.

Shortly after the midpoint of the 83-lap race, Tracy began to come under pressure from Unser for the first time. The Canadian's problem started as he closed up on a dicing Andretti and Fernandez, ready to put them a lap down. Tracy spent three laps trying to find a way past the Mexican, finally diving incisively to the inside at the Keyhole on lap 44, and by then Unser was hot on his heels.

Next in line was Rahal, whose Honda was no match for the Penske-Ilmors in a straight line. As the leaders zoomed past, Unser took the opportunity to take a peek down the inside of Tracy at Turn Five. Not this time. Nor the next lap around, when he actually drew alongside Tracy under braking – but on the outside line. Again, Unser decided discretion was the better part of valor.

The man on the move, however, was Gordon, who had noticed the two Penskes looming ever larger in his mirrors. On lap 46, with the Penskes breathing down his neck, so to speak, Gordon dived underneath Gugelmin under braking for the Keyhole. A few corners later, Mansell also succumbed to the charging Gordon, who defied convention by driving all the way around the outside of the defending series champion at Turn Seven. It was a bold pass, although Mansell said he had been unable to defend himself.

'The car kept changing [balance],' he claimed. 'I mean, we had three different cars out there. It would change with every pit stop. My [lap] times kept changing. Sometimes I would be running in the 1:11s and sometimes in the 1:13s.'

At this point Mansell was closer to 1m 13s, which was no match for Gordon. Or the Penske drivers, for whom Mansell moved aside to enable them to continue their battle for the lead.

By lap 46, only Gordon remained on the same lap as the three Penskes – and although the Californian ran immediately ahead of them on the road, he was not inclined to wave them past. Gordon proceeded to turn his fastest laps of the race, dipping into the 1m 09s range as he battled to stay on the lead lap. He was hoping against hope for a full-course caution, which would enable him to make up most of the lost ground.

As Tracy and Unser stalked the impressive Gordon, Rahal's race ended abruptly with yet another Honda engine failure. The three-time champion made no attempt to hide his frustration.

'I can't sugarcoat this,' said Rahal. 'The car was handling beautifully. It was just slower than molasses on the straightaways and off the corners. Unfortunately, the engine doesn't seem to get any better. When you can't get an engine to go 140 miles, you're in pretty bad shape.'

Gugelmin, too, was in trouble. His brakes had begun to fade badly. The Brazilian soldiered on until his predicament became impossible, whereupon he had no choice but to bring the car into the pits. His fine run was over.

Fabi was also out of contention, having slid off the road at the Keyhole. The Italian, who had been running in tenth, holding onto a long train of cars disputing sixth place, lost four laps before he could resume.

Fabi's incident had more far-reaching effects, however. On lap 53, with the yellow flags waving as the IndyCar Safety Team struggled to pull the Pennzoil Reynard out of the gravel trap, Gordon, still running just in front of the two leaders, was momentarily distracted by the proximity of Dominic Dobson's PacWest Lola, which was about to go two laps down. Gordon left his braking a fraction too late and slid slightly wide on the entry to the corner. Fortunately, Gordon regained control of his car before hitting the safety truck, but by then Tracy had seized the opportunity he had been looking for to slip past on the inside line.

That single pass was to determine the outcome of the race. But not in Tracy's favor. The maneuver, of course, had been made under waved yellow flags, which represented a breach of the rules. After some deliberation, and despite a plea for clemency from Tracy's crew, the officials decided to impose a stop-and-go penalty.

'I thought it was a bad call,' said Tracy, 'because he [Gordon] almost drove off the road, and what was I supposed to do, drive off after him? I wasn't planning on passing him, but he locked up his brakes and almost slid off the turn. He made a mistake. I wasn't under the inside of him under the approach to the corner; I made the pass after the point where the [safety] truck was parked. I didn't think it was an issue.'

Even Unser, who benefited most from the penalty, agreed Tracy was unfortunate to be penalized.

'It was one of those things,' he said. 'The yellows were waving and people were going up in there strong and hard. You didn't really realize where everything was until you got there and everybody started locking up their brakes. The only thing I thought was, it's gonna be close!'

The consensus afterward was that perhaps all three drivers should have been punished for over-driving under the caution flags; there was also widespread criticism of Gordon for not paying more heed to the blue flags. But Gordon steadfastly maintained he had every right to try to defend his position; he was under no obligation to let the leaders pass.

'I wanted to stay on the lead lap,' said Gordon. 'I was waiting for a yellow. I don't think I was holding them up; I was running [laps in one minute] nines. Tracy choked. Because he tried to go inside me.'

Tracy, when informed of Gordon's comments, was not amused. 'The guy's oblivious to flags,' countered the Canadian. 'I was behind him for eight laps and he had so much motor on the straights, I couldn't get by him. He was braking as deep as he could, and he eventually made a mistake and slid out of the way for me.'

Tracy's argument was strengthened over the course of the next half-dozen laps, during which he pulled out more than four seconds over Unser, who remained trapped behind the intransigent Gordon. But it was to no avail. Tracy voluntarily gave up the lead by making a scheduled pit stop for fuel and tires on lap 58, then lost any chance of regaining the advantage (when Unser stopped) by pitting again, to serve his penalty, one lap later. The race for the lead was effectively over. Tracy resumed almost eight seconds in arrears of Unser, who, on full tanks, drove hard to negate the possibility of any counter-attack.

Tracy did have one last hope when the pace car made its one and only appearance of the day on lap 65, after Claude Bourbonnais's Team Losi/In Deck Lola T93/00 ground to a halt out on the track due to yet another transmission failure. The full-course caution erased Unser's advantage, although on the restart Tracy became trapped for several laps behind an unhelpful Stefan Johansson, despite the fact the Swede was running two laps down in 12th place with his Alumax Penske PC22-Ilmor/D.

Once again, Unser was able to stretch his advantage to around six seconds. Unser then maintained a fast sub-1m 10s pace, just to make sure there were no surprises, before easing off over the final couple of laps. He took the checkered flag 1.636 seconds in front of Tracy. Fittipaldi completed the Penske sweep, while Gordon finished a lonely fourth, one lap down.

'There was no catching those [Penske] guys,' he admitted. 'It's great to finish first in our class, but it's still kind of a hollow feeling because we're here to win races, not to be the best of the rest.'

Michael Andretti claimed fifth place, 11 seconds back, by virtue of a superb second pit stop which moved him ahead of the ever-improving Fernandez. The Mexican nevertheless was delighted to earn his highest finish to date.

'I think it was the toughest race I have ever run,' said Fernandez. 'I was battling with Mansell and bumped him a little when he slowed, and I touched wheels with Michael. We were racing hard out there.'

Mansell, who slipped as low as ninth, moved back to seventh at the flag-fall, having passed Raul Boesel's Duracell Lola-Ford shortly after the full-course caution. Try as he did, Boesel was unable to redress the balance.

'Consistency was our ally today,' said Boesel. 'My car was very comfortable to drive and it was very satisfying to move up nine positions from where we qualified.'

Emerson Fittipaldi *(above)* completed another
1-2-3 finish for Marlboro Team Penske.

The impressive Adrian Fernandez took a splendid
sixth, his best finish to date. The young Mexican
driver described his race as the toughest he had
ever run.

SNIPPETS

• Mauro Baldi, replacing injured countryman Alessandro Zampedri in Dale Coyne's Mi-Jack Lola,

thoroughly enjoyed his first single-seater race since driving the Spirit-Hart Formula 1 car at Imola in 1985. Baldi started out steadily and improved as his confidence grew. He rose as high as 17th before unfortunate timing of his second pit stop, immediately before the full-course caution, cost him a lap and dropped him back to 19th.

• Very few cars ventured out during the wet qualifying session on Saturday afternoon. Italian Mimmo Schiattarella, who pitted just before the end of the session, was fastest until being pipped by Fittipaldi on the very last lap. 'I

wanted to run a bit because I have never driven in the wet this year,' said Fittipaldi, who earlier caused some consternation by spinning off directly in front of the Penske pit.

• Buddy Lazier's Financial World Magazine/Leader Card Lola *(below)* benefited from a stunning new Randy Owens paint scheme. Sadly, handling problems narrowly prevented him from making the 28-car starting field.

Photos: Michael C. Brown

PPG INDY CAR WORLD SERIES • ROUND 11

MILLER GENUINE DRAFT 200

MID-OHIO SPORTS CAR COURSE, LEXINGTON, OHIO

AUGUST 14, 83 LAPS – 185.800 MILES

Place	Driver (Nat.)	No.	Team Sponsors Car-Engine	Q Speed (mph)	Q Time	Q Pos.	Laps	Time/Status	Ave. (mph)	Pts.
1	Al Unser Jr. (USA)	31	Marlboro Team Penske PC23-Ilmor/D	119.517	1m 07.773s	1	83	1h 40m 59.436s	110.387	21
2	Paul Tracy (CDN)	3	Marlboro Team Penske PC23-Ilmor/D	119.454	1m 07.809s	2	83	1h 41m 01.072s	110.357	17
3	Emerson Fittipaldi (BR)	2	Marlboro Team Penske PC23-Ilmor/D	119.442	1m 07.815s	3	83	1h 41m 35.611s	109.731	14
4	Robby Gordon (USA)	9	Walker Valvoline/Cummins Special Lola T94/00-Ford	116.857	1m 09.316s	10	82	Running		12
5	Michael Andretti (USA)	8	Ganassi Target/Scotch Video Reynard 94I-Ford	116.968	1m 09.250s	8	82	Running		10
6	Adrian Fernandez (MEX)	7	Galles Tecate/Quaker State Reynard 94I-Ilmor/D	116.541	1m 09.504s	14	82	Running		8
7	Nigel Mansell (GB)	1	Newman-Haas Kmart/Texaco Havoline Lola T94/00-Ford	118.795	1m 08.185s	4	82	Running		6
8	Raul Boesel (BR)	5	Simon Duracell/Fuji Film/Mobil/Sadia Lola T94/00-Ford	116.119	1m 09.756s	17	82	Running		5
9	*Jacques Villeneuve (CDN)	12	Forsythe-Green Player's Ltd. Reynard 94I-Ford	117.405	1m 08.992s	6	82	Running		4
10	Mario Andretti (USA)	6	Newman-Haas Kmart/Texaco Havoline Lola T94/00-Ford	116.145	1m 09.741s	15	82	Running		3
11	*Scott Sharp (USA)	71	PacWest Racing Group Lola T94/00-Ford	116.100	1m 09.767s	18	82	Running		2
12	Stefan Johansson (S)	16	Bettenhausen Alumax Aluminum Penske PC22-Ilmor/D	115.810	1m 09.942s	21	81	Running		1
13	Arie Luyendyk (NL)	28	Indy Regency Eurosport/Boost Monaco Lola T94/00-Ilmor/D	112.352	1m 12.095s	28	81	Running		
14	Jimmy Vasser (USA)	18	Hayhoe Conseco/STP Reynard 94I-Ford	116.703	1m 09.407s	12	81	Running		
15	Dominic Dobson (USA)	17	PacWest Racing Group Lola T94/00-Ford	115.920	1m 09.876s	20	81	Running		
16	*Mimmo Schiattarella (I)	64	Project Indy No Touch/Van Dyne/Marcelo Lola T93/00-Ford	116.140	1m 09.743s	16	81	Running		
17	Eddie Cheever (USA)	14	A.J. Foyt Copenhagen Racing Lola T94/00-Ford	114.576	1m 10.696s	23	80	Running		
18	Hiro Matsushita (J)	22	Simon Panasonic/Duskin Lola T94/00-Ford	113.297	1m 11.493s	26	80	Running		
19	*Mauro Baldi (I)	19	Coyne The Mi-Jack Car Lola T93/00-Ford	112.795	1m 11.812s	27	80	Running		
20	Mark Smith (USA)	15	Walker Craftsman Tools Lola T93/00-Ford	116.051	1m 09.797s	19	80	Running		
21	Teo Fabi (I)	11	Hall Pennzoil Special Reynard 94I-Ilmor/D	116.541	1m 09.504s	13	79	Running		
22	Scott Goodyear (CDN)	40	Budweiser King Racing Lola T94/00-Ford	116.807	1m 09.345s	11	76	Running		
23	*Parker Johnstone (USA)	49	Comptech Racing Acura Lola T93/00-Honda	114.220	1m 10.916s	24	76	Running		
24	*Claude Bourbonnnais (CDN)	30	McCormack Motorsports Team Losi/In Deck Lola T93/00-Ilmor/C+	113.633	1m 11.282s	25	59	Transmission		
25	Mauricio Gugelmin (BR)	88	Ganassi Hollywood Reynard 94I-Ford	117.572	1m 08.894s	5	55	Brakes		
26	Mike Groff (USA)	10	Rahal-Hogan Motorola Lola T94/00-Honda	116.880	1m 09.302s	9	47	Engine		
27	Bobby Rahal (USA)	4	Rahal-Hogan Miller Genuine Draft Lola T94/00-Honda	117.377	1m 09.009s	7	46	Engine		
28	Willy T. Ribbs (USA)	24	Walker Service Merchandise/Bill Cosby Lola T94/00-Ford	115.750	1m 09.979s	22	4	Transmission		
NQ	Buddy Lazier (USA)	23	Leader Card Financial World Lola T93/00-Ilmor/C	111.621	1m 12.567s	29	–	Did not qualify		
NQ	Ross Bentley (CDN)	39	Coyne Agfa Film Lola T92/00-Ilmor/A	110.642	1m 13.209s	30	–	Did not qualify		
NQ	Marco Greco (BR)	25	Simon Arciero Project Indy Lola T94/00-Ford	109.246	1m 14.145s	31	–	Did not qualify		
NQ	Jeff Wood (USA)	50	Euromotorsport Agip/Hawaiian Tropic Lola T92/00-Ilmor/A	107.690	1m 15.216s	32	–	Did not qualify		

* denotes Rookie driver

Caution flags: Laps 64–67, tow/Bourbonnais. Total: one for four laps.

Lap leaders: Paul Tracy, 1–28 (28 laps); Emerson Fittipaldi, 29 (1 lap); Tracy, 30–57 (28 laps); Al Unser Jr., 58–83 (26 laps). **Totals:** Tracy, 56 laps; Unser Jr., 26 laps; Fittipaldi, 1 lap.

Fastest race lap: Al Unser Jr., 1m 08.805s, 117.724 mph, on lap 20.

Championship positions: 1 Unser Jr., 153 pts; **2** Fittipaldi, 117; **3** Tracy, 91; **4** Michael Andretti, 90; **5** Gordon, 87; **6** Mansell, 79; **7** Villeneuve, 54; **8** Fabi, 49; **9** Rahal, 45; **10** Mario Andretti, 43; **11** Boesel, 42; **12** Johansson, 41; **13** Vasser, 36; **14** Goodyear, 30; **15** Gugelmin, 26; **16** Fernandez, 25; **17** Luyendyk, 18; **18** Dobson, 17; **19** M. Groff, 15; **20** Herta, 11; **21** Smith and Sharp, 10; **23** Zampedri, 9; **24** Matsushita, 8; **25** Ribbs, 7; **26** Montermini, 6; **27** Cheever, 5; **28** John Andretti, 3; **29** Greco, 2; **30** Jones, Freon, Till and Danner, 1.

NEW HAMPSHIRE

Michael C. Brown

The Marlboro Team Penske express train sped to its ninth victory of the season in the Slick-50 200 at New Hampshire International Speedway. For the second time in seven days, Roger Penske's cars filled the top three positions – their fourth 1-2-3 sweep this season – and for the seventh time it was Al Unser Jr. who claimed top honors.

'Anytime you win a race it's satisfying,' said Unser, 'and especially with this team. The team has done wonders for me and I really appreciate everything. I was working with the set-up this weekend and you can tell from where I qualified [tenth] that I wasn't happy with my set-up, so I went over to Emerson [Fittipaldi] and he gave me the set-up on his car. So, you know, to have a team do that is great. It was good of the whole team to play ball like this.'

The spirit of co-operation led to an exciting race between the three Penske cars, which, as ever, proved very evenly matched. Fittipaldi, who held the upper hand in qualifying, courtesy of an impressive new track record, saw his challenge for the race victory blunted first by a blistered front tire and then a late pit stop for fuel. Nevertheless, in a thrilling climax, he chased home team-mates Unser and Tracy to the checkered flag. All three were blanketed by a mere 1.75 seconds.

The only real opposition stemmed from Nigel Mansell, who chased hard until being involved in a needless accident while lapping his own Newman-Haas team-mate, Mario Andretti. Mansell's demise allowed Raul Boesel to claim fourth place in Dick Simon's Duracell Lola-Ford/Cosworth, two laps behind the Penskes but just one second ahead of Michael Andretti.

The start *(below left)* was dramatic, with the yellow lights coming on after an accident at the tail of the field which eliminated Jacques Villeneuve and Arie Luyendyk, who are seen against the wall.

Raul Boesel *(right)* strapped in and ready to go in Dick Simon's Duracell/Fuji Film/Mobil/Sadia Lola. The fourth-placed Brazilian was pleased with the car's performance, albeit only in the 'best of the rest' category.

Michael C. Brown

QUALIFYING

Persistent rain on Thursday gave way to overcast skies and pleasantly cool temperatures for the start of official practice the following morning. Bob Bahre's superb New Hampshire International Speedway was in perfect shape for fast lap times. The latest Goodyear tires, featuring a slightly softer compound and stiffer construction, also proved conducive to record speeds. Indeed, by the end of the first 90-minute session, no fewer than seven drivers had eclipsed Nigel Mansell's year-old qualifying standard of 22.504 seconds.

Fastest of all, surprisingly, was Teo Fabi, who carved a startling 22.141 seconds (172.024 mph) in Jim Hall's bright-yellow Pennzoil Reynard-Ilmor, which for this race featured a distinctive 'camel's hump' over its engine bay.

'The car was good,' reported the diminutive Italian, 'apart from just a little bit of understeer on the exit. If we can cure that, I think I can go a little faster – not much but a little.'

True to his word, Fabi found some more time on Saturday as he dipped into the 21-second bracket; but by then several other teams had made more significant gains. Assisted by near-perfect weather conditions, a total of 16 drivers bettered the previous record, with Mansell leading the way on 21.663 seconds (175.818 mph). But significantly, in single-car qualifying, very few were able to match their times set in the cooler morning air.

'It's just the balance,' declared Mansell, who wound up third on the grid. 'If you've got the balance, you can go into the corner and attack it. You have more margin. If you lose the balance, then obviously it just takes a couple of miles per hour off. I had an incredible push in the car. We took a risk by putting more wing in the car, but it still wasn't enough.'

Raul Boesel raised the ire of several rivals, including Mansell, by abandoning his first two qualifying attempts with Dick Simon's Duracell Lola-Ford, then, after a consultation with Chief Steward Wally Dallenbach (and in apparent contravention of the rules), making a third run in which he posted a time 0.001s faster than Mansell. There was much grumbling afterward, but Dallenbach stood by his decision. Boesel would start second on the grid.

It mattered little, for Fittipaldi had blitzed everyone to secure the coveted pole position and the PPG Cup bonus point. The veteran Brazilian was delighted after claiming the 16th pole of his career, and, surprisingly, his first ever on a one-mile oval.

'The whole crew did an incredible job,' said Fittipaldi, smiling even more broadly than usual. 'The car was very smooth and I could lean more on the throttle on my second lap. The balance was perfect.

'We didn't change the car from this morning. I had a good feeling because I did 22.0 with a set of tires that had about 70 laps on them. I knew with fresh rubber I could go quicker. I talked with Paul [Tracy] and Al Jr.; we exchanged information and just got a good set-up.'

Tracy didn't find quite the same amount of grip as Fittipaldi and so had to be content with fourth place, while Unser, who was the first to make a qualifying attempt, set the tenth-fastest time in a characteristically conservative run. He wasn't the least bit upset: 'The Marlboro car ran great. We put it in the show. We're ready for the race.' Uh-oh. Unser's confidence did not bode well for his rivals.

Dominic Dobson (PacWest Lola-Ford) and Adrian Fernandez, in the Galles Reynard, qualified strongly in sixth and eighth, sandwiching Fabi, but perhaps the biggest surprise was to see Michael Andretti a lowly 17th in Chip Ganassi's Reynard-Ford.

'There's just no grip,' complained Andretti. 'I can't get hard on the throttle coming off the corners.'

RACE

The drama on race day began early. Or, to be more precise, it began during the morning warm-up session, which was apparently too early for Robby Gordon. The Californian had struggled all weekend to find a good balance on Derrick Walker's Lola, qualifying unusually poorly in 13th, and when the final practice began at 9 a.m. Gordon was nowhere to be found. Quite simply, he had overslept. Perhaps it was a portent of things to come.

His team was faced with a dilemma, since a new engine had been fitted, routinely, overnight, along with fresh brakes, which needed to be bedded in. Thus, when the transmission in Buddy Lazier's *Financial World* Lola blew asunder early in the session, Walker lost no time in asking the young Colorado driver to take a few laps in Gordon's Valvoline/Cummins car.

'I saw Buddy standing by his car, looking glum,' related Walker. 'I thought, he's the guy!'

Lazier, of course, was delighted to oblige, and despite taking only a bare minimum of laps, he soon circulated faster than he had in his own '93 Lola. 'I could have gone faster,' declared Lazier, grinning from ear to ear, 'but I didn't want to push it. That's not why Derrick asked me to drive the car. But it felt great.' He was impressed, too, with his first experience of the sequential-shift gearbox: 'Awesome!'

The 27-car field (*sans* Lazier, whose car could not be repaired) looked to be in good order on the final pace lap, only for chaos to break out in mid-pack, just as Chief Starter Jim Swintal was preparing to wave the green flag. The incident was triggered when Adrian Fernandez lost control of his Tecate/Quaker State Reynard as he accelerated out of Turn Four. Cold tires. Miraculously, the Mexican didn't hit a thing. Indeed he half-spun the car to the inside of the track, regained control, then drove calmly down the pit lane as if nothing had happened!

Behind, though, Jacques Villeneuve was forced to jump on the brakes in avoidance, which left a close-following Gordon with absolutely nowhere to go but into the back of the Player's Ltd. Reynard. Both cars spun. The luckless Arie Luyendyk also was involved as an innocent victim. Villeneuve and Luyendyk were out even before the race had officially started. Gordon lost two laps before his stalled engine could be re-fired. (Perhaps he should have stayed in bed!)

Following several extra laps behind the pace car, the second attempt at a start was hardly more successful. This time at least the field was greeted by the green flag, only for Stefan Johansson and a fast-starting Eddie Cheever to tangle in Turn Two. Both cars retired soon afterward with suspension damage. On came the yellow lights again.

Then, on lap 13, right after another restart, Mike Groff lost control and spun in Turn Two following contact with Scott Sharp. In what proved to be by far the most serious incident, Sharp's PacWest Lola-Ford clipped Groff's stricken Lola-Honda, then flipped wildly down the back straight before coming to rest upside down. Fortunately, neither driver was hurt. Once again, there was a delay while the track was cleared.

By now, 25 laps were in the books. Only two of them had been run under green flag conditions. But already there had been several significant changes in the order.

Fittipaldi, the pole-sitter, continued to lead, but up into second place had come Tracy – at the expense of both Boesel and Mansell. Mario Andretti held down fifth in the second Newman-Haas car, while, incredibly, up into sixth was Mario's hard-charging son, Michael, who had taken advantage of the various incidents and moved up from 17th. Nevertheless, the younger Andretti soon had his hands full in resisting pressure from

159

Temperatures rise as Goodyear prepares for battle

Emerson Fittipaldi caused quite a furor after the race when he criticized Goodyear for supplying different tires at the race meeting to those on which most teams had tested.

'I'm very disappointed with what Goodyear has done,' said Fittipaldi with uncharacteristic ire. 'We were not given the right assistance this weekend. We came here and tested and had a different tire. For the race we had much softer rubber. Yesterday, when I ran on full tanks, [the Goodyear engineers] were not there to check the tire temperature. I'm very disappointed that I blistered a front tire.'

Goodyear's field manager for Indy Car racing, John Slikkerveer, expressed his surprise at Fittipaldi's outburst, although he freely admitted that several teams did encounter higher than anticipated tire temperatures during practice. Slikkerveer noted that several potential cures for the problem were considered, and that no other team experienced blistering problems during the race.

'Emerson was setting a very quick pace at the start of the race,' he said. 'Unfortunately, it was a little too quick for the suspension set-up he had, and the tires.'

Indeed, eventual winner Al Unser Jr. revealed that he had taken the tire situation into account: 'We had pretty hot right-side tires,' admitted Unser. 'We had to be careful. The final answer is, you've gotta back off and slow down a bit.'

Slikkerveer also alluded to the fact Goodyear was in the midst of preparing for the advent of competition in 1995 from Bridgestone/Firestone, which has mounted a comprehensive test and development program in preparation for Firestone's return to the Indy Car scene after an absence of 20 years.

'Safety, as always, comes first for us at Goodyear,' said Slikkerveer, 'but at the same time, because of the competition, we are beginning to stretch the performance envelope a little more. We have to. And judging by today's results, we're satisfied with what we're seeing.'

Unser, who was also on a forward march. Andretti, though, is never an easy man to overtake. It took Unser ten laps to find a way past.

Once ahead, Unser closed rapidly on papa Andretti, who, likewise, is never one to give up a place without a fight. Finally, on lap 51, Unser moved up into the top five.

Fittipaldi, meanwhile, after setting a torrid pace in the early stages, paid the price when his right-front tire began to show signs of blistering. He was unable to prevent Tracy from slipping through into the lead on lap 47. A handful of laps later, having fallen to fifth, Fittipaldi was forced to make an unscheduled pit stop. He rejoined with a fresh set of Goodyear Eagles and a full tank of fuel, but by now he was 12th, one lap behind the new race leader.

Countryman Boesel continued to run strongly in second, fighting off the advances of Mansell, although it wasn't long before both Lolas came under threat from the fast-rising Unser. This was no contest. By lap 59, Unser had passed both of them.

The PPG Cup points leader then set his sights on Tracy, who clung doggedly to his advantage for several laps. He, too, was fighting a losing battle. Unser's car was more stable, especially in traffic. On lap 69, the #31 Marlboro Penske swept through into the lead.

Mansell, running strongly in his Kmart/Texaco Lola-Ford, also usurped Tracy, while Boesel, struggling with worsening oversteer, fell to fifth behind Mario Andretti.

'I had my hands full,' said Boesel. 'As the rear tires went off, the back end started to get loose. From full [fuel] tanks to half-tanks the Duracell car was handling great, but after half-empty it was a handful.'

Unser commenced the first round of scheduled pit stops when he called in for service on lap 80. Mansell led until making his own stop on lap 85, whereupon Unser regained the upper hand, albeit under renewed pressure from the Englishman.

'My race was going fantastic,' said Mansell. 'After my first stop, I was a little bit quicker than the Penske. Little Al was driving great, but I was hanging on to him.'

By half-distance, lap 100, Tracy had slipped almost half a lap behind the leading duo. Fittipaldi ran in fourth, out of sequence on pit stops, followed by Mario Andretti, who, on lap 104, was lapped by Unser. Boesel followed in sixth, chased by a dicing Michael Andretti and Dominic Dobson, who was maintaining his form from qualifying in the surviving PacWest Lola. Jimmy Vasser, running well in Jim Hayhoe's Conseco/STP Reynard-Ford, and Fernandez, who was experiencing some handling difficulties after his earlier indiscretion, completed the top ten, each of them two laps behind the leaders.

The race by now had settled down into a pattern. All three Penske cars remained in contention for the victory, with the only serious opposition stemming from Mansell, in second place, who was chasing hard after Unser.

'I was trying to be careful,' said Unser. 'I was on full [fuel] tanks and I had a long stint in front of me and I needed the tires to be under me at the end of that stint. I was trying to pull away from Nigel and still take care of the tires at the same time.'

The gap between the two leaders varied as they encountered traffic. And as Mansell accelerated off Turn Four to complete his 108th lap, the next car in front of him was the similar Kmart/Texaco Lola of Newman-Haas team-mate Mario Andretti. Mansell expected no undue problems as he moved to the inside, preparing to put Mario a lap down. Indeed, Mansell seemed to have made the pass cleanly, nosing ahead as they sped toward Turn One. But Mario refused to cede an inch.

Mansell, anxious lest he should lose time to Unser, was forced to dip underneath the yellow line marking the exit of pit lane – and still Andretti left him no room to maneuver. Finally, and inevitably, the two cars made contact. Boom! Andretti was sent into a trajectory toward the wall.

The 54-year-old granddaddy of Indy Car racing remained in the car for several seconds, dazed by the impact. Then, to the relief of everyone, he climbed unsteadily from the car, fortunately suffering no worse than some heavy bruising.

Not surprisingly, the two combatants viewed the incident from rather different perspectives.

'He drove right into me coming off Turn One,' proclaimed Andretti, unconvincingly. 'I thought he was under me and the next thing I know, he just drilled me into the wall.'

'I was alongside, maybe half a car in front going into Turn One,' countered Mansell. 'I don't know whether Mario didn't see me, but then he came across. I tried to give him some room and I was almost into the pit lane. But unfortunately we touched.'

The consensus of opinion afterward placed the blame squarely on Mario's broad shoulders. Surely, one lap behind the leaders, he should have allowed Mansell unhindered passage – especially as he was his team-mate, and still in a position to win the race. Interestingly, however, a contrasting view was expressed by Rick Mears, an acknowledged master of the ovals who retired from driving at the end of the 1992 season and now works as race engineer/driver coach for Penske Racing.

'Nigel should have waited until he was able to make the pass cleanly,' said the universally respected Mears. 'Mario's always a tough guy to pass. But he's generally clean. You just have to make sure you can make it all the way through before you try it. There's no half-measures with Mario. Nigel should have known that.'

Hmmm.

Mansell continued after the collision and remained in second place as the yellow lights flashed on. Soon after the restart, however, he ducked into the pits, complaining of poor handling. Tom Wurtz and the crew changed tires and gave the car a quick once-over but could find nothing obviously amiss. Mansell was sent on his way. He was back shortly afterward, this time for good. The right-side suspension, both front and rear, had been tweaked out of alignment.

Mansell, then, was out, and with him went any semblance of a challenge to the Penske domination. Carl Haas was not amused.

When the race restarted, only the three Penskes remained on the lead lap, Unser ahead of Tracy and Fittipaldi. But when Unser and Tracy made their second pit stops, in tandem and on schedule, with 49 laps remaining, Fittipaldi regained a handsome advantage. The only problem was that, having stopped himself on lap 111, the Brazilian knew he needed one more full-course caution if he was to make it to the finish without having to stop again.

Unfortunately for him, none came.

Marlboro

Above: The Kmart/Texaco Havoline Lola of Mario Andretti emerges from his pit stop as, behind, his son Michael brings in the Ganassi Reynard. In the background Paul Tracy stops for service in his Marlboro Penske.

Left: Hectic action on the banking with Boesel, Mansell, Mario Andretti, Michael Andretti and Dobson running in line astern, while Unser Jr. takes the high line round the outside.

Nigel Mansell, pictured *(left)* battling with Paul Tracy, was very competitive, but a collision with team-mate Mario Andretti eliminated him from contention.

Emerson Fittipaldi *(below)* lost his chance of victory when he had to make a late pit stop for a splash of fuel.

Fittipaldi pulled out almost a full lap over Unser and Tracy, who continued to run in fairly close formation. Then, with just five laps remaining, the race leader gave in to the inevitable. He needed just a splash of fuel.

'We worked out that to come in, slow down, fuel and go out again would cost us 19.8 seconds of track time,' explained Penske Team Manager Chuck Sprague, who calls the shots for Fittipaldi. 'We had 22 seconds on Al at that point. But by the time I had convinced Emerson to stop, Al had taken another four seconds off us.'

Then, excruciatingly, as Emerson began to slow, making his way onto the pit lane, his engine coughed. He was out of fuel. A few precious seconds were lost in coasting in and then refiring the motor, and so, by the time he was back up to speed, Fittipaldi had fallen to third place.

The final few laps provided a thrilling climax as Unser, in the lead, encountered a group of slower cars. Among them was Michael Andretti's Reynard, running fifth and trying as hard as he could to get on terms with Boesel. Just as at the beginning of the race, Unser struggled to find a way by.

'He was running just fast enough that his turbulence was taking downforce off my front end, so I couldn't get past him,' related Unser.

Tracy homed in rapidly from behind. A fired-up Fittipaldi also joined in the chase as the leaders sped into their final couple of laps. But Unser wasn't to be denied. When the checkered flag flew, he remained 0.89 seconds ahead of Tracy, with Fittipaldi a similar distance behind in third.

'I made a mistake at my last [pit] stop,' admitted Tracy. 'During the second segment, the car was a little bit loose. I thought let's take some [front] wing out, and hopefully it will balance out the last 20 laps. The one turn was just way too much and I had bad understeer throughout the rest of the race. I made the call. I over-reacted to what I needed.'

Tracy was nevertheless pleased with second place. Fittipaldi, by contrast, was still angry about losing ground early in the race: 'I'm very disappointed that I blistered a front tire in the first segment. That meant I was out of the fuel window [for making the distance on just two stops]. I had to make an extra stop. It was a shame.'

Fellow Brazilian Boesel, meanwhile, was pleased to finish fourth – 'first in class,' as he put it – narrowly ahead of Michael Andretti.

'I had a good battle with Michael, but I wish it was for first and second instead of fourth and fifth,' said Boesel. 'My car ran well today but I think the Penskes were more consistent throughout the race. They could conserve their tires much better. They always look like they are running on new tires, keeping the balance all the way.'

Dobson, who ran in company with Andretti through most of the race, lost another lap in the frantic final stages but still held on gamely for sixth, showing that his third-place finish at Michigan had not been gained purely through attrition. Even more credibility came with the knowledge that Dobson in fact set the third-fastest race lap, beaten only by Fittipaldi and Unser.

SNIPPETS

instead of sitting around and moping Bentley and wife Robin went to pick it up themselves.

• When Teo Fabi established the fastest time during the first practice session, his efforts provided an appropriate riposte to team owner Jim Hall, who had informed Teo a few days earlier that his services would not be required for next season. 'At least this shows that if the car is performing, I am able to perform too,' said Fabi.

• Computer data from Stefan Johansson's car revealed that this year's aerodynamic rules for the short ovals, requiring smaller two-plane rear wings, resulted in a dramatic increase in straightline speed at NHIS, up to 191 mph from a maximum of 182

• Ross Bentley (above) was sidelined by an engine failure in the first practice session. The only spare motor available to the impecunious Dale Coyne team was due to arrive at Boston airport later in the day, so

last year. Cornering speeds also were improved, due to a combination of a cleaner track surface, a better aerodynamic package and, especially, softer tires. The Swede's Penske PC22 generated a sustained loading of 3.5G.

• After the race at Mid-Ohio, Rahal/Hogan Racing announced it would sever ties with Honda at the end of the season. Nevertheless, Robert Clarke (right), general manager of Honda Performance Development, confirmed that the Japanese auto manufacturer remained committed to Indy Car racing. Commenting on the decision by Rahal/Hogan, Clarke said: 'It's a matter of hopes and expectations. Our hopes were that we'd be further along [in terms of competitiveness]. Our expectations, I think, were

Photos: Michael C. Brown

a little bit behind our hopes. Unfortunately, Rahal/Hogan's expectations were higher than even ours.'

PPG INDY CAR WORLD SERIES • ROUND 12

SLICK-50 200

NEW HAMPSHIRE INTERNATIONAL SPEEDWAY, LOUDON, NEW HAMPSHIRE

AUGUST 21, 200 LAPS – 211.600 MILES

Place	Driver (Nat.)	No.	Team Sponsors Car-Engine	Q Speed (mph)	Q Time	Q Pos.	Laps	Time/Status	Ave. (mph)	Pts.
1	Al Unser Jr. (USA)	31	Marlboro Team Penske PC23-Ilmor/D	170.365	22.357s	10	200	1h 43m 31.594s	122.635	20
2	Paul Tracy (CDN)	3	Marlboro Team Penske PC23-Ilmor/D	173.422	21.963s	4	200	1h 43m 32.485s	122.618	16
3	Emerson Fittipaldi (BR)	2	Marlboro Team Penske PC23-Ilmor/D	175.091	21.753s	1	200	1h 43m 33.344s	122.601	16
4	Raul Boesel (BR)	5	Simon Duracell/Fuji Film/Mobil/Sadia Lola T94/00-Ford	173.856	21.908s	2	198	Running		12
5	Michael Andretti (USA)	8	Ganassi Target/Scotch Video Reynard 94I-Ford	167.848	22.692s	17	198	Running		10
6	Dominic Dobson (USA)	17	PacWest Racing Group Lola T94/00-Ford	172.148	22.125s	6	197	Running		8
7	Jimmy Vasser (USA)	18	Hayhoe Conseco/STP Reynard 94I-Ford	169.861	22.423s	12	195	Running		6
8	Adrian Fernandez (MEX)	7	Galles Tecate/Quaker State Reynard 94I-Ilmor/D	170.978	22.277s	8	195	Running		5
9	Bobby Rahal (USA)	4	Rahal-Hogan Miller Genuine Draft Lola T94/00-Honda	167.262	22.771s	19	193	Running		4
10	Willy T. Ribbs (USA)	24	Walker Service Merchandise/Bill Cosby Lola T94/00-Ford	160.977	23.660s	24	192	Running		3
11	Scott Goodyear (CDN)	40	Budweiser King Racing Lola T94/00-Ford	161.178	23.631s	23	192	Running		2
12	Mark Smith (USA)	15	Walker Craftsman Tools Lola T93/00-Ford	168.697	22.578s	15	192	Running		1
13	Robby Gordon (USA)	9	Walker Valvoline/Cummins Special Lola T94/00-Ford	168.878	22.554s	13	191	Running		
14	Mauricio Gugelmin (BR)	88	Ganassi Hollywood Reynard 94I-Ford	no speed	no time	28	188	Running		
15	Johnny Unser (USA)	19	Coyne The Mi-Jack Car/Ruger Lola T93/00-Ford	160.246	23.768s	25	185	Running		
16	Marco Greco (BR)	25	Simon Arciero Project Indy Lola T94/00-Ford	163.925	23.235s	22	184	Running		
17	Hiro Matsushita (J)	22	Simon Panasonic/Duskin Lola T94/00-Ford	165.031	23.079s	21	153	Engine		
18	Nigel Mansell (GB)	1	Newman-Haas Kmart/Texaco Havoline Lola T94/00-Ford	173.845	21.909s	3	127	Suspension		
19	Mario Andretti (USA)	6	Newman-Haas Kmart/Texaco Havoline Lola T94/00-Ford	172.342	22.100s	5	107	Accident		
20	Teo Fabi (I)	11	Hall Pennzoil Special Reynard 94I-Ilmor/D	171.402	22.222s	7	88	Exhaust header		
21	Eddie Cheever (USA)	14	A.J. Foyt Copenhagen Racing Lola T94/00-Ford	168.796	22.565s	14	63	Suspension		
22	Ross Bentley (CDN)	39	Coyne Agfa Film Lola T92/00-Ilmor/A	153.948	24.741s	27	37	Handling		
23	Stefan Johansson (S)	16	Bettenhausen Alumax Aluminum Penske PC22-Ilmor/D	170.797	22.300s	9	16	Handling		
24	*Scott Sharp (USA)	71	PacWest Racing Group Lola T94/00-Ford	167.446	22.747s	18	12	Accident		
25	Mike Groff (USA)	10	Rahal-Hogan Motorola Lola T94/00-Honda	165.045	23.077s	20	12	Accident		
26	*Jacques Villeneuve (CDN)	12	Forsythe-Green Player's Ltd. Reynard 94I-Ford	170.027	22.401s	11	0	Accident		
27	Arie Luyendyk (NL)	28	Indy Regency Eurosport/Boost Monaco Lola T94/00-Ilmor/D	168.405	22.617s	16	0	Accident		
NS	Buddy Lazier (USA)	23	Leader Card Financial World Lola T93/00-Ilmor/C	159.029	23.950s	26	–	Withdrawn/transmission		
NQ	Jeff Wood (USA)	50	Euromotorsport Agip/Hawaiian Tropic Lola T92/00-Ilmor/A	no speed	no time	–	–	Did not qualify		

denotes Rookie driver

Caution flags: Laps 4–7, accident/Villeneuve and Luyendyk; laps 9–11, accident/Cheever and Johansson; laps 13–24, accident/Groff and Sharp; laps 108–117, accident/Mario Andretti. Total: four for 32 laps.

Lap leaders: Emerson Fittipaldi, 1–46 (46 laps); Paul Tracy, 47–69 (23 laps); Al Unser Jr., 70–81 (12 laps); Nigel Mansell, 82–85 (4 laps); Unser Jr., 86–151 (66 laps); Fittipaldi, 152–195 (44 laps); Unser Jr., 196–200 (5 laps). **Totals:** Fittipaldi, 90 laps; Unser Jr., 83 laps; Tracy, 23 laps; Mansell, 4 laps.

Fastest race lap: Emerson Fittipaldi, 23.157s, 164.479 mph, on lap 162.

Championship positions: 1 Unser Jr., 173 pts; **2** Fittipaldi, 133; **3** Tracy, 107; **4** Michael Andretti, 100; **5** Gordon, 87; **6** Mansell, 79; **7** Villeneuve and Boesel, 54; **9** Rahal and Fabi, 49; **11** Mario Andretti, 43; **12** Vasser, 42; **13** Johansson, 41; **14** Goodyear, 32; **15** Fernandez, 30; **16** Gugelmin, 26; **17** Dobson, 25; **18** Luyendyk, 18; **19** M. Groff, 15; **20** Smith and Herta, 11; **22** Ribbs and Sharp, 10; **24** Zampedri, 9; **25** Matsushita, 8; **26** Montermini, 6; **27** Cheever, 5; **28** John Andretti, 3; **29** Greco, 2; **30** Jones, Freon, Till and Danner, 1.

VANCOUVER

The odds were stacked high against Al Unser Jr. in the Molson Indy Vancouver. Curiously, as in the other Canadian street race in Toronto, the Marlboro Penskes were not on the front-running pace throughout practice and qualifying. Furthermore, a severe case of food poisoning prevented Unser from leaving his hotel room on Friday. Intensive treatment prescribed by IndyCar's Director of Medical Affairs, Dr. Stephen Olvey, ensured that, even in his weakened state, Unser was able to qualify the following day. But the runaway PPG Cup points leader certainly didn't rate his chances too highly for the 102-lap race.

Nevertheless, all the cards fell in his favor. Several of the more fancied contenders ran into either mechanical difficulties or each other, or both, while a couple of inspired strategic decisions by team owner Roger Penske helped him make up ground during his pit stops. Consequently, on lap 77, Unser found himself in the lead.

'The only time I really passed anybody is when they got out of shape and made a mistake themselves. All of the rest of the passing was done by my crew in the pits,' said Unser, who drove flawlessly to claim his third Vancouver victory. 'We watched everybody kind of run into each other out there, and I was just trying to protect what I had.'

Pole-sitter Robby Gordon finished second, despite a lack of third gear in the closing stages, while Michael Andretti, the only other driver to win in Vancouver since the race was first run in 1990, earned the final podium position after, shall we say, a 'robust' performance that brought criticism from several other drivers and earned him a $10,000 fine.

Al Unser Jr. overcame the effects of illness and avoided the many pitfalls, such as a spinning Teo Fabi *(top)*, he encountered during an eventful race to emerge victorious once again.

Father and son. The elder Andretti's portrait gazes down on the circuit as the *'Arrivederci, Mario'* Tour rolls on, while out on the track Michael *(above)* was at the center of a controversy over the forceful tactics which brought him third place.

Photos: Michael C. Brown

| 1st – AL UNSER JR | 2nd – GORDON | 3rd – MICHAEL A |

Pole-sitter Robby Gordon leads from Nigel Mansell on the first lap. The spirited Californian brought the Valvoline/Cummins Lola home in second place after an early puncture and then gearbox trouble had dashed his hopes of scoring his first PPG Cup win.

QUALIFYING

For the second race weekend in a row, the opening practice session ended with a familiar name in an unaccustomed position atop the timing sheets. On this occasion it was Stefan Johansson who posted the quickest time, narrowly ahead of Nigel Mansell.

'That's the nice thing about this championship,' declared the Swede. 'It goes to show the strength of its rules stability when you can still do well in a year-old car. You can at least get up there sometimes.'

Johansson also proved the effectiveness of the spring-less, progressive-rate Quantum shock absorbers fitted exclusively to his Alumax Penske PC22-Ilmor/D, since the extraordinarily bumpy 1.653-mile circuit always places a premium on suspension settings. As usual, however, lap times tumbled in the after-noon qualifying session, during which Johansson's efforts were thwarted by a problem with fifth gear.

Instead, Gordon and Mansell vied for the honor of quickest time. The two Lola-Ford/Cosworths, which, coincidentally, also had set the pace in Toronto, again proved evenly matched. Gordon, who had switched briefly to his back-up Valvoline/Cummins car in the morning due to a cracked heat exchanger, showed there had been no ill effects by bouncing to the top of the charts early in the session. Mansell responded with a slightly faster time, only for Gordon to post a sensational 54.570 seconds on his very last lap.

'It was a lot of fun, trading positions with Nigel,' said an excited Gordon. 'Once it got down to 30 seconds to go, I went for it, and that was a perfect lap. It was a good one.'

Mansell was impressed: 'I was out there trying my hardest and I couldn't get near it.'

Most drivers improved their times the following day. Even so, no one approached Gordon's Friday best. Pole number two for the rapidly maturing Californian was assured.

'As I said in Toronto when we got the pole, we like the beer here in Canada. That must be why we go faster,' quipped car owner Derrick Walker after securing his team's third straight pole north of the border.

Mansell found a couple of tenths to retain the other front row position, narrowly eclipsing Michael Andretti's best in Chip Ganassi's Target/Scotch Video Reynard-Ford, while a flu-ridden Scott Goodyear, who, driving for Walker, had claimed last year's pole in Vancouver, found a substantial improvement in the closing moments to leap all the way from 18th to fourth! Goodyear had experimented with a radical set-up on his Bud-weiser Lola on Friday morning, but immediately felt more at home after switching to the team's back-up car, which was in virtually 'stock' specification. He then fine-tuned the settings and was able to reap the benefits.

Teo Fabi also made a huge leap at the end of the final session, lodging the fifth-fastest time in his Pennzoil Reynard-Ilmor. Paul Tracy, relegated to sixth, had lost his opportunity to improve when he slid into a wall after encountering a large puddle of water dislodged from the tire barriers moments earlier by Michael Andretti. Johansson, seventh, had again set fastest time in the morning practice session, although for the race he was forced into his back-up car due to a crash in the final warm-up. Unser was one place behind, having risen from his sick bed to set an impressive eighth-best time inside a bare minimum of laps.

The racing was close-fought and there were plenty of incidents. *Left:* Teo Fabi is about to be helped into a spin by the Miller Genuine Draft Lola-Honda of Bobby Rahal.

Below: The Marlboro Penskes of Emerson Fittipaldi and Paul Tracy are chased by Rahal, who lost his chance of a good placing when he slid up an escape road, rejoining to finish seventh.

Bottom: Michael Andretti is ahead of trouble on this occasion as Stefan Johansson, close behind Scott Goodyear, locks his brakes, runs into the wall and is eliminated.

Michael C. Brown

Scott Goodyear was the beneficiary of the late-race coming-together between Emerson Fittipaldi and Nigel Mansell, the Budweiser King Racing Lola emerging with fourth place.

RACE

The presence of three of the most aggressive and uncompromising drivers in Indy Car racing at the sharp end of the grid led many among the record-sized crowd of more than 70,000 to expect some fireworks at the start. Surprisingly, however, the first lap was remarkably clean. The top positions remained unaltered as the 28-car field sped along bumpy Pacific Boulevard, then funneled into the tight, right-handed hairpin at Turn Three. Gordon duly completed lap one a commanding 1.83 seconds ahead of Mansell.

Andretti, Goodyear, Fabi and Tracy followed in line astern, while Johansson, who had lost out to Unser in the initial burst, regained seventh place by driving calmly around the outside of the series points leader at Turn Three.

Gordon's early spurt took him fully 3.46 seconds ahead of Mansell after one more lap, whereupon Andretti decided he had had enough of following the Englishman. Fortunately for him, Andretti's task of making the pass was eased considerably when Mansell missed a gear shift right in front of the pits. A grateful Andretti scooted past and set off in pursuit of Gordon.

Andretti's chase wasn't very fruitful. Even with a clear road, he was unable to make any impression on Gordon, who had set off at a startling pace. Gordon turned three of the fastest laps of the entire race as he eked out a margin of more than six seconds by lap nine.

Mansell, meanwhile, had fallen a further ten seconds adrift, simply unable – or, at least at this early stage in the race, unwilling – to match their pace. The major excitement instead was focused on the battle for fourth as Goodyear struggled to stay ahead of Fabi, Tracy and Johansson. Mario Andretti, who had moved up a couple of places in the early laps, Jacques Villeneuve (Player's Reynard-Ford) and a cautious Unser rounded out the top ten.

'If anyone attempted to poke a nose in front of me, it was their corner,' said Unser, who had managed to regain much of his strength after following Dr. Olvey's regime. 'I wasn't 100 per cent but I'd say I was 80 per cent. I felt a hell of a lot better than I did yesterday. We just went out there to do the best job we could.'

As usual, it was pretty good.

The first respite for the drivers came on lap ten, when a spectacular fire aboard Alessandro Zampedri's Mi-Jack Lola-Ford ensured the first full-course caution.

Immediately after the restart, Andretti began to place Gordon under pressure for the first time. The youngster held up well, though, and in fact it was Andretti's challenge that wilted, victim of a shredded right-rear tire on lap 19.

'It just blew,' said Andretti. 'I had no warning. I thought I was done because the car started to head right for the wall in that very fast corner before the hairpin. I was just lucky. I had my eyes closed the whole time.'

Andretti limped into the pits for fresh rubber, rejoining immediately ahead of Gordon on the road, albeit down in 21st position. Even farther behind, having pitted as a result of making contact under braking for Turn Ten a couple of laps earlier, were Michael's father, Mario, and Villeneuve.

Michael Andretti's delay allowed Mansell to move up into second place, followed by Fabi and Tracy, both of whom had found a way past Goodyear a couple of laps earlier.

For the next dozen laps, Gordon maintained a lead of around one second over Mansell. The Briton's fears about fuel consumption, on a circuit that traditionally provides problems, had been eased by the early caution. For now he was content to bide his time. Fabi, meanwhile, resisted continuous attempts by Tracy to move into third place – until lap 32, when the Canadian executed a clean pass under braking for Turn Three.

Injudiciously, Fabi tried to regain the position under braking for the following chicane. He was never likely to succeed. Instead, Fabi hit the rear of Tracy's car, ripping off his own nose cone. He also stalled. The pace car was summoned again while the yellow Reynard was tow-started.

This time all the leaders took the opportunity to make their first scheduled pit stops. Save Unser, that is, who had stopped, at Penske's command, under green, a couple of laps earlier. It turned out to be a shrewd move. Unser had resumed in 12th place after taking on service, then was able to hustle through the order as everyone else pitted under the yellow. Only Gordon and Mansell remained ahead as the field re-formed behind the pace car.

Tracy, meanwhile, had lost valuable time in the pits as a crewman struggled to refasten his seatbelts, which had earlier fallen loose. But a broken locking pin ensured the efforts were in vain. Tracy not only fell from third to eighth, behind team-mate Emerson Fittipaldi, he also had to contend with the fact his belts remained loose.

One lap after the restart, striving to put some distance between himself and Mansell, Gordon made a mistake as he braked too late on the approach to Turn Ten. Instinctively, rather than risk spinning the car with the entire field bearing down upon him, Gordon took to the escape road, which doubled as the pit entry lane.

'I take all the blame for it,' said Gordon. 'Nigel was pretty close to me on the restart. I tried to go in pretty deep, I started to lock up the front tires and I said, OK, instead of flat-spotting the tires, I'll go into the pits.'

Gordon also had the presence of mind to adhere to the pit lane speed limit of 80 mph during his enforced detour, from which he emerged in fifth place behind Mansell, Unser, Goodyear and Johansson. Next in line, though, was Adrian Fernandez, who inadvertently made light contact with the rear of Gordon's car as they swept toward the braking area for Turn Three.

'I don't know what he was thinking,' said Gordon, 'because there was no chance he was going to go underneath me.'

Again Gordon came out the loser. A rear tire was punctured. Gordon headed for the pits once more. He rejoined in 17th.

Gordon's adventures elevated Mansell into the lead.

Disregarding the solitary laps he led in Detroit and Cleveland, and his brief moments atop the lap chart amid pit stops in New Hampshire, this was only the fourth time Mansell had held the point this year. He was determined to make the most of it.

By lap 40, Mansell led Unser by 2.29 seconds. A dicing Goodyear and Johansson were a similar margin behind. The man to watch, however, was Michael Andretti, who was making rapid progress toward the front.

On lap 45, Andretti moved from fifth to third, having despatched Johansson and Goodyear with two brilliantly incisive moves on the same lap. Next time around, Johansson threw away his hopes of a strong finish when he locked up his front brakes in pursuit of Goodyear and slid into the wall on the entry to Turn Three. His Penske suffered extensive damage to its left-front suspension. Johansson was out.

Andretti continued his charge by erasing a three-second deficit to Unser inside just three laps. Then, without further ado, he nipped neatly into second place in Turn Ten. Only Mansell now lay ahead, although the deficit had grown to over 11 seconds. Furthermore, Andretti was due to make another pit stop. His opportunity came on lap 52, when the pace car was sent out again after Willy T. Ribbs spun and stalled at the second chicane. The out-of-sequence pit stop saw Andretti fall to 11th. But only briefly. After the restart, Andretti quickly picked off Raul Boesel, Mauricio Gugelmin and Bobby Rahal. He also moved up a place when Tracy locked up his rear brakes and spun in Turn Three just moments after finally finding a way past Fittipaldi, who had been fighting an unco-operative Marlboro Penske all weekend. The error dropped Tracy to 11th.

On lap 59, the caution flags were out again, this time after Dominic Dobson's Vancouver Grizzlies/PacWest Lola stalled on the exit of the Turn Five chicane following an incident with Jimmy Vasser's Conseco/STP Reynard. The pair had been disputing tenth until a gear-linkage failure suddenly left Dobson without drive. Poor Vasser, with nowhere to go, bumped up onto the back of Dobson's car, losing a lap before he could resume.

The yellows flew just as the race leaders were approaching the final turn. Mansell, unfortunately, was already past the pit entrance. Unser, though, heeded a frantic call from Penske and dived into the pits for service. Unser lost only three places, and now was in a position to attempt to run the rest of the way without stopping again. It was a pivotal point in the race.

'I saw the yellow,' related Unser, 'but I didn't see the double yellow

Michael Andretti *(right)* takes the outside line while Emerson Fittipaldi is nudged from behind by team-mate Paul Tracy – one of many such incidents on the testing Vancouver street circuit.

Michael C. Brown

[indicating a full-course caution]. Roger made the call. He called a beautiful race today. He was really, really sharp today and I especially want to thank him.'

Most of the other cars on the lead lap took the opportunity to pit. Mansell, therefore, was left in the lead, followed by Fernandez and Arie Luyendyk. Both had moved up steadily, also eschewing a pit stop at this stage. Michael Andretti was elevated to fourth place by the pit stops, although soon after the restart he encountered a serious vibration. A slow puncture was suspected. He, too, would need an extra stop.

In fact, upon inspection, all four tires were found to be properly inflated. His team later speculated that the imbalance had been caused by excessive pick-up of debris during the caution period. Once again, Andretti found himself mired deep in the pack as he rejoined in 13th, the last man on the lead lap.

Mansell continued to run out in front, chased by Fernandez, Luyendyk and Unser. By lap 73, the top four cars each were separated by around five seconds, but all bar Unser were due to make another pit stop.

Luyendyk was the first to call in for service, on lap 74. Two laps later, Mansell pulled onto pit lane, elevating Fernandez into the lead of an Indy Car race for the first time in his career. Tragically, however, less than a quarter-mile into its 77th lap, the Mexican's Tecate/Quaker State Reynard-Ilmor suddenly coughed, spluttered and died. There was no coaxing it back to the pits. The fuel tank was dry. Fernandez was out.

'We weren't even thinking about stopping,' claimed Galles Team Manager Owen Snyder. 'That's how far off the computer was. There was no warning. The pick-up's almost too good now. These cars are real efficient. It coughs once and it's out.'

Yet another caution, the fifth of the day, was called to remove Fernandez's stalled car. The relaxed pace helped to allay the fears of several drivers about being able to reach the finish without a final splash-and-go. Among them was Unser, who had now taken over in the catbird seat. Fittipaldi, after an unspectacular run, assumed second place, chased (as he had been in Toronto) by Rahal.

Close behind at the restart, though, was Gordon, who immediately addressed that situation by passing Rahal in a breathtaking outside-line maneuver going into the

Drawing the line

Incredibly, Michael Andretti's Target/Scotch Video Reynard-Ford escaped unscathed from its contact with Paul Tracy's Marlboro Penske-Ilmor on lap 94, although afterward Andretti came in for a verbal lashing from a distinctly unhappy Tracy.

'This is the second time in Canada this year Michael's taken me out of the race,' declared Tracy. 'He ran straight into the back of me.'

'He has every right to be mad,' agreed Andretti, 'but it wasn't done on purpose. I feel very bad. I wasn't even trying to pass him, but I was having real problems with my rear brakes.'

'Why then,' queried Tracy upon being informed of Andretti's admission, 'didn't he back off a bit earlier?'

Good question. The IndyCar stewards apparently agreed with Tracy's viewpoint, later slapping Andretti with a $10,000 fine under a new provision citing 'unjustifiable risk, rough driving and unsportsmanlike driving.' The ruling had been instituted following the infamous incident at Mid-Ohio, where Robby Gordon, fighting to stay on the lead lap, made a mistake during a localized yellow caution flag and was inadvertently passed by the race leader, Paul Tracy.

Andretti was reportedly involved in as many as 11 incidents of contact with other cars during the Vancouver race, and indeed his car bore numerous scars.

More controversially, Tracy was fined an identical amount under the same provision after he, too, was reported as having come into contact with other competitors. The consensus afterward was that, while Andretti's punishment was just, Tracy's was unfortunate; and Mansell was lucky to escape a similar fine following his last-corner fracas with Fittipaldi.

---

flat-out Turn One. Moments later, when Fittipaldi momentarily bogged down on the exit of Turn Three, Gordon took full advantage to regain second place. And then, as if to maintain the drama, Rahal locked up his tires under braking for Turn Five and slid into the escape road. Rahal was obliged by the regulations to come to a complete halt before resuming, thereby falling to ninth.

Unser, meanwhile, blessed with a clear track, pulled out a lead of more than three seconds. But with 20 laps remaining, he knew he faced a tough battle if he was to keep the charging Gordon at bay: 'Man, I thought, this is going to be a heck of a finish.'

Sadly, the critical loss of third gear was costing Gordon valuable momentum every time he tried to accelerate away from the slow corners. Try as he did, there was no way he could mount a serious challenge for the lead.

Instead the focus of attention was now on the battle for third place. And what a battle it was. Fittipaldi could do nothing about Gordon but he wasn't about to let Tracy through without a struggle. A frustrated Mansell, too, was close behind, soon to be joined by Michael Andretti, who passed Goodyear and Gugelmin immediately after the yellow.

On lap 88, Tracy out-dragged Fittipaldi along Pacific Boulevard, repeating the move he had pulled earlier in the race, only this time he made no mistakes under braking for Turn Three. Tracy was back up to third. At Turn Ten, Mansell also grasped an opportunity to pass Fittipaldi by diving down the inside under braking. Nice move. And as if falling from third to fifth in one lap wasn't bad enough, Fittipaldi was passed by the charging Andretti next time around.

Andretti continued his action-packed afternoon by diving inside Mansell under heavy braking for

Turn Three on lap 93. Again, it was a beautifully judged maneuver. Mansell had no option but to capitulate.

Andretti was now close behind Tracy, battling for third place. Right ahead of the pair of them was Mario Andretti, still one lap down after his early delay but able to run at a good pace. Tracy, after briefly looking to the inside of Mario under braking for Turn Ten, realized he wasn't close enough to pass, so quickly tucked back into line . . . only to be slammed from the rear by the other Andretti.

Adding insult to injury (or should that be the other way around?), Tracy's car was clipped again by Michael as he tried to find a way past, inflicting enough damage to put the irate Canadian out of the race. Mansell, running close behind, was forced to a complete halt. By the time his path had cleared, Mansell had lost three places to Fittipaldi (again!), Gugelmin and Goodyear.

A couple of laps later, the sixth and final full-course caution was made necessary when Fabi spun (after an assist from Rahal) and stalled in Turn Three. Curiously, as Michael Andretti made his way around Fabi's stationary car, Fittipaldi took the opportunity to nip through into third place – under caution but without receiving any kind of penalty from the officials.

In reality, it didn't matter too much. On the final restart, with four laps remaining in this incredible contest, Andretti immediately redressed the situation, thereafter holding on to his hard-earned third position.

Fittipaldi seemed to be headed for fourth place going into the last corner, only to have to contend with an ambitious move by Mansell, who, after charging by Gugelmin and Goodyear, still reckoned there was plenty of fight left in his Kmart/Havoline Lola. Braking impossibly late, and from some dis-

tance behind, Mansell lunged to the inside in a surprisingly desperate maneuver which never looked like succeeding.

As Mansell himself said: 'He [Emerson] had the choice of letting me go or crashing. So we crashed.'

It was an entirely inappropriate ending to the afternoon for the two former champions. And Fittipaldi left Mansell in no doubt as to who he felt was to blame.

'He tried to use my brakes to slow his car,' asserted an angry Fittipaldi. 'My car is not a ghost. Between my car and the wall there was not enough gap for him to go through, and he just made a big judgment mistake. A great champion like Nigel should never try to make a pass like that.'

Goodyear gratefully accepted fourth place amid the acrimony that followed Mansell's ill-judged pass, followed by Gugelmin, then Luyendyk and Rahal, who, without rancor, traded places just a couple of laps from the finish. Mark Smith moved into eighth, his Craftsman Lola-Ford the only other unlapped finisher after a strong performance.

Much the same can be said of Unser's winning drive. Unser didn't overtake another car at any stage in the race. But then, he didn't need to. Instead he parlayed brilliant strategy and consistency into his record-tying eighth win of the season. 'That was our plan today,' he revealed, 'to stay out of trouble and finish the race.' Mission accomplished.

Robby Gordon, meanwhile, would have to wait a little longer before notching what was now a long overdue first victory.

'It's frustrating for me and the whole Walker team,' said Gordon. 'They gave me a car that was awesome. I think this race we really earned it. We showed we have the speed; now we just have to have a flawless race.'

SNIPPETS

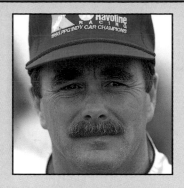

• Carl Haas confirmed prior to the race weekend that, by mutual consent, Nigel Mansell *(above)* would not be fulfilling the final year of his contract with Newman-Haas Racing. Haas also said Mansell would be free to contest the final three Formula 1 races of the season, once his Indy Car commitments had been completed.

• Construction of General Motors Place, the future home arena for the latest National Basketball Association franchise, the Vancouver Grizzlies, caused a slight re-alignment of the second chicane at Turn Seven.

• Bobby Rahal used the latest 'spec five' Honda engine in qualifying but reverted to the trusty, but less powerful, '3D' motor for the race. The newer specification employs a conventional firing order, in contrast to the 3D 'big bang' version, which boasts a distinctive, throatier sound.

• Michael Andretti arrived in Vancouver suffering from the effects of a heavy crash while testing Chip Ganassi's Reynard at Nazareth Speedway. Andretti had been knocked unconscious in the incident and spent a night in hospital.

• All season, the all-conquering Penske team has employed a suspension device aimed at reducing the chassis's pitch-sensitivity by controlling the ride-height. At Vancouver, however, the arrangement was discarded after practice. 'Any bumpy tracks you can't use it because it makes the ride so harsh you can't drive it,' said Paul Tracy *(below)*. Rival Lola and Reynard teams, which have developed their own so-called 'third-spring' derivative, reached the same conclusion.

Photos: Michael C. Brown

PPG INDY CAR WORLD SERIES • ROUND 13
MOLSON INDY VANCOUVER

B.C. PLACE CIRCUIT,
VANCOUVER, BRITISH COLUMBIA, CANADA

SEPTEMBER 4, 102 LAPS – 168.606 MILES

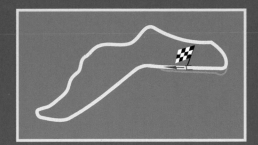

Place	Driver (Nat.)	No.	Team Sponsors Car-Engine	Q Speed (mph)	Q Time	Q Pos.	Laps	Time/Status	Ave. (mph)	Pts.
1	Al Unser Jr. (USA)	31	Marlboro Team Penske PC23-Ilmor/D	107.510	55.351s	8	102	1h 53m 27.345s	89.166	20
2	Robby Gordon (USA)	9	Walker Valvoline/Cummins Special Lola T94/00-Ford	109.049	54.570s	1	102	1h 53m 29.584s	89.136	17
3	Michael Andretti (USA)	8	Ganassi Target/Scotch Video Reynard 94I-Ford	108.592	54.799s	3	102	1h 53m 34.428s	89.073	14
4	Scott Goodyear (CDN)	40	Budweiser King Racing Lola T94/00-Ford	108.096	55.051s	4	102	1h 53m 39.797s	89.003	12
5	Mauricio Gugelmin (BR)	88	Ganassi Hollywood Reynard 94I-Ford	107.013	55.608s	13	102	1h 53m 40.161s	88.998	10
6	Arie Luyendyk (NL)	28	Indy Regency Eurosport/Boost Monaco Lola T94/00-Ilmor/D	106.207	56.030s	18	102	1h 53m 42.198s	88.972	8
7	Bobby Rahal (USA)	4	Rahal-Hogan Miller Genuine Draft Lola T94/00-Honda	106.756	55.742s	15	102	1h 53m 45.020s	88.935	6
8	Mark Smith (USA)	15	Walker Craftsman Tools Lola T94/00-Ford	106.720	55.761s	16	102	1h 53m 59.660s	88.744	5
9	Emerson Fittipaldi (BR)	2	Marlboro Team Penske PC23-Ilmor/D	107.151	55.537s	12	101	Accident		4
10	Nigel Mansell (GB)	1	Newman-Haas Kmart/Texaco Havoline Lola T94/00-Ford	108.734	54.728s	2	101	Accident		4
11	Mario Andretti (USA)	6	Newman-Haas Kmart/Texaco Havoline Lola T94/00-Ford	107.367	55.425s	10	101	Running		2
12	*Scott Sharp (USA)	71	PacWest Racing Group Lola T94/00-Ford	106.884	55.675s	14	101	Running		1
13	*Parker Johnstone (USA)	49	Comptech Racing Acura Lola T93/00-Honda	104.487	56.953s	25	101	Running		
14	Mike Groff (USA)	10	Rahal-Hogan Motorola Lola T94/00-Honda	105.607	56.348s	21	101	Running		
15	Jimmy Vasser (USA)	18	Hayhoe Conseco/STP Reynard 94I-Ford	105.502	56.404s	22	101	Running		
16	Marco Greco (BR)	25	Simon Arciero Project Indy Lola T94/00-Ford	105.267	56.531s	23	100	Spin		
17	Eddie Cheever (USA)	14	A.J. Foyt Copenhagen Racing Lola T94/00-Ford	106.263	56.001s	17	99	Running		
18	Teo Fabi (I)	11	Hall Pennzoil Special Reynard 94I-Ilmor/D	107.887	55.158s	5	98	Running		
19	Dominic Dobson (USA)	17	PacWest Racing Group Lola T94/00-Ford	106.022	56.128s	19	96	Running		
20	Paul Tracy (CDN)	3	Marlboro Team Penske PC23-Ilmor/D	107.562	55.324s	6	94	Suspension		
21	*Claude Bourbonnais (CDN)	30	McCormack Player's Ltd. Lola T93/00-Ilmor/C+	105.009	56.669s	24	88	Transmission		
22	Adrian Fernandez (MEX)	7	Galles Tecate/Quaker State Reynard 94I-Ilmor/D	107.365	55.426s	11	76	Out of fuel		
23	Raul Boesel (BR)	5	Simon Duracell/Fuji Film/Mobil/Sadia Lola T94/00-Ford	105.747	56.274s	20	68	Engine		
24	*Jacques Villeneuve (CDN)	12	Forsythe-Green Player's Ltd. Reynard 94I-Ford	107.499	55.357s	9	53	Exhaust header		
25	Willy T. Ribbs (USA)	24	Walker Service Merchandise/Bill Cosby Lola T94/00-Ford	104.395	57.003s	26	52	Handling		
26	Stefan Johansson (S)	16	Bettenhausen Alumax Aluminum Penske PC22-Ilmor/D	107.550	55.331s	7	45	Accident		
27	Buddy Lazier (USA)	23	Leader Card Financial World Lola T93/00-Ilmor/C	104.180	57.120s	27	16	Half-shaft		
28	*Alessandro Zampedri (I)	19	Coyne The Mi-Jack Car Lola T93/00-Ford	103.008	57.770s	28	8	Fire		
NQ	*Franck Freon (F)	50	Euromotorsport Agip/Hawaiian Tropic Lola T92/00-Ilmor/A	102.187	58.235s	29	–	Did not qualify		
NQ	Ross Bentley (CDN)	39	Coyne Agfa Film Lola T92/00-Ilmor/A	102.129	58.268s	30	–	Did not qualify		
NQ	Hiro Matsushita (J)	22	Simon Panasonic/Duskin Lola T94/00-Ford	100.180	59.401s	31	–	Did not qualify		

* denotes Rookie driver

Caution flags: Laps 10–13, fire/Zampedri; laps 32–35, spin/Fabi; laps 51–54, spin/Ribbs; laps 59–61, tow/Dobson; laps 77–80, tow/Fernandez; laps 95–97, tow/Tracy. Total: six for 22 laps.

Lap leaders: Robby Gordon, 1–36 (36 laps); Nigel Mansell, 37–75 (39 laps); Adrian Fernandez, 76 (1 lap); Al Unser Jr., 77–102 (26 laps). **Totals:** Mansell, 39 laps; Gordon, 36 laps; Unser Jr., 26 laps; Fernandez, 1 lap.

Fastest race lap: Robby Gordon, 55.786s, 106.672 mph, on lap 6.

Championship positions: 1 Unser Jr., 193 pts; 2 Fittipaldi, 137; 3 Michael Andretti, 114; 4 Tracy, 107; 5 Gordon, 104; 6 Mansell, 83; 7 Rahal, 55; 8 Villeneuve and Boesel, 54; 10 Fabi, 49; 11 Mario Andretti, 45; 12 Goodyear, 44; 13 Vasser, 42; 14 Johansson, 41; 15 Gugelmin, 36; 16 Fernandez, 30; 17 Luyendyk, 26; 18 Dobson, 25; 19 Smith, 16; 20 M. Groff, 15; 21 Herta and Sharp, 11; 23 Ribbs 10; 24 Zampedri, 9; 25 Matsushita, 8; 26 Montermini, 6; 27 Cheever, 5; 28 John Andretti, 3; 29 Greco, 2; 30 Jones, Freon, Till and Danner, 1.

ROAD AMERICA

There were, in effect, two winners in the Texaco/Havoline 200. Jacques Villeneuve *(left)* ensured a breath of fresh air for the PPG Cup series by scoring a sensational maiden success, while the season's dominant driver, Al Unser Jr., also was in a mood to celebrate following a close second-place finish, which was enough to clinch his second championship title.

After a truly magnificent drive, Villeneuve joined Nigel Mansell in becoming only the second driver to win a race during his rookie season since Teo Fabi in 1983. At the same time, the French-Canadian confirmed the immense promise he has shown ever since enrolling as a 15-year-old with the Jim Russell Racing Drivers School at St. Jovite, Quebec, in 1986.

Villeneuve's success was a testament not only to his own consummate skills but also the strategy of his team, Forsythe-Green Racing, which had gambled on applying a low-downforce set-up to his Player's Ltd. Reynard-Ford/Cosworth XB. The ploy paid off late in the race when, following a full-course caution, Villeneuve used his straightline speed advantage to draft past both Paul Tracy, who had led convincingly from the start, and his Marlboro Penske team-mate Al Unser Jr. Once in front, Villeneuve belied his relative inexperience by making not the hint of a mistake.

'He's definitely one of the best rookies we've had,' asserted the new series champion graciously. 'What I was hoping to do was to push him into a mistake; but he didn't make any. He drove a perfect race.'

Michael C. Brown

Robby Gordon performs a tire-smoking spin-turn in his Lola after an off-course excursion during Saturday practice.

QUALIFYING

Gorgeous fall weather greeted the Indy Car teams as they assembled under clear blue skies in rural Wisconsin. As seems to be the case every year, several improvements had been made to the challenging Road America circuit since the series' previous visit, including the provision of extended run-off areas and larger gravel traps in some of the more precarious locations. A good crowd, too, was on hand for the start of official practice on Friday morning. It was a perfect setting.

Paul Tracy, in particular, has developed a close affinity for the four-mile track, and indeed the talented Canadian set the pace from the get-go.

'This is one of my favorite tracks,' he confirmed. 'It's a joy to drive here. It seems to suit my style. There's lots of room and you can afford to let the car slide and hang out. You can dip a wheel off if you have to and really use the road.'

Tracy proved the veracity of his statement by sliding off at Turn Six during the first qualifying session. His PC23 escaped serious damage, although its trip into the gravel resulted in some debris being ingested by the Ilmor/D engine. The subsequent loss of power restricted Tracy to third-best time. Nevertheless, on Saturday, he bounced back to claim his third consecutive pole on what has come to be regarded as one of the most popular and demanding road courses in the world.

'This place brings out the best in Paul,' declared race engineer Nigel Beresford. 'He's young and he's brave. He really makes up time through the fast corners.'

Tracy's quickest lap, in 1m 45.416s, represented an improvement by almost 1.7 seconds over Bobby Rahal's long-standing record, set in 1991. It was also more than a half-second faster than his nearest challenger, countryman Villeneuve.

'We had a pretty strong car from the beginning and we just made it better,' said Villeneuve, who had enjoyed a fruitful test at Road America earlier in the summer. 'We took some wing out, so now we're quite fast on the straights; and the interesting thing is that we didn't lose a lot of time under braking.'

Villeneuve was indeed fast on the straightaways. In fact, his Reynard alone reached 200 mph, leaving most other cars breathless at around 190–195 mph.

Third place on the starting grid was taken by Nigel Mansell, who lost valuable track time in the first session after over-revving an engine. He also missed the final part of qualifying on Saturday due to another Ford/Cosworth failure.

'The last change we made to the chassis was very, very good,' claimed Mansell. 'We bolted on new tires and I was on a really fantastic lap, but then the engine had a little problem.'

Series leader Al Unser Jr. ended up with the fourth-fastest time, having been quickest on Friday in his Marlboro Penske-Ilmor. Afterward he thought he should have done better.

'I've been trying to improve the car, trying to make it better for the race, and I slowed it down,' he said candidly. 'So tomorrow I'm going back to how it was. I was tryin' a little bit harder, too, and I made some mistakes.'

Robby Gordon overcame an engine problem on Saturday morning to qualify fifth in his Valvoline/Cummins Lola, while Adrian Fernandez maintained his recent form to be sixth on the grid in Rick Galles' Tecate/Quaker State Reynard-Ilmor. Other strong efforts were posted by Mark Smith, a season-high eighth in his Craftsman Tools Lola-Ford; Eddie Cheever, 11th in his best showing at the wheel of A.J. Foyt's Copenhagen Lola-Ford; and the two PacWest drivers, Dominic Dobson and Scott Sharp, who were separated by a scant 0.018s in 12th and 13th places.

RACE

The warm, sunny conditions from practice rolled over into race day, helping to attract another record crowd. Almost every vantage point was taken. The circuit's concession stands, famed for their bratwurst, corn and beer, conducted a roaring trade.

Paul Tracy, who last year sped to a virtually unchallenged victory at Road America, set off this time with every intention of providing a repeat performance. He jumped clear of fellow front-row qualifier Villeneuve almost as soon as he had exited Turn 14, and was already a car length or two ahead by the time he could see the starter's waving green flag.

It was a good job he took off so soon, because when Tracy reached the braking area for Turn One, Villeneuve's aerodynamically unencumbered Player's Reynard was snapping at his Marlboro Penske's rear wing. Tracy, though, was able to

maintain his advantage. Villeneuve was obliged to follow.

Behind, Mansell took advantage of Tracy's fast getaway to nose ahead of fellow second-row starter Unser on the front straightaway. Unser, however, proved to be the more aggressive under braking for Turn One, drawing calmly alongside on the outside line and retaking third position. Gordon also seized an opportunity to slide past Mansell on the downhill run toward Turn Three. Inside a couple of hundred yards, the 1993 champion had slipped from third to fifth. Mansell's team-mate, Mario Andretti, showed that he was in a racy mood too, neatly out-braking Fernandez at Turn Five for sixth position.

Tracy set a stunning pace in the opening stages. He completed the first lap a full 1.8 seconds clear of a dicing Villeneuve and Unser. The next time around, Tracy increased his lead to 2.6 seconds, and for the next half-dozen circuits he padded his cushion by as much as one second per lap.

'My car was perfect,' said Tracy. 'I was running comfortably and the fuel mileage was good. Really, I was cruising.'

Villeneuve was having to work harder in keeping Unser at bay, while Gordon was holding on in fourth place. Until lap nine, that is, when he suddenly lost almost five seconds. Gordon was obviously in trouble, as he continued to lose ground, yet he remained ahead of Mansell, who was unable to muster enough speed to make a pass.

Finally, on lap 15, Gordon left his braking a fraction too late in Turn Eight. Mansell was alongside him in a flash, then past. Farther around the lap, Gordon slowed to a crawl.

'I felt second gear go about lap nine or ten and I'm pretty sure it broke clean in half,' explained Gordon. 'We tried to run as long as we could, to pick up some points, but a few laps later the whole [gearbox] went.'

Gordon wasn't the only top-ten contender in trouble. As early as lap eight, Cheever's race had ended with an engine failure. Shortly afterward, Smith's Ford/Cosworth also succumbed to the rigorous demands imposed by the circuit's long straightaways.

The problem is exacerbated at Road America by the fact fuel consumption is also a factor, especially since the four-mile lap affords no margin for error in terms of making pit stops. Thus, many teams opted to lean out the fuel mixture with the intention of

ensuring better mileage. Tracy, however, obviously had no such concerns, because he was one of only a half-dozen drivers to stretch their first stint to a full 17 laps. Everyone else stopped one lap sooner.

Tracy was able to take on fresh tires and a full load of fuel without losing his lead. By lap 20, his margin of superiority had stabilized at around seven seconds. But now up into second place was Unser, profiting from an unusual slip by Villeneuve, who, quite simply, forgot to engage first gear during his pit stop. Fortunately, Villeneuve lost only one position.

Mansell, hindered almost from the start by a misfiring engine, ran all alone in fourth, more than ten seconds adrift of Villeneuve and almost as far ahead of Mario Andretti. Fernandez and a fast-closing Emerson Fittipaldi were next, the Brazilian's Penske transformed overnight by the adoption of Tracy's set-up.

'I was struggling all weekend,' said Fittipaldi. 'I couldn't get the car to work in Turn Five, the Carousel and the kink, but today it was much better. The car was running strong.'

Sure enough, on lap 25, Fittipaldi executed a clean pass in Turn Five when he outbraked Fernandez.

Teo Fabi, too, had made good progress in the early stages. Having started 15th in his Pennzoil Reynard-Ilmor, Fabi was up to eighth by lap 18, his cause aided considerably by an excellent pit stop by Jim Hall's team. PacWest team-mates Dobson and Sharp remained tied together in their dice for ninth, while Bobby Rahal and Arie Luyendyk also were in close contention.

By lap 25, the race had developed into something of a procession. The top five contenders were spaced well apart. But then came the first of two full-course cautions, when a transmission problem forced Alessandro Zampedri to abandon Dale Coyne's Mi-Jack Lola in the gravel trap at Turn Six.

Interestingly, Unser, Mansell and Fernandez all took the opportunity to take on service, despite the fact they had stopped only ten laps earlier. Their strategy ensured they would need to pit again before the finish. Nevertheless, since each of them held a clear lead over his nearest pursuer, the initial delay would cost very few, if any, positions. Furthermore, the timing would ensure extra flexibility in the event of any further cautions toward the end of the race. Sure enough,

Michael C. Brown

Right: Just behind the leaders, the pack jockey for position on the first lap of the Texaco/Havoline 200 on the magnificent Road America circuit. Emerson Fittipaldi leads Eddie Cheever (14), Dominic Dobson (17), Raul Boesel, Scott Sharp (71), Teo Fabi (11), Scott Goodyear (40) and the rest.

Adrian Fernandez *(below)* was again in the points with a fifth-place finish in the Tecate/Quaker State Reynard.

Unser lost only one place, to Villeneuve, while Mansell fell behind only Andretti and Fittipaldi. Fernandez resumed in tenth.

Tracy rocketed away once more when the green flag was waved. Inside one lap he had stretched more than three seconds clear of Villeneuve. But then, three laps later, the yellows were out again, this time after Luyendyk lost control of his 11th-placed Eurosport/Boost Monaco Lola-Ilmor at the infamous kink on the back straightaway.

'I made contact with Rahal the lap before, so I may have picked up a slow puncture,' related Luyendyk, who was fortunate to emerge shaken but unhurt from the high-speed incident. His Lola also escaped serious damage. 'The car was real loose and I was struggling anyway. Coming out of the kink I spun and hit the wall. I saw cars coming by on both sides of me and I thought, "Oh, @*&#!" '

Miraculously, no one else was involved. Rahal and Stefan Johansson both squeaked by unscathed, but the most impressive maneuver was performed by Christian Danner, who reckoned he must have benefited from some divine intervention.

'I was *that* close,' stressed the German, indicating the minutest gap between his thumb and forefinger. He was still wide-eyed a half-hour after the incident. 'I had four wheels on the grass in top gear. I tell you, it was not funny. All I know is that some chap up there above the clouds kept us apart.'

The entire field pitted under the ensuing caution period, although both PacWest drivers missed their cue and ended up completing an extra lap before making their stops.

'We'd been having radio problems all day long,' explained Sharp, who had finally gotten past his team-mate a couple of laps before the caution. 'I just never heard the call.'

Strangely, although Sharp and Dobson led past the start/finish line as everyone else made their way onto pit road, they were not credited with leading the lap. And by the time they had rejoined, Sharp and Dobson had fallen from eighth and ninth (before the yellow) to 16th and 17th.

They weren't the only drivers to encounter problems during the pit stops. Villeneuve, incredibly, negated his crew's fine work by stalling his engine, although once again he was fortunate in that he lost only one place. Rahal also killed his motor and fell a couple of positions.

But the biggest drama occurred at the front of the field. Unser had been stationary for only a few seconds, long enough simply to replenish his almost-full tank. The time saved by not changing tires enabled him to leave his pit before Tracy's service was completed. Unser seemed to have claimed the advantage; but no one told Tracy, who lit up his tires and powered past his team-mate under full acceleration. Unser could hardly believe his eyes. Surely, he thought, Tracy would be penalized for exceeding the pit lane speed limit. But no. Tracy was adamant that he had kept below the 80 mph maximum. And whether or not he did so remained a moot point, since the IndyCar officials later admitted their speed monitoring device had malfunctioned! There would be no penalty.

Unser wasn't too impressed.

'I felt Paul had exceeded the limit going out of the pits when he passed me, and I was a little excited,' admitted Unser. 'The CART officials, they didn't catch it or they didn't see it, and Roger [Penske] came back on the radio and said, "Settle down, settle down." I got back and said I definitely want to have the #1 on my car and that's more important than winning the race today; and he came back and said, "Ten-four!" '

The order behind the pace car therefore saw Tracy back out in front, followed by Unser, Villeneuve and Fittipaldi. Next were Andretti, Fabi, Mansell and Fernandez, with Johansson and Raul Boesel completing the top ten.

The restart came with 35 laps in the books, leaving 15 to go. Tracy, of course, was planning to hot-foot away into the distance, just as he had following the earlier restart. Unfortunately, as he came around Turn 14, Tracy suddenly realized he hadn't left enough room for the pace car to clear his path. And instead of keeping his right foot planted on the throttle, he had to ease off a fraction, enabling those behind to gain a slight advantage. Tracy did manage to lead across the start/finish line, but Unser was closing fast.

Tracy knew he was in trouble. He made sure he kept to the middle of the road, thereby forcing Unser to take the outside line if he was to take the lead. Which he duly did. But only briefly. Villeneuve, too, had gotten a good jump, making it three wide at close to 190 mph as the leaders sped toward Turn One.

'I got a great tow and there was room to go to the inside, so I went for it,' said Villeneuve.

It was a bold maneuver, brilliantly executed. Unser was impressed, although, at the same time, he sensed a recipe for disaster.

'I looked in my mirror and I knew it was going to get real crowded there in Turn One,' said Unser, who still had his focus firmly fixed on the championship title, 'so I got on the brakes because I didn't have any control over them. I knew they were plannin' on outbrakin' me into that corner. At least I could control the situation when they were in front of me.'

Sagely, Unser backed out early and had a bird's eye view as Tracy and Villeneuve duked it out. Surprisingly, all three made it through the corner cleanly, despite the fact the two Canadians were in side-by-side formation.

Villeneuve's better acceleration enabled him to nose clear on the exit, whereupon Tracy gave him a nudge, just to let Jacques know he was there. As if he didn't know!

'Paul hit me from behind but I managed to hold on and then get to the inside [for Turn Three],' related Villeneuve. 'I was a little bit lucky not to go off when I was touched.'

Lucky or not, Villeneuve was in the lead. And Tracy was back to second. Unser, meanwhile, after poking his nose ahead for perhaps 100 yards, had been shuffled back to third, just ahead of Fittipaldi. There was action behind, too, as Fabi braved it out around the outside of Mario Andretti at Turn Five to take over in fifth place. Nice move.

'Mario is always tough to go by,' noted Fabi. 'He is a hard racer, but actually he is very fair. He tried to hold his position but he didn't try to hit me.'

Right behind this pair, Mansell radioed in to report a puncture, then brought his car onto pit road. All four wheels were changed, but no tire problems were detected. Mansell resumed, at the tail of the lead lap, then proceeded to lap faster than anyone, despite his intermittently misfiring engine. (The problem later was traced to a cracked electronic sensor.) Unfortunately, all hopes of a good placing had long since disappeared.

'I'm very sad because the car was fantastic,' said Mansell, who finished just out of the points in 13th. 'The team did a fantastic job, because we really got the chassis right, but I was only pulling a bit over 12,000 rpm on the straight. If we could have fixed the engine, we could have flown.'

Villeneuve, meanwhile, really was flying. He was also battling mightily

Teo Fabi *(above)* put in a committed performance to secure fourth in the Pennzoil Reynard after handling problems had hampered his efforts in qualifying.

Right: Seeing double! Two Andrettis, father and son, run side by side. On this occasion, neither finished.

Left: Celebration time as newly crowned champion Al Unser Jr. and his charming wife Shelley pose with the PPG Cup.

Michael C. Brown

to stay ahead of Tracy and Unser. He did a fine job. Tracy chased hard, until suddenly he felt his engine begin to lose power. An exhaust header cracked through, leaving him powerless to defend himself. Tracy had no alternative but to pull into the pits.

But was Villeneuve able to relax? Not at all. Because as one Marlboro Penske pulled off, another one began to loom larger in his mirrors. And there were still seven laps to go.

'When you've got Junior in your mirrors and he's faster than you, that was tough,' said Villeneuve. 'We lost a little under braking and cornering, but if I didn't make any mistakes, it was easier to stay in front because we were fast on the straights. All I wanted to do was not make a mistake.'

He didn't. Villeneuve drove superbly in those closing stages, absorbing the pressure more like a seasoned veteran than a raw rookie. The pace increased substantially, such that both Villeneuve and Unser set their fastest laps on the very last circuit. Villeneuve, though, was not to be denied. The victory was his, by a scant 0.609s.

Incredibly, the drama didn't end there, as Villeneuve slowed immediately after taking the checkered flag. He was out of fuel!

'I started to run out just as I came up to the start/finish line, so I switched it off because if you stop out on the circuit at this place, it's a long walk home,' said Villeneuve, calm as can be. 'For the last few laps I could see the [fuel] numbers on the dash, so I knew it was going to be close.'

As Villeneuve walked back to the pits, waving in acknowledgment of the cheers of the crowd, Unser returned to accept the plaudits from his team. Mansell, the out-going champion, also hustled across to offer his congratulations. The championship was won. Unser was content to accept second place this day.

'We were trying as hard as we could to stay with Jacques, let alone pass him,' said Unser with a smile. 'We could get close enough, but as soon as his car started taking my downforce away, that was it. He was awfully quick down the straightaways, so we could only get so close and that was it. He did a great job.'

Fittipaldi also offered high praise to both Villeneuve and Unser after finishing third, while Fabi was pleased to claim fourth, his car handling far more consistently than it had during practice and qualifying. Mario Andretti, sadly, lost fifth place when his engine failed shortly before the finish, handing the position to a grateful Fernandez.

Boesel took sixth, despite being assessed a stop-and-go penalty for inadvertently running over an air hose in Luyendyk's pit during his first stop, and Scott Goodyear parlayed a planned three-stop strategy into seventh.

Johansson, Rahal and Sharp crossed the line in tight formation after an absorbing battle in the closing stages, followed by an out-of-fuel Dobson and Danner, who was delighted to earn the final PPG Cup point – his second in only two starts this season. 'Mission accomplished,' declared Danner.

Similar sentiments were shared by Unser after clinching not only his second PPG Cup title but also a record-extending ninth for team owner Roger Penske.

'I'm just so proud of my guys,' said Unser. '[Crew chief] Richard Buck and all of Marlboro Team Penske. It takes a whole team to do this.'

Michael C. Brown

SNIPPETS

• Seen on a bumper sticker in the Road America infield: 'Life's too short to drink cheap beer.'

• Stefan Johansson (right) confirmed he will remain with Tony Bettenhausen's Alumax Aluminum-backed team for the next two seasons. The Swede will have a pair of this year's Penske PC23 chassis at his disposal in 1995.

• The effects of Nigel Mansell-fever seem to have worn off, at least in rural Wisconsin. Prior to the race weekend, a scheduled one-hour appearance by the 1993 PPG Cup champion at a Kmart store in nearby Plymouth was curtailed after 40 minutes due to a lack of autograph-seekers.

• Jacques Villeneuve's uncle, also named Jacques, scored his first (and only) Indy Car victory at Road America in 1985.

• Several drivers encountered tire failures during the race weekend. Some were attributed to drivers running wide onto the flinty 'marbles'

at the exit of several corners, while others were caused by overheating, especially on the right-rear corner. The Goodyear engineers kept a close watch on temperatures and made strict recommendations concerning tire pressures and the amount of camber run on some cars. They also cut some rubber away from the inside shoulders to assist in the heat-dissipation process. Michael Andretti, who was never close to the front-running pace but had suffered no tire problems in practice, blew two tires inside 15 laps on race day. Later, after adjusting the pressures, he faced no further problems – at least not from the tires. In the end he was forced out by a broken exhaust header.

Michael C. Brown

PPG INDY CAR WORLD SERIES • ROUND 14

TEXACO/HAVOLINE 200

ROAD AMERICA, ELKHART LAKE, WISCONSIN

SEPTEMBER 11, 50 LAPS – 200.000 MILES

Place	Driver (Nat.)	No.	Team Sponsors Car-Engine	Q Speed (mph)	Q Time	Q Pos.	Laps	Time/Status	Ave. (mph)	Pts.
1	*Jacques Villeneuve (CDN)	12	Forsythe-Green Player's Ltd. Reynard 94I-Ford	135.864	1m 45.988s	2	50	1h 42m 37.930s	116.922	20
2	Al Unser Jr. (USA)	31	Marlboro Team Penske PC23-Ilmor/D	135.598	1m 46.196s	4	50	1h 42m 38.539s	116.911	16
3	Emerson Fittipaldi (BR)	2	Marlboro Team Penske PC23-Ilmor/D	133.656	1m 47.739s	9	50	1h 42m 40.543s	116.873	14
4	Teo Fabi (I)	11	Hall Pennzoil Special Reynard 94I-Ilmor/D	132.603	1m 48.595s	15	50	1h 43m 01.809s	116.471	12
5	Adrian Fernandez (MEX)	7	Galles Tecate/Quaker State Reynard 94I-Ilmor/D	134.623	1m 46.965s	6	50	1h 43m 05.553s	116.400	10
6	Raul Boesel (BR)	5	Simon Duracell/Fuji Film/Mobil/Sadia Lola T94/00-Ford	133.638	1m 47.754s	10	50	1h 43m 09.966s	116.317	8
7	Scott Goodyear (CDN)	40	Budweiser King Racing Lola T94/00-Ford	132.781	1m 48.449s	14	50	1h 43m 11.961s	116.280	6
8	Stefan Johansson (S)	16	Bettenhausen Alumax Aluminum Penske PC22-Ilmor/D	132.031	1m 49.065s	19	50	1h 43m 14.120s	116.239	5
9	Bobby Rahal (USA)	4	Rahal-Hogan Miller Genuine Draft Lola T94/00-Honda	132.538	1m 48.648s	16	50	1h 43m 14.925s	116.224	4
10	*Scott Sharp (USA)	71	PacWest Racing Group Lola T94/00-Ford	132.854	1m 48.390s	13	50	1h 43m 15.349s	116.216	3
11	Dominic Dobson (USA)	17	PacWest Racing Group Lola T94/00-Ford	132.876	1m 48.372s	12	50	1h 43m 30.488s	115.933	2
12	Christian Danner (D)	64	Project Indy No Touch/Van Dyne/Marcelo Lola T93/00-Ford	131.376	1m 49.609s	21	50	1h 43m 41.712s	115.724	1
13	Nigel Mansell (GB)	1	Newman-Haas Kmart/Texaco Havoline Lola T94/00-Ford	135.829	1m 46.016s	3	50	1h 44m 04.143s	115.308	
14	Hiro Matsushita (J)	22	Simon Panasonic/Duskin Lola T94/00-Ford	128.123	1m 52.392s	27	49	Running		
15	*Giovanni Lavaggi (I)	23	Leader Card Financial World Lola T93/00-Ilmor/C	127.695	1m 52.769s	28	49	Running		
16	Mario Andretti (USA)	6	Newman-Haas Kmart/Texaco Havoline Lola T94/00-Ford	133.986	1m 47.474s	7	47	Engine		
17	Michael Andretti (USA)	8	Ganassi Target/Scotch Video Reynard 94I-Ford	132.028	1m 49.068s	20	46	Exhaust		
18	Paul Tracy (CDN)	3	Marlboro Team Penske PC23-Ilmor/D	136.602	1m 45.416s	1	43	Engine		2
19	Mauricio Gugelmin (BR)	88	Ganassi Hollywood Reynard 94I-Ford	130.427	1m 50.407s	25	40	Engine		
20	Mike Groff (USA)	10	Rahal-Hogan Motorola Lola T94/00-Honda	132.148	1m 48.969s	18	38	Engine		
21	Marco Greco (BR)	25	Simon Arciero Project Indy Lola T94/00-Ford	126.813	1m 53.553s	29	38	Running		
22	Arie Luyendyk (NL)	28	Indy Regency Eurosport/Boost Monaco Lola T94/00-Ilmor/D	132.404	1m 48.758s	17	30	Accident		
23	Alessandro Zampedri (I)	19	Coyne The Mi-Jack Car Lola T93/00-Ford	129.385	1m 51.296s	26	24	Transmission		
24	Willy T. Ribbs (USA)	24	Walker Service Merchandise/Bill Cosby Lola T94/00-Ford	130.481	1m 50.361s	24	19	Engine		
25	Robby Gordon (USA)	9	Walker Valvoline/Cummins Special Lola T94/00-Ford	134.685	1m 46.916s	5	16	Transmission		
26	Mark Smith (USA)	15	Walker Craftsman Tools Lola T94/00-Ford	133.982	1m 47.477s	8	12	Engine		
27	Eddie Cheever (USA)	14	A.J. Foyt Copenhagen Racing Lola T94/00-Ford	133.310	1m 48.019s	11	8	Engine		
28	Jimmy Vasser (USA)	18	Hayhoe Conseco/STP Reynard 94I-Ford	130.584	1m 50.274s	22	6	Vibration		
29	*Franck Freon (F)	50	Euromotorsport Agip/Hawaiian Tropic Lola T92/00-Ilmor/A	122.085	1m 57.951s	31	2	Electrical		
30	*Claude Bourbonnais (CDN)	30	McCormack In Deck/Team Losi/Lola T93/00-Ilmor/C+	130.558	1m 50.296s	23	0	Accident		
NS	Ross Bentley (CDN)	39	Coyne Agfa Film Lola T92/00-Ilmor/A	125.783	1m 54.483s	30	–	Did not start/bellhousing		

denotes Rookie driver

Caution flags: Laps 25–27, tow/Zampedri; laps 32–34, accident/Luyendyk. Total: two for 6 laps.

Lap leaders: Paul Tracy, 1–35 (35 laps); Jacques Villeneuve, 36–50 (15 laps). **Totals:** Tracy, 35 laps; Villeneuve, 15 laps.

Fastest race lap: Nigel Mansell, 1m 48.004s, 133.328 mph, on lap 44.

Championship positions: 1 Unser Jr., 209 pts; **2** Fittipaldi, 151; **3** Michael Andretti, 114; **4** Tracy, 109; **5** Gordon, 104; **6** Mansell, 83; **7** Villeneuve, 74; **8** Boesel, 62; **9** Fabi, 61; **10** Rahal, 59; **11** Goodyear, 50; **12** Johansson, 46; **13** Mario Andretti, 45; **14** Vasser, 42; **15** Fernandez, 40; **16** Gugelmin, 36; **17** Dobson, 27; **18** Luyendyk, 26; **19** Smith, 16; **20** M. Groff, 15; **21** Sharp, 14; **22** Herta, 11; **23** Ribbs, 10; **24** Zampedri, 9; **25** Matsushita, 8; **26** Montermini, 6; **27** Cheever, 5; **28** John Andretti, 3; **29** Greco and Danner, 2; **31** Jones, Freon and Till, 1.

NAZARETH

1st – TRACY

2nd – AL UNSER JR.

3rd – FITTIPALDI

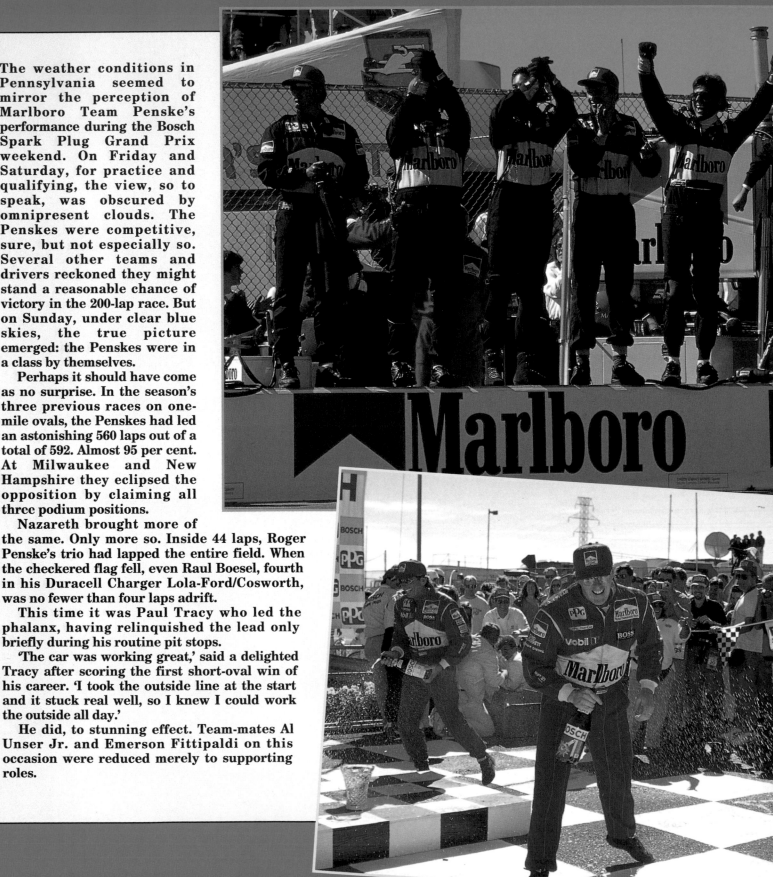

The weather conditions in Pennsylvania seemed to mirror the perception of Marlboro Team Penske's performance during the Bosch Spark Plug Grand Prix weekend. On Friday and Saturday, for practice and qualifying, the view, so to speak, was obscured by omnipresent clouds. The Penskes were competitive, sure, but not especially so. Several other teams and drivers reckoned they might stand a reasonable chance of victory in the 200-lap race. But on Sunday, under clear blue skies, the true picture emerged: the Penskes were in a class by themselves.

Perhaps it should have come as no surprise. In the season's three previous races on one-mile ovals, the Penskes had led an astonishing 560 laps out of a total of 592. Almost 95 per cent. At Milwaukee and New Hampshire they eclipsed the opposition by claiming all three podium positions.

Nazareth brought more of the same. Only more so. Inside 44 laps, Roger Penske's trio had lapped the entire field. When the checkered flag fell, even Raul Boesel, fourth in his Duracell Charger Lola-Ford/Cosworth, was no fewer than four laps adrift.

This time it was Paul Tracy who led the phalanx, having relinquished the lead only briefly during his routine pit stops.

'The car was working great,' said a delighted Tracy after scoring the first short-oval win of his career. 'I took the outside line at the start and it stuck real well, so I knew I could work the outside all day.'

He did, to stunning effect. Team-mates Al Unser Jr. and Emerson Fittipaldi on this occasion were reduced merely to supporting roles.

Below: An ecstatic pit crew greet Paul Tracy's first win since Detroit and the first short-oval victory of the Canadian's career. The fifth Penske clean-sweep of the year prompted enthusiastic celebrations on the podium *(bottom).*

Photos: Michael C. Brown

QUALIFYING

The opening practice session was only 12 minutes old when Tracy became the first driver to dip beneath the official track record of 181.435 mph (19.842 seconds), set in 1992 by nearby resident Michael Andretti. (Last year, incidentally, qualifying was rained out.) The speeds continued to increase, with Robby Gordon circulating at 183.939 mph on Saturday morning, despite the fact his regular race engineer, Tim Wardrop, had flown home to England a few days earlier to be with his 4-year-old son, Timmy, who was suffering from viral meningitis.

'Hopefully it says something about the depth of this team,' said Walker Racing's other resident engineer, Rob Edwards, standing in for Wardrop and working in partnership with data acquisition expert Ron Ruzewski. 'I've worked with Robby before, during some tests, so it's not as if we're breaking any new ground. But I will say it's damn good fun!'

Gordon, as usual, exhibited his preference for running a high groove, which resulted in some spectacular viewing on the quirky, three-cornered 'oval.' In Turn Two, especially, Gordon would run as much as a car width or so 'higher' than most other drivers. Periodically, however, Gordon's car would effectively jump the cushion, resulting in a big lift from the throttle and a huge sideways moment for the driver. Later both he and Edwards admitted they needed to work on the car's balance.

'He's fast, but what we're trying to do is make the car more consistent,' said Edwards, 'mainly with a view to the race.'

Gordon, like many other drivers, complained of a tendency toward looseness (oversteer). The phenomenon was attributed primarily to the latest Goodyear tires, which produced a slightly larger stagger (the difference in circumference between the left- and right-side rear tires, used as an aid to cornering on the left-turn-only ovals) than had been run during recent testing.

Some drivers were rather more vocal than others on the matter, although Stefan Johansson spoke for most when he admitted: 'We didn't come here testing but if we had done I'd be really mad, because you spend all that time and money and then come here with totally different tires. It's ridiculous. Everything you'd learned in testing you'd have to throw completely out of the window.'

In hazy, warmer conditions for qualifying, the first few drivers failed to improve upon their morning speeds. Among them was Unser, who set a conservative 175.220 mph, more than 4 mph shy of his previous best. With the benefit of hindsight, much of the deficit was put down to his decision to run brand-new tires. Those on scrubbed rubber appeared to fare better.

Local hero Mario Andretti, in his penultimate Indy Car start and appearing before his hometown crowd for the last time, elicited a huge cheer when he became the first to officially break son Michael's record. Ultimately, though, and surprisingly, Mario was relegated to fifth on the starting grid.

Newman-Haas team-mate Nigel Mansell was the first to eclipse Mario's speed, whereupon Tracy turned an impressive 184.818 mph, faster by more than 1.2 mph (or 0.2 seconds) than his previous best. Tracy seemed to have a lock on the pole. But he had reckoned without the third Penske driver, Fittipaldi, who proceeded to knock almost 0.4 seconds from his personal best and claim the pole with a sensational 185.600 mph (19.397s).

'I went much faster in Turn Two [than before] and the car accept,' said Fittipaldi in his familiar accented voice. 'That's where I gained a lot of speed. The track was cool. I think there was more rubber down. Conditions were very good when I went out.'

RACE

Tracy regained the upper hand by setting easily the fastest time in the race morning warm-up, while Fittipaldi was content to take just a few laps. The Penske team was entirely confident.

Eddie Cheever, meanwhile, made his presence felt for the first time by posting a lap at 176.516 mph – considerably faster than his qualifying time and, indeed, better than he had managed throughout the previous two days of practice.

'We made a mistake in qualifying,' explained Cheever. 'We went the wrong way and it was a little loose. We went back to where we started and we're just working with that a little bit.'

Nevertheless, the omens looked good for Cheever. The same could not be said for Dominic Dobson, who crashed his Bank of America/PacWest Lola-Ford heavily on the exit of Turn Two. Dobson, who had lapped comfortably inside the top ten early in the session, had been caught out on a fresh set of tires which possessed significantly more stagger than the first.

'I was virtually on the straightaway and it just swapped ends,' lamented Dobson. 'I'm just really unhappy with the tire situation.'

Damage to the car was extensive. Nevertheless, with his spare chassis set up entirely differently, the decision was taken to cannibalize the engine and rear end of the secondary car and transplant it onto his primary machine. Impressively, Russell Cameron's crew completed the task in time for the #17 car to take up its place on the grid.

Fittipaldi and Tracy paced the field neatly toward the starter's waiting green flag, and according to proper protocol it was Fittipaldi, the pole-sitter, who led the 26 starters into Turn One. A couple of hundred yards later, however, at the crest of the hill in Turn Two, Tracy decided it was time to assert his authority, and calmly drove around the outside to assume the lead. The pass was completed with clinical precision.

'I had already decided to let Emerson go at the first corner, but I took the outside line in Turn Two and it stuck real well,' said Tracy, 'so I knew I could work the outside all day.'

Tracy's maneuver was to set the tone for the remainder of the afternoon.

In Turn Three, Gordon also moved around the outside of Mansell, thereby completing the first lap in third place. Mario Andretti also was snapping at his team-mate's heels. It was the start of a downhill slide for Mansell, whose performance was far removed from his commanding drive at Nazareth one year earlier. By the end of lap four he had slipped from third to eighth.

'The car was fine on the first lap, and then it went into massive oversteer,' he said. 'Every time I went into the corner it wanted to spin.'

Tracy and Fittipaldi remained firmly in the lead. Gordon, who clung on in pursuit of the Penskes during the opening stages, soon fell into the clutches of Jacques Villeneuve and Boesel, who, amid some lapped traffic, had exchanged positions on lap ten, at the same time as finally finding a way past Mario Andretti.

'I was much faster than Mario, but each time I tried to pass, he chopped me off,' said Boesel, who had been pressuring the veteran since the

The face of experience. The penultimate Indy Car race of Mario Andretti's distinguished career was also his last appearance at his hometown track.

Even Al Unser Jr. was forced to play second fiddle to the dominant Tracy. *Below:* The PPG Cup champion is given a reminder to reset his fuel meter during a routine pit stop.

start of the race. To his intense frustration, Boesel found Villeneuve no easier to pass.

Stefan Johansson followed in seventh place at the ten-lap mark. He, too, passed Mario next time around. Then came Mansell and Mark Smith, who for the second straight race was maintaining his qualifying form by running comfortably inside the top ten.

Adrian Fernandez also looked confident, tenth in his Reynard, followed by Jimmy Vasser, Arie Luyendyk and Unser, who was making slow but steady progress from 18th on the grid.

'At the beginning of the race when everybody had fresh tires we were being extremely careful because you don't know what's going to happen when you start that far back,' explained the newly crowned PPG Cup champion. 'I had a push in my car at the very beginning, so they could pull me a little bit because they were better balanced than I was. But when they started to get loose, I began to start passing a lot of people.'

Too true. Unser moved from 13th to eighth between laps 12 and 18, demoting Luyendyk, Vasser, Smith and then the fading Andretti and

Mansell in quick succession. Fernandez, however, proved a slightly tougher nut to crack, having himself passed both Newman-Haas cars.

By lap 25, amazingly, the dicing Fernandez and Unser were firmly in the sights of Tracy, who seemed intent upon lapping the field at a record rate. But that served only to spur on Unser, who had no intention of joining those a lap down.

'I can tell how he feels by the way he answers Roger [Penske] on the radio,' revealed Unser's race engineer, Terry Satchell. 'When Roger told him Paul was only four seconds behind, he just came back on and said, "OK." '

Inside another eight laps, he had made short work not only of Fernandez but also of Gordon, Johansson, Boesel and Villeneuve. Now Unser was in third, with only Tracy and Fittipaldi ahead.

Also on a charge was Cheever, who by lap 19 had moved stealthily from 23rd to ninth. Gordon, who in common with the Newman-Haas duo was slipping inexorably backward, was Cheever's next victim on lap 25. Fernandez capitulated on lap 27. Next time around, all of them had been lapped by the flying Tracy.

The only constant at this stage was the dominance of the Penske team. Virtually everyone else was struggling to maintain a consistent balance on their car. On lap 44, Tracy swept past the fourth-placed Villeneuve. Now only the Penskes remained on the lead lap.

Then came the first of only two full-course cautions. There was a collective groan from the crowd when it became apparent Mario Andretti was the cause of the yellow, having collided with Cheever on the exit of Turn Two. Andretti, having made two pit stops in a vain attempt to cure the oversteer, was already four laps off the pace in 23rd. Cheever, meanwhile, was in seventh, chasing after a dicing Villeneuve, Boesel and Johansson, when he went to make the ill-fated move on the outside line.

'I was passing a group of cars,' related Cheever. 'Mario was being lapped. He just put me in the wall. I'm sure he didn't see me. If he did, he absolutely wouldn't do anything as silly as that.'

Andretti admitted he hadn't seen Cheever as the Copenhagen car moved alongside on the downhill back straightaway.

'I'm sorry,' he said. 'Cheever had a

good race going. I don't really know what happened.'

Andretti's Kmart/Texaco Havoline car was pitched hard into the outside retaining wall. Its occupant was lucky to escape injury. Cheever managed to maintain control and bring his Lola back into the pits, but his race, too, was over.

The caution enabled everyone else to make a pit stop. For some, like the Penskes, it was a chance to take on regular service, fuel and fresh tires. No big deal. For others it was a welcome respite, an opportunity to make an adjustment to their ill-handling cars. For the likes of Gordon and Mansell it was of little consequence, since they were already three laps behind.

'We started pretty strong and were running with the Penskes the first five laps, but right after that the car went loose,' said Gordon. 'We kept trying to make adjustments and hang in there for points.'

But the changes brought no respite, and it wasn't until Gordon stopped again on lap 63 that the real problem was diagnosed: a broken wheel bearing. Mansell didn't make it much farther before also parking his car for good.

'We had taken six turns of [front]

wing out and the car still had massive oversteer,' reported Mansell. 'Something's not right. Mario's car was the same. I had three moments where I almost caught the wall.' Mansell decided to withdraw rather than risk a similar fate.

Unser led for three laps under the yellow before making his own stop, resuming in third place, as before, behind Tracy and Fittipaldi. Boesel was fourth, a lap down, followed by Johansson, Fernandez and Villeneuve. The French-Canadian was on the tail end of the lap, having been trapped behind the pace car after his stop took a little longer than usual due to a change of wicker bill on the rear wing. Teo Fabi (Reynard-Ilmor) and Bobby Rahal (Lola-Honda) led those two laps in arrears, each having gained several positions during the pit stops.

Right away after the restart, on lap 56, Johansson was back in the pits after being assessed a stop-and-go penalty for using the designated warm-up lane in avoidance of some debris from the Andretti/Cheever incident. The Swede was not a happy camper.

'Totally ridiculous' was his description of the ruling. 'I don't know what [the officials] wanted me to do. It was

debris. They told us in the drivers' meeting, they said we could use the warm-up lane if necessary. We didn't gain anything. There was no relevance to the race, safety or anything.'

Johansson's Alumax Penske PC22 lost an extra lap by making the enforced pit stop, falling from fifth to seventh.

The race had by now settled down into a familiar pattern.

The Penskes, of course, were long gone. On lap 98, just before the halfway mark, Tracy lapped Boesel for a second time.

'The car was balanced all day long,' reported the Brazilian.

'The car was pretty neutral. Every set of tires, the same balance.'

The gaps between the three leaders varied according to traffic. By lap 75, Tracy had stretched some six seconds clear of Fittipaldi, who in turn had come under increasing pressure from Unser. Five laps later, while lapping a group of slower traffic, Unser seized his opportunity to take over in second place.

'I had to go on the grass,' said Fittipaldi. 'I was lucky I didn't spin.'

Tracy increased his lead over Unser to as much as 11 seconds on lap 86; then, slowly but surely, the margin began to diminish once again. By lap

100, the two leaders were separated by 4.5 seconds, with Fittipaldi a similar distance back in third.

By lap 104, even Boesel, in fourth, was on a lap by himself. Villeneuve and Fernandez, meanwhile, were enjoying one of the best battles of the race. Villeneuve had made up for his earlier delay by passing Fernandez for fifth place on lap 80, only for the favor to be returned on lap 107. Then Villeneuve's Player's Reynard began to run increasingly loose. He was lapped a fourth time on his 120th circuit, and next time around he lost sixth place to Johansson.

On his 131st lap, Fernandez gave up a hard-earned fifth position by stopping for regular service. Villeneuve, seventh, another lap in arrears, stopped at virtually the same time. Sadly, just a few laps later, the youngsters collided when Fernandez tried to make an outside pass on Villeneuve, ironically not for position, on the exit of Turn Two. The initial impact was remarkably similar to the earlier crash involving Cheever and Andretti. This time, though, the right-front wheel was torn from Fernandez's Tecate/Quaker State Reynard in its first contact with the wall. The Mexican's car skewed wildly across the track,

totally out of control and now, of course, without any brakes, before slamming into the inside guard rail and then continuing its destructive course by bouncing back over into the outside wall.

It was a big accident.

'I'm not sure exactly what happened,' said Fernandez, dazed but thankfully suffering no other injury. 'It seemed like Villeneuve came right into me, but I don't know. That's the hardest I have hit in my career. It's a shame because we were running well and we were headed for another good finish.'

To his credit, Fernandez refused to blame Villeneuve for the incident.

'It was a racing accident for sure,' he said. 'Just one of those things that happens out there.'

Villeneuve, having been hit from behind, was rather more forthright: 'I took my line. He wasn't even next to me. He shouldn't have been on the outside. There's no grip there. He hit my right-rear. I couldn't even see his car next to me,' declared the French-Canadian, who, even more fortunately, was able to continue after a pit stop had revealed no significant damage.

More than 20 laps of yellow-flag running were required to clear away

Boesel 'best of the rest'

Bottom: Jacques Villeneuve speeds past the industrial backdrop of Nazareth, which offers a sharp contrast with the scenic road courses such as Road America and Laguna Seca.

the considerable debris from Fernandez's wrecked car. The restart came on lap 160, with Tracy, Unser and Fittipaldi equally spaced about three seconds apart, albeit with various lapped cars between them. Thankfully, even though the Penskes were a class apart, they were still putting on a show for the fans.

Unser gradually inched closer to Tracy, reducing the margin to 1.84 seconds on lap 168, with Fittipaldi only another one second back in third. This was looking like quite a contest. For the next dozen laps, Unser and Fittipaldi were locked in combat, the Brazilian anxious to redress the situation from earlier in the race. Their dice, however, along with Tracy's uncompromising bravery in heavy traffic, saw the Canadian gradually move away.

Tracy raced as much as 11.58 seconds clear, almost half a lap, on lap 177, and even though that margin had been halved, to 5.54 seconds, just six laps later Tracy maintained his edge and went on to score a thoroughly well-earned victory.

'It's great to get my first oval win,' said Tracy, whose previous six Indy

Car victories all had come on street or road circuits. 'I got a little loose in high traffic but the car was really great. We compensated this morning on the set-up. I didn't want to have the same problem as last year, when the car went loose after a couple of laps, so we set the car up accordingly.

'I was thinking about making a change at the last stop, but I didn't want to dial myself out and risk losing the race on a bad decision.'

Unser, whose car seemed slightly quicker on a clear track, took the flag 8.459 seconds in back of Tracy, having eased off in the final laps. Fittipaldi was a further 5.7 seconds in arrears.

'I was very unlucky in traffic today,' reflected Fittipaldi after earning his tenth podium finish of the season. 'I always hit traffic in the wrong place, but I was running strong all day and I'm very happy.'

Boesel, too, was content with fourth place – apart from the fact he was lapped a fourth time a half-dozen tours short of the flag. Johansson was equally pleased with fifth, one more lap behind and himself a lap clear of Fabi.

'My car was consistent but loose,'

Raul Boesel, working well with team owner Dick Simon and regular race engineer Chuck Matthews, continued his strong form on the ovals by claiming a fourth-place finish. It was the second time this year Boesel had finished 'first in class' behind the dominant Penskes.

'It was a strange race,' said Boesel. 'My car was handling well and some people were so slow I had to look to see if there was a yellow! I had to make sure it was green, because I didn't know why everybody was backing off.'

Unlike most other contenders, Boesel's car maintained its consistency throughout.

'I was just waiting for my car to go loose, for lap after lap, because I could see the other cars going loose. So I was careful to conserve my tires, especially the rears. But it stayed OK. Dick asked me if I wanted to change the car at all during my pit stops, but

I said, "No, no, leave the car as it is. Just make sure you give me identical tires." '

Boesel admitted to being 'discouraged' by the disparity between the Penskes and the rest of the field, although he echoed Al Unser Jr.'s comments by suggesting it was the Penske team's chassis which has proved the deciding factor.

'I don't think it's the engine,' he asserted. 'It's the whole package. They conserve their tires well. I think that was the biggest difference here. Like when you go in Turn Two, for example, if you want to pass on the outside, you go in, your car gets unbalanced a bit in the middle of the corner, and you don't know exactly what the car's going to do. Their car seems to be balanced around the whole corner. They need just a little bit of tarmac; we need the whole track!'

said Fabi. 'We had to look after the rear tires.'

Villeneuve, seven laps off the lead, did well to bring his ill-handling Reynard to the finish, earning valuable short-oval experience, while Scott Goodyear moved up to eighth following an excellent pit stop on lap 134 which moved him ahead of the battling Chip Ganassi team-mates, Michael Andretti and Mauricio Gugelmin, who exchanged places several times. Mike Groff also drove well in his Motorola Lola-Honda,

easily out-pacing team-mate Rahal.

'It was a mess today,' admitted Rahal, who finished 14th. 'The rear end just wouldn't hold throughout the race. I think the other guys had the same problem, but I was close to pulling the car in several times.'

The Penskes, of course, had no such problems. Their cars were perfectly balanced and closely matched. 'The Marlboro car was definitely hands and feet better than any car out there today,' confirmed Unser, a gleam in his eye.

SNIPPETS

• Alessandro Zampedri, injured in a huge practice crash at MIS in late July, finally made his oval track race debut at the wheel of Dale Coyne's year-old Mi-Jack Lola-Ford. The personable Italian *(above)* lost 14 laps due to a broken turbo boost adjuster but was delighted to finish, albeit in 20th place. 'I was really comfortable,' he said. 'I figured out how to pass some drivers. I really enjoyed my first oval.'

• The latest Goodyear tires left several drivers struggling to find a balance on their cars. The most obviously affected was Canadian Jacques Villeneuve, who had everyone covered during a recent test session when he lapped at 19.6 seconds, then struggled to break 20.6s in official practice. 'Terrible,' declared Villeneuve on Friday. 'When we tested it was perfect, but today it was loose from apex to exit, and at the same time we had understeer on the turn-in.' Fortunately, race engineer Tony Cicale was able to translate Villeneuve's information into an effective cure, resulting in an improvement to 19.9s on Saturday morning.

• Paul Tracy had quite a week. In addition to earning his first oval win and receiving a firm offer to test the current Formula 1 World Championship-leading Benetton B194-Ford Zetec-R at Estoril, Portugal, the 25-year-old Canadian and his wife Tara celebrated the birth of their second child, a baby boy, Conrad James Anthony, the previous Tuesday.

• Mauricio Gugelmin *(below)* also was pleased to earn his first points on a short oval. 'I'm starting to learn more about the ovals and what they want in terms of set-up,' said Gugelmin after finishing tenth, close behind teammate Michael Andretti. 'These places are weird. You do things to the car you think are going to work and they just don't. You just need experience basically.'

Photos: Michael C. Brown

BOSCH SPARK PLUG GRAND PRIX

NAZARETH SPEEDWAY, NAZARETH, PENNSYLVANIA

SEPTEMBER 18, 200 LAPS – 200.000 MILES

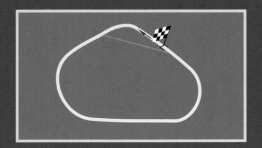

Place	Driver (Nat.)	No.	Team Sponsors Car-Engine	Q Speed (mph)	Q Time	Q Pos.	Laps	Time/Status	Ave. (mph)	Pts.
1	Paul Tracy (CDN)	3	Marlboro Team Penske PC23-Ilmor/D	184.818	19.479s	2	200	1h 31m 30.292s	131.141	21
2	Al Unser Jr. (USA)	31	Marlboro Team Penske PC23-Ilmor/D	175.220	20.546s	18	200	1h 31m 38.751s	130.939	16
3	Emerson Fittipaldi (BR)	2	Marlboro Team Penske PC23-Ilmor/D	185.600	19.397s	1	200	1h 31m 44.451s	130.803	15
4	Raul Boesel (BR)	5	Simon Duracell/Fuji Film/Mobil/Sadia Lola T94/00-Ford	181.919	19.789s	6	196	Running		12
5	Stefan Johansson (S)	16	Bettenhausen Alumax Aluminum Penske PC22-Ilmor/D	178.966	20.116s	10	195	Running		10
6	Teo Fabi (I)	11	Hall Pennzoil Special Reynard 94I-Ilmor/D	179.257	20.083s	9	194	Running		8
7	*Jacques Villeneuve (CDN)	12	Forsythe-Green Player's Ltd. Reynard 94I-Ford	179.758	20.027s	7	193	Running		6
8	Scott Goodyear (CDN)	40	Budweiser King Racing Lola T94/00-Ford	173.614	20.736s	21	191	Running		5
9	Michael Andretti (USA)	8	Ganassi Target/Scotch Video Reynard 94I-Ford	175.090	20.561s	19	191	Running		4
10	Mauricio Gugelmin (BR)	88	Ganassi Hollywood Reynard 94I-Ford	177.780	20.250s	14	190	Running		3
11	Mike Groff (USA)	10	Rahal-Hogan Motorola Lola T94/00-Honda	174.981	20.574s	20	190	Running		2
12	Mark Smith (USA)	15	Walker Craftsman Tools Lola T94/00-Ford	179.568	20.048s	8	189	Running		1
13	Jimmy Vasser (USA)	18	Hayhoe Conseco/STP Reynard 94I-Ford	178.739	20.141s	12	189	Running		
14	Bobby Rahal (USA)	4	Rahal-Hogan Miller Genuine Draft Lola T94/00-Honda	178.737	20.141s	13	188	Running		
15	*Scott Sharp (USA)	71	PacWest Racing Group Lola T94/00-Ford	176.211	20.430s	17	187	Running		
16	Hiro Matsushita (J)	22	Simon Panasonic/Duskin Lola T94/00-Ford	172.585	20.859s	22	186	Running		
17	Marco Greco (BR)	25	Simon Arciero Project Indy Lola T94/00-Ford	171.259	21.021s	24	185	Running		
18	Willy T. Ribbs (USA)	24	Walker Service Merchandise/Bill Cosby Lola T94/00-Ford	170.303	21.139s	25	182	Running		
19	Dominic Dobson (USA)	17	PacWest Racing Group Bank of America Lola T94/00-Ford	176.241	20.427s	16	182	Running		
20	*Alessandro Zampedri (I)	19	Coyne The Mi-Jack Car Lola T93/00-Ford	168.928	21.311s	26	174	Running		
21	Adrian Fernandez (MEX)	7	Galles Tecate/Quaker State Reynard 94I-Ilmor/D	178.826	20.131s	11	134	Accident		
22	Nigel Mansell (GB)	1	Newman-Haas Kmart/Texaco Havoline Lola T94/00-Ford	184.162	19.548s	3	87	Handling		
23	Robby Gordon (USA)	9	Walker Valvoline/Cummins Special Lola T94/00-Ford	182.389	19.738s	4	63	Wheel bearing		
24	Eddie Cheever (USA)	14	A.J. Foyt Copenhagen Racing Lola T94/00-Ford	172.231	20.902s	23	45	Accident		
25	Mario Andretti (USA)	6	Newman-Haas Kmart/Texaco Havoline Lola T94/00-Ford	182.302	19.747s	5	40	Accident		
26	Arie Luyendyk (NL)	28	Indy Regency Eurosport/Boost Monaco Lola T94/00-Ilmor/D	177.686	20.260s	15	23	Transmission		
NQ	Buddy Lazier (USA)	23	Leader Card Financial World Lola T93/00-Ilmor/C	160.352	22.451s	27	–	Did not qualify		
NQ	Ross Bentley (CDN)	39	Coyne Agfa Film Lola T92/00-Ilmor/A	157.790	22.815s	28	–	Did not qualify		
NQ	Jeff Wood (USA)	50	Euromotorsport Agip/Hawaiian Tropic Lola T93/00-Ilmor/C	no speed	no time	29	–	Did not qualify		

* denotes Rookie driver

Caution flags: Laps 45–55, accident/Mario Andretti; laps 138–159, accident/Fernandez. Total: two for 33 laps.

Lap leaders: Paul Tracy, 1–47 (47 laps); Al Unser Jr., 48–50 (3 laps); Tracy, 51–124 (74 laps); Unser Jr., 125–126 (2 laps); Emerson Fittipaldi, 127–129 (3 laps); Tracy, 130–200 (71 laps). **Totals:** Tracy, 192 laps; Unser Jr., 5 laps; Fittipaldi, 3 laps.

Fastest race lap: Emerson Fittipaldi, 20.578s, 174.941 mph, on lap 121.

Championship positions: 1 Unser Jr., 225 pts; **2** Fittipaldi, 166; **3** Tracy, 130; **4** Michael Andretti, 118; **5** Gordon, 104; **6** Mansell, 83; **7** Villeneuve, 80; **8** Boesel, 74; **9** Fabi, 69; **10** Rahal, 59; **11** Johansson, 56; **12** Goodyear, 55; **13** Mario Andretti, 45; **14** Vasser, 42; **15** Fernandez, 40; **16** Gugelmin, 39; **17** Dobson, 27; **18** Luyendyk, 26; **19** Smith and M. Groff, 17; **21** Sharp, 14; **22** Herta, 11; **23** Ribbs, 10; **24** Zampedri, 9; **25** Matsushita, 8; **26** Montermini, 6; **27** Cheever, 5; **28** John Andretti, 3; **29** Greco and Danner, 2; **31** Jones, Freon and Till, 1.

LAGUNA SECA

Michael C. Brown

Mario Andretti held the spotlight throughout the pre-race festivities at Laguna Seca Raceway. Perfect California weather ensured an entirely appropriate send-off for one of auto racing's most beloved, successful and enduring characters, who was finally hanging up his helmet after a record 407 Indy Car starts spanning 31 seasons.

During the race itself, however, Paul Tracy laid claim to the headlines by scoring his second clear victory in succession. The Canadian was never headed as he ran away from the field to win by more than 21 seconds.

'The car was excellent all day,' reported Tracy. 'I never had any problems in traffic or anything. The car was just magic.'

Several drivers took turns at leading the fruitless chase of Tracy, including his own team-mate, Al Unser Jr., who charged through the field superbly following a first-lap incident. But even Unser was unable to mount a serious challenge, and ultimately his hopes of beating Michael Andretti's single-season records for PPG Cup race wins (eight) and total points (234) were thwarted by a broken transmission.

Raul Boesel posted another fine drive, finishing a strong second in his last appearance for Dick Simon Racing, while Jacques Villeneuve rounded out his impressive rookie season by securing the final podium position.

The Indy Car family honors its favorite son

Left: Signing off in style. Paul Tracy's splendid end-of-season form continued, the Canadian scoring a runaway win on what was to be his final appearance for Marlboro Team Penske.

QUALIFYING

Laguna Seca Raceway has become the traditional venue for the PPG Cup season finale. As one of the world's most scenic and challenging race tracks, set high among the coastal hills that also offer a sensational view over nearby Monterey Bay, it fits the bill perfectly. This year, of course, the premier championship positions had already been settled, so there was a palpable end-of-term party atmosphere for the Toyota Grand Prix of Monterey, featuring the Bank of America 300. The feeling was heightened as cloudless blue skies prevailed throughout the race weekend.

Nevertheless, several drivers traveled to California intent on making their presence felt. Nigel Mansell, for example, was looking to end what had been a thoroughly disappointing, winless season on a positive note. Mario Andretti, his Newman-Haas team-mate, also held high hopes of concluding his stellar career with a strong performance. Others such as Paul Tracy, Michael Andretti, Teo Fabi and Raul Boesel were intent upon one more solid result as they prepared to switch teams over the winter.

Mansell and Tracy duly headed the times after the opening 90-minute practice session on Friday, although in the afternoon Tracy turned up the wick as he posted a lap in 1m 10.058s, well inside Emerson Fittipaldi's existing track record and almost exactly a full second faster than anyone else.

'The car is quite well balanced,' said Tracy, who since his victory at Nazareth had enjoyed a thoroughly impressive test in Portugal with the Benetton Formula 1 team. 'I'm trying to finish off the season with a good result to finish third in the championship. It was a good lap. It seems the last few races the first day has been quicker, so I really wanted to have a go.'

Sure enough, when the ambient temperature proved appreciably higher on Saturday, very few drivers were able to match their times from the first qualifying session.

'That lap Paul did was pretty amazing,' commented Jacques Villeneuve, who started alongside on the front row in his Player's Ltd. Reynard-Ford. Villeneuve, though, like everyone else in the field, was struggling to gain any consistency from his Goodyear tires.

'The car's great on new tires,' he

confided, 'and terrible once they get worn – which is quickly.'

Tracy's margin of superiority was all the more remarkable for the fact the next four drivers on the grid – Villeneuve, Mansell, Unser and Robby Gordon – were separated by little more than one-tenth of a second. Then, following a gap of 0.4s back to Stefan Johansson's year-old Alumax Penske-Ilmor, a large group comprising 16 cars was blanketed by a fraction over 0.8s.

Johansson, like several others, felt he had lost the opportunity to improve his time due to a couple of red-flag incidents during the faster period of qualifying. First of all, Mauricio Gugelmin made a rare mistake by spinning his Hollywood Reynard-Ford backward into the barriers at Turn Nine. A few minutes later Dominic Dobson lost control of his Bank of America/PacWest Lola-Ford after straying two wheels onto the dirt on the exit of Turn Four. On each occasion, Johansson had just embarked upon a fast lap. Thus, when he finally had the opportunity to get up to speed, his tires were past their best.

'The car feels good when you've got new tires on,' said Johansson, 'but like everyone else, once the tires wear, you're sliding all over the place.'

RACE

Johansson's bad luck continued into Sunday morning, when his warm-up session ended amid a cloud of smoke. A broken oil line resulted in a brief fire and a lengthy clean-up operation by Steve Ritenour and the rest of Tony Bettenhausen's team.

'It always looks more dramatic than it really is,' reported race engineer Ken Anderson, 'but the biggest problem is that you've got to clean off all the oil, because if the car's smoking on the first lap [of the race], the officials will black-flag you.'

Happily, the car was back in (almost) pristine condition in time to join the other 28 qualifiers on the starting grid.

The tributes to Mario Andretti continued as his #6 Kmart/Texaco Havoline Lola-Ford/Cosworth was parked proudly at the front of the field. Andretti's daughter, Barbie, a professional singer, then gave a splendidly robust rendition of the National Anthem. A few minutes later, wife Dee Ann and twin brother Aldo issued the time-honored command for Mario to fire up his engine

Despite Paul Tracy's masterful performance, Mario Andretti still garnered most of the attention during the final Indy Car race of his remarkable career. And justifiably so. Andretti was feted at all manner of events during the days preceding the race and gladly answered myriad questions during a rigorous series of appearances, interviews and press conferences.

On race morning, after the final warm-up, he was greeted by mechanics from every team on pit road, all of them wearing '*Arrivederci, Mario*' tee-shirts. Shortly afterward he received a standing ovation during the regular drivers' briefing. At the end of the race, accompanied by his family, the greatly respected veteran took one final ceremonial lap of honor aboard a special-edition Oldsmobile painted in 'Andretti Red,' a color developed in appreciation of his career by PPG Automotive Refinishes. Andretti

was also delighted that Nick Fornoro, former Chief Starter for IndyCar, agreed to come out of retirement and fly the breadth of the country to flag one final race.

'Nicky's probably started three or four hundred races that I've run in,' said Andretti. 'When CART brought him out here, that was extra-special.

'I feel like today is the most important day of my career, just because of everything that's happened. The tributes in the drivers' meeting and so on and so forth, it's a great feeling. I truly am very happy and satisfied, and I will always feel I owe everybody. It will take a long time to thank everybody.

'That display of affection, it tops everything. There's so much competition among the teams – there's a war going on out there – but there are times when we come together like a big family. It's been a great day.'

And a great career.

for the very last time. Respectfully, the remainder of the field followed suit a few seconds later.

Andretti's emotional roller-coaster persisted as he led the field around the first parade lap, waving to the huge crowd throughout, before taking up his correct position of 12th in the starting line-up. Appropriately, right alongside was his eldest son, Michael, making his final start for Chip Ganassi before taking over his father's position at Newman-Haas Racing, the team with which Michael won the 1991 PPG Cup championship.

The start itself was clean, with Tracy taking charge of the uphill drag race past the start/finish line. The Canadian's Marlboro Penske maintained its advantage over the crest of the hill in Turn One and then down again into the braking area for the left-handed Turn Two hairpin. Villeneuve tucked in close behind his countryman, while Gordon displayed his customary aggression by taking to the outside of Unser. Unfortunately, the pair made heavy contact on the exit of the corner, resulting in front suspension damage on both cars.

'Junior didn't want to give me any room,' said Gordon. 'I was on the outside with my tires against the dirt. I think he just got a little loose and we hit.'

Gordon moved through into third place, while Unser lost momentum

on the outside line, then found his car unwilling to turn right at the next corner. As Unser slid off into the dirt, Michael Andretti tried to take advantage of the melee in his Target/Scotch Video Reynard-Ford. But having passed Fittipaldi's Penske and then slipped beneath Arie Luyendyk's Eurosport/Boost Monaco Lola-Ilmor, Andretti locked up his rear brakes and spun.

He quickly realized that facing the wrong way did not offer a good perspective. Andretti winced as several cars took to the dirt in avoidance, then shut his eyes when he saw Bobby Rahal, who was in the midst of attempting to pass Gugelmin on the outside, was about to collide with his stationary car. Pow! Their left-front wheels came into heavy contact, causing extensive damage to the suspension. Both were out.

'Well, that's kind of the way our season went,' summarized Rahal. 'I was on the outside of the turn and I couldn't move down to avoid Michael. There wasn't anywhere to go.'

The running order changed dramatically during several laps behind the pace car. Tracy and Villeneuve remained out front, followed by Mansell, Johansson, Fabi, Boesel and Eddie Cheever, who had moved up from 17th to seventh in A.J. Foyt's Copenhagen Lola-Ford. Mario Andretti, Fittipaldi and Luyendyk all fell to the back of the pack after pitting to replace punctured tires as

Michael C. Brown

Young lions Adrian Fernandez and Andrea Montermini battle in midfield. The Mexican took seventh place in the Tecate/Quaker State Reynard, while the Italian, this time racing the Project Indy Lola, claimed ninth spot.

Inset right: Raul Boesel, who was leaving Dick Simon Racing to join Rahal/Hogan in 1995, gave the team a great farewell with a strong drive into second place.

Undoubtedly the new star of Indy Car racing, rookie Jacques Villeneuve rounded off a brilliant debut season with another mature performance to finish in third place at Laguna Seca.

a result of the opening-lap fracas, there to be joined by Unser, who needed attention to a broken nose cone and right-front steering arm. Richard Buck and the crew set into the repair with remarkable rapidity and precision, allowing Unser not only to remain on the lead lap but to do so with a car that displayed no appreciable after-effects. Unser was impressed.

'Richard and the crew have been just unbelievable all year,' praised the new PPG Cup champion. 'I could never have asked for anything more.'

Gordon also made for the pits, although, unfortunately, he lost a lap while the left-front top wishbone was replaced. He was never able to overcome that handicap, although he drove with his customary verve to finish a disappointed 13th, delayed still further by a pair of tire-consuming spins and another off-course excursion in Turn Six.

Once the race finally had gotten under way, Tracy lost no time in underscoring his dominance. Inside three laps he had pulled an astonishing 5.95 seconds clear of Villeneuve, who was under attack from Mansell.

'The key thing for me was that I knew Michael [Andretti] was involved in the first-lap incident and so that assured me of third place in the championship,' noted Tracy. 'That meant I was able to concentrate on winning the race instead of trying to finish the race.'

Tracy's margin was erased by a second full-course caution on lap 17, after Scott Goodyear found himself edged off-line by Dobson under braking for Turn Six and promptly slid off into the tire barrier. Mansell took the opportunity to make a pit stop, as did Unser, who slipped briefly to 22nd after having worked his way impressively through to 13th before the interruption.

Johansson also stopped. But the Swede's exit from his pit was hindered by Fernandez's Tecate/Quaker State Reynard-Ilmor, which was being serviced in the adjoining stall. Johansson inadvertently nudged into Mitch Davis, who was on his knees, changing the right-rear wheel

on the Mexican's car, whereupon a justifiably irate Davis promptly attempted to block Johansson's path still further by placing the discarded wheel in front of the Alumax Penske.

The two wrongs, predictably, did not make a right. Both drivers lost time during their stops, and both were assessed stop-and-go penalties for what were euphemistically described as 'pit lane safety violations.' Their respective crews, too, were reprimanded, although in truth the whole incident was effectively caused by the track's notoriously small pit working areas. Incidentally, an angry Johansson then received a second penalty after exceeding the pit lane speed limit. He rejoined in a distant 22nd, last of those on the lead lap.

The restart, at the end of lap 22, saw Tracy again run away into the distance. Inside five laps, his margin over Villeneuve had risen to nine seconds. Five laps more and his lead was up to 17.4 seconds, albeit now over Fabi, who slipped ahead on lap 28 when Villeneuve succumbed to intense pressure from the Italian and slid sideways under braking for Turn Four.

Tracy made his first routine pit stop after 34 laps. He rejoined behind Villeneuve, who promptly handed the lead back to Tracy by stopping next time around. Mansell now ran in second, under siege from the charging Unser, although moments later the double yellow flags were displayed again when Franck Freon punctuated his strong run in a second Indy Regency Lola-Ilmor (run by Steve Erickson's Autosport Specialists team) by making contact with the rear of Jimmy Vasser's Reynard in Turn Two. The Frenchman spun and stalled. Vasser went off later on the same lap due to a deranged suspension.

The line-up for the restart saw a familiar sight with two Marlboro Penskes at the front of the field. Villeneuve and Fabi were next, the Canadian having regained the advantage when Fabi lost a few extra moments in the pits while his crew effected a wing change. They

were followed by Fittipaldi, who had moved up steadily, then Boesel, Mansell (after a slow stop caused by a recalcitrant wheel nut on the right-rear corner) and Gugelmin. Fernandez and Luyendyk had battled back inside the top ten following their early delays, to be pursued by Mario Andretti.

Intriguingly, having just taken on a full load of fuel and fresh tires, Tracy was in the lead, while Unser, who had not stopped, had the advantage of a lighter fuel load. It proved to be no big deal. Tracy pulled away by a half-second or so for each of the next few laps, then more rapidly as Unser's tires deteriorated.

'I knew he was out of sequence on his pit stops,' said Tracy. 'He stayed close when he was on a light fuel load, but after a few laps I was able to pull away. Once I knew we could do that, I knew we pretty much had everyone covered.'

Even on full tanks, Tracy was able to circulate in the 1m 13s range, significantly faster than any of his rivals. By lap 52, when Unser pitted again for fuel and tires, Tracy was lapping comfortably at around 1m 14s or 1m 15s. Villeneuve and Fabi, still running in close company, could keep pace with that, but they were already more than 15 seconds in back of the race leader. Tracy was under no threat whatsoever.

On lap 64, right on cue for Tracy, who was due to make his second scheduled pit stop, the pace car was pressed back into action when Scott Sharp's PacWest Lola-Ford was stranded by a broken engine at the top of the hill. Tracy never even lost the lead. Barring any disasters, this race was in the bag.

Unser, having stopped only a dozen laps earlier, regained second place when the other cars in front of him pitted. Fittipaldi, also out of sequence, took over in third ahead of Villeneuve, Boesel and Fabi, who had lost more time when he was forced to enter his pit at an oblique angle (again due to the cramped space) and the fuel hose wouldn't quite reach the car. Luyendyk, Fernandez and Mario Andretti resumed

next ahead of Mansell, who had fallen several more positions in the pits due to a balky wheel nut. Andrea Montermini (No Touch/Van Dyne Lola T93/00-Ford) and Willy T. Ribbs (Service Merchandise Lola-Ford) had run strongly in eighth and ninth prior to the caution, but were unfortunate to lose a lap while making their pit stops.

Right away after the restart, Mario Andretti showed there was still plenty of life in the old dog as he relieved Fernandez of eighth place with a daring maneuver around the outside at the final hairpin, Turn 11.

'It was an opportunity,' reasoned Andretti, who inwardly derived a great deal of pleasure from what was to prove his final pass for position in Indy Car racing. 'He's a clean little driver. I knew I could trust him so I just did it. I thought it was a good pass.'

Fernandez thought so, too.

'We were passing a back-marker – I don't remember who it was – as we came into Turn 11,' he related. 'I chose the inside to pass him and the guy pulled down to the inside, so I had nowhere to go. I was a little bit blocked and Mario took advantage. We were really close and I thought, whatever you do, don't hit Mario! This was his show. After that I pushed him hard and he was driving very well. It was a great feeling to race with him.'

Unfortunately, the pass brought no reward. Ten laps later, Andretti's engine expired in a cloud of smoke.

'It was coming down to a decent finish but it wasn't to be,' said Andretti philosophically. 'The timing chain on the engine let go – for the umpteenth time on those things. I couldn't believe it.'

A handful of laps earlier, Unser's hopes of a second-place finish also crumbled due to a ring-and-pinion failure. Unser never came close to challenging Tracy, having slipped more than 18 seconds in arrears during the seven laps immediately following the final restart, but he surely had the legs on anyone else.

On lap 72, Fittipaldi had been thrown out of his stride when Villeneuve executed a brave pass, with two wheels on the dirt, under heavy braking for Turn Three. Fittipaldi had no recourse. Two corners later, Fittipaldi lost another place to Boesel, who dived incisively for the inside, totally undeterred by his countryman's attempt to defend the line.

'It was quite exciting. We will probably exchange a few Brazilian

Photos: Michael C. Brown

The tortuous curves of the Laguna Seca road course are further contorted in photographer Michael C. Brown's fish-eye shot of Eddie Cheever, Scott Goodyear and Alessandro Zampedri battling for position early in the race.

words,' admitted Boesel, grinning broadly. 'I think I caught him a little bit by surprise.'

Truth be told, Fittipaldi wasn't too amused.

Two laps after disposing of Fittipaldi, Boesel grasped an opportunity to slip past Villeneuve when the French-Canadian made a mistake under braking for Turn Five while trying to put a lap on Dobson.

'He was slowing everybody down,' explained Villeneuve, 'and, trying to get by him, I braked too late and locked up the brakes and ran off the corner; and Raul got by me.'

Boesel capitalized on his unaccustomed mix of aggression and good fortune to pull out a slight breathing space. He then maintained a cushion of one second or so until the checkered flag. At the same time he had managed to keep pace with Tracy.

Notwithstanding the fact Tracy was some 20 seconds or so farther up the road, this was a good performance by Boesel, who claimed his best result of the year and the fifth second-place finish in his Indy Car career.

'It was a great way to finish the season,' said Boesel, who confirmed the previous week he would join Rahal/Hogan Racing in 1995. 'The first set of tires I pushed too hard at the beginning, and the next two sets I tried to conserve the rears more; and I think it paid off. At the end my car was very good. I'm very pleased. The team has worked very hard. This is a good result for myself and for Dick Simon Racing.'

Villeneuve, battling some understeer in the final segment, was content to claim his third podium finish of the year. It was enough to elevate him to sixth in the seasonal point standings. Behind, a disgruntled Fittipaldi narrowly held off a charging Fabi for fourth.

'Without Tracy today, I think my car was as good as any other car in the race,' said Fabi of his Pennzoil Reynard. 'The pit stops were just poor racing luck. I'm sorry I couldn't finish better but we had a good race.'

Luyendyk also was content with sixth following a consistent drive. Fernandez was the final unlapped runner. Among the other contenders, Cheever's fine early charge was negated by persistent electrical gremlins and Gugelmin succumbed to a broken exhaust header after running as high as sixth. Mansell's pit stop woes restricted him to eighth, one lap off the pace, while Montermini delighted Andreas Leberle's Project Indy crew with a solid ninth-place finish, narrowly ahead of a dicing Dobson and Ribbs, who also finished his season on a strong note. A frustrated Johansson claimed the final point.

All eyes, though, were on Tracy, who ended his tenure with Penske Racing in the best possible style, and Mario Andretti, who had displayed great tenacity in fighting his way from 24th to as high as sixth. He deserved better than to be watching from the pits as the final laps unfolded.

'It's been really a special day,' concluded Andretti. 'It's disappointing not to finish but I feel very satisfied with myself. I tried hard. I think I drove decent, so I have to be satisfied with that.' And so he should be. *Arrivederci*, Mario!

Michael C. Brown

SNIPPETS

• Paul Tracy's dominating success ensured quite a windfall. In addition to securing third place in the PPG Cup standings, worth $300,000, Tracy claimed the $25,000 Marlboro Pole Award for most poles in the season, plus a $75,000 accumulated bonus for winning from the pole. Tracy *(center)* also scooped $9000 from race sponsors Bank of America, which he duly presented to the charity run by Father Phil De Rea. At a Marlboro party (much) later in the evening, Eric Silverman, President of Boss USA, sportingly agreed to match that donation.

• Chip Ganassi confirmed at a press conference that Bryan Herta will drive his Target/Scotch Video Reynard-Ford/Cosworth in 1995, replacing Michael Andretti.

• A variety of honorable guests graced the garage area, including Dan Gurney, whose All American Racers team is deep into a test and development program on behalf of Toyota, in anticipation of entering the Indy Car fray some time in 1995. Ferrari's Formula 1 technical chief, John Barnard, whose glorious Chaparral 2K design dominated both the Indianapolis 500 and the PPG Cup title-chase in 1980 with Johnny Rutherford at the helm, also was paying close attention to proceedings on behalf of the legendary Italian company.

• Mauricio Gugelmin's Hollywood Reynard sported several developmental components due to be run on the 1995 chassis, including the so-called 'shortitudinal' gearbox, which is 30 lbs lighter than the existing transmission, revised brake ducts and new WP shock absorbers produced in Holland. Incidentally, Gugelmin's crew chief, Grant Weaver, was a surprised (and popular) recipient of the Championship Association of Mechanics' top award as Chief Mechanic of the Year.

Michael C. Brown

TOYOTA MONTEREY GRAND PRIX/ BANK OF AMERICA 300

LAGUNA SECA RACEWAY, MONTEREY, CALIFORNIA

OCTOBER 9, 84 LAPS – 185.976 MILES

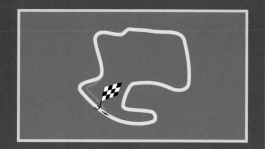

Place	Driver (Nat.)	No.	Team Sponsors Car-Engine	Q Speed (mph)	Q Time	Q Pos.	Laps	Time/Status	Ave. (mph)	Pts.
1	Paul Tracy (CDN)	3	Marlboro Team Penske PC23-Ilmor/D	113.768	1m 10.058s	1	84	2h 00m 00.763s	92.978	22
2	Raul Boesel (BR)	5	Simon Duracell/Fuji Film/Mobil/Sadia Lola T94/00-Ford	111.350	1m 11.579s	8	84	2h 00m 22.179s	92.702	16
3	*Jacques Villeneuve (CDN)	12	Forsythe-Green Player's Ltd. Reynard 94I-Ford	112.244	1m 11.010s	2	84	2h 00m 23.248s	92.689	14
4	Emerson Fittipaldi (BR)	2	Marlboro Team Penske PC23-Ilmor/D	110.942	1m 11.843s	9	84	2h 00m 26.353s	92.649	12
5	Teo Fabi (I)	11	Hall Pennzoil Special Reynard 94I-Ilmor/D	111.357	1m 11.576s	7	84	2h 00m 27.040s	92.640	10
6	Arie Luyendyk (NL)	28	Indy Regency Eurosport/Boost Monaco Lola T94/00-Ilmor/D	110.764	1m 11.959s	10	84	2h 00m 35.851s	92.527	8
7	Adrian Fernandez (MEX)	7	Galles Tecate/Quaker State Reynard 94I-Ilmor/D	110.416	1m 12.185s	16	84	2h 00m 45.741s	92.401	6
8	Nigel Mansell (GB)	1	Newman-Haas Kmart/Texaco Havoline Lola T94/00-Ford	112.146	1m 11.072s	3	83	Running		5
9	Andrea Montermini (I)	64	Project Indy No Touch/Van Dyne/Marcelo Lola T93/00-Ford	108.966	1m 13.146s	25	83	Running		4
10	Dominic Dobson (USA)	17	PacWest Racing Group Lola T94/00-Ford	110.516	1m 12.120s	14	83	Running		3
11	Willy T. Ribbs (USA)	24	Walker Service Merchandise/Bill Cosby Lola T94/00-Ford	109.189	1m 12.996s	23	83	Running		2
12	Stefan Johansson (S)	16	Bettenhausen Alumax Aluminum Penske PC22-Ilmor/D	111.454	1m 11.513s	6	83	Running		1
13	Robby Gordon (USA)	9	Walker Valvoline/Cummins Special Lola T94/00-Ford	112.030	1m 11.146s	5	82	Running		
14	Mark Smith (USA)	15	Walker Craftsman Tools Lola T94/00-Ford	110.543	1m 12.102s	13	82	Running		
15	Mike Groff (USA)	10	Rahal-Hogan Motorola Lola T94/00-Honda	109.175	1m 13.006s	24	82	Running		
16	*Alessandro Zampedri (I)	19	Coyne The Mi-Jack Car Lola T93/00-Ford	108.300	1m 13.595s	29	82	Running		
17	*Parker Johnstone (USA)	49	Comptech Racing Acura Lola T93/00-Honda	108.942	1m 13.162s	26	81	Running		
18	*Franck Freon (F)	29	Indy Regency/Autosports Specialists Lola T94/00-Ilmor/D	108.828	1m 13.239s	27	81	Running		
19	Mario Andretti (USA)	6	Newman-Haas Kmart/Texaco Havoline Lola T94/00-Ford	110.619	1m 12.053s	12	80	Engine		
20	Al Unser Jr. (USA)	31	Marlboro Team Penske PC23-Ilmor/D	112.056	1m 11.129s	4	74	Transmission		
21	*Scott Sharp (USA)	71	PacWest Racing Group Lola T94/00-Ford	110.269	1m 12.281s	20	59	Engine		
22	Mauricio Gugelmin (BR)	88	Ganassi Hollywood Reynard 94I-Ford	110.339	1m 12.236s	19	51	Exhaust header		
23	Hiro Matsushita (J)	22	Simon Panasonic/Duskin Lola T94/00-Ford	109.296	1m 12.925s	22	48	Electrical		
24	Marco Greco (BR)	25	Simon Arciero Project Indy Lola T94/00-Ford	108.593	1m 13.397s	28	44	Transmission		
25	Eddie Cheever (USA)	14	A.J. Foyt Copenhagen Racing Lola T94/00-Ford	110.386	1m 12.205s	17	36	Electrical		
26	Jimmy Vasser (USA)	18	Hayhoe Conseco/STP Reynard 94I-Ford	110.436	1m 12.172s	15	35	Accident		
27	Scott Goodyear (CDN)	40	Budweiser King Racing Lola T94/00-Ford	110.191	1m 12.332s	21	16	Accident		
28	Michael Andretti (USA)	8	Ganassi Target/Scotch Video Reynard 94I-Ford	110.687	1m 12.008s	11	0	Accident		
29	Bobby Rahal (USA)	4	Rahal-Hogan Miller Genuine Draft Lola T94/00-Honda	110.353	1m 12.227s	18	0	Accident		
NQ	*Giovanni Lavaggi (I)	23	Leader Card Financial World Lola T93/00-Ilmor/C	107.175	1m 14.368s	30	–	Did not qualify		
NQ	Ross Bentley (CDN)	39	Coyne Agfa Film Lola T92/00-Ilmor/A	105.295	1m 15.696s	31	–	Did not qualify		
NQ	Jeff Wood (USA)	50	Euromotorsport Agip/Hawaiian Tropic Lola T93/00-Ilmor/C	103.523	1m 16.992s	32	–	Did not qualify		

* denotes Rookie driver

Caution flags: Laps 1–5, accident, Michael Andretti/Rahal; laps 17–21, accident, Goodyear; laps 35–39, tow, Gordon; laps 53–66, tow, Sharp. Total: four for 19 laps.

Lap leaders: Paul Tracy, 1–84 (84 laps). *Total:* Tracy, 84 laps.

Fastest race lap: Paul Tracy, 1m 12.959s, 109.244 mph, on lap 9.

Championship positions: 1 Unser Jr., 225 pts; **2** Fittipaldi, 178; **3** Tracy, 152; **4** Michael Andretti, 118; **5** Gordon, 104; **6** Villeneuve, 94; **7** Boesel, 90; **8** Mansell, 88; **9** Fabi, 79; **10** Rahal, 59; **11** Johansson, 57; **12** Goodyear, 55; **13** Fernandez, 46; **14** Mario Andretti, 45; **15** Vasser, 42; **16** Gugelmin, 39; **17** Luyendyk, 34; **18** Dobson, 30; **19** Smith and M. Groff, 17; **21** Sharp, 14; **22** Ribbs, 12; **23** Herta, 11; **24** Montermini, 10; **25** Zampedri, 9; **26** Matsushita, 8; **27** Cheever, 5; **28** John Andretti, 3; **29** Greco and Danner, 2; **31** Jones, Freon and Till, 1.

by Jeremy Shaw

TASMAN TAKEOVER

The Tasman trio who all tasted victory in 1994 *(left to right)*: Steve Robertson, Andre Ribeiro and Eddie Lawson. The talented Ribeiro *(below)* is stepping up to the PPG Cup with the Tasman team in 1995.

Steve Horne's Tasman Motorsports Group maintained its stranglehold on the PPG-Firestone Indy Lights Championship in 1994. The team has only been in existence for two seasons, yet from a total of 24 races, Tasman drivers have won no fewer than 19 times. They have also claimed two championships, with Steve Robertson taking over the mantle of Bryan Herta and emerging with his first title since winning the 1988 British Formula Ford 2000 series.

'We went in with reasonably high expectations, and we tried over the off-season to make sure we weren't complacent,' said Horne, who also guided Didier Theys to the 1987 Indy Lights (American Racing Series) title as manager/co-owner of TrueSports Racing. 'We did a lot of work on making sure all the ingredients were in place.'

Horne, aided and abetted by his three partners, team manager Jeff Eischen and businessmen Ben Dillon and Stan Ross, continued his tried and tested formula of leaving no stone unturned in the pursuit of excellence. The team secured an ample but by no means extravagant budget from its three drivers – Robertson, Andre Ribeiro and Eddie Lawson – and conducted a corresponding amount of testing.

Around the paddock area, there's no doubt the Tasman team set the standard for others to follow. The cars, the crew and the equipment were always immaculately presented. The results followed.

'To be honest, I think our biggest advantage was the drivers,' declared Horne. 'We had a very strong combination and they all worked very well together. Having said that, the competition was probably three times as strong as in '93.'

The trio of Tasman drivers each gained a taste of victory, with prodigiously talented teenaged Canadian Greg Moore the only other man to break into Victory Circle. Nevertheless, in addition to Moore, three other drivers – Pedro Chaves, Alex Padilla and Bob Dorricott Jr. – grasped a taste of glory by annexing one pole position apiece.

The battle for championship honors boiled down to a duel between Robertson and Moore. Englishman Robertson had proved to be one of Herta's toughest challengers in 1993, and was expected to continue the rich vein of success in a renewed partnership with the Tasman team. Robertson did not disappoint. The 29-year-old from Chigwell, Essex,

England, was able to deal with the pressure of being a championship contender – and the inevitable few disappointments along the way – without the signs of petulance that had marked his initial foray into North American racing. He listened intently to the sage advice from Horne and capitalized on his own experience by opening up a commanding points lead in the early part of the season. Consecutive victories in Long Beach, Milwaukee and Detroit, in addition to his runner-up finish in the opener at Phoenix, ensured a lead he was never to lose.

'He did everything we asked of him,' summarized Horne, who also acted as Robertson's race engineer. 'We had to teach him how to win a championship, and the strategy we used all the time was: "Maximize your opportunities and minimize your mistakes." '

Robertson followed the credo admirably. He was a consistently strong qualifier (with an average grid position of 2.5) and made only a couple of mistakes, spinning at Portland and Mid-Ohio. Even with minor mechanical problems at Cleveland (misfire) and Laguna Seca (gearshift), Robertson's Guess Men's Classics Lola-Buick finished every lap of every race – a remarkable tribute to the Tasman team's meticulous preparation, and in particular his crew chief Steve Ragan. Robertson finally clinched the crown with a steady-as-she-goes run to fourth place at Nazareth.

'I can't say enough about the team,' said Robertson, who in addition to maturing greatly as a driver also proved far more adept in dealing with fans, sponsors and the media. 'We set a goal at the start of the season and worked hard to achieve it. To reach that goal is a dream come true.'

While Moore provided Robertson's sternest challenge through the first half of the season, it was Ribeiro who emerged to claim second place in the standings. The personable Brazilian finished either first or second in each of the last six races, and in addition to earning the Turbo-Mac Rookie of the Year Award Ribeiro also deserved unofficial honors as Most Improved Driver.

The 28-year-old Brazilian truly came of age during 1994. His confidence blossomed, at least in part due to his excellent rapport with race engineer Don Halliday. His technical feedback, reportedly, was phenomenal. Ribeiro, a very talented and charming young man who had shown his speed before in British Formula 3, finally put all the ingredients together and marked himself as a potential star of the future. Next year he will graduate into the PPG Cup series along with his sponsors (which include Marlboro, Regino, Sadia and Pizza Hut) and the Tasman team. It promises to be a formidable partnership.

Mistakes by Moore at Toronto, where he had won the pole, and at Mid-Ohio eventually restricted him to third place in the series standings. Nevertheless, this 19-year-old has a bright future ahead of him. He is mature beyond his years, both in and out of the car. He possesses good technical knowledge and excellent car control. His form on the ovals, in particular, has been sensational – witness his wins at Phoenix, New Hampshire and Nazareth to easily claim the Bosch Speedway Challenge bonus.

Thus far, his small, family-run team has been limited by financial constraints, although with Tasman graduating into the Indy Car ranks next season, he should have an opportunity to continue his winning ways.

Photos: Michael C. Brown

Left: Canadian Greg Moore *(on left)* produced some stunning performances throughout the year. Particularly strong on the ovals, the 19-year-old took wins at Phoenix, New Hampshire and Nazareth, where he is seen on the podium with another promising driver, Jeff Ward.

After twice taking the runner-up spot in his Brian Stewart Racing Castrol-Benetton Lola, Pedro Chaves *(below left)* was still chasing his first Indy Lights win. The personable Portuguese driver is a strong contender for outright success in 1995.

World Champion will achieve everything of which he is capable.

Pedro Chaves was the 'nearly man' of 1994. Twice he finished as runner-up, four times more in third place with Brian Stewart Racing's Castrol-Benetton Lola.

'Tasman!' exclaimed the likable Portuguese at Laguna Seca after taking his ninth podium finish in two years. 'They are the only reason we cannot win races. The difference is the car. They never break. They don't do any mistakes. They have good set-up, good everything.'

In 1995, he along with Moore and Lawson must start as firm favorites for seasonal honors. That first win cannot be far away.

Nick Firestone endured a disappointing year with Dick Simon Racing, earning only one podium finish in his Montgomery Ward Auto Express/Firestone Vineyards car, while ex-Barber Saab stand-out Alex Padilla made good progress with Mark Weida's Leading Edge team, run nowadays in conjunction with Mike Collier. Formula 2000 graduates Dave DeSilva and Doug Boyer both overcame numerous expensive incidents during the season as they attempted to become acquainted with the big leagues of auto racing. Both showed well on occasion. Next season should see their true colors emerge.

Other promising performances were posted by former motocross star Jeff Ward, who finished a strong third in his first Indy Lights race of the season at Nazareth; former German F3 contender Markus Liesner, who, sadly, ran out of money after only one race; and Canadians Patrick Carpentier and Trevor Seibert, who are likely to emerge as serious championship contenders if Canaska Racing can attract a full budget.

The Indy Lights series continued its gradual upward trend in 1994, with entries almost reaching an average of 20 for the first time. Mechanical problems, once again, were rare, with an impressive overall finishing record of 78.07 per cent throughout the 12-race season.

Significantly, IndyCar President Andrew Craig has affirmed his support for the PPG Cup circuit's 'Official Development Series.' That news, together with renewed backing from Lola Cars, which offers the series champion the loan of a new Indy Car chassis, and Firestone, which adds a bonus of $100,000, along with a much-improved television package, should set the stage for Indy Lights to enjoy further growth in the years ahead.

Fourth place was taken by the third Tasman driver, Eddie Lawson, who showed on several occasions he has the talent to achieve as much in the world of four-wheel racing as he did during a magnificent career on motor cycles. One slight slip was all it took for Lawson to miss out on what would have been a well-earned maiden victory at Long Beach, but he was a consistently solid contender. The only surprise was that Lawson had to wait until Cleveland – the 100th race in the history of Indy Lights – to break through with his first win. It should be the first of many.

Lawson is at pains to point out the fact he has a lot to learn in auto racing, yet there's no doubt he possesses the skills. Money, patience and opportunity, however, will determine whether the four-time 500 cc

1994 PPG-FIRESTONE INDY LIGHTS CHAMPIONSHIP
Final point standings, after 12 races:

1.	Steve Robertson (GB), Guess Men's Classics	179
2.	Andre Ribeiro (BR), Marlboro/Sadia/Banespa	170
3.	Greg Moore (CDN), Viper/Hugo Boss/Mobil 1	154
4.	Eddie Lawson (USA), Diehard/Crane & Shovel Sales	139
5.	Pedro Chaves (P), Castrol/Benetton	132
6.	Nick Firestone (USA), Montgomery Ward Auto Express	72
7.	Alex Padilla (USA), Team Sacramento/Bail America	63
8.	Doug Boyer (USA), Red Line Oil/BTU Stoker	47
9.	Dave DeSilva (USA), Oliver DeSilva/STP/Guess	46
10.	Buzz Calkins (USA), Bradley Food Marts/Total Oil	41
11.	Scott Schubot (USA), Transatlantic Racing	26
12.	Rob Wilson (NZ), Team Leisy/SCP	22
13.	David Pook (USA), Makita Tools/Ecology Pure Air	18
	Bob Dorricott Jr. (USA), Sunnyvale Valve	18
15.	Jeff Ward (USA), Primm/Nature's Recipe/Oakley	16
16.	Dr. Jack Miller (USA), Waterpik/Aquafresh	14
17.	Bob Reid (USA), Ingersoll-Rand/W.W. Grainger	12
18.	Markus Leisner (USA), John Martin Racing	10
19.	Christopher Smith (USA), Earl's Perf. Products	9
20.	Rick Hill (USA), Kids on Track	8

Driver	Wins	Poles
Ribeiro	4	4
Robertson	4	2
Moore	3	2
Lawson	1	1
Chaves	–	1
Dorricott	–	1
Padilla	–	1

(all run identical Lola T93/20-Buicks)

by Jeremy Shaw

EFFECTIVE

Michael C. Brown

EMPRINGHAM

David Empringham overcame the odds to become only the fourth driver in 21 years to claim consecutive Formula Atlantic Championship crowns. In doing so he joined an exclusive club comprising Bill Brack, who won the first two titles in 1974 and '75, and the two Villeneuve brothers, Gilles and Jacques.

The 28-year-old from Willowdale, Ontario, began the season as a hot favorite to retain his Player's Ltd. Toyota Atlantic Championship, especially having transferred his Motomaster sponsorship to the crack

BDJS Racing team managed by the vastly experienced Kiwi Dave McMillan. Nevertheless, Empringham fared badly in the first two races and it wasn't until the fourth round in Milwaukee, where he placed second, that he finally enjoyed a trouble-free race.

'At that point in the year I didn't expect to end up as the champion,' admitted Empringham, 'so it's a pretty remarkable result.'

Fortunately, Empringham regained the consistency which has been a hallmark of his career to date as he

recorded six top-two finishes (including two wins) in seven races to take the points lead for the first time following the penultimate round at Nazareth. Empringham clinched the title, by a scant two points, with a conservative run to fourth in the season finale at Laguna Seca.

Empringham's triumph came after a thrilling three-way contest with two extremely talented Americans, Richie Hearn and Greg Ray. Each shone at various times during the year, although ultimately, perhaps, it was the Canadian's experience

which enabled him to win through.

Nevertheless, Hearn, 23, from Arcadia, California, can rightly claim to be unfortunate to have missed out on the title. He was consistently fast in John Della Penna's Food 4 Less/Lynx Racing Ralt and could – or should – have scored more than his final tally of four victories. Next year, the former Elf-Winfield School winner plans to be back with the same team. He will take some beating.

Ray also shone in his rookie season. The least experienced of the

191

Pretenders to Empringham's throne: gifted Californian Richie Hearn *(near right)* and exciting rookie Greg Ray. Hearn took four wins in his Food 4 Less/Lynx Racing Ralt *(bottom)* but it could have been more . . .

Photos: Michael C. Brown

three title protagonists, in only his third season of auto racing, Ray, 28, from Plano, Texas, began the year sensationally by claiming pole in the first four races with Angelo Ferro's Mercury Outboards/Genoa Racing Ralt. Ray sped to victory in three of the four races, although mistakes on the streets in Toronto and Trois Rivieres blunted his title challenge.

Series veteran Colin Trueman provided a good basis from which to judge the ability of the other major contenders, and indeed his Hogan Motor Leasing/TrueSports Ralt RT41 was generally 'best of the rest' – except at his home track, Mid-Ohio, where Trueman sped to an accomplished victory.

The only other race winner was Mark Dismore, who made a sensational return at Nazareth with Bill Fickling's 1987-vintage P-1 Racing Swift DB-4. The vastly underrated Dismore scored an emotional victory in his first Toyota Atlantic start in over a year. It was also the 1990 West Coast champion's record 15th Atlantic win.

Bobby Carville and Peter Faucetta Jr. were consistent point scorers in an 11-race season which was marred by several small fields. Nevertheless, the quality was high, with Canadian Patrick Carpentier, Englishman Jeremy Cotterill and young Californ-ian Clint (son of Rick) Mears also displaying good form. In addition, Frank Allers ran well in his updated Reynard 92H and Paul Dallenbach enjoyed a couple of good outings in Jim Griffith's under-developed Raven chassis, which provided a welcome respite from the flock of Ralts. Last but not least, Texas-based Canadian Bernie Schuchmann claimed seasonal honors in the concurrent series run for older cars.

Michael C. Brown

1994 PLAYER'S LTD. TOYOTA ATLANTIC CHAMPIONSHIP
Final point standings, after 11 races:

1.	David Empringham (CDN), Motomaster Ralt RT41	162
2.	Richie Hearn (USA), Food 4 Less Ralt RT40/1	160
3.	Greg Ray (USA), Mercury Outboards Ralt RT41	148
4.	Colin Trueman (USA), Hogan Motor Leasing Ralt RT41	135
5.	Bobby Carville (USA), Sentry Custom Services Ralt RT40	100
6.	Peter Faucetta Jr. (USA), Brut/Kodak/Snapple Ralt RT40	83
7.	David Myers (USA), Sammons Enterprises Ralt RT41	51
8.	Frank Allers (CDN), Keen Engineering Reynard 92/3H	47
9.	Patrick Carpentier (CDN), Plastifab/Cari-All Ralt RT40	40
10.	Jim Ward (USA), The Crossings Swift DB-4	40

Driver	Wins	Poles
Hearn	4	4
Ray	3	5
Empringham	2	2
Trueman	1	–
Dismore	1	–